What Works in Foster Care?

What Works in Foster Care?

Key Components of Success From the Northwest Foster Care Alumni Study

PETER J. PECORA
RONALD C. KESSLER
JASON WILLIAMS
A. CHRIS DOWNS
DIANA J. ENGLISH
JAMES WHITE
KIRK O'BRIEN

UNIVERSITY PRESS
2010

OXFORD

UNIVERSITY PRESS

Oxford University Press, Inc., publishes works that further
Oxford University's objective of excellence
in research, scholarship, and education.

Oxford   New York
Auckland   Cape Town   Dar es Salaam   Hong Kong   Karachi
Kuala Lumpur   Madrid   Melbourne   Mexico City   Nairobi
New Delhi   Shanghai   Taipei   Toronto

With offices in
Argentina   Austria   Brazil   Chile   Czech Republic   France   Greece
Guatemala   Hungary   Italy   Japan   Poland   Portugal   Singapore
South Korea   Switzerland   Thailand   Turkey   Ukraine   Vietnam

Published by Oxford University Press, Inc.
198 Madison Avenue, New York, New York 10016
www.oup.com

Library of Congress Cataloging-in-Publication Data

What works in foster care? : key components of success from the Northwest Foster Care
Alumni Study / Peter J. Pecora ... [et al.].
    p. cm.
Includes bibliographical references and index.
ISBN 978-0-19-517591-2
1. Foster children—United States.   2. Foster home care—United States.
I. Pecora, Peter J.
HV863.W43 2010
362.73'30973—dc22
2009002643

9 8 7 6 5 4 3 2 1

Printed in the United States of America
on acid-free paper.

Acknowledgments

Special thanks to the staff members and agency collaborators of the Northwest Foster Care Alumni Study for their efforts in making this book possible. We especially appreciate the foster care alumni and foster parents who helped design the study, shared their stories, and interpreted the findings; the Casey, Oregon State, and Washington State staff who helped us locate alumni; and the Survey Research Center study leaders (Nat Ehrlich, Nancy Gebler, Tina Mainieri, and Alisa McWilliams) and interviewers at the University of Michigan who assisted us with the study.

Sara Colling, Justin Rathburn, Justin Anderson, and Delia Armendariz helped manage the editing and formatting of the manuscript. We appreciate the technical advice from John Emerson and Debbie Staub regarding education issues and the astute revisions to the manuscript contributed by Catherine Roller White of Casey Research Services. Richard Barth, Natasha Bowen, Robin Nixon, Janet Preston, Octavia Nixon, Lissa Osborne, and James Whittaker provided expert consultation for the first technical report; all remaining errors are the responsibility of the authors.

Editorial Advisory Board

We especially want to thank the following people who helped review and edit some of the book chapters.

- Carol Brandford (formerly Washington Department of Social and Health Services, Children's Administration, Division of Children and Family Services, Office of Children's Administration Research)
- Wai Tat Chiu (Department of Health Care Policy, Harvard Medical School)
- Nathaniel Ehrlich (Michigan State University Institute for Public Policy and Social Research)
- Nancy Gebler (University of Michigan, Survey Research Center)
- Anne Havalchak (Casey Family Programs)
- Steve Heeringa (University of Michigan, Survey Research Center)
- Eva Hiripi (formerly Department of Health Care Policy, Harvard Medical School)
- Catherine Roller White (Casey Family Programs)
- Dan Torres (Center for the Study of Social Policy)
- Tamera Wiggins (Psychology Department, Royal Brisbane and Women's Hospital and Queensland Health, Australia)

Contents

PART I

INTRODUCTION

1

Study Background, Rationale, and Participating Agencies

An interviewer reported interviewing a young woman who had been molested and raped from the age of two throughout her childhood. She was not removed from [her birth parent's] home until high school. She has spent her whole life climbing the ladders to overcome the backlash of her childhood. She is now employed at a drug and alcohol treatment center, has gotten her eating disorders at bay, and in her spare time makes bean bag couches. Then, life put another ladder in front of her: she now has multiple sclerosis. "We sat in her apartment while she walked me through her childhood pain. Soft saxophone jazz and giant cups of herb tea were an ironic calm to the storm of her life. In this humble interviewer's opinion, I met a remarkable woman this day."

This book focuses on how a group of young adults functioned years after leaving foster care. It also examines what made a difference in their lives. The research team investigated the role that quality services can play in helping children who spent time in foster care as adolescents become successful adults. The findings have much practical value for policymakers, administrators, line workers, and communities concerned about supporting children in foster care and young adults who have left foster care. More specifically, The Northwest Foster Care Alumni Study (Northwest Alumni Study) examined outcomes for adults who were placed in family foster care as children (here referred to as *alumni*). The investigation included adults who were between the ages of 20 and 33 during the interviewing period (September 2000 through January 2002), who had been placed in family foster care between 1988 and 1998, and who were served by one of three agencies: *(1)* Casey Family Programs; *(2)* the Oregon Department of Human Services, Division of Children, Adults, and Families; or *(3)* the Washington Department of Social and Health Services, Children's Administration, Division of Children and Family Services.

The primary research questions were:

1. How are maltreated youth who were placed in foster care faring as adults? To what extent are they different in their functioning from other adults?
2. Are there key factors or program components that are linked with better functioning in adulthood?

To answer these and other questions, case records were reviewed for 659 alumni. An attempt was made to track these alumni, and interviews were conducted with 479 alumni. Although the in-person interviews explored retrospectively some experiences while the alumnus or alumna was in care (e.g., educational services, therapeutic services, and therapeutic supports), they focused primarily on current adult outcomes including mental health, education, and employment and finances. Subsequent chapters, in addition to describing demographics, birth-family strengths and risk factors, agency membership, foster care experiences, and outcomes, present data explicating the relationship between foster care experiences and outcomes. These analyses will prove extremely useful for practitioners and policymakers as they work to improve services that will enhance the lives of youth in care.

This chapter begins by presenting data on the number of youth in care in the United States and how long they receive services. Next come a description of family foster care and a summary of the expectations of care. Then findings from foster care studies, research limitations, and the financial costs of providing care are presented. Conclusions about foster care are then drawn, followed by the rationale of the Northwest Alumni Study. The chapter concludes with a brief description of each chapter of this book. Quotes from alumni are included throughout the book to provide a first-person context; these were taken from interviewers' notes.

Foster Care by the Numbers

Placement of Children as a Consequence of Child Maltreatment

Every child has a right to a childhood experience that promotes healthy growth and development (United Nations, 1990). However, nearly 50,000 children come to the attention of child protective service agencies throughout the United States each week (U.S. Department of Health and Human Services, 2006). In 2007, approximately 5.8 million U.S. children were reported to child protective services as possible victims of abuse and neglect, with 794,000 confirmed victims (U.S. Department of Health and Human Services, 2009). When birth parents or other caregivers do not provide adequate protection and nurturance, city, county, or state governments intervene *in loco parentis* to care for the child (Wald, 1975).[1]

In 2006, an estimated 312,000 children received foster care services as a result of investigation for child abuse or neglect (U.S. Department of Health and Human Services, 2008c). About 783,000 children, or 1% of the nation's children, are served in foster care settings at some point during each year, including children who return home but reenter foster care (U.S. Department of Health and Human Services, 2008d). At any one time during the year, nearly 500,000 children are living in out-of-home care.

Though preventing the placement of children in foster care and minimizing their length of stay is a child welfare priority, many children will spend a substantial amount of their childhood in foster care (U.S. Department of Health and Human Services, 2006). Nearly half of the children placed in foster care will remain there for a year or longer, with an average length of stay of two years. More specifically, of those children in foster care as of September 30, 2006, 58% had been there for 12 months or longer. Of those leaving care in fiscal year 2006, 49% had been in care for 11 months or less, but 16% had been there for three years or more. Over 26,000 older youth emancipate to adulthood from a foster care setting every year (U.S. Department of Health and Human Services, 2008c). While many children reunite with their birth parents or are adopted, some children remain in care until their 18th birthday, the time of emancipation.

In Oregon, one of the two states in the study, 6,199 children entered foster care in fiscal year 2006, with a total of 11,021 children in care on September 30, 2006. In Washington, the other state in the study, 7,004 children entered foster care in fiscal year 2006, with a total of 10,068 children in care on September 30, 2006 (U.S. Department of Health and Human Services, 2007b).

Duration of Stay in Foster Care

As discussed below, a primary goal of foster care is achieving a permanent living situation for the child. Despite the efforts of family-based service placement prevention programs (e.g., Walton, Sandau-Beckler, & Mannes, 2001), family reunification programs (e.g., Pine, Healy, & Maluccio, 2002; Walton, Fraser, Lewis, Pecora, & Walton, 1993), aggressive adoption and guardianship programs (Stein, 1998; Testa, 2002), and an emphasis by child welfare policymakers on shortening the length of placements,[2] many children will spend a substantial amount of their childhood in the foster care system (Wulczyn & Brunner, 2002) (See Figure 1.1). Nationwide, the median length of stay for children in care on September 30, 2006, was 15.5 months (U.S. Department of Health and Human Services, 2008b). In Oregon, the median length of stay for children in care in 2005 was 14.4 months (NDAS: http://ndas.cwla.org/data_stats). In Washington, the median length of stay for children in care in 2007 was 17.5 months (National Resource Center for Family-Centered Practice and Permanency Planning, 2008a, 2008b).

Foster Care: Goals, Objectives, and Key Outcomes

What Is Family Foster Care?

We believe that communities should be willing to invest as much to keep a family together as they would pay for placing a child. Despite this approach, many children are served by foster care, and many stay for an extended period of time. But what exactly constitutes family foster care? When a child's safety in the home is not guaranteed or the parents are unable to care for the child,

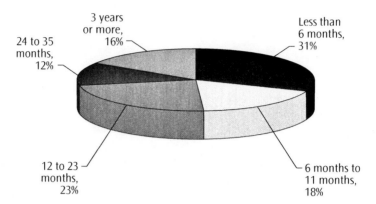

Figure 1.1. Duration of Stay for Children Exiting Foster Care During Federal Fiscal Year 2006 (Note that entry cohort statistics are more accurate.)

alternate systems of care come into play. The term *foster care* is generally used to encompass not only family foster care, but also placement of children and youth in group homes and residential settings—a topic covered later in this chapter. Family foster care, which is the focus of this chapter, has been defined as

> ...the provision of planned, time-limited, substitute family care for children who cannot be adequately maintained at home, and the simultaneous provision of social services to these children and their families to help resolve the problems that led to the need for placement.
>
> (Blumenthal, 1983, p. 296)

The above definition reflects various principles that are well accepted in the field of child welfare, as exemplified by the "CWLA Standards of Excellence for Family Foster Care" (Child Welfare League of America, 1995), although not fully realized in policy or practice. First, family foster care is conceptualized as a comprehensive family support service, and the family is regarded as the focus of attention. Second, family foster care is carefully planned to be short term and to provide access to time-limited services and opportunities that can help families to become rehabilitated and children to grow up and develop into healthy adults. In some cases, however, longer-term services may be needed by families. And the sense of urgency to move children into a more permanent living situation has increased over the past 20 years.

The major functions of family foster care include emergency protection, crisis intervention, assessment and case planning, reunification, preparation for adoption, and preparation for independent living. To implement such functions, diverse forms of foster care are required, including emergency foster care, kinship foster care, placement with unrelated foster families, treatment foster care, foster care for medically fragile children, shared family foster care, and small-family group home care. Also, long-term family foster care is an option for a small number of youth for whom family reunification, kinship care, or adoption are not viable permanency planning options.

In addition, there are indications that family foster care is responding to the substantial behavioral health needs of the children in care and becoming more treatment oriented. Specialized family foster care programs—particularly treatment foster care—for children and youth with special needs in such areas as emotional disturbance, behavioral problems, and educational underachievement are gaining significant use (e.g., Chamberlain, 2003).

Family foster care is sometimes provided as a multifaceted service, including specialized or therapeutic services for some children, temporary placements for children in "emergency" homes, and supports to relatives raising children through kinship care (Maluccio, Pine, & Tracy, 2002). (While there is little descriptive data on services to children in foster care, our experience is that much foster care is delivered without significant services for children other than basic health care and referral to mental health agencies for treatment.) In this book, *foster care* refers to both family and nonfamily types of out-of-home care, including shelter care, group homes, and residential treatment centers.

Current Goals, Objectives, and Key Outcomes of Foster Care

Although some of the current system goals, objectives, and key outcomes were not outlined explicitly during the time youth were in care during this study, similar principles were in place as the alumni had to have been in foster care as an adolescent between the years of 1988–1998 but they actually could have been in care as early as 1970 or in some form of transition services in 1999. This section places foster care in Oregon and Washington in the political context in which it functioned during the period of the study. Because foster care practice and programs have been governed by an intricate set of policies and laws at the federal, state, and local levels (Curtis, Grady, & Kendall, 1999; Lindsey & Schwartz, 2004; Pew Commission on Children in Foster Care, 2004), evaluation of such a piecemeal system has been extremely challenging.[3]

Historically, child welfare reviews focused on case record documentation (process) rather than on the capacity of state or local child welfare service agencies to create positive outcomes for children and families. Since March 25, 2002, the federal government has changed its approach to assessing state child welfare programs with the introduction of child and family services reviews. These reviews examine the outcomes of services provided to children and families served by state child welfare agencies. These outcomes fall into three categories—safety, permanence, and well-being—which are described below:

Child Safety

- Preventing further child maltreatment by birth family members and others while the child is placed in foster care

Child Permanence

- Achieving a more permanent living situation for the child through reunification; adoption by relatives, foster parents, or nonrelatives; guardianship; or other methods
- Minimizing movement of the child from one home to another and from one school to another

Child and Family Well-Being

- Restoring and strengthening birth family functioning
- Maintaining family, school, and other connections
- Stabilizing or improving the child's emotional, social, and cognitive functioning
- Enabling positive ethnic identification
- Addressing physical health and mental health care (U.S. Department of Health and Human Services, 2003a)[4]

These three domains encompass what might be termed *immediate concerns* and are necessary considerations regardless of the length of stay in foster care. Other concerns surface as the length of stay for a youth increases. Duration of care can be triaged into the following groups:

1. *Group A:* Roughly one-third of the child and family situations are resolved quickly and permanently through reunification, adoption, or some other means.
2. *Group B:* About 18% of the children stay in foster care for six months to one year (U.S. Department of Health and Human Services, 2008b). Although more complicated, these situations usually are resolved with the same sorts of permanent placements described for Group A.
3. *Group C:* The remaining situations (about half of all situations) last for more than one year. Some of these youth are eventually placed in a permanent home. Unlike the cases in Groups A and B, a significant proportion of these cases are closed when the child reaches the age of majority (emancipation) rather than through a permanent placement. Also included in this group are those cases in which reunification was attempted unsuccessfully and an ensuing second or third foster care placement took place. These youth, who did not achieve a stable home, represent the failure of prompt or successful permanency planning.

All participants in the Northwest Alumni Study were Group C situations. In addition to the immediate concerns of child safety, child permanence, and child and family well-being, youth experiencing longer durations of care have additional outcomes with which agencies providing care must be concerned, including emotional, physical, and cognitive development. Specifically, the following outcomes are considered important for youth in long-term care (American Academy of Pediatrics Committee on Early Childhood Adoption and Dependent Care [AAP], 2000; Berrick, Needell, Barth, & Jonson-Reid, 1998; Casey Family Programs, 2001, 2003a; Wulczyn, Barth, Yuan, Harden, & Landsverk, 2005):

- Reduction in the emotional trauma of child maltreatment
- Healthy physical development through regular checkups and adequate medical, dental, and vision care
- Avoidance of teen pregnancy
- Life-skills development
- High school graduation
- Healthy socialization
- Healthy adult relationships

Why Should Society Care About Foster Care Outcomes?

Why should society care about how youth formerly in care function as adults? And why should evaluation research be conducted to assess outcomes? First, a significant number of children and families are affected by child maltreatment and, consequently, are served in foster care every year. Second, existing research has found that outcomes are good in some areas and poor in others. Third, there are many gaps in the research on the effects of foster care and what factors are associated with positive outcomes. Finally, the financial costs of foster care are substantial, with over $20 billion spent every year. The next sections discuss each of these reasons in more detail.

Large Numbers of Children and Families Are Served in Foster Care

The number of children remaining in foster care at the end of the federal fiscal year has risen substantially since 1980. As described previously, in 2007 about 783,000 children (including re-placements) were served during that fiscal year, with 496,000 children remaining in care at the end of that federal measurement cycle—September 30, 2007 (U.S. Department of Health and Human Services, 2008d). The increase in placement rates over time and the lack of more substantial decreases may be due to cuts in preventive services, frequent agency leader turnover, dramatic increases in crack/cocaine and methamphetamine abuse, reduction in public housing and an increase in homelessness, continuing unemployment in many geographical areas and in some ethnic communities, and other factors. Studies have indicated that foster care *reentry* (Wulczyn, 1991), weak reunification efforts (Wulczyn, 2004), and parent substance abuse and mental health disorders (Besharov & Hanson, 1994; Marsh & Cao, 2005) have also contributed to the rise in foster care numbers. In fact, various studies have estimated that between 50% and 80% of parents involved with child welfare agencies are having difficulty with substance abuse (Bruni & Gillespie, 1999; Child Welfare League of America, 1998). Community-based prevention initiatives need to be strengthened.

Foster Care Outcomes Are Mixed

How is the child welfare field doing in terms of achieving key outcomes for children served in foster care? Results are mixed and, as will be documented in Chapter 2, in some areas, such as postsecondary educational achievement and employment earnings, the results are unacceptably poor. The evidence from some recent studies has indicated that some children who received foster care services were at greater risk of being arrested or incarcerated, of having lower high school graduation rates, of experiencing lower employment rates, of suffering from depression more frequently, and of being overrepresented among the homeless when compared to the general population (Buehler, Orme, Post, & Patterson, 2000; English, Widom, & Brandford, 2002; Pecora et al., 2003a; Widom, 1989a) or when compared (in some cases) to children from families with similar income or other demographic characteristics but who experienced no foster care placement (see, e.g., Minty, 1999; Pecora & Wiggins, 2009).

In contrast, other studies have found that certain alumni outcomes were reasonably positive: Youth in care exhibited improvements in physical health, emotional adjustment, school performance, and behavioral functioning (Berrick et al., 1998; Biehal & Wade, 1996; Coulling, 2000; Goerge, Wulczyn, & Fanshel, 1994). Due to the mixed results of foster care studies, additional research is necessary to identify more clearly areas of success and areas requiring attention.

Methodological Limitations of Research on the Effectiveness of Foster Care

Concrete information explaining why some studies demonstrate successful outcomes and others do not is lacking. Possible explanations include different levels of rigor in study methodology and the fact that some services work better for some children than others. Ultimately, broad conclusions about foster care outcomes from existing studies cannot be made because of the following methodological issues (some exceptions noted):

1. Comparison groups, matched on variables such as family background, pre-placement child adversity, age, ethnicity, and gender were not used. Further, data have not been statistically adjusted for variables such as these.
2. Few quasi-experimental or experimental studies exist. Control groups permit valid comparisons to the general population of children or to subgroups of children with similar family or child characteristics who have not been placed (Barth, 1990; Holdaway & Ray, 1992; Jacobson & Cockerum, 1976; Jones & Moses, 1984; Rice & McFadden, 1988).
3. General population or other benchmarks were not used to place findings in context.

4. Sample sizes were too small to support meaningful conclusions.
5. The field has overrelied on cross-sectional ("snapshot") or exit data instead of longitudinal cohort data (Courtney, Needell, & Wulczyn, 2004a). Exceptions include the National Survey of Child and Adolescent Well-being (NSCAW) and LONGSCAN, a longitudinal study of child maltreatment (Blome, 1994; Kohl, Gibbons, & Green, 2005; Runyan et al., 1998b; Starr & Wolfe, 1991; Usher, Randolph, & Gogan, 1999).
6. Few studies have collected detailed service data that permit analyses of services related to outcomes.
7. Important functional measures of child or adult well-being such as mental health diagnoses, employment, parenting as adults, and community service were not used.
8. Most follow-up studies collected incomplete educational achievement data because they did not follow alumni long enough to capture high school completion with a graduate equivalency degree (GED) or college completion when the individuals were in their mid- to late 20s.
9. A common set of standardized diagnostic measures that assess behavior, educational functioning, satisfaction, self-esteem, and other central dependent variables were used infrequently. Thus, comparisons to other populations are limited.
10. Youth in care, caregivers, alumni, and front-line staff were not often involved in study design and data interpretation, which would have helped ensure that researchers gathered meaningful information in respectful ways.
11. For new or underexplored problem areas, few qualitative studies were completed that would help the field better understand the program model, the dynamics of treatment, consumer perceptions of service, and what is working for whom and why.

The Financial Costs to Society Are Substantial

In addition to the large number of children served and the mixed outcomes they experience, society should also be concerned with foster care because of the financial costs of providing services. Foster care services represent a major societal investment. As with any investment, Americans have a right to know the economic return on that investment. From the moment that calls are screened by an agency charged with initiating an assessment of possible abuse or neglect, through removal and placement of children in substitute care, to pursuing permanency options (such as reunification or adoption), to emancipation, to the ultimate disposition of cases, the full range of child welfare services to children and families is covered through a multi-billion-dollar patchwork of federal, state, and local funding. For example, in state fiscal year 2006, $25.1 billion was spent, including $12.4 billion from federal funds, $10.6 billion from state sources, and $2.6 billion from local governments (DeVooght, Allen, & Geen, 2008).[5]

Other, more general costs to society have been estimated by various experts. For example, the *direct costs to society* due to hospitalization, chronic health problems, mental health care, child protective services, family support, foster care, law enforcement, and the judicial system have been conservatively estimated at $24.3 billion (Fromm, 2001). This must be a conservative estimate, as federal, state, and local funding in state fiscal year 2006 was estimated at $25.7 billion alone (DeVooght, Allen, & Geen, 2008). The *indirect costs* in terms of special education, later mental health and physical health care, juvenile delinquency, lost productivity to society, and adult criminality were estimated at an additional $69.7 billion, for a total cost estimate of *$94.1 billion annually* (Fromm, 2001).

The costs for treatment and other services may not be surprising, given national data that establish a strong link between childhood adversity and later adult psychiatric disorders (Kessler, Davis, & Kendler, 1997). So, the overall social and fiscal significance of this program area is high. Children are traumatized, parents suffer, and agencies have been sued when their responsibilities for child safety, stability, and nurturing were not fulfilled. For example, thousands of individual lawsuits and over 25 child welfare–related class action lawsuits have been filed against states in the past 20 years based on maltreatment of children while in care, inadequate provision of mental health services, frequent placement moves, and other practice deficiencies that led to a child's injury or poor development. When these societal costs are added to those described above, the overall costs are extraordinarily high.

The Condition of Foster Care

Practice experiences; research findings[6] from landmark studies such as those of Fanshel and Shinn (1978), Maas and Engler (1959), and the National Survey of Child and Adolescent Well-Being (NSCAW) (U.S. Department of Health and Human Services, 2001b); a long history of research in other countries;[7] and more recent critiques of foster care have underscored a number of points concerning foster care in the United States.

First, despite its temporary intent, foster care has become a permanent status for many children entering the system. Further, until the mid-1980s, many children "drifted" in foster care, going from one placement to another, with little sense of stability or continuity in their living arrangements. Although more attention has been paid to permanency planning recently, the latest federal outcome data document that some children continue to experience too many placement changes.[8]

Second, family supports remain inadequate and unforgiving (Curtis & Denby, 2004). For example, because of time limits placed upon public assistance provided by Temporary Assistance for Needy Families (TANF; five-year limit) and parent rehabilitation before termination of parental rights imposed by the Adoption and Safe Families Act (ASFA), many families lack the resources and time needed to rehabilitate (U.S. Department of Health and Human Services, 2003a). Indeed, many children placed in foster care come from poor families that are barely managing to survive on limited income from public assistance programs (Lindsey, 2004).

Third, children of color are disproportionately represented in foster care in many communities, and they experience less positive outcomes. This is especially true of African American, Latino, and American Indian/Alaska Native children (Hill, 2001, 2007; U.S. Government Accountability Office, 2007). To date, the factors that drive disproportionate representation and outcomes are not fully understood and programs are only beginning to address the issue.

Fourth, as discussed above, data on the effectiveness of foster care are mixed. Improving a system of care with such mixed outcomes is a challenge because, until recently, the data haven't suggested where to target interventions. However, this study and others (Courtney et al., 2005a, 2007) suggest that addressing the mental health needs of youth in care may be the place to start. Further, underresearched areas remain. For example, there is some evidence that keeping siblings together has beneficial effects in terms of placement stability and other outcomes (Hegar, 2005; Leathers, 2005), but more data are needed.

Finally, common standards of care and performance targets are new to foster care. Built on the collection of common child demographics and general rates of child maltreatment, formal expectations of foster care now exist. For example, recent legislative action has focused on introducing key measures or outcome indicators that are customized according to the population and type of service being provided, emphasizing such important areas as length of care, freedom from child maltreatment, placement stability, and permanency (U.S. Department of Health and Human Services, 2000, 2001b, 2007a).

Unfortunately, recent reviews of state performance have revealed continuing problems in program performance (U.S. Department of Health and Human Services, 2003b). Consequently, pressure from private and public agencies, juvenile court judges, physicians, and other stakeholder groups is being applied (Wulczyn et al., 2005). In response to this poor program performance and poor foster care outcome data, questions about the effectiveness of the child welfare system continue to be raised. Suggested potential solutions include better community-based family support programs, lowering child welfare worker caseloads, providing more thorough worker training and supports to increase retention rates, more support of foster parents, and more explicit foster care practice philosophies and guidelines (Casey Family Programs, 2000, 2003a).

Rationale of the Northwest Alumni Study

The number of children in long-term (greater than one year) foster care is troubling, especially given a child's elongated sense of time and need for enduring positive relationships with caring adults (Berrick et al., 1998). As a child's time in care increases, the nature of a program's accountability shifts to focus more on long-term needs and development. Unfortunately, the data on how children who have experienced long-term foster care develop and function as young adults are lacking. More information is needed to determine what experiences and services best result in adult success.

Research on the consequences of maltreatment (see Pecora, Wiggins, Jackson, & English, 2009b) indicates that many children in foster care have had significant preexisting physical and mental health, education, and behavioral problems that may be exacerbated by their placement experience and lack of services. Services provided to address these needs while a child is in foster care, however, may have important mediating effects upon the effects of maltreatment. While some studies have addressed drug abuse, alcoholism, and depression as consequences of maltreatment, there is little research regarding the post–foster care impact of maltreatment on education, employment, and social relationships. And, with few exceptions, standardized diagnostic measures, longitudinal approaches, retrospective studies, and experimental designs have not been used to answer two important questions: *(1)* How are maltreated youth placed in foster care faring as adults? *(2)* Are there key factors or program components linked with better functioning in adulthood? To begin to address these questions, findings must be compared to similar data for other populations (benchmarks). For the few studies that have examined the long-term effects of foster care, comparisons with other alumni of foster care studies, general population, mental health, or Census Bureau studies have been rare.

In sum, while there is much more research about child maltreatment and its effects and about the general trends of children placed in foster care, there is a dearth of rigorously gathered outcome data concerning youth in foster care, and there remain many unexamined questions regarding the long-term effects of placement and how certain elements of foster care might help youth overcome the effects of maltreatment and grow to become successful adults. The Northwest Alumni Study has attempted to address these and other questions.

The next section summarizes the program mission, goals, resources, and foster care practice models that were operational in the three agencies involved in the Northwest Alumni Study during the study period 1988–1998:

1. Casey Family Programs (Casey)
2. Oregon Department of Human Services, Children, Adults and Families (Oregon DHS)
3. State of Washington Department of Social and Health Services, Children's Administration, Division of Children and Family Services (Washington CA/DCFS)

Description of Casey Family Programs

Overview

Casey is a privately endowed operating foundation, established in 1966 by Jim Casey, the founder of United Parcel Service (Kupsinel & Dubsky, 1999). Casey began by providing planned long-term foster care to youth in Seattle,

Washington. Based on a business model, the explicit goal of the program was to support foster children's development by focusing on education, social achievement, and the long-term success of each child. Individual self-sufficiency, a primary focus of Casey programs, was different from that of most child welfare agencies of the time, which were more concerned with children's adjustment to foster care. Casey staff members were expected to contribute to the development of new techniques of providing foster care by carefully matching youth with foster families who wanted to raise one or two children to adulthood.

Business and organizational values of United Parcel Service were transferred to Casey. These values included an emphasis on the following:

- *A primary focus.* There was a concentrated focus on one service: long-term family foster care.
- *Maintenance and improvement of service.* Youth, families, and staff played active roles in maintaining and improving the quality of service.
- *A culturally diverse and experienced staff:* Small, direct-service units (divisions) were intentionally composed of well-trained, culturally diverse, and experienced staff (with caseloads averaging 15–17 per worker).
- *Team decision making and shared responsibility.* The work style in these divisions reinforced team decision making and shared responsibility for work with youth and families.
- *Staff reward and development.* Staff retention and internal promotion opportunities were supported through fringe benefits and a focus on professional development.
- *Quality improvement:* Improvement of public and private services for children and youth was advocated, particularly for the nation's out-of-home care systems.
- *Use of resources.* Funds were invested to increase the organization's ability to serve as a nationally recognized information and learning center in the field of child welfare (Casey Family Programs, 1995).

Program Focus and Design

There were few changes in the core Casey program mission during the study period, with the exception of the development of life-skills tools and training (e.g., Ansell-Casey Life Skills Assessment [ACLSA]) in the mid-1990s. Early in the study period (1990–1992), Casey systematically reviewed best practices in foster care and developed a manual for child assessment and case planning: *Practice Guidelines for Clinical Practice and Case Management.* The manual was used agencywide, along with standardized child assessment instruments to help gauge the needs of children (e.g., the Ansell-Casey Life Skills Checklist and the Achenbach Child Behavior Checklist, Teachers Report Form, and Youth Self-Report). Eight case-planning factors were used to organize and guide assessments of each child's strengths and deficits (Perry, Pecora, & Traglia, 1992):

- Emotional health
- Family adjustment and other relationships

- Cultural identification
- Competence and achievement
- Physical health
- Educational development
- Self-sufficiency
- Legal involvement

The initial and ongoing service planning was driven by quarterly assessment of each of these case-planning factors. Outcomes were determined by the use of subjective and objective measures, including normed educational and behavioral reports, DSM-III clinical diagnostics and assessments, as well as periodic child and family self-reports of behaviors and relationships (e.g., the Child Behavior Checklist). Additionally, Casey staff placed great emphasis on ensuring that youth, foster parents, and other caregivers were full partners in the development of service plans.

To facilitate comprehensive case-planning policies and guidelines, Casey staff had access to greater financial resources to ensure that children's social, emotional, and behavioral needs were met. Services included a broad array of normalizing child developmental experiences—art, music, group activities (e.g., Boys and Girls Clubs, scouting)—as well as child-specific therapeutic services. Further, Casey aides assisted by transporting youth to activities and to tutoring sessions.

Work in extending services beyond age 18 was initiated early in the 1990s, depending on the youth's needs and his or her level of investment in further work to prepare for the future. Providing youth with an organizational anchor was intended to extend surrogate parental involvement into young adulthood, to help youth cope with unfinished or delayed development tasks, especially in completing education. To further help youth, Casey provided a postsecondary educational scholarship program—Continuing Education and Job Training (CEJT). CEJT scholarships were offered to any past or current youth from care through age 22 who had been the recipient of Casey services for one year or more. Youth applied for one of three different program scholarships:

1. The Jim Casey Scholarship (for full-time schooling at vocational and technical schools, undergraduate schools, and apprenticeship and/or entrepreneurial training)
2. The Marguerite M. Casey Scholarship (for full-time graduate schooling toward a master's degree, doctorate degree, or professional certificate)
3. The Henry J. Casey Scholarship (for part-time vocational or undergraduate schooling requiring a stable, long-term job, held either full-time or part-time; may also apply to college classes taken while still in high school)

In addition to extending services to youth beyond foster care, Casey emphasized recruitment, development, ongoing training, and retention of foster parents. The program actively recruited families that were willing to embrace the values of the organization by conducting a comprehensive assessment of prospective foster families. Foster families were assessed on their motivation to be foster parents, ability to work with Casey, personal history of caregiving, family values and beliefs, family system functioning, and parenting skills. After the family was accepted, Casey staff disclosed to foster families all the essential elements of a child's background that were directly relevant to the child's successful adjustment to the home.

During the study period, a greater focus on preserving kinship systems and recruiting extended family members to be caregivers to children who could not remain with their biological parents was established. For example, in 1992, nearly 25% of children were in relative placements; in 1996, that proportion increased to 31%. For both kin and nonrelated foster families, the goal was to nurture and support multiple healthy caregivers to children, including respite providers and Casey aides. By doing this, staff and foster families were offering each youth a network of caregivers, the same idea portrayed in the African proverb "It takes a village to raise a child."

Lastly, stable, well-trained staff members were a key component of Casey Family Programs. During the study period, Casey had a 6%–10% turnover rate, which was lower than that of most public child welfare agencies (Russell, 1987, p. 36). Factors contributing to the low staff turnover were the rewards and opportunities for professional development provided to Casey staff.

Characteristics of the Casey Foster Care Population

During the study period of 1988–1998, Casey recruited children from the nation's public child welfare system. Youth requiring long-term foster family care were usually referred by county or state foster care systems, with community sanction and oversight almost always provided by the legal system. The main intake criteria were as follows (Perry et al., 1992):

- Children accepted into Casey were between the ages of 6 and 15 years.
- Long-term foster family care was the plan of choice for the child at the time of intake. Children whose placement needs could best be met by any other permanent plan, including adoption or return to birth parents, were not appropriate for placement with Casey.
- The child must have been capable of self-sufficiency as a young adult. The program was not intended to serve children with disabling conditions at the time of intake that would interfere substantially with their likelihood to attain self-sufficiency.
- Community sanction must have been secured for all placements made with Casey Family Programs. *Community sanction* was legal recognition by the community that Casey was responsible for the care of a child (the day-to-day case management authority to make a variety of decisions and plan for the welfare of the child), regardless of the agency, entity, or individual with ultimate legal responsibility.

As displayed in Table 1.1, the Casey program model during the time of the study was long-term in nature, with workers having reasonable caseloads

Table 1.1. Characteristics of Services Provided by Casey Family Programs and the State Agencies During Most or All of the Study Period of 1988–1998

Characteristic	Casey	Oregon DHS	Washington CA/DCFS
Average size of foster care caseloads	Low: 15–17	Moderate: 25	High: 31[a]
Staff education:			
MSW level staff	Over 90%	20%	23%[c]
MSW and/or MA in another field	Over 98%	36.5%[b]	42%
Frequency with which children and foster parents were seen	Monthly	Monthly for children	Every 90 days
Worker turnover	Low (6–10%)[d] per year	Statistic not available	High (24.6% in 1999)[e]
Monthly foster parent retention payment (about $100 per month)	Yes	No	No
Child clothing allowance	Substantial	Moderate	Moderate
Foster parent satisfaction	High[f]	Moderate—High[g]	Moderate[h]
Foster parent training hours	Generally at or above the state minimum requirements[i]	Most foster parents met the annual training requirements	Most foster parents met the annual training requirements[j]
Foster parent turnover	10–12%[f]	32%[k]	28%[l]
Availability of supplemental services such as mental health counseling and employment experience	High[m]	Moderate	Generally low but varied by region[n]
Access to mental health counseling during the course of their time in the foster care program. (Note: All Casey youth had access to supplemental services, while youth in the public systems had less access due to funding limitations [expressed in percent])	98.6% (0.5)[o]	98.6% (0.7)[o]	92.6% (0.9)[o]
Use of mental health counseling during the course of their time in the foster care program (expressed in percent)	75.8% (2.4)[o]	70.8% (5.8)[o]	66.0% (1.8)[o]
Access to alcohol or drug treatment programs during the course of their time in the foster care program (expressed in percent)	98.5% (0.5)[o]	95.2% (1.4)[o]	91.2% (1.1)[o]
Use of alcohol or drug treatment programs during the course of their time in the foster care program (expressed in percent)	12.4% (1.6)[o]	13.5% (2.4)[o]	14.7% (1.3)[o]

(continued)

Table 1.1.　Continued

Characteristic	Casey	Oregon DHS	Washington CA/DCFS
Access to employment training or location services in the last placement longer than three months (expressed in percent)	89.9% (1.5)[o]	84.9% (2.4)[o]	81.3% (1.5)[o]
Use of employment training or location services in the last placement longer than three months (expressed in percent)	48.1% (2.8)[o]	51.2% (3.5)[o]	45.8% (1.9)[o]
Cost per day (1998)[p]	$82.00	$49.16	$50.53
Mean time in care (in years)	9.8	4.4	5.3

[a]Washington State, Department of Social and Health Services. (Undated). *DCFS case count percentage comparison FY 1994—FY 1999* (Carol Brandford, personal communication, November 7, 2005).

[b]Oregon data are taken from a study of the Oregon CPS system conducted by the University of Southern Maine (Hornby & Zeller, 1992).

[c]November 2000 data.

[d]See Ezell et al. (2002).

[e]November 2000 data. The social worker turnover rate includes promotions, transfers, demotions, reassignments, retirements, deaths, and so on.

[f]Estimated by senior staff working in the Casey Family Program offices during the time of the study. See Doucette, Tarnowski, and Baum (2001); Le Prohn, Barenblat, Godinet, Nicoll, and Pecora (1996); Le Prohn and Pecora (1994); Vaughn (2002).

[g]Hornby and Zeller (1992) noted that 70% of the families who stopped fostering did so as a result of a change in their family circumstances and not as a result of their relationship with the agency (satisfaction).

[h]Washington State Department of Social and Health Services (1996) (Carol Brandford, personal communication, November 7, 2005).

[i]Le Prohn et al. (1996); Le Prohn and Pecora (1994).

[j]For example, annual governor's recognition event, steady increase in foster parents trained (e.g., in 1988, 342 trained; in 1998, 3,790 trained). In 1994, CA/DCFS received enhancement dollars to increase workshops for foster parents on special topics, worked collaboratively with the Foster Parent Association of Washington State (FPAWS) on preservice training—15 hours, 60 hours of a basic foster parent training course, and a special topic workshop (Sharon Newcomer, Washington State Department of Social and Health Services, Children's Administration Program Manager, personal communication, November 7, 2005).

[k]Compared to a Child Welfare League of America national average of 40%. See Hornby and Zeller (1992). Hornby and Zeller noted that 70% of the families who stopped fostering did so as a result of a change in their family circumstances and not as a result of their relationship with the agency (satisfaction).

[l]See footnote h above and Washington State Department of Social and Health Services. (Undated). *Report to the legislature: Recruitment of adoptive and foster homes 07/98—06/99. Olympia, WA: Author.*

[m]See Le Prohn et al. (1996); Le Prohn and Pecora (1994).

[n]Washington State Department of Social and Health Services (2004a). *Washington DSHS has made improvements in this area* (Carol Brandford, personal communication, November 7, 2005).

[o]Data taken from the Northwest Alumni Study alumni interviews. Numbers in parentheses are standard errors.

[p]The year 1998 was chosen for calculating the cost per day because this was the last year of the ten-year study period and cost data were more likely to be located. Neither Casey nor state costs include mental health costs, because the State of Oregon could not calculate these costs (Edgbert et al., 2004).

(averaging 16 youth per worker); low staff turnover (averaging 8.2% for 1995 to 1998 and 10% in 1998); good foster parent retention; and a variety of mental health, education, and other services available to the youth in care. The 1998 cost per child per day for Casey family foster care was $82.00 (not including physical health and mental health costs).

Description of the Oregon Department of Human Services, Children, Adults, and Families

Overview

Oregon child welfare services were state-administered and provided comprehensive programming in local communities. Between 1988 and 1998, the State of Oregon reorganized the delivery of child welfare services from what was called the Children's Services Division by creating three separate state agencies with overlapping responsibilities.[9] The Oregon State Office for Services to Children and Families (SOSCF) was part of this state-administered system, providing programming in local communities throughout the state. Its programs were governed by federal and state legislation, as well as state-specific policies and program guidelines.

Program Focus and Design

At the time of the study, SOSCF under the direction of the Department of Human Services (DHS) was the entity primarily responsible for child protection, foster care, residential treatment, and adoption services. The Oregon Commission for Children and Families (OCCF) developed programming at the state and local levels that responded to traditional family preservation and prevention services. The third entity created, the Oregon Youth Authority was mandated to work with juvenile corrections and focus on youth who had been adjudicated delinquent and who were in the juvenile justice system.

Oregon law assigned to SOSCF, the child protection organization, a broad mission in the area of child protective services. This organization was tasked with preventing child abuse and neglect, protecting children who had been maltreated, and, when possible, rehabilitating families in which children had been maltreated. More specifically, it was designed to provide a wide range of services to families and children, to take custody of endangered and maltreated children when necessary, to regulate private agencies dealing with endangered or maltreated children, to investigate and assess child maltreatment cases, to administer programs for foster care and adoption, and to play a key role in court proceedings on behalf of maltreated children.

The legal mission of SOSCF was balanced between child protection and family preservation. At least three separate legislative statements expressed basic policy concerning the mission of SOSCF. First, in listing its basic powers, ORS418.005(1) stated that such powers had been created "in order to establish, extend and strengthen welfare services for the protection and care of homeless, dependent, or neglected children." Second, ORS418.745 provided that "the Legislative Assembly finds that for the purpose of facilitating the use of protective social services to prevent further abuse, safeguard and enhance the welfare of abused children, and preserve family life when consistent with the protection of the child by stabilizing the family and improving parental capacity, it is necessary and in the public interest to require mandatory reports and investigations of abuse of children." Third, ORS418.485 established policy concerning the purchase of care and services, providing in part, that "it is the policy of the State of Oregon to strengthen family life and to insure the protection of all children either in their own homes or in other appropriate care outside their homes."

During the study period, one of the major initiatives in Oregon was the development and expansion of the use of family decision meetings. Originally called *family unity meetings,* the purpose of these meetings was to focus on the needs of the child and to provide a forum to elicit the best thinking from a significant group of people on the safety and permanency needs of the child. Oregon became known for conducting multiple family decision meetings with families.

During the early 1990s and into the middle of the decade, SOSCF in Multnomah County expanded the role and accessibility of child welfare services to the community. One such function was in the decentralization of the single Multnomah County office into five separate neighborhood-based branches throughout the county. Each of the separate branch offices was staffed as a full-functioning, independent office under one judicial jurisdiction.[10] The branch office boundaries were based on the public school districts and the school catchment areas, which enabled the educational system to have a single point of entry into child welfare services. This configuration is important to note because this structure naturally lent itself to the practice of identifying school liaisons within child welfare. School staff then had a child welfare professional whom they could consult about specific children and families. Child abuse calls and mandatory reporter laws still required a formal process, but the liaisons provided a sounding board and troubleshooter for the schools.[11]

Throughout this period, SOSCF strengthened services to address the growing concerns about parent drug and alcohol abuse. Teams consisting of a caseworker, a drug counselor, and a community health nurse were established in order to provide a comprehensive approach to the issues involved in families struggling with drug dependency. These *Family Support Teams* were established in a number of the larger local offices across Oregon, including the Multnomah County Juvenile Court (the Portland site for the Northwest Alumni Study toward the end of the study period).

Toward the end of the study period, SOSCF entered into a settlement agreement with a group of child advocates to address a series of common concerns in the child welfare protective services and foster care systems. This agreement resulted in SOSCF implementing a series of child welfare reforms called *System of Care* (SOC). It was based on a strengths/needs-based practice approach that addressed children's safety, permanency, and well-being needs, including attachment through more integrated services.

Characteristics of the Oregon State Foster Care Population

During the study period, Oregon's child welfare system continued to serve a wide range of children and families. Approximately half of the children and families served received in-home services and half were served in substitute care. Youth requiring long-term foster care, the population for this study, represented one group of the youth served in substitute care. The number of children in foster care grew during this period from 4,266 on December 31, 1988, to an average daily population of 6,543 in December 1998. Throughout this period, approximately 30% of the children in family foster care were placed with relatives. One-third of the children in foster care were between the ages of 0 and 5 years, one-third were between 6 and 12 years, and one-third were over 12 years. Lastly, in 1988, the median length of stay for children in out-of-home care was 49 days (the mean was 228 days). By 1998, the median length of stay had risen to 139 days (the mean was 404 days).[12]

In sum and as displayed in Table 1.1, Oregon's state family foster care program model focused on child safety and rehabilitating families. The average caseload for workers was moderate (averaging 25 youth per worker); foster parent retention was moderate; and there was high availability of mental health, education, and other services available to the youth in care. (Note that the staff turnover rate for this time period was not available.) The 1998 cost per child per day for Oregon family foster care was $49.16 (not including physical health and mental health costs).

Description of Washington State Department of Social and Health Services, Children's Administration

Overview

The Washington State Department of Social and Health Services, Children's Administration, Division of Children and Families (CA/DCFS) is part of a state-administered and state-provided child welfare service delivery system. Children and families enter CA/DCFS through three primary program areas: *(1)* Child Protective Services (CPS), *(2)* Child Welfare Services (CWS), and *(3)* Family Reconciliation Services (FRS). These programs are responsible for the investigation of child abuse and neglect complaints, child protection, family preservation, family reconciliation, in-home services, foster care, group care, adoption services, and independent living services for children ages 0 to 18 years.[13] At the time of the study, the CWS program provided both permanency planning and intensive treatment services for children and families when children were in out-of-home care, dependents of the state, or legally free for adoption. The Office of Foster Care Licensing within the Division of Licensed Resources was responsible for the licensing and monitoring of out-of-home care facilities, including foster care, group care, and child placement agencies.

Program Focus and Design

Since 1987, the State of Washington's vision for child welfare services provided by the CA/DCFS has been described in mission statements that focus on protecting children, supporting the ability of families to care safely for their own children, ensuring that children are provided quality care in permanent family settings in a timely manner, and involving child welfare stakeholders (i.e., communities and tribes) in the state's efforts (Washington State Department of Social and Health Services, 1987, 1989, 1991, 1993, 2004b, 1995b).

Specifically, the mission of the CA/DCFS was to provide a comprehensive range of services that protected children from abuse, neglect, and exploitation; rehabilitated youthful offenders while providing community support and protection; and promoted healthy child growth and development. Services were intended to promote preservation, rehabilitation, and reunification of families to the maximum extent possible while providing services in the least intrusive and restrictive means possible.

Between 1988 and 1998, the goals and objectives for the CA/DCFS were identified as prevention, placement, substitute care, permanency, effective service to minorities, community support, and administrative practice (Washington State Department of Social and Health Services, 1987, 1989, 1991, 1993, 1995b). With regard to prevention, the CA/DCFS pursued ongoing goals of improving preventative services by implementing intensive placement prevention units and services, and by increasing funding for and availability of home-based placement prevention services (Washington State Department of Social and Health Services, 1987, 1989, 1991, 1993, 1995b).

A focus on placement decision making included expansion of Child Protection Teams to review decision making related to placement, developing tools to assess relatives as a placement resource, and regulating evaluation of local placement practices (Washington State Department of Social and Health Services, 1987, 1989). The primary goal of the service delivery system was to reduce placement rates overall while ensuring that children remained safe from serious maltreatment during and subsequent to involvement with child welfare services (Washington State Department of Social and Health Services, 1989, 1995b).

During this time period, the CA/DCFS pursued several objectives to meet the goals of improving social work practices and services for children removed from parental custody (foster and relative care) and to ensure that the agency had a stable pool of well-trained foster and adoptive parents (Washington State Department of Social and Health Services, 1987, 1989, 1991, 1993, 1995b). The focus of CA/DCFS services was on dual case-planning processes. Principles of practice included work to increase the number of foster care and adoptive homes available to children in need of placement and to create permanent homes while simultaneously reducing the number of children in care.

Further, during this period, the agency worked on objectives to cultivate an atmosphere of teamwork between social workers and foster parents, to increase reimbursement rates for foster parents, and to improve foster parent training, particularly for difficult-to-care-for children (Washington State Department of Social and Health Services, 1989, 1993). Additionally, a foster parent/birth parent mentoring program was established to enhance the ability of birth parents to care safely for their children by using resources provided by foster parents more effectively (Washington State Department of Social and Health Services, 1993). Also, procedures for licensing nontraditional foster and adoptive parents were developed. Finally, during this time period, the CA/DCFS implemented an Independent Living Program (ILP) to help youth aging out of foster care to transition to independence (Washington State Department of Social and Health Services, 1987, 1989, 1993).

Consistent with federal and state policies mandating that permanency planning include prevention, family reunification, and postreunification services, in addition to foster care and adoption, policies and practices were developed to improve permanency planning decisions (Washington State Department of Social and Health Services, 1987, 1989). Additionally, the agency developed program accountability mechanisms, initiated a self-assessment process to identify service limitations and needs, examined and reduced worker caseloads, developed procedures to incorporate family strengths in the decision process, and encouraged joint Children's Administration and parent decision making. Further, the CA/DCFS improved staff training and retention, analyzed worker stress, and developed a staff retention plan (Washington State Department of Social and Health Services, 1987, 1989, 1993).

Case practice was based on goal-oriented permanency planning and a family-centered practice model. Goal-oriented permanency planning involved using placement only as a last resort, placing children in the least restrictive environment available, and planning to return the child home or to a permanent and stable family environment as quickly as allowed by the issues surrounding the child's safety and the family's ability to reunify. The family-centered practice model directed social workers to recognize a broad definition of *family*, to provide holistic services to the family unit rather than to individuals, and to involve families in planning, delivering, and evaluating services tailored specifically to individual families.

Upon referral and once the child's safety had been established, placement prevention was the primary goal of the social worker. When a child entered placement, an individual service plan was created and great attention was given to addressing the issues that had led to placement so that the child could be reunified with his or her family. If reunification was not an option, the social worker sought to implement an alternate permanency plan. A permanency plan had to be completed for a child in out-of-home care by his or her 18th month in placement or by the 12th month if the child was 10 years old or younger. Acceptable permanency plans included maintaining a child in or returning a child to the home of a parent; relative guardianship; relative placement with a written permanency agreement; adoption or foster parent guardianship; family foster care with a written permanency agreement; and independent living if appropriate and if the child was 16 years of age or older.

Placement with relatives was the preferred type of out-of-home care. Foster adoption was another type of placement that was intended for children who were unlikely to return home. Children were placed with an adoptive family who was licensed to provide foster care and who had had an approved adoptive home study. The intent of this type of placement was to reduce the number of moves a child had to make and to increase stability (Washington State Department of Social and Health Services, 1995a). An ILP assessment was completed for all children who were in placement after their 16th birthday. The objective of the ILP was to assist youth in attaining independence and self-sufficiency in the community. Youth were assessed on their ability to attain educational goals, manage income, attain vocational goals, secure adequate housing, and develop daily living skills and interpersonal skills. Independent living skills services were then provided to eligible youth.

In 1999, Washington's annual turnover rate for child welfare service workers was 24.6% (this included promotions, transfers, demotions, reassignments, retirements, and death). These workers spent an average of 4.1 years in their position. Over half of the workers who worked with youth in foster care had a bachelor's degree only, while 24% had a master's in social work (MSW) degree (in 2000, it was 23%), 17% had a master of arts (MA) degree, 1% had a doctoral degree (PhD), and 1% had an associate arts (AA) degree. The average caseload for child welfare social workers in 1998 was 27 (Child Welfare League of America National Data Analysis System, 2004; see http://ndas.cwla.org).

During this time period, improved procedures for recruiting and assessing foster families were developed. A Foster Home Assessment was implemented to include an evaluation of the family's character, personal history, relationships, trauma and crises, coping skills, child care skills, and experience (Washington State Department of Social and Health Services, 1995a). Foster families were assessed and relicensed every three years and every time they changed their residence. Foster families received multifaceted training before licensing, including child behavior management, understanding sexual abuse, dealing with a child's separation from his or her parents, substance abuse, and stress related to caring for foster children. Foster parents were eligible to receive ancillary support services that included recreational activities, a clothing allowance, and transportation reimbursements, as well as social supports including peer support from other foster parents.

Characteristics of the Washington State Foster Care Population

The number of Washington children in out-of-home care increased from over 7,700 at the beginning of 1988 to nearly 8,900 by 1998. Of these children, 5,600 were in foster homes or relative care in 1988 (Washington State Department of Social and Health Services, 1989), and 7,600 were in this type of care in 1998. The percentage of children in relative placements increased from 11% of all out-of-home placements in 1988 (Washington State Department of Social and Health Services, 1989) to 28.6% of all out-of-home placements in 1998 (see the Child Welfare League of America National Data Analysis System at http://ndas.cwla.org for these statistics).

The average age of children in foster care shifted during this period, with the largest cohort of children being 12- to 18-year-olds (37%) in 1988 (Washington State Department of Social and Health Services, 1989) and 0 to 6-year-olds (38%) in 1998 (U.S. Department of Health and Human Services, 1999). In 1988, the median length of stay for children in out-of-home care was 12 months (Washington State Department of Social and Health Services, 1989). By 1998, the median length of stay had risen to 17 months, and the proportion of children with a length of stay of one year or more had increased from 50% to 62% (Child Welfare League of America National Data Analysis System, http://ndas.cwla.org).

In sum and as displayed in Table 1.1, the State of Washington's family foster care program model focused on promoting healthy growth and development and returning children to their biological or other family connections. The average caseload for workers was high (averaging 31 youth per worker); staff turnover was high (almost one in four per year in 1999); the foster parent retention turnover rate was 28%; and relatively good access to mental health, education, and other services was available to the youth in care (with variability by region in the state). The 1998 cost per child per day for Washington DSHS family foster care was $50.53 (not including physical health and mental health costs).

Summary of the Differences Between Casey and State Agencies

Key differences between the Casey and state agencies are summarized in Table 1.1 and highlighted below:

- Casey had a specific focus on long-term foster care. For state agencies, foster care was one component of programming in a larger mandate for child protection and family reunification. For example, state agencies provided short-term as well as longer-term foster care.
- State agencies had additional areas of focus, including family preservation, family reunification, and providing care in the least restrictive setting, while

Casey focused primarily on permanent long-term foster care and pursued other forms of permanency planning only if the child's situation changed.

- All children were served in state agency programs, including children with disabilities and unaccompanied minors. Casey did not serve children with mental, emotional, or physical disabilities so severe that they could not be expected to live independently in the community upon reaching adulthood.
- Because of state legislative and federal program funding priorities, fewer resources were available to staff for Oregon DHS and Washington CA/ DCFS, while Casey staff had greater access to additional therapeutic, recreational, educational, and life-skills preparation services. (But note that 93%–99% of the alumni from foster care served by all three organizations rated access to these services as fairly high.)
- A much higher proportion of Casey social workers had obtained MSW degrees than had workers in the public agencies.
- All agencies had a case-planning process; however, Casey had implemented a more comprehensive child assessment and planning approach (involving cultural, emotional, and independent living skills) earlier in the study period.
- Children and foster parents were seen by caseworkers less frequently in Washington than in Oregon or by Casey.
- Worker turnover was higher in Washington and Oregon compared to Casey.
- Foster parent turnover was lower in Casey compared to the two state agencies.
- Foster parent satisfaction was higher in Casey compared to the state agencies.
- Casey provided more supplemental services and supports to foster parents, such as recognition and training, and child enrichment activities, such as music lessons and summer camps.

Summary

At any one point during the year, nearly 500,000 children are in foster care in the United States. Of the youth exiting care each year, one-half have been in care for a year or longer. The needs of these youth are slightly different from those of youth with shorter stays. In addition to the immediate concerns of child safety, child permanence, and child and family well-being for all youth entering care, youth experiencing longer durations of care have additional short- and long-term outcomes with which agencies providing care must be concerned, including emotional, physical, and cognitive development. Given the time spent in care and the federal, state, and local financial investment in caring for these children, it would be expected that more conclusive research would be available on the outcomes of these children after leaving care.

Unfortunately, the relative lack of research and the methodological limitations of existing research have hampered conclusions concerning long-term outcomes and the effectiveness of care that foster youth received. The Northwest Alumni Study was designed to address the lack of objective data about adolescents who were placed in foster care for longer time periods in the Northwest. By examining extensive information collected through case records and interviews, the Northwest Alumni Study sought to understand how youth formerly in foster care were faring as adults and what experiences in care related to long-term success. The study also sought to discover if there were agency differences in service delivery quality, process, and outcomes— and what factors might account for those differences. This study, therefore, examined the efficacy of a high-quality long-term family foster care program in the particular context of the American Northwest. As such, this is an example of what Donald Campbell called a *local molar causal validity* study (Campbell, 1986). Although this study took place in only two states, these states are similar to many other states in terms of family demographics and service delivery structures. So, we are cautiously optimistic that readers will be able to generalize the findings to other jurisdictions.

Organization of the Book

This chapter sets the stage for the current state of foster care and why a study such as this was necessary. A list of conceptual units and a description of all chapters are provided below.

1. *Introduction to the Northwest Alumni Study*
   a. Chapter 1 (this chapter) describes the current state of foster care in terms of how many youth are served, how much society invests in them, the lack of conclusive data on their long-term functioning, and the program models for the programs in which young adults were served.
   b. Chapter 2 describes how past research informed the choice of a conceptual and theoretical framework for the Northwest Alumni Study, including the main research questions and hypotheses of the study.
2. *Study Methodology*
   a. Chapter 3 presents the sample characteristics and response rates of the three foster care agencies that participated in the study.
   b. Chapter 4 summarizes the data sources, variables, and measures, as well as the data collection procedures and data weighting methods.
3. *Risk Factors*
   a. Chapter 5 details factors that put alumni at risk during childhood, including demographics and maltreatment.
   b. Foster care experiences are presented in Appendix C. A separate Working Paper No. 4 further describes the foster care experiences of alumni while in care. The first part of this working paper focuses on placement history, while the second part focuses on other dimensions of care, including access to mental health and educational services and preparation for leaving care (see Williams, Herrick, Pecora, & O'Brien, 2008).

4. *Outcome Findings*

   Alumni prevalence rates and comparison benchmarks are presented in Chapters 6–9 for the following outcome domains:
   a. Chapter 6: mental health and physical health
   b. Chapter 7: education
   c. Chapter 8: employment and finances
   d. Chapter 9: relationships and social supports

5. *Relationships With Outcomes*

   The relationship between each area listed below, and alumni outcomes are detailed in Working Paper No. 6 and Chapters 10–12:
   a. Summary of the effects of demographics and risk factors on alumni outcomes (O'Brien et al., 2008b)
   b. Chapter 10: agency program model
   c. Chapter 11: the effects of foster care experiences are summarized in Working Paper No. 7 (O'Brien et al., 2008c).

6. *Optimization Analyses*

   a. Chapter 12 presents results from statistical simulations examining the possible effects on outcomes had a higher-quality foster care experience been provided.

7. *Discussion and Implications*

   a. Chapter 13 discusses the implications of findings for improving foster care and related services.

Note that while gender and ethnicity were used in the multivariate equations as control variables, the research team is currently analyzing the data to further explore racial/ethnicity differences when other variables are used as controls. This includes exploring differences for the largest ethnic groups of color in the study sample: African American, Hispanic/Latino and American Indian/Alaska Native. Those results will be published in peer-reviewed journals and working papers posted on the Casey Family Programs website (http://www.casey.org).

Acknowledgment.   Anne Havalchak contributed to this chapter.

2

Theoretical and Conceptual Frameworks and Past Research

They're my family. I was with one family from 7th grade to when I graduated from high school. That was where I went during summers when I came home from college. When I tell people about my family, I include them. They had three daughters and a brother and I associate with them just as much as I do with my biological family.

I don't feel that I have succeeded in my life the way that I would have liked. For one thing, I had a kid when I was very young. I believe that because I lived in foster care and a treatment center up to about a month before I turned 18, during that time I didn't get to date, go out with friends to the movies, go shopping at the mall, dances, or parties like normal kids do. And when I turned 18 and moved out of my grandmother's and moved in with my brother, I let loose and did all those things that I had been denied. I feel that if I had been allowed to do normal teenage things, my life would have been different.

Overview

The Northwest Alumni Study examined the intermediate and long-term outcomes for 659 children placed in foster care. Data from case records and interviews were collected to examine the relationship between foster care experiences and adult outcomes (e.g., mental health, education, and employment and finances). Further, additional information concerning demographics and risk factors was collected and examined. In addition to the agency through which alumni were served (Casey or the state agencies in Washington or Oregon), demographics and risk factors were controlled. Eligible participants had to *(1)* have spent 12 months or more in family foster care between the ages of 14 and 18 years; *(2)* have been placed by the state agency or Casey in Seattle, Tacoma, or Yakima, Washington or Portland, Oregon, between January 1, 1989, and September 30, 1998; *(3)* have been placed because of child maltreatment or child behavior problems and not as an unaccompanied refugee minor; and *(4)* have no major physical or developmental disability (e.g., an IQ of less than 70). Youth who had severe physical disabilities and those with an IQ of less than 70 were excluded from the sample due to their likelihood of needing extended care following emancipation. Before samples were drawn and prior to analyses, steps were taken to increase comparability and minimize preexisting differences (e.g., demographic differences) between Casey and state alumni. Specifically, matching and data weighting techniques were implemented (see Chapters 3 and 4, respectively).

To understand the context and environment of the alumni while in foster care and their influence on adult outcomes, this chapter is divided into four sections:

1. *Foster care research.* Prior research informing this study's research questions and hypotheses is discussed. This section begins by presenting findings on the impact of child maltreatment on later development (for more detail, see Pecora et al., 2009).
2. *Landsverk's conceptual framework.* This model describing critical factors impacting youth development in foster care is presented.
3. *Developmental theories and conceptual models.* Theories and conceptual models explaining child growth and development and informing the Northwest Alumni Study are discussed.
4. *Research questions and hypotheses.* This chapter concludes by presenting the primary and secondary research questions and hypotheses.

Collaborators in the Northwest Alumni Study

To ensure objectivity and examine a representative sample of alumni, the University of Washington, Harvard Medical School, and the University of Michigan Survey Research Center collaborated with three social service organizations to conduct the Northwest Alumni Study:

1. Casey Family Programs (Casey), with participating offices in Seattle, Tacoma, and Yakima, Washington, and Portland, Oregon; 111 children from Casey Washington and 44 children from Casey Oregon were included in the study.
2. The Oregon Department of Human Services, Division of Children, Adults and Families, Community Human Services (Oregon DHS), with participating offices in Portland; 171 children from DHS were included in the study.
3. The State of Washington Department of Social and Health Services, Children's Administration, Division of Children and Family Services (Washington CA/DCFS), with participating offices in the areas of Seattle, Tacoma, and Yakima; 333 children from CA/DCFS were included in the study.

A full list of project staff and key advisors is presented in Appendix A.

Past Research About Foster Care Outcomes

Overview

Table 2.1 presents a cross section of recent research studies on outcomes in foster care conducted in the United States in two major areas:

- Progress and outcomes of children while in foster care
- Follow-up studies on youth status and functioning after discharge from foster care[14]

Table 2.1.   A Cross Section of Foster Care Outcome Data[22]

Overview

Studies have demonstrated that, after leaving foster care, many alumni are coping well with the effects of child maltreatment, but a substantial proportion are struggling. The field needs to pay attention to the many alumni success stories while learning from areas where services were less effective. This table provides a concise summary of the outcome data from recent and classic foster care studies conducted in the United States. Note that in many cases the foster care alumni data have not been compared with data on nonplaced youth of similar racial, economic, family background, and other relevant variables, but comparisons with general population data have been used where possible. Caution is needed, as the studies vary in terms of the age at which the data were collected, geographic areas covered, method of data collection, and sample size. Thus the averages provided are rough estimates.

During-Care Outcomes

Education

What is the high school graduation rate for youth placed in foster care? How many youth complete high school with a diploma? With a GED? How many alumni have enrolled in college? How many alumni received a BA or higher degree? There are no simple answers to this set of crucial questions because many youth complete high school later than age 18—often after leaving foster care. And yet, most outcome monitoring by agencies stops at youth discharge. Furthermore, most follow-up studies include alumni at age 19, 20, or 21 instead of at ages 23–25, when many people complete high school with a GED, or at ages 23–30, when many would have had time to receive a college degree. Given those limitations, when the most relevant studies are identified in terms of including alumni of a suitable age and reasonable sample size, estimates to help address each of the questions can be derived, with the caveat that few national studies have been done and the age range of the alumni included in these studies varied.

Compared to the general population, fewer youth placed in foster care complete high school, but as mentioned above, these data are limited because dropout rates have not been carefully tracked and follow-up studies beyond age 22 are rare. While about one-third of alumni lack a high school diploma or GED at discharge, about 74% or more later complete high school or earn a GED.[23]

Very few studies have tracked the proportion of youth in foster care who earn a GED versus a high school diploma because the most accurate data need to be collected from alumni who are 24 and older, as many people complete a GED at age 20 or later. For example, a study of alumni aged 20–51 (averaging 30 years old) found that 16.7% of them completed high school with a GED, a rate that is more than three times higher than the general population rate of 5%.[24]

Gaps in development of life skills for independent living exist, and these skills need to be taught more intensively and earlier in a child's life.[25]

Health and Safety

Substantiated rates of foster parent maltreatment are generally low; 0.7% for foster care nationally in 2000.[26] However, major differences have been found between the rates reported while youth are in foster care versus retrospective reports from alumni. What reasons are offered for this difference in rates? The reported in-care child maltreatment rates often include reported and substantiated reports of abuse and/or neglect. Although some studies used a standardized case record review instrument, the reports were not necessarily screened or assessed using a consistent standard of proof. The reasons for those differences need to be understood before any firm conclusions are drawn.

(continued)

Table 2.1.   Continued

Over the past 10 years, teen pregnancy while in foster care has been much higher than in the general population, but there are signs that this rate may be decreasing among youth in certain agencies.[27] However, rates of teen pregnancy within a few years of leaving foster care remain high in the few studies that have measured this outcome.[28]

Permanence

Placing children with relatives or other kin has increased in recent years, but even more children might be placed with relatives if the right supports were made available.[29] More siblings could be placed together, and agencies are increasing their focus on this aspect of practice.[30] Evidence is growing that placement stability is linked with positive short- and long-term youth outcomes and therefore should be maximized.[31] Adoption delays are decreasing but are still too long for some children.[32]

Postdischarge Outcomes

Education

Early studies of 19- and 20-year-old alumni estimated that about 50%–60% obtained a high school diploma. However, more recent studies that have followed youth further after leaving care have found higher rates of high school completion; a more reasonable estimate would be about 74%.[33]

A substantial proportion of alumni (about 37%) attend college or some kind of vocational degree program, but few obtain a four-year degree.[34] While the BA college completion rate has averaged about 3% across some of the most recent studies of older alumni, a study that contacted some of the oldest alumni ever interviewed found that, for alumni of ages 25 and older, the BA or above completion rate was 10.8%, with over 12% of alumni still in school of some kind.[35] Thus, vocational training and college completion rates, while low compared to those of the general population, may be higher than the rates previously reported.[36]

Transition Services and Preparation for Independent Living

A substantial number of alumni report being inadequately prepared for emancipation.[37] Of alumni from care, 12%–44% have experienced homelessness after discharge, with rates varying by study sample and the definition of homelessness.[38]

Employment and Self-Sufficiency

Some alumni have difficulty finding work and have employment rates lower than that of the general population.[39] Disproportionately high numbers of alumni receive public assistance,[40] are struggling to earn a living wage, or do not have health care benefits.[41] Compared to the general population of children with similar family backgrounds, a higher proportion of alumni have spent time in jail.[42]

Mental Health, Parenting, and Community Involvement

Over one-third of alumni have at least one serious mental health condition or have experienced emotional problems since leaving foster care.[43] Few alumni have had their own children placed in foster care, but the rate is higher than that of the general population.[44] Community involvement and volunteer rates may be substantial among youth in foster care and alumni, but these are rarely tracked.[45] Good citizenship in the form of voter registration and voting is an important indicator; however, it has been measured in only a few studies.[46]

In-Care Findings

Most studies of foster care have focused on the needs, behaviors, and outcomes of the children while they are in care using cross-sectional surveys and qualitative case studies. Relatively few studies have employed experimental designs. Until recently, this research has been limited by the poor agency management information systems that have been in place, poor staff training, inconsistent recording of data, and a growing but slow realization that there are key functional or developmental outcomes that should be tracked in addition to various "status" outcomes such as permanency status and living situation restrictiveness. There are pockets of positive findings, however—especially among the programs with higher-quality services.

Postdischarge Findings

As described in Table 2.1, some key large-scale follow-up studies have been conducted using quantitative research approaches to measure the postdischarge functioning of youth who had been placed in foster care. Some of these follow-up studies have been limited by a lack of agency funding, as well as staff time and expertise to conduct these evaluations. Until recently, little consensus existed about how and when to measure alumni functioning. These results have been sobering reminders of the agencies' need to do more regarding teaching of independent living skills, employment training, relationship formation, and mental health counseling. More studies using multiple time points and longer-term follow-up are needed.

Wider Reflections on Foster Care Outcomes[15]

Practice experiences, research findings from landmark studies such as those of Maas and Engler (1959) and Fanshel and Shinn (1978), as well as more recent critiques of foster care, have underscored a number of points:

- Some children still experience too many placement changes, as the latest federal outcome data document, but permanency planning has reduced this problem.[16]
- Earlier, children were inappropriately moved out of their homes—with little effort to help their parents to care for them. If anything, the system encouraged parents to abandon their children, which is less the case now—especially with the emphasis upon kinship care by relatives if the birth parents are unable or unwilling to care for the child adequately. However, there are disturbing reports that a new wave of child relinquishments is emerging due to the more restrictive Temporary Assistance to Needy Families (TANF) public assistance program's five-year lifetime limit and the 1997 Adoption and Safe Families Act's 18-month time limit for parent rehabilitation before termination of parental rights (Raymond Kirk, personal communication, June 15, 2004).

- Children from minority families—especially black, Hispanic, and American Indian/Alaska Native families—are represented in foster care at disproportionately high rates, and many have had less positive service outcomes (Hill, 2001; see http://racemattersconsortium.org).
- Relatively little attention has been directed to gender differences in foster care services or outcomes.
- Most of the children placed in foster care came from poor families—often families that were barely managing to survive on limited income from public assistance programs (U.S. Department of Health and Human Services, 2001a).
- Although some children were effectively helped through placement in foster care, for others the separation from their families had adverse consequences, including losing track of siblings, a feeling of inadequacy, unplanned school changes, mental health problems, and disrupted relationships.

As a result of these and other findings, as well as the rapid increase in the number of children entering foster care that has only recently slowed, questions have been raised about the effectiveness of the child welfare system. One partial response has been the development of more evidence-based treatment foster care models (e.g., Chamberlain et al., 2008; Meadowcroft, Thomlison, & Chamberlain, 1994; Meadowcroft & Trout, 1990) and more explicit foster care practice philosophies and guidelines (e.g., Casey Family Programs, 2000, 2003b). The need for treatment fidelity measurement is being more widely recognized. In both areas of research that we reviewed earlier, there are many research gaps and areas where the evaluations could be strengthened. Suggested refinements are presented in the next section.

Which Foster Care Experience Processes Remediate the Effects of Maltreatment and Removal From the Birth Home?

While family foster care is intended to be a temporary living arrangement for a child, for most of the time period of this study, placements for nearly half of the children lasted for more than a year and for almost one in five children, placements lasted for three years or more (U.S. Department of Health and Human Services, 1999). If children spend a year or more in foster care, the services and supports they receive can be potentially powerful interventions for remediating the effects of maltreatment and removal from the birth home.

Each of the following sections describes an area of the foster care experience that is hypothesized to have a positive effect on outcomes when seen in its positive form (e.g., low placement change rate, greater access to services and supports, greater involvement with the foster family). These areas were considered important in influencing adult outcomes for alumni of foster care. A brief rationale for each area follows. Note that there is little research on the long-term effects of many of these factors because older alumni have not been interviewed or studied.

Placement History

There is a growing body of evidence that associates placement stability and youth behavior while in care and afterward (e.g., Redding, Fried, & Britner, 2000; Rumberger & Larson, 1998; Ryan & Testa, 2004; Widom, 1991). Changing homes because of placement disruption compounds the sense of loss that children being placed must face by leaving behind parents and often siblings and friends. Festinger's (1983) landmark study of 277 alumni of care, entitled *No One Ever Asked Us,* revealed that most alumni experienced placement changes as unsettling and confusing. When rating their perception of foster care, alumni satisfaction was inversely related to the number of placements they had experienced. Additional research has found that multiple placements increase child behavior problems (Newton, Litrownik, & Landsverk, 2000) and that these changes are associated with decreased school performance and increased delinquent behavior (Ryan & Testa, 2004).

Second, the experiences of these children while in care have important ramifications throughout their development. For young children, Wulczyn, Kogan, and Harden emphasize that, "multiple placements are thought to have a pernicious impact on the development of attachment to primary caregivers, an early developmental milestone thought to be essential for the achievement of later developmental tasks" (2002, p. 2). School performance problems may be compounded by school changes related to placement changes (Rumberger & Larson, 1998). Multiple placement moves before age 14 are associated with delinquency filings after age 14 for males only (Ryan & Testa, 2004, 2005). Lastly, Pecora et al. (2003b) found that less placement change was associated with success in a sample of alumni ranging in age from 20 to 51.

Placement changes also disrupt service provision, distress foster parents (thereby lowering retention rates), cost precious worker time, and create administrative disruptions (James, 2004). Finally, because we know so little about what causes placement change—a variety of child, family, social worker, and agency factors have been discussed—the field is less able to predict and therefore prevent it.

The dynamics of these changes are important, and their exploration can have important practice implications. For example, Leathers (2005) found that adolescents who were placed alone after a history of joint sibling placements were at greater risk for placement disruption than those who were placed with a consistent number of siblings (not necessarily all of them). This association was mediated by a weaker sense of integration and belonging in the foster home. In addition, James (2004) found that child behavior problems, while significant, constituted the reason for the move in only 19.7% of the situations, as contrasted with "system or policy-related" reasons (70.2%), such as a move to a short-term or long-term care facility, a placement with a sibling or relative, group home closure, or a move to be closer to a relative or a certain school (p. 612). Some of these system or policy-related reasons stem from what might be thought of as sound practice decisions to help a child reach a more permanent or developmentally appropriate living situation. Similarly, as a result of their longitudinal study, Taber and Proch (1987) noted that "placement disruption may be a function primarily of the service system, not the child" (p. 436).

Educational Services and Experience

Many studies have documented the disproportionate rates of learning disabilities among children entering care and the extra educational supports they need because they are often one or more grade levels behind in school (often because of changing schools as a result of changing placements), with partial school records and incomplete educational plans. Foster youth have been found to *(1)* have lower scores on tests of academic achievement, *(2)* be more likely to have cognitive delays, *(3)* be placed in special education classes, *(4)* be absent from school, *(5)* be held back a grade, *(6)* display behavioral loss of control at school, and *(7)* drop out before obtaining a high school diploma or GED (Courtney et al., 2007; Horwitz, Simms, & Farrington, 1994; Shin, 2004; Wyatt, Simms, & Horwitz, 1997; Zetlin et al., 2004).

Therapeutic Service and Supports

The literature on child maltreatment clearly documents that children and youth enter foster care with higher levels of physical disabilities and mental health impairments compared to children and youth not in state care. A recent national study reported that 47.9% of 3,803 youth aged 2 to 14 who were subjects of a completed child protective services investigation had clinically significant emotional or behavioral problems (Burns et al., 2004). Another study found that 41.8% of dependents of the court met DSM-IV diagnostic criteria with at least one moderate level of diagnostic-specific functional impairment. The most common disorders were Attention Deficit Hyperactivity Disorder (20.8%), Conduct Disorder (16.1%), Oppositional Defiant Disorder (13.5%), Major Depression (4.7%), and Separation Anxiety (4.6%) (Garland et al., 2001). Another study found that up to 80% of youth in foster care had at least one psychiatric diagnosis (Zima, Bussing, Yang, & Belin, 2000). All of these studies underscore the importance of therapeutic services and supports.

Activities With the Foster Family

Recreational, spiritual, and other activities that foster families do together are recognized as helpful, but there is less firm research evidence of how much impact they have on youth outcomes (Berrick et al., 1998; Festinger, 1983; White, Havalchak, Jackson, O'Brien, & Pecora, 2007). However, based on ecological models (see below), the literature suggests that foster families can act as a powerful protective mechanism for development, especially when the youth is engaged in the foster family and is an active participant in the foster care experience.

Preparation for Leaving Care

Educational supports and career planning are two of the many contributors to life-skills preparation (also known as *independent living skills* or *transition skills*). These skills are intended to prepare youth for later success. Some of the most important skills include (Casey Family Programs, 2001):

- Goal setting and attainment
- Problem solving and decision making
- Self-advocacy
- Personal health and safety awareness (e.g., pregnancy, sexually transmitted diseases, human immunodeficiency virus infection, and other health and mental health issues)
- Employment readiness (e.g., workplace skills, job placement, job coaching, and preparation of young women for nontraditional careers)
- Self-sufficiency and knowledge of how to secure safe and stable housing
- Ability to establish social support networks

Leaving Care Resources

When most children leave home, they have concrete resources that are needed to function with greater independence. In most communities, that means having a Social Security card, a driver's license, cash savings for rent and utility deposits, and bedding and kitchen utensils (Carnegie Council on Adolescent Development, 1989; Casey Family Programs, 2001). Having obtained these resources is likely an indicator of greater preparation for leaving care.

Foster Family and Other Nurturing Support While in Care

Children entering care are in desperate need of nurturing adults who can help them begin to overcome the effects of child maltreatment by providing a warm, stable, and consistent environment (Wind & Silvern, 1994). Interviews with alumni from foster care have illustrated the importance of caring relationships with adults. For example, when youth from care were asked in the mid-1990s what was the most positive or helpful factor or experience in foster care, a significant proportion identified a feeling of belonging and an emotionally supportive relationship with the foster family, social worker, or caseworker (Wedeven, Pecora, Hurwitz, Howell, & Newell, 1997).

Maintaining positive connections to birth parents, siblings, and other kin is also critical in the development of youth regardless of how long they have been in out-of-home care before achieving permanency.[17] While the research base is not extensive, practice wisdom has emphasized, and some studies have shown, that youth in out-of-home care who are placed with their siblings and who have contact with their birth parents while in out-of-home care have better outcomes than youth who do not (Barth, 1986). It is thought that this effect occurs because interacting with birth families provides youth with a greater sense of identity, a sense of cultural self, and a historical connection.[18] Healthy families and supportive parents also shape the values and behaviors of youth in enduring ways.

During analyses, the relation between the areas described in this section and outcomes was examined after controlling for demographics and risk factors (including child maltreatment by the birth family). Although much of the research presented does not relate these areas directly to adult outcomes, it is thought that if they affect short-term outcomes, they are likely to have an impact on long-term (adult) outcomes as well. A key aspect that separates the foster care experience areas from demographics and risk factors is the ability of the intervening agency (Casey or the state agencies of Oregon and Washington) to influence these areas. This influence may be seen in programs or policies and can impact each foster care experience area to a greater or lesser degree. For example, to positively affect the placement history, an agency could provide greater training and incentives to foster parents and caseworkers to remain with the agency, thereby reducing the number of placements and providing a stable presence in the youth's life which helps lower the likelihood of child placement disruption.

Future Research Directions

As in other areas of human services, rigorous research on the outcome of family foster care is limited due to such factors as insufficient funding and the complexities of the problems under study. It is critical that this important gap in research be closed in order to provide data that can be used for rational program planning. For this reason, we offer a few suggestions:

1. Implement new studies of youth outcomes during and after care for all types of substitute care populations.
2. Use standardized diagnostic measures that assess behavior, educational functioning, satisfaction, self-esteem, and other central dependent variables.
3. Involve more youth in care, caregivers, alumni, and front-line staff in study design and data interpretation to help ensure that researchers gather meaningful information in respectful ways.
4. Conduct longitudinal research aimed at evaluating model foster care programs. This will enhance efforts to delineate program components that should be required of service contractors or incorporated into revised state models of foster care.
5. Conduct experimental and quasi-experimental program studies to evaluate different models of family foster care and other interventions to help children.

6. Add to the few studies that have examined mental health disorders other than drug and alcohol use or depression.

7. Provide comparisons with the general population of youth of similar age, ethnicity, and gender, along with the use of benchmarking data from similar programs and service populations. For example, we could explore the proposition that placement in family foster care, in conjunction with mental health, education, tutoring, and other services, may have a protective mediating effect upon the sequelae of child maltreatment.

8. For more efficient collection of certain kinds of outcome data, use administrative databases, such as those on employment (Goerge et al., 2002).

9. Involve young people more actively and consistently in planning foster care (see Sinclair, 1998, and http://www.casey.org).

10. Conduct further research on the impact of services to enable children to remain in foster care beyond age 18 which has substantial economic benefits (Courtney, Dworsky, and Peters, 2009), and postpermanency services (Freundlich & Wright, 2003).

Summary

The scope of family foster care in the United States is extensive—with over 800,000 children served each year, some as a result of failed reunifications or adoptions. Considerable amounts of money are invested to care for these children and the data suggest that we have achieved mixed results, some of which are no doubt due to the early adversities experienced by these children.

A huge number of areas need to be explored more extensively, such as assessment methods to help place children in the most appropriate foster homes, interventions to help stabilize youth while in care, strategies for achieving permanency, methods to help youth reach key developmental milestones and gain life skills, and methods to determine what life-skills development approaches will help youth make a successful transition from foster care to living on their own. Our research evidence base is thin in most of these areas, with few national studies, as most research has been based on limited geographic areas. Consequently, the field lacks a firm empirical foundation upon which to base policies and practice guidelines. Fortunately, the sophistication of the research is growing, more cohort studies are being conducted, agency management information systems are improving, and there is more consistency in some of the variables being used. As mentioned above, a variety of research efforts could be launched to build on this foundation. Given current fiscal constraints, these studies most likely will need to be true collaborations with mixed method evaluations and blended/pooled funding.

Landsverk's Conceptual Framework

The conceptual framework of the Northwest Alumni Study was informed by past research and by the work of John Landsverk and his colleagues at the Child and Adolescent Services Research Center in San Diego. Using some of the background information already discussed, Landsverk developed a comprehensive approach to mapping critical factors influencing youth development in foster care. His framework has been used to guide other research on victims of child maltreatment placed in foster care (Landsverk, Clausen, Ganger, Chadwick, & Litrownik, 1995a; Landsverk et al., 1995b). The framework of the Northwest Alumni Study followed closely from this body of research, which addressed the mental health needs of youth in foster care in ways that had been neglected by most previous research (Landsverk, 1999). (See Fig. 2.1 for a diagram of the conceptual framework.) The framework placed the Northwest Alumni Study in a developmental context and highlighted the interactive effects that birth family characteristics, child characteristics, community ecology, and foster families can have on the development of children. Mediating factors, including interactions with extended family and service delivery systems, are important determinants as well. (The study design did include a small group of mediators in the area of foster care services and experiences of the alumni, and the effects of some of these mediators and moderators are examined in Chapters 10 and 11.)

The elements of this framework, which are described below, related directly to existing theories of development (summarized later in this chapter), to the variables/measures, and to the hypotheses of this investigation. For example, attachment theory, risk/protective models, and Erikson's theory all include constructs emphasizing that stable and emotionally nurturing care will lead to better overall adult outcomes.

- *Child characteristics.* Factors inherent in children (e.g., age, gender, disability) are emphasized by risk/protective factor theories as contributors to the treatment youth receive.
- *Child abuse and neglect.* Briere's theoretical perspectives (1992, 2002) related to post-abuse trauma offer extensive predictions about the impact of the type, severity, onset, duration, number of perpetrators, and frequency of abuse and neglect. Moreover, Briere discusses the negative consequences of undetected abuse and delays in intervention. Risk/protective factor theories also emphasize abuse and neglect as significant risk factors for negative adult outcomes. Finally, extrapolations from Erikson's theory (Downs & Pecora, 2004) indicate that the impact of abuse and neglect can be expected to vary as a function of the youth's developmental maturity at the time of the abuse.
- *Birth family characteristics.* Attachment theory predicts that the responsiveness of caregivers to infants (including abuse patterns) directly affects infant and early child development. Erikson's theory makes comparable predictions about family members' responses to children's attempts to master various tasks across developmental stages.
- *Family-of-origin characteristics.* Ecological theories argue that cultural and familial traditions shape the context and interpretation of patterns of interaction, including abuse and neglect, with children. What is regarded as unacceptable practice in some family contexts is seen as acceptable in others.

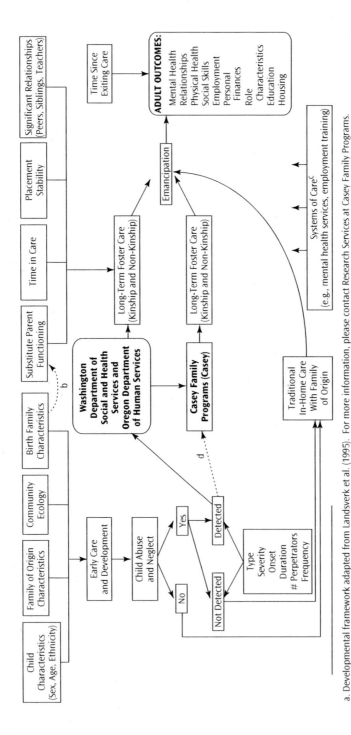

Figure 2.1. Developmental Framework for the Alumni Studies

a. Developmental framework adapted from Landsverk et al. (1995). For more information, please contact Research Services at Casey Family Programs.

b. Birth families often influence foster parent service delivery and functioning (e.g., visitation).

c. The Northwest Alumni Study focuses only on a few systems of care variables, including mental health services, group work, and employment training.

d. A small percentage, about 2%, of Casey's youth are not referred by public child welfare agencies and instead might be referrals directly from kinship care providers.

- *Community ecology.* Ecological and risk/protective factor theories posit that community settings influence the contexts for and risks associated with abuse and neglect; youth in isolated communities may be more likely to experience abuse.
- *Type and quality of long-term foster care.* Some attachment theorists (e.g., Hazan & Shaver, 1987) argue that earlier disrupted patterns of attachment may be ameliorated by later high-quality care. Briere's theory also emphasizes the type and quality of interventional care. Erikson's theory stresses the critical role of environmental support (in this case, high-quality out-of-home care) in repairing negative outcomes from earlier stages. All of these views predict that the higher the quality of care, the better the adult outcomes. For example, placement stability is related to Erikson's notion of the availability of time periods (moratoria) to examine old and new identity constructs. Significant relationships with teachers, peers, and siblings can also help to improve interpersonal functioning while in care. Further, educational and occupational services have been hypothesized to be critical factors for both risk and resilience in foster youth (Anctil, McCubbin, O'Brien, Pecora, & Anderson-Harumi, 2007; Shin, 2004; Zetlin et al., 2004).
- *Systems of care.* Attachment theory, Briere's theory, risk/protective factor models, and Erikson's theory all include constructs leading to the hypothesis that the availability and quality of a range of systems of care (e.g., mental health services, employment training, group work) can help remediate the earlier effects of abuse and neglect, and they may enhance the impact of out-of-home care.
- *Time since exiting care.* Erikson emphasizes that experiences in later adolescence and early adulthood can build on or undo earlier development. Consequently, adult outcomes can be affected by the foster home placement, other interventions, and experiences that alumni have after care.
- *Adult outcomes.* Attachment theory emphasizes the effects of early attachment patterns and abuse on adult relationships, social skills development, and role characteristics. Briere and other researchers, such as Kendall-Tackett and Giacomoni (2003), have documented how abuse and neglect patterns and their after effects are related to later mental health, cognitive functioning, physical health, relationships, and social skills. Risk/protective factor frameworks posit all of the adult outcomes listed as important variables to be examined in light of the risk and protective factors examined. Erikson's theory indicates that the impact of earlier abuse and neglect, coupled with knowledge of the timing of that abuse and of the quality and timing of therapeutic intervention, will lead to varying predictions about the quality of adult outcomes listed (see Downs & Pecora, 2004).

How Risk and Protective Factors Research Provided a Basis for Selection of Some Variables

Overview

A growing body of research informed the selection of some of the controls and other variables for the Northwest Alumni Study. For example, the

LONGSCAN study found the following risk factors for maltreatment during the child's first four years of life:

- Maternal depression
- Alcohol use by one or more caregivers
- Psychosomatic complaints of caregiver
- Family receipt of Aid to Families with Dependent Children (AFDC) or another form of cash assistance
- More than one dependent child
- Mother separated from her own mother at age 14 or earlier
- Use of physical discipline as a punishment strategy[19]

The LONGSCAN study's conceptual framework was used to help inform the Northwest Alumni Study in other areas. For example, child exposure to domestic violence or intimate partner violence (IPV) had been recognized as an important risk factor for later difficulties, such as increased risk of child maltreatment. For co-occurring kinds of maltreatment, the risk factors were mother's depression and harsh parenting. In contrast, parent separation (most of the time) and social involvement (e.g., religious activities, grandparent involvement) acted as protective factors for children.

Factors associated with verbal discipline were African American race, higher maternal education, and female gender. In general, harsher physical discipline is more likely to occur in families that are not on welfare. Limit setting was used less often when the biological father was in the home. Mild spanking was used less often by mothers who had been victimized, but it was used more often by African Americans and families reported for maltreatment.

In families where the teen mother has a male partner, there were more maltreatment reports before age four, and maltreated children were more likely to have behavior problems. The mothers who reported negative partner relationships were more likely to report more child behavior problems, regardless of maltreatment status, and to be depressed. In families where the teen mother was living with her own mother, the teen mother was less likely to live with a man. If maltreatment was present, child behavior problems were worse in three-generation households (Hunter & Knight, 1998; LONGSCAN investigators, 2006).

Foster Care Research

In addition to the developmental theories and models and Landsverk's conceptual framework, a brief discussion of prior foster care research will contribute further background for the Northwest Alumni Study's research questions and hypotheses. This section begins by summarizing research on the effects of child maltreatment on outcomes, a variable that will be used both as a control (when perpetrated by the birth family—labeled as a *risk factor*) and as a predictor (when perpetrated by the foster family or other caregiver). Although this is a risk factor, because it occurred while under agency supervision, it was usually labeled as a *foster care experience*. (For a more complete summary, see Pecora et al., 2009a.) This section concludes by summarizing research on the effects of child maltreatment and foster care experiences on outcomes.

The Effects of Child Maltreatment

Numerous researchers and clinicians have documented the importance of intervening to prevent or stop child maltreatment and to treat both perpetrators and victims (e.g., Briere, 1992; Kendall-Tackett & Giacomoni, 2003; Polansky, Chalmers, Buttenweiser, & Williams, 1981). While some maltreated children function well as adults, others are at high risk for adverse adult outcomes, possibly related to negative consequences of both the abuse and, in some cases, removal from the home (Becker et al., 1995; Briere, 2002, 2004; Cicchetti, 1994; Cicchetti & Lynch, 1993; Cicchetti & Toth, 1995; Lamphear, 1985; Widom, 1989b).

These consequences, in turn, are dependent upon a number of factors, including the type, severity, frequency, number of perpetrators, and developmental timing of the abuse or neglect. For example, some research shows that physically abused boys placed in family foster care are at higher risk of poor outcomes such as adult violence and criminality than girls (Fanshel, Finch, & Grundy, 1990, p. 205). Further, some factors appear to have more impact than others, including youth's age at onset, chronicity of abuse, and maltreatment by a primary caregiver (Cicchetti, 1989, 1994; English & the LONGSCAN investigators, 1997).

There is a growing recognition and some convergence of research indicating that various forms of child maltreatment have a dynamic and interactive effect on development *over time*. Specifically, reactions to victimization, accommodation to ongoing abuse, and long-term elaboration and secondary accommodation may each emerge at any point in later development rather than in only one particular developmental period (e.g., Briere, 1992; Erikson, 1968; Wolfe & McGee, 1994). For these and other reasons, fully understanding the impact that child maltreatment plays in development is a great challenge.

Developmental Theories and Conceptual Models

Research questions and hypotheses were built on developmental theories and conceptual models, Landsverk's conceptual framework, and past research. This section presents several theories that help explain child growth and development. Given previous research on the effects of foster care (and child maltreatment) on adult outcomes, the Northwest Alumni Study collected case record and interview data on three classes of variables: *(1)* demographics and risk factors (e.g., gender, parents' health, and parents' criminal problems); *(2)* characteristics of the foster care experience (e.g., placement history, preparation for independent living); and *(3)* outcomes (e.g., mental health, education). In addition to Landsverk's conceptual model and earlier research, developmental theories and conceptual models informed the variables selected for examination. For each theory or model listed below, examples are presented to show how the theory or model informed the selection of variables used in the Northwest Alumni Study. Additional information of this nature is provided in the discussion of Landsverk's conceptual model, which interweaves many of the theories and models described in this section.

Attachment Theory

This theory is particularly useful for addressing relationships and traumas occurring prior to age two and for understanding how adult outcomes and relationships can be influenced by bonds broken though maltreatment (Ainsworth, 1989; Ainsworth, Blehar, Waters, & Wall, 1978; Bowlby, 1982; Bretherton, 1992; Goldberg, Muir, & Kerr, 1995; Hazan & Shaver, 1987; Sroufe, 1990; Weinfield, Ogawa, & Sroufe, 1997).

How was it used in the Northwest Alumni Study? Attachment theory was particularly relevant for inclusion of child maltreatment and a positive relationship with an adult while growing up. For child maltreatment, extensive information was collected on maltreatment perpetrated by the birth family (a risk factor) and the foster family or other caregiver (an experience while in care).

Trauma Theory

Briere (2002) and others have examined the effects of abuse and neglect and offered explanations for variations in the types and impact of abuse and the impact of immediate or delayed intervention. Thus, both the type and number of types of child maltreatment were assessed.

How was it used in the Northwest Alumni Study? Among the extensive information collected about child maltreatment regardless of perpetrator, the type of maltreatment was detailed (see Chapter 5). Specifically, the LONGSCAN approach to categorizing maltreatment was implemented. Based on extensive research, this approach combines sexual abuse, physical abuse, physical neglect, and emotional maltreatment to examine the relationship with outcomes (Runyan et al., 1998b).

Risk and Protective Factor Frameworks (Including Noam and Hermann's [2002] Application of the Developmental Resilience Framework to Foster Youth With Impairments)[20]

These frameworks are useful for explaining resilience and for identifying predictors of adult outcomes (e.g., Catalano & Hawkins, 1996; Coie et al., 1993; Jessor, Van Den Bos, Vanderryn, Costa, & Turbin, 1995; Rutter, 1989a,

1989b, 2001; Werner, 1989). For example, this research underscores the value of living situation stability, positive adult relationships, connections to the community via extracurricular activities, and positive peer networks.

In addition, Luthar and Cicchetti (2000) defined resilience as "a dynamic process wherein individuals display positive adaptation despite experiences of significant adversity or trauma" (p. 858). Although resilience has been found to be related to biological factors like temperament or environmental factors such as attachment, researchers have also found that new strengths or vulnerabilities can appear in an individual as age- and gender-related physical and psychological changes occur or as life circumstances change (Luthar & Cicchetti, 2000).

Recent research attempts to gain an understanding of resilience as a process rather than a set of traits or factors. This notion is focused on the role of the environment and context in the development of resilience, and it allows for the provision of services to enhance evidenced-based protective factors in children and adolescents who may not have had a resilient outlook previously because of the multiple community and individual risk factors they have experienced. For example, a child can encounter multiple community risk factors, such as low neighborhood socioeconomic status, poor school climate, and limited social resources, and individual risk factors including antisocial relationships with peers, negative family involvement, or maltreatment (Jensen & Fraser, 2006).

Noam and Hermann (2002) identified important factors that they believed are predominantly influential in the development of resilience and that are important for practitioners to attend to when working with at-risk youth:

> 1) Self-reflection and meaning-making about the self and important relationships; educational and occupational successes and security; 2) individuals' capacity to use symptoms, risk, and problems to motivate themselves to reflect, to test new thoughts and behaviors, and to gain insight from trauma...; and 3) the capacity to engage in productive relationships and to be supported by people and institutions that are attentive and make a positive contribution to an individual's development and well-being. (pp. 870–871)

The developmental resilience model appears to be particularly suited to the unique needs of children in foster care who have physical and psychiatric impairments, since it encompasses developmental stages, accounts for individual differences in development, and allows for adaptation to meet the special needs of youth in care (who are likely to have been maltreated, to suffer from various mental and physical health conditions, and to already be experiencing educational or social difficulties) (Courtney, Piliavin, Grogan-Kaylor, & Nesmith, 2001; Rashid, 2004; Shin, 2004; Zetlin et al., 2004).

How was it used in the Northwest Alumni Study? While a particular risk and protective factor framework was not used in the study, this perspective did inform the variables that were chosen. For example, the presence of enduring connections with adults through a stable living situation (placement stability), the influence of educational advisors, therapeutic services, and other supports were examined. According to this perspective, these kinds of services and supports should alleviate the impact of some risk factors (e.g., child maltreatment, physical or learning impairments) on outcomes. (This is described more fully later in this chapter.)

> *An interviewer recalled a respondent who told of her mother, who was a drug dealer and was incarcerated when the respondent was nine. The foster mother who took her in also took her three siblings and immediately made them all a part of the family. Her older, grown children accepted them as new brothers and sisters, and they all knew they were loved and were very well cared for.*

Ecological and Risk-Based Developmental Models

These models complement the risk and protective factor theories discussed above because they stress the importance of individual, familial, and social contexts (e.g., Bronfenbrenner, 1979; Bronfenbrenner & Morris, 1998; Garbarino, 1982). When examining life outcomes and mental health functioning of alumni from foster care, it is important to note that child characteristics interact with the experience of child maltreatment (risk) and foster care (protection) to produce outcomes. These characteristics could include genetic factors; risk factors such as poverty, racism, and dangerous living environments; and family-of-origin characteristics and functioning (Belsky, 1980; Cicchetti & Lynch, 1993; Plomin & Nesselroade, 1990).

Additionally, foster family characteristics and functioning, other child/family supports, the quality and nature of services provided by various community agencies, and other factors interact with the experience of child maltreatment and foster care to produce certain alumni outcomes (Barber & Delfabbro, 2003; Chamberlain, 2003; Walsh & Walsh, 1990; Widom, 1989b).

How was it used in the Northwest Alumni Study? From an ecological and protective factors perspective, in addition to the services and supports mentioned above, foster families can act as a powerful microsystem intervention that can have important protective and ameliorative functions for the youth. Therefore, data were collected on how engaged the youth was in his or her foster family (including participation in enjoyable and religious activities). To test this model, these variables were examined in relation to outcomes.

Erikson's Developmental Theory

This enduring theory (Erikson, 1956, 1963, 1964, 1968, 1974, 1975, 1985), coupled with refinements by Marcia (1966, 1976, 1980; Orlofsky, Marcia, & Lesser, 1973), is directly relevant to many of the constructs identified in the Northwest Alumni Study's conceptual framework. Specifically, information on the timing of abuse or neglect is known and consequently can be juxtaposed to the timing of outcomes found in Erikson's eight developmental stages. Such developmental cross-matching has been cited as useful in understanding and predicting adjustment sequelae (Wolfe & McGee, 1994).

A more thorough description of the application of Erikson's theory to foster care research is found in Downs and Pecora (2004).

How was it used in the Northwest Alumni Study? Erikson's theory indicates that the impact of earlier abuse and neglect, coupled with knowledge of the timing of that abuse and of the quality and timing of therapeutic intervention, would lead to varying predictions about the quality of adult outcomes listed (see Downs & Pecora, 2004). Thus, access to therapeutic services and supports, which may remediate the effects of child maltreatment, was measured.

Social Support Theory

Research suggests that having a caring adult in a child's life and stable support networks are important determinants of health and well-being. The importance of a caring adult for child well-being was underscored by the findings of a recent study: If abused children with two short alleles (genes) saw the adults they counted on daily or almost daily, their depression scores were very close to the scores of abused children with two long protective alleles—and within reach of the scores of children who had not been abused. The children with the protective version of the gene were far less affected by a lack of contact with their primary adult caregiver. The study indicates that good support ameliorates the effect of abuse and the vulnerability produced by the high-risk genotype (Kaufman et al., 2006). This brief example is presented to illustrate that research about the interaction of genetics and behavior, as well as other social science research, is documenting the value of positive relationships with adults, peers, and others. Consequently, the association between placement stability to help children maintain their support networks and adult achievements and functioning is important. Fewer turnovers among placements therefore may be linked with greater proportions of alumni reporting ongoing relations with supportive adults and peers, as well as other positive effects on adult outcomes.

How was it used in the Northwest Alumni Study? Comprehensive information on placement was collected as part of this study, including number of placements, length of time in care, placement change rate, number of reunification failures, number of runaways, and the number of unlicensed living situations with friends or relatives (this is not considered *kinship care,* which is a licensed living situation). In addition to placement information, educational stability was assessed (i.e., the number of school changes). Combined, this information is important for understanding relationships and social supports and may have important implications for other adult outcomes.

Research Questions and Hypotheses

This study was informed by developmental theories and conceptual models, Landsverk's conceptual framework, and foster care research. Many of the questions and hypotheses concern functioning for certain outcomes (e.g., prevalence rates: how many alumni have experienced posttraumatic stress disorder in the past 12 months?), while other questions concern relations among variables (e.g., what is the effect of child maltreatment on outcomes?). Data presented in subsequent chapters provide answers to many questions that are not presented in the sections below. Similarly, only a sampling of all questions and hypotheses is presented.

As discussed previously, the relation between the foster care experience and outcomes is a primary focus because of its ability to be influenced by agency intervention (subsequent chapters focus on these analyses, and most recommendations concern enhancing the foster care experience). However, some hypotheses (and questions) concern demographics, risk factors, the intervening agency, and their relationship to outcomes. In general, lower levels of risk factors and higher levels of a positive foster care experience are hypothesized to be more closely related to positive outcomes. For example, it was expected that alumni with fathers not involved in the criminal justice system (a lower level of a risk factor) would exhibit more positive outcomes than alumni with fathers involved in the criminal justice system. Further, it was expected that alumni with fewer placements while in care (a more positive foster care experience) would exhibit more positive outcomes than alumni with more placements. Although demographic comparisons were made, specific hypotheses were not made for comparing groups. For example, it was not expected that females would exhibit more positive outcomes than males. In sum, fewer expectations were placed on the relation between demographics and outcomes due to differential expectations based on specific outcomes.

Primary Research Questions

As described above, the primary research questions of the Northwest Alumni Study concern both prevalence rates and relationships between demographics, risk factors, the intervening agency, foster care experiences, and outcomes. The primary research questions are as follows:

1. How are maltreated youth placed in foster care faring as adults? To what extent are they different in their functioning from other adults?
2. Which youth are most at risk for poor long-term outcomes based on risk factors that affected them at the time of first placement?
3. Is one foster care program approach better than another in terms of outcomes?
4. Are there key factors or program components that are linked with better functioning in adulthood? [21]

Hypotheses

As discussed earlier in this section, few expectations were placed on the relationship between demographics and outcomes. However, we hypothesized that, in general, lower levels of risk factors and higher levels of a positive foster care experience would be related to positive adult outcomes. In addition, because of additional resources and financial capacity, we hypothesized that, in general, Casey alumni would exhibit more positive outcomes than state alumni. These hypotheses were informed by developmental theories and conceptual models, Landsverk's conceptual framework, previous foster care research, and differences between agencies' resources and functioning (described in Chapter 1). Due to the large quantity of data and large number of relationships among variables (see Chapters 6–9), only a small set of hypotheses is presented here for each primary research question (repeated below):

1. How are maltreated youth placed in foster care faring as adults? To what extent are they different in their functioning from other adults?
   • *Hypothesis:* Alumni will exhibit functioning lower than that of general population comparisons but comparable to or better than that of alumni from other studies.
2. Which youth are most at risk for poor long-term outcomes based on risk factors that affected them at the time of first placement?
   • *Hypothesis:* Lower levels of risk factors such as good parents' health and fewer parents' criminal problems will be related to more positive outcomes (e.g., education and mental health).
3. Is one foster care program approach better than another in terms of outcomes?
   • *Hypothesis:* In general, Casey alumni will exhibit more positive outcomes than state alumni.
4. Are there key factors or program components that are linked with better functioning in adulthood?
   • *Hypothesis:* Higher levels of a positive foster care experience are related to more positive outcomes.
   • *More specific hypotheses for this section.* The following experiences while in care were hypothesized to be related to more positive outcomes:
   (1) A more stable placement history
   (2) More access to educational tutoring supports and educational stability
   (3) More access to therapeutic services and supports
   (4) More involvement with the foster family
   (5) Greater preparation for leaving care (e.g., employment training and support)
   (6) More tangible resources upon leaving care (e.g., $250 in cash and a driver's license)
   (7) A positive relationship with an adult while growing up

Summary

To set the context for the research questions and hypotheses for the Northwest Alumni Study, this chapter summarizes developmental theories and conceptual models, Landsverk's conceptual framework, and foster care research. Developmental theories and conceptual models informing the study include trauma theory, Erikson's developmental theory, and ecological and risk-based developmental models. Landsverk, in an attempt to map critical factors influencing youth development in foster care, integrated these theories and other experiences into a conceptual framework. Also informing questions and hypotheses was research on the impact of foster care on outcomes. Specific areas of importance included placement history and experience, educational services and experience, and therapeutic services and supports. Based on this background information, questions and hypotheses for the Northwest Alumni Study were generated. Primary research questions included the following:

1. How are maltreated youth placed in foster care faring as adults? To what extent are they different in their functioning from other adults?
2. Are there key factors or program components that are linked with better functioning in adulthood?

It was hypothesized that alumni would exhibit functioning that was lower than that of the general population comparisons but comparable to or better than that of alumni from other studies. Further, it was hypothesized that, in general, lower levels of risk factors and higher levels of a positive foster care experience would be related to more positive outcomes.

Acknowledgment.   Steve Heeringa, Nancy Gebler, and Carol Brandford contributed to this chapter.

PART II

STUDY METHODS

3

Study Sample and Demographics
of the Participating Agencies

I don't know if it was just the agency that was with me or the whole foster system all around. I felt that they could give kids hands-on training, even stuff like working with knives, how to run a mower, how to run a weed eater. Stuff that foster care won't even let you touch because they're afraid you're going to get hurt with it. I mean all the little tiny stuff that most kids get the advantage of doing throughout the day. A social worker should be more prone to listen to your problems and actually, you know, act like they care.

Overview

As discussed in Chapter 1, while family foster care is intended to be a temporary living arrangement for a child, placements for nearly half of the children who exited care in 2003 lasted for more than a year, and for almost one in five children, placements lasted for three years or more (U.S. Department of Health and Human Services, 2005a). This chapter provides the background for two research questions concerning youth spending extended periods of time in care: *(1)* Are there key factors or program components linked to better functioning of youth from care as they reach adulthood? *(2)* Is one family foster care program approach more successful than another in helping youth achieve desired outcomes? Although Casey Family Programs has traditionally devoted more resources to family foster care than state agencies have, there are also commonalities to the experiences and services provided while in care that may predict adult success. Additionally, there are programmatic differences that may be more indicative of later success. Answers to these questions could be used by policymakers to promote changes in public and voluntary foster care programs.

This chapter consists of two sections. The first section (Sample Characteristics and Matching Criteria) explains how the Northwest Alumni Study sample was formed, including eligibility, sample matching, data weighting, and power analyses. The second section (Alumni

Demographics: Ethnicity, Gender, and Age at the Time of the Interview) provides demographic information on the Northwest alumni including ethnicity, gender, and age.

Sample Characteristics and Matching Criteria

Sample Eligibility, Development, and Matching Criteria

As summarized in Table 3.1, the study team drew a stratified random probability sample (Schlesselman, 1982) of Washington and Oregon State alumni, which was matched with the sample of Casey alumni based on the following samplewide eligibility characteristics:

1. *Geographic location.* Samples were matched based on the agency office from which they emancipated or otherwise left care. Casey's offices in Washington (Seattle, Tacoma, and Yakima) were matched with Washington State offices in the geographic areas. Casey's Oregon office in Portland was matched with the Oregon State sample from Multnomah County (including the city of Portland).
2. *Length of service.* Youth who lived in family foster care for 12 months or more were included in the sample. Youth who only had other types of out-of-home care (e.g., residential care) were excluded from the sample.
3. *Age.* Alumni turned 18 years old on or before September 30, 1988, so the age group of the alumni interviewed ranged from 20 to 33 years.

Table 3.1.   Sample Eligibility for the Northwest Alumni Study

1. Born on or before September 30, 1980.
2. Placed in family foster care for 12 or more consecutive months between January 1, 1988, and September 30, 1998. Disruption of more than 14 days made the placement ineligible.
3. Placement of 12 or more consecutive months occurred when the alumnus or alumna was between 14 and 18 years of age. Using ages 14–18 *(a)* limited the sample to those whose foster care experience occurred during adolescence, *(b)* increased accuracy of recall for interviews, and *(c)* yielded a sample of alumni who were in foster care later and were therefore easier to find.
4. Foster placement was in the Portland, Seattle, Tacoma, or Yakima area.
5. Physical disability/developmental delay was not the primary reason for foster placement (i.e., the youth was not severely physically disabled to the point where he or she could not be expected to live independently as an adult, or the youth had an IQ below 70). In the original data pulls, this criterion was used to query the state information systems. Casey did not have this information available in a central Management Information System (MIS). Other alumni with officially diagnosed severe disabilities were eliminated when files were reviewed.
6. Oregon and Washington state alumni were not placed with Casey between January 1, 1988, and September 30, 1998.

4. *Disabilities.* Children with mental or physical disabilities so severe that they could not live independently as adults (such as those with an IQ lower than 70) were excluded from this study.

Sample Formation

The specific procedures for drawing each of the samples are detailed below.

State of Washington

The Washington state sample was identified from the Social Service Payment System (SSPS) database that included payments for children in foster care. Youth who met the study criteria were included in the initial sample population. Foster placement for the sample was restricted to the Seattle, Tacoma, and Yakima areas with a 2:1 Washington State to Casey sample of alumni. A review by hand of the case records was conducted on the sample to remove any youth who had also been placed with Casey.

State of Oregon

The Oregon State sample was identified using the agency's Integrated Information System (IIS). This system contained the history for families and individuals who were referred to the Oregon child welfare system. The IIS contains information on referrals, assessments, case openings and closings, plans, services, and substitute care placements. Programs were written to extract records for any youth who met the sample eligibility criteria. A list was produced that included the youth's name, date of birth, gender, ethnic heritage, and case name. This list was used randomly to select a 3:1 Oregon State to Casey sample of alumni. A 3:1 sample was used in Oregon to increase the statistical power to detect meaningful differences in the outcomes of alumni. Although the study team also wanted a 3:1 ratio in Washington, permission from the state agency was obtained for only a 2:1 ratio.

Casey

All the Casey youth who met the sampling criteria were included in the study to help maximize the Casey sample size for statistical analysis purposes. The statistically matched sample of cases and controls was designed to enable efficient adjustment for geographic, demographic, and programmatic effects in multivariate logistic and linear regression analyses. In sum, matching criteria were used to select the samples so that they would be similar. To further align samples, weighting procedures adjusted for differences between the Casey and state samples. The statistical matching and weighting criteria are as follows:

1. *Sample matching criteria* were used to initially select cases for matching using computerized and paper case records. These criteria included

(a) geographic location, (b) 12 or more months spent in family foster care, and (c) no severe physical or intellectual disabilities. Youth placed by the state agency solely because of family violence or unaccompanied minor refugees were dropped from the study because Casey did not serve these youth.

2. *Case record demographic and risk factor weighting criteria* included (a) ethnicity, (b) gender, (c) reason(s) for placement, (d) birth parent characteristics, (e) birth family abuse history, and (f) physical disabilities. These variables were selected from case records (see Chapter 4 for more detail).

Final Sample Characteristics

In summary, to participate, alumni had to *(1)* have spent 12 months or more in family foster care between the ages of 14 and 18 years; *(2)* have been placed by the state agency or Casey located in Seattle, Tacoma, and Yakima, Washington, or Portland, Oregon, between January 1, 1989, and September 30, 1998; *(3)* have been placed because of child maltreatment or child behavior problems and not as an unaccompanied refugee minor; and *(4)* not have a major physical or developmental disability (e.g., an IQ of less than 70). Youth who had severe physical disabilities and those with an IQ of less than 70 were excluded from the sample due to their likelihood of needing extended care following emancipation. Thus, the study focused on former youth from care who had spent at least a year in care during adolescence.

The different agency samples were further aligned by adjusting them to eliminate potential participants who were over age 16 at the time of their first placement. A small number of alumni from the state agencies were also eliminated because they were unaccompanied refugees, a type of foster youth rarely served by Casey. Interviews took place from September 2000 to January 2002. At that time, participants were aged 20–33. Eligibility criteria are summarized in Table 3.1. Note that the sample matching criteria were designed to maximize the ability to compare the Casey alumni with the public agency alumni. That is, the sampling approach was tied most directly to the research question regarding which program models work best.

During data collection, a number of prospective sample members who lived in prisons or in psychiatric or other restrictive institutions were deemed ineligible for interviews, as determined by the human subjects review boards that approved the investigation. These restrictions caused 20 potential sample members who were in prison and 1 living in an institution to become ineligible. Thus, while case records were reviewed for 659 alumni, 479 alumni who were located subsequently were interviewed. The breakdown is as follows:

1. Casey Oregon: Case records with 44 alumni, interviews with 29
2. Casey Washington: Case records with 111 alumni, interviews with 82
3. Oregon DHS: Case records with 171 alumni, interviews with 126
4. Washington CA/DCFS: Case records with 333 alumni, interviews with 242

Protections Against Selection Bias

Despite the investigators' attempts at scientific precision, especially when preparing the matched sample, challenges to the sampling strategy remained prior to the initiation of interviewing. Equivalence of the samples from the agencies had to be virtually identical in order to have confidence that observed differences were most likely due to foster care treatment rather than to preexisting sample differences or selection bias. In addition to the sample matching criteria and weighting approaches described above, three additional factors minimized this threat to the study's internal validity.

First, virtually all Casey youth were originally served by the State of Washington or the State of Oregon and were referred to Casey by staff members from those state agencies. If an opening existed at the time of the referral, Casey accepted them if the youth could best be served through long-term family foster care and had the potential to live independently in the community as adults after emancipation. Casey staff was vigilant about pursuing reunification or adoption if the child's circumstances changed.

Second, a pilot study of case records found no significant differences between randomly selected cases from Casey (n = 24) and the State of Washington (n = 23) in ethnicity, disabilities (including drug exposure, fetal alcohol exposure/effect, fetal alcohol syndrome, physical impairments, learning disabilities), primary reason for placement, or rates of sexual or emotional abuse. The few differences that existed between these samples indicated greater frequencies of physical abuse, neglect, number of abuse perpetrators, and number of foster care placements among Casey alumni compared with Washington State alumni.

Third, an additional pilot study was conducted to test the idea that Casey accepted only certain prospective youth who were more likely to succeed instead of youth who might prove difficult or unlikely to emancipate successfully. To test this notion, extensive case record reviews of 40 youth who were accepted in Casey care and 40 youth who were not accepted were compared. No differences beyond chance expectations (5%) were found, meaning that there were no apparent differences between the youth that Casey accepted and the youth that Casey did not accept. Nevertheless, when comparisons were subsequently made for the obtained sample, some agency-based differences were identified. Thus, Harvard Medical School statisticians who were part of the Northwest Alumni Study team used various statistical weighting approaches that were highlighted earlier in this chapter and that will be described in more detail in Chapter 4. See also Pecora et al. (2009a).

Response Rates

As noted, the study started with a sample of 659 and interviewed 479 of these alumni. Not every alumnus could be located or interviewed because of human subjects protection restrictions and/or a lack of timely location information. Very few who were found refused to participate.

> An interviewer reported having to reschedule an appointment with a young man recently released from prison. When he called to reschedule, he was concerned and apologetic, worried that he'd "lose my chance to tell my story." The interviewer assured him that was not a problem and she would be happy to accommodate his schedule, that we did not want to lose the opportunity to include his perspectives. The respondent replied, "Really? I mean, you really *do* want to hear what I have to say?" The interviewer told him indeed we did and that she was very much looking forward to talking with him. "Wow," he said, "thanks!"

> Team leaders contact about 15% of the respondents who have completed interviews and ask them a few questions in order to verify the interview. During these verifications, respondents are asked about how long the interview took and if they thought the length was "too long," "about right," or "too short." Despite the length of the interview and the fact that respondents remember pretty accurately how long it took, they most often report that the length was "about right." Some even say it was so interesting that it could have gone on longer. Team leaders are also getting compliments on the interviewers during the verifications.

To calculate the response rate, this study used the *minimum response rate* (RR1) as defined by the standard definitions manual of the American Association for Public Opinion Research. Using this definition, 26 (4.0%) respondents, including deceased alumni and those who were in prisons or psychiatric institutions at the time of the interviews, were ineligible. After removal of these alumni, the response rate was 75.7% (see Table 3.2). With the exception of a landmark study in New York City (Festinger, 1983) and the more recent longitudinal cohort studies in the Midwest (Courtney, Terao, & Bost, 2004b), this response rate is much higher than the response rates that have been obtained in other alumni follow-up studies, which are typically about 55% or less. A variety of innovative alumni location and engagement strategies were used to achieve this high response rate (see Williams, McWilliams, Mainieri, Pecora, & La Belle, 2006, for more information).

Alumni Demographics: Ethnicity, Gender, and Age at the Time of the Interview

During the interviews, over half of the alumni identified themselves as people of color (total: 54.4%; Casey: 53.9%; state: 54.5%). A person's primary ethnicity was determined from self-report interview data.[47] The majority of alumni were women (Total: 60.5%; Casey: 54.8%; state: 62.3%).[48] (See Table 3.3 and Figure 3.1.)

As seen in Table 3.3, alumni were between the ages of 20 and 33 at the time of the interview. Their average age was 24.2 years, an older age at the

Table 3.2. Alumni Disposition at the Time of Interview, Response Rates, and Sample Size

Disposition at Time of Interview, Response Rates, and Sample Size	Washington		Oregon		Combined		
	Casey (%)	State (%)	Casey (%)	State (%)	Casey (%)	State (%)	Total (%)
Disposition at the time of interview							
Deceased	2.7	0.3	0.0	0.6	1.9	0.4	0.8
In prison	2.7	2.7	2.3	4.1	2.6	3.2	3.0
In a psychiatric or other institution	0.0	0.0	0.0	0.6	0.0	0.2	0.2
Not locatable	17.1	17.4	22.7	18.1	18.7	17.7	17.9
Refusals	3.6	6.9	9.1	2.9	5.2	5.6	5.5
Interviewed (unadjusted response rate)	73.9	72.7	65.9	73.7	71.6	73.0	72.7
Response rates							
RR1[a]	78.1	74.9	67.4	77.8	75.0	75.9	75.7
Sample sizes							
Interview sample size (n)	82	242	29	126	111	368	479
Total sample size (n)	111	333	44	171	155	504	659

[a]Due to human subjects restrictions, alumni in mental health or correctional institutions could not be interviewed. This "traditional" response rate subtracts those in prison, those in psychiatric institutions, and the deceased from the sample size: interviews ÷ (sample—deceased—in institution—in prison).

Table 3.3. Demographics for the Northwest Alumni

Demographics	Washington		Oregon		Combined		Total
	Casey	State	Casey	State	Casey	State	
Ethnicity							
Hispanic	11.1 (2.7)[a]	14.0 (1.4)	4.8 (2.0)	4.7 (1.4)	9.4 (2.1)	10.8 (1.0)	10.5 (0.9)
Non-Hispanic black	23.0 (2.4)	16.3 (1.4)	24.9 (6.8)	28.8 (3.2)	23.5 (2.5)	20.6 (1.4)	21.3 (1.2)
Non-Hispanic other	21.7 (3.4)	27.6 (1.7)	18.7 (4.1)	14.5 (2.4)	20.9 (2.7)	23.1 (1.4)	22.6 (1.2)
Non-Hispanic white	44.2 (3.2)	42.1 (1.9)	51.6 (6.4)	52.0 (3.5)	46.1 (2.9)	45.5 (1.7)	45.6 (1.5)
Age at time of interview							
20–22	17.7 (2.8)	37.4 (1.9)[†]	18.8 (5.2)	24.7 (3.0)[†]	18.0 (2.5)	33.0 (1.6)[†]	29.6 (1.4)
23–25	33.0 (2.9)	39.4 (1.9)	24.6 (5.5)	42.4 (3.5)	30.8 (2.6)	40.4 (1.7)	38.2 (1.4)
26–33	49.3 (3.3)	23.2 (1.6)	56.6 (6.4)	32.9 (3.3)	51.2 (3.0)	26.5 (1.5)	32.2 (1.4)
Mean age at time of interview	25.2 (0.2)	23.7 (0.1)*	25.4 (0.3)	24.2 (0.2)*	25.2 (0.1)	23.8 (0.1)*	24.2 (0.1)
Sample size	82	242	29	126	111	368	479
Gender							
Males	45.9	38.4 (0.7)*	43.2	36.3 (2.4)*	45.2	37.7 (1.0)*	39.5 (0.7)
Females	54.1	61.6 (0.7)	56.8	63.7 (2.4)	54.8	62.3 (1.0)	60.5 (0.7)
Sample size	111	333	44	171	155	504	659

Note. As will be detailed in Chapter 4 to reflect data as if all youth had been interviewed, a nonresponse weight was used to adjust data for those who were or were not interviewed.

[a] The numbers in parentheses are standard errors. For some Casey data, standard errors are not reported because the use of the full Casey sample represents the total Casey population.

*Statistically significant Casey and state difference at $p < .05$. Washington, Oregon, and Combined tested separately.

[†] Significance when the variable has more than one level, $p < .05$. Washington, Oregon, and Combined tested separately.

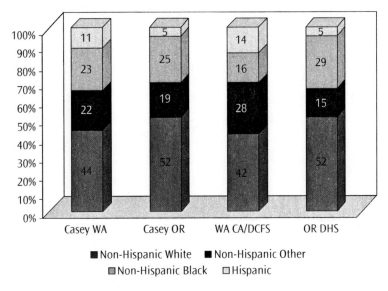

Figure 3.1. Ethnic Composition of the Interviewed Sample

time of follow-up when compared to many previous alumni studies (e.g., Cook, 1991; Courtney et al., 2004b, 2005b). The age distribution for the Casey and state alumni differed somewhat as Casey youth were, on average, older at the time of the interview (25.2 versus 23.8 years).

Summary

Foster care services are one component of a larger child welfare services system that provides prevention, child protective services, family preservation, reunification, and out-of-home care services, including foster care and independent living services. The primary mandate of public agency services for children removed from parental custody is family reunification if it is safe to return the child to the family. If a court or another decision maker determined that it was not safe to return a child to the biological family or a relative, services to families to resolve the safety issues were provided first. Only after it was found that the family was unable or unwilling to provide for the safety of the child was it determined that the child was eligible for an alternative permanent plan, including adoption, guardianship, long-term foster care services, or others.

Each of the agencies that participated in the Northwest Alumni Study was governed by similar federal statutes/policies regarding foster care. Casey's intake criteria and approach were similar to those for the small proportion of youth who needed a more long-term out-of-home placement in the state systems. As discussed in Chapter 1, important differences between Casey and care provided by the state systems of Oregon and Washington were the Casey focus on long-term care, lower caseworker turnover, higher foster parent retention, and higher daily costs per child.

Both sampling and data weighting techniques were used to account for preexisting differences between Casey and state youth. The final sample included 60.5% women, 54.4% people of color, and an alumni average age at the time of the interview of 24.2 years.

Acknowledgment.   Carol Brandford contributed to this chapter.

4

Data Sources, Variables, and Data Collection Procedures

Every interviewer is hearing fascinating stories of people's lives. Many are about respondents who have overcome horrible abuse and other adversity to achieve success in their lives today. One interviewer encountered resistance from a respondent who said she had decided she did not want to participate because the memories were just too bad and too difficult for her to deal with. The interviewer convinced her to do the interview by telling her that we hope that this study's results will make changes that help children coming into the system. Another respondent was excited about the interview, and told the interviewer that she has opened up her house as a foster home for cats that are available for adoption from the cat rescue group she works with. At the time of the interview she had seven cats and an interviewer who was allergic to them!

Overview

This chapter discusses the two means of data collection (case record reviews and interviews); the description of study variables, predictors, and outcomes; and the response rate, the handling of missing data, and how the data were weighted to adjust for interview nonresponse.[49]

Case Record Reviews (CRRs)

The study reviewed archival records for the 659 alumni selected to participate in the study. Trained raters individually read and recorded on standardized forms case record information, which included demographics; reason(s) for original placement; dates of entry into and exit from foster care; type and length of each living situation during care; foster family background; type of exit from care; history of child maltreatment; and information about birth parents, including family composition and functioning (including drug and alcohol usage and termination of parental rights). A version of the Maltreatment Classification Scheme, initially developed by Barnett, Manly, and Cicchetti and modified by the LONGSCAN Group, was used to record and classify maltreatment experiences (Barnett, Manly, & Cicchetti, 1993; Lau et al., 2005). Only variables with acceptable interrater reliability were used in subsequent analyses (for more information on reliability, please see Pecora et al. (2009a).

Interviews and Data Collection Measures

Professional interviewers from the University of Michigan Survey Research Center (SRC) conducted interviews with 479 alumni in person or by phone between September 2000 and January 2002. Interviewers were not aware of the study hypotheses. The interview protocol contained several standardized scales and covered a wide range of areas, including mental health, education, employment and finances, marriage and relationships, and parenting. The interviewers also asked open-ended questions that focused on the alumnis' perceptions of agency services, how their foster parents could have done better, how the transition to independent living could have been improved, and which people or services had the most influence on their success.

Based on advice from alumni of foster care and foster parents, the interview was organized and administered to maximize participant comfort and honesty. Interviewers were trained to build rapport and encourage honesty in reporting. To start and finish on a positive note, more benign questions were placed at the beginning and end, while more difficult and personal items were placed in the middle of the interview. The next sections summarize the main data collection measures that were used.

Composite International Diagnostic Interview

An important feature of this interview was the use of several sections from the Composite International Diagnostic Interview (CIDI). The CIDI is a World Health Organization (WHO)–approved psychiatric diagnostic interview that was developed to facilitate psychiatric epidemiological research without the need for clinician interviewers. It generates mental health diagnoses for conditions such as depression, anxiety, and substance addiction. Sections of the CIDI 2.1, supplemental sections from the CIDI 2.0 and 3.0 (Kessler, 1991; Kessler & Magee, 1994; Kessler & Üstün, 2004; Kessler & Walters, 2002; Robins et al., 1989; World Health Organization, 1996), and other supplemental interview questions from the University of Michigan Institute for Social Research were used. This version of the CIDI has been shown to have high reliability and validity indices (e.g., Haro et al., 2006; World Health Organization, 1996).

This compilation of CIDI items was used to compare the outcomes for alumni in the Northwest Alumni Study to the outcomes for adults in the National Comorbidity Study Replication survey (NCS-R; Kessler & Merikangas, 2004). The NCS-R was conducted with a nationally representative sample of 10,000 respondents in 2001–2002. Participants in the two studies were matched on age, ethnicity, and gender to help make the studies more comparable. This enabled detailed comparisons based on poststudy stratified data from a unique nationally representative data set.

Short Form Health Survey 12

The interview included the Short Form Health Survey 12 (SF-12®) to assess overall mental and physical health. The SF-12® was developed to be a shorter, yet valid, alternative to the SF-36® for use in large surveys of general and specific populations as well as for large longitudinal studies of health outcomes (Ware, Kosinski, & Keller, 1998, pp. 11, 60). A score of 50 or higher indicates good physical or mental health (depending upon the particular SF-12 subscale).

Conflict Tactics Scale (CTS)

The CTS is a 19-item, 7-point Likert-scale questionnaire that measures reasoning (not used in the current study), verbal aggression, and physical aggression in reaction to family members. It has internal reliabilities ranging from 0.42 to 0.88. The original factor structure has been repeatedly confirmed, and concurrent validity indices have been high (Gelles & Straus, 1988; Straus, 1979; Straus & Gelles, 1989; Straus, Gelles, & Steinmetz, 1980). Further, it has been successfully adapted for studies of victims of maltreatment (Benedict, Zuravin, & Stallings, 1996; Zuravin, McMillen, DePanfilis, & Risley-Curtiss, 1996). The present study used the original CTS *psychological aggression* and the *physical assault* items.

Rosenberg Self-Esteem Scale (RSE)

The Rosenberg Self-Esteem Scale (Rosenberg, 1965) was used as a measure of psychological health and well-being.[50] The RSE is a widely used measure of self-esteem, with excellent test-retest reliability and internal consistency (Corcoran & Fischer, 2000). Unfortunately, one item from the original scale ("I feel I do not have much to be proud of") was accidentally omitted from the interview form. Therefore, the RSE results were not used in multivariate analyses; only a scale score constructed from the nine items used was reported.

Home Environment Questions

A revised and shortened set of items from the NCS-R was used to assess the nature of the birth and foster family environments in which the alumni lived. The home environment data were bolstered by CRRs.

Ethnic Identity Questions

Six ethnic identity questions were drawn from two main bodies of work. The first four items were derived from the WHO World Mental Health 2000 Survey questionnaire (Demyttenaere et al., 2004) originally developed by Jackson (1994) for the National Survey of Black Americans. The final two questions were drawn from work by Cauce (Cauce & Gonzales, 1993; Gonzales & Cauce, 1995), modified to use a 5-point scale.

Description of Study Variables

The study obtained some information on demographics, risk factors, and foster care experiences through case records. It obtained information on service access, extent of use, and outcomes primarily through interviews. This section of the report groups the items that were used in the analyses into *predictor variables* and *outcome variables*. To simplify explanations of subsequent analyses, predictor variables were categorized as demographics, risk factors, intervention group, or foster care experiences. A wide range of outcome variables was assessed, including mental health, education, and employment. For example, the study addressed the extent to which alumni from foster care experienced any of the major types of psychological and behavioral disturbance that are frequently found among adolescents and adults in the general population who were abused in childhood (e.g., post-traumatic stress disorder [PTSD], depression, panic disorder). Table 4.1 lists predictors and outcomes and provides detail on the domain the variable is part of, a description of the variable, and the source of the information.

Missing Data

The study used two procedures to impute data missing from otherwise complete archival records (Ford, 1983). The first method was *hot-deck imputation*, which matched the participant for whom a data element was missing with respondents who had complete data for that element. The matching was based on other variables that were present in all sample case records and were strongly related to the missing data element. Once matches were made, the data were drawn from a randomly selected matching case record to impute the missing data element. The second method was *mean imputation*, which was used to impute values to variables with small amounts of missing data that were not considered central to the analysis. In this situation, we assigned the mean value from respondents who had data for the variable to the missing case.

Table 4.1. Predictors and outcomes for the Northwest Alumni Study

Variable	Description	Source
	Predictors	
Demographics		Interview
Ethnicity	Participant identified as Hispanic, non-Hispanic white, non-Hispanic black, non Hispanic other	
Gender	Participant identified as male or female	
Age	Based on participant report of birth date	
Risk Factors: Living Arrangements Before Care		
Mother and father employment	Participant was asked whether the parent was employed part-time, full-time, or not at all	Interview
Age entered child welfare system	Based on case record information	Case record
Number of places lived before foster care	Based on self-report	Interview
Knew birth mother and birth father	Participant was asked whether he or she knew the mother, knew the father, knew neither, or knew both	Interview
Risk Factors: Parent Functioning		Interview
Mental health	Participant was asked if the parent had good mental health	
Physical health	Participant was asked if the parent had good physical health	
Substance abuse	Participant was asked if the parent had a substance abuse problem	
Criminal behavior	Participant was asked if the parent was involved in the criminal justice system	
Risk Factors: Parenting Style of Birth Parents		Interview
Mother and father warmth	Participant was asked if the parent exhibited warm behaviors	
Mother and father overprotection	Participant was asked if the parent exhibited overprotective behaviors	
Both parents' neglect	Participant was asked about the degree of neglect experienced from birth parents	
Risk Factors: Child Maltreatment by Birth Parents		Case record
Type of abuse/neglect	Case record information concerning emotional, physical, sexual, neglect was reviewed	
Number of abuse/neglect types experienced	Based on type pulled from case records, participants were assigned a number (0 to 4)	
Risk Factors: Reasons for Initial Placement		Case record
Placement reasons	Case record information concerning child behavior problems, maltreatment, and parents' substance abuse was reviewed	

(continued)

Table 4.1. Continued

Variable	Description	Source
Number of reasons	Based on reasons pulled from case records, participants were assigned a number (0 to 3)	
Risk Factors: Mental/Physical Health Problems Diagnosed Before or During Care		Case record
Attention deficit hyperactivity disorder (ADHD)	Based on case record information	
Physical or learning disability	Based on case record information	
Other impairments	Case record information that included drug exposure as an infant, fetal alcohol effect, fetal alcohol syndrome, vision or hearing impairment	
Intervention Group		Case record
Agency	Based on case record information, participants were designated as Casey or state alumni	
Foster Care Experiences and Services: Placement History		Case record
Number of placements	All information in this section came from case records. Living situations and placements are defined differently, depending on the federal rules, viewpoints (e.g., youth, agency, or researcher), and other conceptual frameworks being considered. The Northwest Alumni Study defined a child's living situation as the place where the youth lived and what was viewed by the caseworker as the child's home—temporary or not. Following most of the federal and Child Welfare League of America National Data Analysis System work group definitions (Woodruff, 2004), the study considered the following living situations to be distinct placements:	

- Initial shelter care
- Foster care
- Kinship care
- Treatment foster care
- Group homes
- Residential treatment
- Independent living placements
- Adoptions
- Juvenile justice placements once the youth is under child welfare agency supervision (not as an initial placement).

(continued)

Table 4.1. Continued

Variable	Description	Source
	Although recorded in the case records, the following living situations were not counted as placements:	

- Returning to or living with birth parents
- Running away from a current placement
- Visits to medical hospitals
- Respite care
- Living with unlicensed friends or relatives
- Unless recorded as the first placement in the log, stays at psychiatric institutions for fewer than 30 days (i.e., stays at the beginning of the placement log or 30 days or longer) were counted
- A stay in a juvenile justice or correctional facility that was recorded in the log as the first placement

Variable	Description	Source
Length of time in care	Based on case record information	
Placement change rate	The ratio of number of placements to length of time in care	
Number of reunifica-tion failures	Based on case record information, this is the number of times a participant was returned to the birth home for more than two weeks and was subsequently removed.	
Number of runaways	Based on case record information, this is the number of times a participant ran away from a placement	
Number of unlicensed living situations with friends or relatives	Based on case record information, this is the number of times a participant resided with an unlicensed friend or relative (not a kin placement)	

Foster Care Experiences and Services: Educational Services and Experience   Interview

Variable	Description	Source
Could participate in supplemental educational services/tutoring (access)	Based on self-report	
Total number of school changes from elementary through high school	Based on self-report	

Foster Care Experiences and Services: Therapeutic Service and Supports   Interview

Variable	Description	Source
Could participate in therapeutic service and supports (access)	Participant reported that he or she could access all of the following services: *(1)* counseling or other mental health services, *(2)* alcohol or drug treatment programs, and *(3)* group work or group counseling	

(continued)

Table 4.1.   Continued

Variable	Description	Source
Foster Care Experiences and Services: Activities with Foster Family		Interview
Participated frequently in activities with foster family	Participant reported participating in both enjoyable and religious activities with foster family	
Foster Care Experiences and Services: Preparation for Leaving Care		Interview
Degree of preparation for leaving care	Participant reported that he or she *(1)* could participate in employment training or job location services, *(2)* could participate in independent training groups or workshops, *(3)* was somewhat or very well prepared for independent living, and *(4)* had health insurance at exit—participants were assigned a number (0 to 4)	
Foster Care Experiences and Services: Preparation for Leaving Care		Interview
Resources upon leaving care	The leaving care resources included possession of *(1)* a driver's license, *(2)* $250 in cash, and *(3)* dishes and utensils—participants were assigned a number (0 to 3)	
Foster Care Experiences and Services: Foster Family and Other Nurturing Support While in Care		Interview
Positive parenting by foster parents	Positive parenting was trichotomized into high, medium, and low based on alumni reports of foster parents' parenting style—authoritative, authoritarian, permissive, disengaged, or "other" (Baumrind, 1995). High positive parenting occurred only when two foster parents were present in the identified home and they were both authoritative or one was authoritative and one was other. Medium positive parenting occurred when both were other or one was authoritative and one was authoritarian, permissive, or disengaged or only one foster parent was present and s/he was authoritative. Low positive parenting occurred when one parent was other and one was authoritarian, permissive, or disengaged or when both were authoritarian, permissive, or disengaged or when only one foster parent was present and s/he was authoritarian, permissive, disengaged, or other.	
Felt loved while in foster care	Based on self-report	
Overall, foster parents were helpful	Based on self-report	
Foster family helped with ethnic issues	Based on self-report	
Had a close relationship with an adult while growing up	Based on self-report	

(continued)

Table 4.1.   Continued

Variable	Description	Source
Maltreatment by foster parent or other caregiver	Based on self-report, maltreatment was categorized as sexual, physical abuse, or physical neglect	

Outcomes

Mental Health	Based on self-report	Interview
No 12-month CIDI diagnosis *Total number of 12-month CIDI Diagnoses was fewer than three* *No major depression in past 12 months* *No panic syndrome in last 12 months* *No social phobia in last 12 months* *No alcohol dependence in last 12 months* *No drug dependence in last 12 months* *No PTSD in last 12 months* *No generalized anxiety in last 12 months*	Each diagnosis and sum score was generated based on a series of questions asked of the participant— based on responses, diagnoses were generated	
SF-12®—Short Form Health Survey 12—mental health score of 50 and above	Based on participant's responses to a series of questions, a score between 0 and 100 was given. A score of 50 or above is commonly considered good mental health	
Physical Health	Based on self-report	Interview
SF-12® physical health score of 50 or above	Based on participant's responses to a series of questions, a score between 0 and 100 was given. A score of 50 or above is commonly considered good physical health	
No chronic physical disorder *Does not smoke currently* *Smokes fewer than 10 cigarettes per day* *Does not drink currently* *Drinks fewer than 150 drinks per year*		

(continued)

Table 4.1.   Continued

Variable	Description	Source
Education	Based on self-report	Interview
Completed high school—high school diploma or General Equivalency Diploma (GED)		
Completed high school—high school diploma only		
Any education past high school (any type of postsecondary education)		
Completed any degree/ certificate beyond high school (vocational, BA, etc.)		
Completed college or more (has BA or more)		
Employment and Finances	Based on self-report	Interview
Alumnus or alumna was not homeless within one year after leaving foster care		
Alumnus or alumna was never on public assistance after age 18		
Alumnus or alumna currently does not receive cash public assistance (Temporary Assistance to Needy Families [TANF])		
No one in the house- hold of the alumnus or alumna received a form of public aid (TANF, General Assistance) in the past 6 months		
Household income above the poverty level	Household income of participants was compared to national poverty levels to determine relative position	
Household income greater than three times the poverty level		

(continued)

Table 4.1. Continued

Variable	Description	Source
Has health insurance of any kind		
Owns house or apartment		
Employed or self-employed		
Relationships and Social Supports	Based on self-report	Interview
Alumnus or alumna married or cohabitating		
No violence in relationship	Based on responses to the Conflict Tactics Scale (Straus, Hamby, Boney-McCoy and Sugarman (1996)	
Very satisfied with marriage or cohabitating relationship		
Not socially isolated (number of friends is not in lowest 25% of sample)	Based on self-report and distribution of the sample's data	
Not socially isolated (number of friends is not in lowest 25% of sample)	Based on self-report and distribution of the sample's data	
No serious fighting with anyone in past 12 months		
Negative social support (receives low demands, stress, and arguments from friends and relatives)	Based on self-report and distribution of the sample's data	
Positive social support (receives high understanding, help from friends and relatives)	Based on self-report and distribution of the sample's data	
No children before age 18		
No children before marriage		
Engages in many activities with children		
Frequent displays of nurturance/affection with children		
Did not have a child of his or her own placed in foster care		

Weighting Data

During analyses, additional steps were taken to match Casey and state samples and to account for the youth who were not interviewed. The sample data were weighted using archival data on preplacement characteristics to adjust for systematic nonresponse. Propensity score adjustment (Rosenbaum & Rubin, 1984) was implemented by estimating a logistic regression equation (Hosmer & Lemseshow, 1989) separately within the Casey and public system target samples that distinguished survey respondents from nonrespondents (treated as a dichotomous dependent variable) based on preplacement characteristics. The predicted probabilities generated from these equations were used to weight the data without case-level matching so that survey respondents had distributions on preplacement characteristics comparable to those of the original target sample. Weighted Casey and state samples were then compared within each state to generate a second propensity score weight that adjusted for baseline differences (i.e., at first placement) between Casey and public program alumni.

This matching improved the ability to generalize to the population from which the sample was drawn. In both cases, propensity score matching was used to weight the data so that differences between the samples did not bias the results (Braitman & Rosenbaum, 2002). Weights were used to estimate data as if there had been no preexisting differences between Casey and the state samples and as if the entire sample of 659 had been interviewed. Thus, all of the outcome data presented in this report are based on weighted data to adjust for these sample differences, small as most of them were. Case record data for the full sample of 659 are not weighted.

Limitations

Findings should be viewed with some caution because of the following potential study limitations:

1. Comparisons between Casey and the state agencies should be interpreted with caution because Casey field offices were not operating under the workload pressures of achieving a permanent placement in the same way that the public agency staff were. Namely, because the children referred to Casey were those that the state agency and the juvenile court determined were unable or unwilling to be adopted or be reunified with their parents, Casey staff had the goal of stabilizing and preserving the placement.
2. The Northwest Alumni Study focused on alumni who had spent one year or more in foster care as adolescents. Many of these youth tend to stay in care for longer periods of time or enter care as adolescents (e.g., at age 16) and emancipate from foster care in *both* public and private systems. This was a study of a group of alumni who spent a year or more in care as *adolescents;* therefore, participants do not represent the full spectrum of children served in foster care.

3. There were differences between Casey and state alumni in certain risk factors and foster care experiences. For example, Casey alumni stayed in care an average of two years longer than state alumni, and there were differences in child maltreatment history in the birth family (e.g., more Casey youth had been sexually abused than youth in the state agencies). Weighting and propensity score matching were conducted to minimize these differences; however, the full range of differences may not have been addressed by these statistical techniques.

Summary

This study has a number of distinguishing methodological aspects, which are summarized as follows:

What Was Most Unique About This Study?	Significance
United three public and voluntary child welfare agencies and three universities in a six-year research collaboration.	Enabled a joint research project to conduct an objective study with findings that are useful for guiding program design.
Used standardized measures of outcomes, including the mental health assessment that is used for the U.S. national prevalence studies (CIDI).	Facilitated comparisons to the general population. The NCS-R provided unique comparison data because it was stratified poststudy to match the Northwest Alumni Study's distribution of ethnicity, sex, and age.
Obtained an unusually high response rate (75.7%) for alumni interviews, which resulted in a larger, more representative sample than most previous research.	Provided a more complete picture of alumni functioning than past studies.
Interviewed alumni further into adulthood than in previous studies (alumni averaged 24 years of age [ranging from 20 to 33] vs. 19 to 21 years of age in other studies).	Offered a more comprehensive picture of development than short-term studies because alumni are further along in their lives (e.g., more time for college enrollment and completion).

The following chapters present selected childhood experiences that may have acted as risk or protective factors. Chapters also describe foster care placements and services received by the alumni.

Acknowledgment. Nancy Gebler, Eva Hiripi, Wai Tat Chiu, Nathaniel Ehrlich, and Carol Brandford contributed to this chapter.

PART III

RISK FACTORS

5

Risk Factors

I will never forget age four. I still lived with my birth mother then. She had an addiction, too. She was addicted to men. She couldn't be without men and it didn't matter what kind: She would take anyone, drug dealer or user, pimp, thief, or child abuser. She needed them so badly she'd go deep into their wayward world and forget that there were children left alone in the apartment that she had not visited in over a week. So, yes, the day the police finally figured out that at four years old, I cooked for my older brother and cleaned house instead of watching Sesame Street, I was glad. Maybe things would change for the better.

Question: If you could tell children coming into the foster care agency anything right now, what would you tell them?

Answer: Let them know they're in a position now to make a decision—they can either use the stuff that has happened in their life as a crutch or as a stepping stone.

Overview

This chapter summarizes the risk factors for adverse adult outcomes that Northwest alumni faced before or during care. These included the number of places lived before foster care, parents' health and criminal problems, and abuse/neglect. In this volume, the term *risk factors* refers to those descriptors, aside from demographic variables, largely in effect before the alumni entered foster care and certainly before they became eligible for the study. Thus, risk factors are here differentiated from factors the agencies could likely control or influence. As detailed in later chapters, the risk factors described here play an important role in later adult functioning (see Chapters 6–9; Rutter, 2001; Widom, 1989a). This chapter presents prevalence data on many risk factors that will later be associated with outcomes (see O'Brien et al., 2009b) and will later be used as controls prior to examining the relationship between foster care experiences and outcomes (see Chapters 11 and 12). This chapter provides the context for experiences that placed alumni at risk for poor long-term outcomes.

Living Arrangements Before Foster Care

For the purpose of the Northwest Alumni Study, parents' employment, age when youth entered the child welfare system and foster care, places lived before foster care, and relationship with birth parents defined the conceptual factor of Living Arrangements before Foster Care. Different combinations of specific levels of these factors can describe childhoods before foster care that vary widely in parenting and attachment, privation, stability, and other aspects important to development. Differences in age at entry can mark very different histories in terms of maltreatment, child protective services (CPS) involvement, services received, and home stability. For example, the National Survey of Child and Adolescent Well-Being (U.S. Department of Health and Human Services, 2001b) found that, among children examined during their first year in foster care, those who were oldest at the time of placement (age 11 or older) were more likely to have experienced multiple previous incidents of maltreatment. Child removal and placement in care immediately after the first call to CPS may indicate an unprecedented experience of severe maltreatment, while a long interval between case opening (the first CPS report) and entry into care might indicate parents who struggled to overcome financial, emotional, or substance difficulties (see Pecora, Wiggins, Jackson, & English, 2009b,c, for a discussion of differential effects of child maltreatment). Thus, it is important to account for such childhood variables when examining long-term outcomes. These variables are reported in this section.

The alumni in this sample were, on average, 9.6 years old at the time of first contact with the child welfare system (when their case was first opened; see Table 5.1a). This was generally the first report of harm to CPS regarding the child. Nearly one-quarter of these children were less than 6 years old, but over 41% were 12 years or older at first contact with the child welfare system.

Placement for these children typically occurred within two years of first contact with the child welfare system: The average time between case opening and first placement was 1.5 years, with 37% of the sample being removed from their homes and placed immediately upon case opening. The mean age at first out-of-home placement varied widely in this sample, from infancy to 16 years, with an average of 11.1 years. Casey alumni were younger than state alumni on average at both case opening and entry into placement. These differences may possibly reflect Casey's focus on long-term foster care and early identification of children who would not be returning to their families of origin (e.g., due to more severe maltreatment or chronic parental drug abuse). In contrast, state youth may have had more preservation efforts prior to removal and therefore entered the child welfare system and placement later. These differences may be key to future outcomes. Disruptions of attachment relationships with primary caregivers can result in serious problems for children or, depending on the timing, may have provided an opportunity for the youth to develop attachment relationships with new and more permanent primary caregivers.

Reported in Table 5.1b are alumni recollections of their birth parents' employment while the alumni were growing up. Alumni were more likely

Table 5.1a. Living Arrangements Before Foster Care

Living Arrangements		Washington		Oregon		Combined		
		Casey %	State % (SE)	Casey %	State % (SE)	Casey %	State % (SE)	Total % (SE)
Age in years at child welfare case opening	5 or younger	35.1[a]	19.2 (0.7)†	34.1	23.4 (2.2)†	34.8	20.6 (0.9)†	24.0 (0.7)
	6–11	41.4	37.2 (0.8)	50.0	21.6 (2.1)	43.9	31.9 (0.9)	34.7 (0.7)
	12 or older	23.4	43.5 (0.7)	15.9	55.0 (2.5)	21.3	47.4 (1.0)	41.3 (0.7)
Mean age at child welfare case opening		8.1	10.0 (0.1)*	7.9	10.4 (0.2)*	8.0	10.2 (0.1)*	9.6 (0.1)
Age entered foster care	5 or younger	27.9	10.2 (0.5)†	29.5	11.7 (1.6)†	28.4	10.7 (0.6)†	14.9 (0.5)
	6–11	42.3	26.4 (0.8)	43.2	18.7 (2.0)	42.6	23.8 (0.9)	28.2 (0.7)
	12 or older	29.7	63.4 (0.8)	27.3	69.6 (2.3)	29.0	65.5 (0.9)	56.9 (0.7)
Mean age entered foster care		8.9	11.7 (0.1)*	8.4	12.1 (0.2)*	8.7	11.8 (0.1)*	11.1 (0.1)
Sample size		**111**	**333**	**44**	**171**	**155**	**504**	**659**

[a] The numbers in parentheses are standard errors. For some Casey data, standard errors are not reported because the use of the full Casey sample represents the total Casey population.

*Statistically significant Casey and state difference at $p < .05$. Washington, Oregon, and Combined tested separately.

†Significance when the variable has more than one level, $p < .05$. Washington, Oregon, and Combined tested separately.

Table 5.1b. Living Arrangements Before Foster Care

Living Arrangements		Washington		Oregon		Combined		
		Casey % (SE)	State % (SE)	Casey % (SE)	State % (SE)	Casey % (SE)	State % (SE)	Total % (SE)
Birth mother's employment	Unemployed	63.9 (3.2)	47.4 (1.9)†	52.6 (6.4)	33.9 (3.3)†	61.0 (2.9)	42.8 (1.7)†	47.0 (1.5)
	Part-time	8.5 (1.5)	13.3 (1.3)	8.2 (2.8)	21.6 (2.9)	8.4 (1.3)	16.1 (1.3)	14.3 (1.1)
	Full-time	27.6 (3.0)	39.4 (1.8)	39.2 (6.6)	44.4 (3.5)	30.7 (2.9)	41.1 (1.7)	38.7 (1.5)
Birth father's employment	Unemployed	57.6 (3.3)	41.0 (1.9)†	50.7 (6.4)	36.0 (3.4)	55.8 (2.9)	39.2 (1.7)†	43.1 (1.5)
	Part-time	5.0 (1.1)	8.0 (1.1)	7.2 (2.5)	8.5 (1.9)	5.6 (1.1)	8.2 (1.0)	7.6 (0.8)
	Full-time	37.4 (3.2)	51.0 (1.9)	42.1 (6.2)	55.5 (3.5)	38.6 (2.9)	52.6 (1.7)	49.3 (1.5)
Relationship with birth parents	Knew mother only	30.3 (2.8)	24.9 (1.8)†	28.5 (6.2)	21.9 (3.0)†	29.9 (2.6)	23.9 (1.6)†	25.3 (1.3)
	Knew father only	2.8 (0.8)	4.2 (0.7)	10.3 (3.5)	3.4 (1.3)	4.8 (1.1)	3.9 (0.6)	4.1 (0.6)
	Knew neither	12.8 (2.6)	6.3 (0.9)	—	3.8 (1.3)	9.4 (2.0)	5.5 (0.7)	6.4 (0.7)
	Both	54.1 (3.3)	64.5 (1.9)	61.1 (6.4)	70.9 (3.3)	55.9 (2.9)	66.7 (1.7)	64.2 (1.5)
Number of places lived per year before foster care	Low (less than 0.25)	32.6 (3.1)	33.8 (1.8)	29.5 (6.2)	24.8 (3.0)	31.8 (2.8)	30.7 (1.6)	31.0 (1.4)
	Medium (0.25 to 0.66)	28.8 (2.7)	34.2 (1.8)	39.8 (6.4)	37.5 (3.4)	31.6 (2.6)	35.4 (1.7)	34.5 (1.4)
	High (more than 0.66)	38.7 (3.4)	31.9 (1.7)	30.6 (5.1)	37.7 (3.4)	36.6 (2.9)	33.9 (1.6)	34.5 (1.4)
Sample size		82	242	29	126	111	368	479

*Statistically significant Casey and state difference at $p < .05$. Washington, Oregon, and Combined tested separately.

†Significance when the variable has more than one level, $p < .05$. Washington, Oregon, and Combined tested separately.

to report that their birth mothers were mostly unemployed (47.0%) than employed full-time (38.7%). Nearly half (49.3%) of birth fathers were employed full-time, while 43.1% were unemployed. Both the birth fathers and birth mothers of state alumni were more often recalled as employed full-time and less often unemployed compared to Casey alumni. The majority of the young adults in this study (64.2%) knew both of their biological parents while growing up (state youth were more likely to know both), 10 times the proportion who knew neither (6.4%).

Another risk factor in Living Arrangements before Foster Care is pre–foster care residential instability. Research suggests a link between the stability and predictability of the environment, changes in the structure of the family, or relocation of the family and negative outcomes for children (e.g., Adam, 2004; Amato & Keith, 1991). For example, several studies have identified a link between residential instability and impairment in children's academic and emotional adjustment and behavioral problems (Eckenrode, Laird, & Doris, 1993; Haveman & Wolfe, 1994; Humke & Schaefer, 1995; McLoyd & Wilson, 1991; Reider & Cicchetti, 1989). It follows that placement instability prior to care may have a significant impact on later functioning. According to Table 5.1b, almost equal numbers of alumni experienced less than 0.25 (31.0%), 0.25 to 0.66 (34.5%), and more than 0.66 (34.5%) places lived per year before foster care with no agency differences. That is, nearly 35% of the sample reported having two or more different living arrangements—moving at least twice—every three years.

Birth Parent Availability During Care

Continuity of relationships is an important factor in healthy child growth and development (e.g., Berrick et al., 1998). An important aspect defining a youth's time in foster care is the relationship with the birth parents. Some youth want little to do with their birth parents, while others want to maintain some semblance of continuity via occasional birth family contact. Decisions about visitation should be made carefully on an individual basis (American Academy of Pediatrics Committee on Early Childhood Adoption and Dependent Care [AAP], 2000). Birth parent involvement has not been found to be associated with the child's adaptation to foster care placement (Leathers, 2002), yet it tends to be a focus of caseworkers because of its association with reunification.

Birth parent availability, as noted in case records during the alumni's time in care, is presented in Table 5.2. The identity and location were known more for alumni's birth mothers (96.3%) than birth fathers (79.9%), indicating more contact with mothers than with fathers. Fewer than 1 in 25 case records (3.7%) indicated that the birth mother's location or identity was unknown, while 20% of records indicated that the birth father was unknown or not locatable, with statistically significant differences by agency and by

Table 5.2. Birth Parent Availability During Care

Birthparent Availability		Washington		Oregon		Combined		
		Casey % (SE)	State % (SE)	Casey % (SE)	State % (SE)	Casey % (SE)	State % (SE)	Total % (SE)
Birth mother	Location or identity unknown	9.0	2.0 (0.6)*	0.0	3.5 (0.9)*	6.5	2.7 (0.5)*	3.7 (0.4)
	Deceased	9.9	11.4 (1.3)	6.8	4.1 (1.0)*	9.0	8.3 (0.9)	8.5 (0.6)
	Parental rights terminated	19.8	13.3 (1.4)*	22.7	4.1 (1.0)*	20.6	9.4 (0.9)*	12.5 (0.7)
Birth father	Location or identity unknown	26.1	13.5 (1.4)*	20.5	25.1 (2.2)*	24.5	18.4 (1.2)*	20.1 (0.9)
	Deceased	19.8	8.6 (1.2)*	4.5	8.2 (1.4)*	15.5	8.4 (0.9)*	10.4 (0.7)
	Parental rights terminated	16.2	14.8 (1.5)	18.2	4.1 (1.0)*	16.8	10.3 (0.9)*	12.1 (0.7)
Primary caregiver	Incarcerated	7.2	7.2 (1.1)	6.8	4.1 (1.0)*	7.1	5.9 (0.7)	6.2 (0.5)
	Deceased	9.0	10.6 (1.2)	6.8	3.5 (0.9)*	8.4	7.6 (0.8)	7.8 (0.6)
Sample size		**111**	**232**a	**44**	**171**	**155**	**403**a	**558**a
Birth mother incarcerated		13.3 (1.9)	23.1 (1.6)*	22.2 (5.4)	27.4 (3.1)	15.6 (2.0)	24.6 (1.5)*	22.5 (1.2)
Birth father incarcerated		18.2 (2.8)	26.2 (1.6)*	29.4 (5.7)	27.2 (3.1)	21.1 (2.5)	26.5 (1.5)	25.2 (1.3)
Sample size		**82**	**242**	**29**	**126**	**111**	**368**	**479**

aThe Washington State Institutional Review Board did not permit collection of a small number of variables without consent (provided during the interview). Therefore, the sample size is smaller.

*Statistically significant Casey and state difference at p < .05. Washington, Oregon, and Combined tested separately.

†Significance when the variable has more than one level, p < .05. Washington, Oregon, and Combined tested separately.

state ($p < .05$, two-tailed). Meanwhile, less than 10% (8.5%) of birth mothers were deceased (no Casey/state difference), while about one in 10 (10.4%) birth fathers were deceased, with Casey alumni's fathers more often deceased than those of state alumni. Parental rights had been officially terminated for a substantial percentage of the birth mothers (12.5%) and birth fathers (12.1%) of the alumni, with a higher percentage for Casey alumni, consistent with its historical focus on long-term care.

In another perspective on parental availability, about one in four alumni reported in the interview that their birth mothers (22.5%) and birth fathers (25.2%) had been incarcerated at some point, with a higher percentage of state alumni's birth mothers having been incarcerated—a factor that influences a child's support network and often results in substantial emotional distress (Gabel & Johnston, 1997). In the case records, a small percentage of alumni had a primary caregiver noted as being incarcerated (6.2%) or deceased (7.8%) before or during their time in care.

Household Arrangements

Table 5.3 provides data on the alumni family situation at the time of initial placement as recorded in the case file. Three arrangements were examined: the alumnus lived in a household with (1) birth parents living together, (2) a single parent, or (3) a primary caregiver, such as the birth mother, who was living with a stepparent, partner or paramour, relative, or friend. About one in eight alumni (12.2%) lived in a home with both birth parents; a little over one-third of alumni (35.6%) lived in a single-parent household; and a little over one-third of alumni (36.4%) lived in a home with a primary caregiver living with a stepparent, partner or paramour, relative, or friend. Only alumni living in a single-parent home differed by agency, with significantly more state alumni in this type of household arrangement. As discussed above, household structure represents another factor influencing alumni outcomes (e.g., Adam, 2004; Amato & Keith, 1991). For example, Zimiles and Lee (1991) found that students living with both parents were less likely to drop out of high school than students living with a single parent or in a blended (step) family, while Frost and Pakiz (1990) demonstrated relationships between parental marital disruption and antisocial and delinquent behavior among 14- to 16-year-olds.

Parent Functioning

Evidence from several studies suggests that parental substance abuse is related to child maltreatment, especially neglect (Ammerman, Kolko, Kirisci, Blackson, & Dawes, 1999; Brown, Cohen, Johnson, & Salzinger, 1998; Chaffin, Kelleher, & Hollenberg, 1996; Olsen, Allen, & Azzi-Lessing, 1996). Further, the Foster Care Mental Health research project (Besinger,

Table 5.3. Household Arrangements

Household Arrangements	Washington		Oregon		Combined		
	Casey %	State % (SE)	Casey %	State % (SE)	Casey %	State % (SE)	Total % (SE)
Birth parents living together	14.4	10.8 (1.4)*	6.8	14.0 (1.8)*	12.3	12.2 (1.1)	12.2 (0.8)
Single-parent household	22.5	40.7 (2.0)*	20.5	40.9 (2.5)*	21.9	40.8 (1.6)*	35.6 (1.1)
Primary caregiver living with a stepparent, partner, or paramour, relative, or friend	34.2	34.2 (1.9)	47.7	38.0 (2.5)*	38.1	35.8 (1.5)	36.4 (1.1)
Sample size	**111**	**232**[a]	**44**	**171**	**155**	**403**[a]	**558**[a]

[a]The Washington State Institutional Review Board did not permit collection of a small number of variables without consent (provided during the interview). Therefore, the sample size is smaller.

*Statistically significant Casey and state difference at $p < .05$. Washington, Oregon, and Combined tested separately.

Garland, Litrownik, & Landsverk, 1999) found that children in care who had a substance-abusing caregiver were more likely to have been removed due to neglect and less likely to have been removed due to physical or sexual abuse than children in care who did not have a caregiver with alcohol or drug problems. Different maltreatment histories may, in turn, contribute to different outcome profiles. Additionally, Hillis and colleagues (Hillis, Anda, Felitti, & Marchbanks, 2001) found that both household substance abuse and having an incarcerated family member (as well as physical, verbal, and sexual abuse) were predictive of future sexually risky behavior, with risk increasing with the number of types of adverse childhood experiences. Thus, parental substance abuse is an important marker of family conditions and risk factors. As seen in Table 5.4, alumni reported that their birth fathers had no substance abuse problems over half of the time (54.9%), with Casey alumni reporting no substance abuse more often. In comparison, alumni reported that their birth mothers had no substance abuse problems just over a third of the time (35.4%) (no Casey/state difference). While birth fathers were less likely to be reported as having substance abuse problems, recall that the alumni were less likely to have contact with their fathers than with their birth mothers while in care.

Another factor associated with poor alumni outcomes was the criminal justice problems of their birth parents. Over six in 10 alumni reported that their birth mother and birth father were not involved in the criminal justice system (65.0% and 63.3%, respectively), with no agency differences found. Finally, alumni were more likely to rate their birth father's mental (89.0%) and physical health (95.6%) as good compared to their birth mother's (77.4% and 88.0%, respectively), with state alumni rating their birth mother's physical health as good more often than Casey alumni.

Parenting Style of Birth Parents

The parenting behavior or style of the birth parents is naturally an important risk or protective factor for future emotional and other problems. The presence of an adequate amount of household resources during childhood is widely regarded as another important factor in development. Resource deprivation during childhood—not getting enough nutritious food, suffering from lack of heat in the home, not receiving important routine and emergency medical care, lacking appropriate clothing, and so on—may be due to poverty or to neglect on the part of the parents. (Here, this will be referred to as the more neutral *resource availability*, with reported neglect appearing in the next section.) Warmth and overprotection of the birth mother and birth father, as well as a retrospective assessment of resource availability, were trichotomized into low, medium, and high (see Table 5.5). Agency differences were found for birth father warmth and overprotection and birth mother overprotection. State alumni were more likely to have fathers high and low in warmth and more likely to have fathers high in overprotection. They were more likely to recall their mothers as high in overprotection.

Table 5.4. Parent Functioning

Parent Functioning		Washington		Oregon		Combined		
		Casey % (SE)	State % (SE)	Casey % (SE)	State % (SE)	Casey % (SE)	State % (SE)	Total % (SE)
Birth mother	Had good mental health	80.7 (2.3)	78.0 (1.6)	61.1 (6.0)	78.1 (2.8)*	75.6 (2.3)	78.0 (1.4)	77.4 (1.2)
	Had good physical health	83.6 (2.2)	90.2 (1.2)*	77.8 (5.4)	89.2 (2.1)*	82.1 (2.2)	89.8 (1.1)*	88.0 (1.0)
	Had no substance problems	46.3 (3.4)	37.6 (1.9)*	13.7 (4.0)	29.1 (3.2)*	37.7 (2.8)	34.7 (1.7)	35.4 (1.4)
	Had no criminal problems	69.8 (3.1)	66.4 (1.8)	49.3 (6.4)	62.9 (3.4)	64.5 (2.9)	65.2 (1.6)	65.0 (1.4)
Birth father	Had good mental health	91.9 (1.5)	87.0 (1.3)*	84.7 (3.7)	92.1 (1.8)*	90.0 (1.4)	88.7 (1.0)	89.0 (0.9)
	Had good physical health	97.1 (0.9)	95.2 (0.8)	92.8 (2.5)	95.9 (1.4)	96.0 (0.9)	95.4 (0.7)	95.6 (0.6)
	Had no substance problems	65.0 (3.4)	53.9 (1.9)*	57.8 (5.9)	49.6 (3.5)	63.2 (2.9)	52.4 (1.7)*	54.9 (1.5)
	Had no criminal problems	69.0 (3.1)	63.1 (1.8)	63.9 (6.0)	60.1 (3.4)	67.6 (2.8)	62.0 (1.7)	63.3 (1.4)
Sample size		82	242	29	126	111	368	479

*Statistically significant Casey and state difference at $p < .05$. Washington, Oregon, and Combined tested separately.

†Significance when the variable has more than one level, $p < .05$. Washington, Oregon, and Combined tested separately.

Table 5.5. Parenting Style of Birth Parents

Parenting Style of Birth Parents		Washington		Oregon		Combined		
		Casey % (SE)	State % (SE)	Casey % (SE)	State % (SE)	Casey % (SE)	State % (SE)	Total % (SE)
Birth mother warmth	Low	30.4 (2.8)	34.4 (1.8)	43.8 (6.3)	32.2 (3.3)	33.9 (2.7)	33.7 (1.7)	33.7 (1.4)
	Medium	27.3 (3.0)	31.0 (1.7)	31.4 (5.3)	34.2 (3.3)	28.4 (2.6)	32.1 (1.6)	31.2 (1.4)
	High	42.3 (3.4)	34.6 (1.8)	24.7 (6.2)	33.6 (3.3)	37.7 (3.0)	34.2 (1.7)	35.0 (1.5)
Birth father warmth	Low	27.2 (3.0)	33.5 (1.8)†	27.3 (4.8)	32.6 (3.2)	27.2 (2.6)	33.2 (1.6)†	31.8 (1.4)
	Medium	54.6 (3.3)	38.7 (1.9)	33.1 (6.3)	33.0 (3.4)	48.9 (2.9)	36.7 (1.7)	39.6 (1.5)
	High	18.2 (2.3)	27.8 (1.6)	39.7 (6.4)	34.4 (3.3)	23.8 (2.5)	30.1 (1.6)	28.6 (1.3)
Birth mother overprotection	Low	38.6 (3.3)	32.3 (1.8)†	40.2 (5.8)	29.5 (3.2)	39.0 (2.8)	31.4 (1.6)†	33.1 (1.4)
	Medium	38.3 (3.4)	34.5 (1.8)	26.8 (5.7)	30.1 (3.2)	35.3 (2.9)	33.0 (1.6)	33.5 (1.4)
	High	23.1 (2.4)	33.1 (1.8)	33.0 (6.7)	40.4 (3.5)	25.7 (2.6)	35.6 (1.7)	33.3 (1.4)
Birth father overprotection	Low	34.1 (3.4)	28.6 (1.7)†	43.5 (6.2)	25.8 (3.0)†	36.5 (3.0)	27.7 (1.5)†	29.7 (1.4)
	Medium	48.6 (3.3)	37.9 (1.9)	31.9 (6.3)	35.1 (3.4)	44.2 (2.9)	36.9 (1.7)	38.6 (1.5)
	High	17.3 (2.1)	33.4 (1.8)	24.6 (5.5)	39.1 (3.4)	19.2 (2.1)	35.4 (1.6)	31.6 (1.4)
Resource availability	Low	31.8 (3.1)	32.4 (1.8)	45.0 (6.1)	28.9 (3.2)†	35.2 (2.7)	31.2 (1.6)	32.1 (1.4)
	Medium	34.4 (3.1)	36.9 (1.9)	27.9 (6.4)	27.9 (3.1)	32.7 (2.8)	33.8 (1.6)	33.5 (1.4)
	High	33.8 (3.2)	30.7 (1.8)	27.1 (6.2)	43.3 (3.5)	32.1 (2.8)	35.0 (1.7)	34.3 (1.5)
Sample size		82	242	29	126	111	368	479

†Significance when the variable has more than one level, p < .05. Washington, Oregon, and Combined tested separately.

Child Maltreatment[51]

Currently, there is no commonly agreed-upon systematic method for describing and/or classifying a child's maltreatment experience. However, there is an emerging consensus (and evidence) on the dimensions of maltreatment that should be examined. These dimensions include severity, frequency, chronicity, duration, type, age of onset, and perpetrator (Barnett et al., 1993; English, Bangdiwala, & Runyan, 2005; Hanson, Smith, Saunders, Swenson, & Conrad, 1995; National Research Council, 1993).

For the purposes of this study, three dimensions of child maltreatment perpetrated by the birth family are reported: *(1)* breakdown of four basic types of maltreatment (sexual abuse, physical abuse, physical neglect, and emotional maltreatment); *(2)* the number of these basic types experienced (ranging from zero to four); and *(3)* the Expanded Hierarchical Categorization scheme for type of maltreatment. These were developed from a version of the Maltreatment Classification Scheme (MMCS), initially developed by Barnett et al. (1993) and modified by the LONGSCAN Group (Lau et al., 2005). In addition to no abuse, the Expanded Hierarchical Categorization produces the following mutually exclusive categories:

1. Sexual abuse only (with or without emotional maltreatment)
2. Sexual abuse and other (besides emotional maltreatment)
3. Physical abuse only (with or without emotional maltreatment)
4. Physical neglect only (with or without emotional maltreatment)
5. Physical abuse and physical neglect (with or without emotional maltreatment)
6. Emotional maltreatment only

Of the four basic types of abuse measured, over half of the alumni experienced sexual abuse (53.6%); around two-thirds experienced physical abuse (64.6%) and physical neglect (67.4%); and 84.5% experienced emotional maltreatment (Table 5.6). Casey alumni were more likely than state alumni to have been reported as sexually abused and emotionally maltreated. Almost one in four alumni (23.2%) experienced all four abuse types, while almost one in five (19.0%) had none or one type recorded in their case files. More Casey alumni experienced all four types, while more state youth experienced none or one type.

Based on the Expanded Hierarchical Categorization scheme, the most common category of abuse alumni experienced by the birth family was sexual abuse and other (49.2%), followed by physical abuse and physical neglect (16.7%) and physical neglect only (10.8%). One in 15 (6.7%) alumni experienced no maltreatment. There was a significant agency effect as Casey alumni were more likely to experience sexual abuse and other maltreatment than state alumni.

Since for many years the majority of children in foster care have been victims of neglect as opposed to other types of maltreatment (U.S. Department

Table 5.6. Child Maltreatment

Child Maltreatment	Washington		Oregon		Combined		
	Casey %	State % (SE)	Casey %	State % (SE)	Casey %	State % (SE)	Total % (SE)
Type of abuse/neglect							
Sexual abuse	61.3	54.1 (0.8)*	63.6	45.0 (2.5)*	61.9	51.0 (1.0)*	53.6 (0.8)
Physical abuse	66.7	65.8 (0.6)	61.4	62.0 (2.5)	65.2	64.5 (0.9)	64.6 (0.7)
Physical neglect	62.2	73.0 (0.5)*	79.5	56.7 (2.5)*	67.1	67.5 (0.9)	67.4 (0.7)
Emotional maltreatment	82.9	86.5 (0.4)*	93.2	79.5 (2.1)*	85.8	84.1 (0.7)*	84.5 (0.6)
Number of abuse/neglect 0 or 1	18.0	16.8 (0.4)†	13.6	25.1 (2.2)†	16.8	19.6 (0.8)†	19.0 (0.6)
types 2	26.1	20.4 (0.5)	20.5	27.5 (2.3)	24.5	22.8 (0.8)	23.2 (0.6)
3	38.7	36.3 (0.8)	22.7	31.6 (2.4)	34.2	34.7 (1.0)	34.6 (0.7)
4	17.1	26.4 (0.7)	43.2	15.8 (1.9)	24.5	22.8 (0.8)	23.2 (0.6)
Expanded Hierarchical Categorization							
No child maltreatment	5.4	6.6 (0.3)†	4.5	8.2 (1.4)†	5.2	7.1 (0.5)†	6.7 (0.4)
Sexual abuse only (with or without emotional abuse)	8.1	3.6 (0.3)	—	4.7 (1.1)	5.8	4.0 (0.4)	4.4 (0.3)
Sexual abuse and other (besides emotional abuse)	53.2	50.5 (0.8)	63.6	40.4 (2.5)	56.1	47.0 (1.0)	49.2 (0.8)
Physical abuse only (with or without emotional abuse)	5.4	6.3	4.5	16.4 (1.9)	5.2	9.7 (0.6)	8.6 (0.5)
Physical neglect only (with or without emotional abuse)	8.1	10.8 (0.3)	15.9	11.1 (1.6)	10.3	10.9 (0.6)	10.8 (0.4)
Physical abuse and physical neglect only (with or without emotional abuse)	17.1	18.9 (0.8)	4.5	15.2 (1.8)	13.5	17.7 (0.8)	16.7 (0.6)
Emotional maltreatment only	2.7	3.3	6.8	4.1 (1.0)	3.9	3.6 (0.3)	3.6 (0.3)
Sample size	**111**	**333**	**44**	**171**	**155**	**504**	**659**

*Statistically significant Casey and state difference at $p < .05$. Washington, Oregon, and Combined tested separately.
†Significance when the variable has more than one level, $p < .05$. Washington, Oregon, and Combined tested separately.

of Health and Human Services, 2001a, 2005b, 2008c), the alumni in the sample are less representative of youth in foster care as a whole because the rate of sexual abuse appears higher than what most states have reported. Comparisons should be made with great caution, however, because the timing and methods for data collection about sexual abuse differ between this study and federal studies.[52] Note, however, that such differences are to be expected among a sample drawn from those who have experienced long-term foster care as opposed to most youth who are in care for short periods of time.

Reasons for Initial Placement

Maltreatment is often the key reason that children are removed from parental care and placed in foster care, either directly (detected maltreatment leading to removal) or indirectly (behavior problems resulting in part from earlier maltreatment leading to removal). About one-fifth of reported child maltreatment victims are placed in out-of-home care by government officials as a result of a CPS services investigation (U.S. Department of Health and Human Services, 2005). Because youth could have been placed for multiple reasons, the following reasons were examined separately:

1. Child behavior problems
2. Maltreatment
3. Birth parents' substance abuse problems
4. Other (including caregiver(s) unable/unwilling to care, family stress, and any other reason; these were reported less frequently and combined into one category)

In addition to specific reasons for placement, the number of reasons was examined (ranging from one to four).

As reported in Table 5.7, the most common reason alumni were placed was maltreatment (64.3%), followed by birth parents' substance abuse (28.5%) and child behavior problems (19.6%). Agency differences were found for all four reasons. State alumni were more often placed because of child behavior problems, while Casey alumni were more often placed for the other three reasons. About half of the alumni (49.5%) were placed for only one reason, and two in five (40.2%) had two reasons for placement noted in their case files. The agencies differed in the number of reasons alumni were placed, as state alumni were more likely than Casey alumni to be placed for just one reason.

Mental/Physical Health Problems Diagnosed Before or During Care

Mental and physical health problems were professionally diagnosed and could have developed at any point in the individual's childhood, including before placement and up to case closure. As seen in Table 5.8, the following problems were examined separately for ease of analysis:

1. Attention deficit hyperactivity disorder (ADHD)

Table 5.7. Reasons for Initial Placement

Reasons for Placement		Washington		Oregon		Combined		
		Casey %	State % (SE)	Casey %	State % (SE)	Casey %	State % (SE)	Total % (SE)
Placement reasons (alumni could have more than one reason)	Child behavior problems	17.1	16.2 (0.4)*	11.4	29.8 (2.3)*	15.5	20.8 (0.8)*	19.6 (0.6)
	Maltreatment	60.4	64.0 (0.6)*	84.1	62.6 (2.5)*	67.1	63.5 (0.9)*	64.3 (0.7)
	Birth parents' substance problems	42.3	25.2 (0.7)*	61.4	17.5 (1.9)*	47.7	22.6 (0.8)*	28.5 (0.6)
Number of reasons	None or one	44.1	51.4† (0.8)	22.7	56.1† (2.5)	38.1	53.0 (1.0)	49.5 (0.8)
	Two	40.5	39.0 (0.8)	45.5	40.9 (2.5)	41.9	39.7 (1.0)	40.2 (0.8)
	Three	15.3	9.6 (0.5)	31.8	2.9 (0.9)	20.0	7.3 (0.5)	10.3 (0.4)
Sample size		**111**	**333**	**44**	**171**	**155**	**504**	**659**

*Statistically significant Casey and state difference at p < .05. Washington, Oregon, and Combined tested separately.
†Significance when the variable has more than one level, p < .05. Washington, Oregon, and Combined tested separately.

Table 5.8. Mental/Physical Health Problems Diagnosed Before or During Care

Mental/Physical Health Problems Diagnosed Before or During Care	Washington		Oregon		Combined		
	Casey %	State % (SE)	Casey %	State % (SE)	Casey %	State % (SE)	Total % (SE)
ADHD	22.5	11.7 (0.6)*	15.9	11.1 (1.6)*	20.6	11.5 (0.7)*	13.7 (0.5)
Physical or learning disability	28.8	9.6 (0.4)*	13.6	9.4 (1.5)*	24.5	9.5 (0.6)*	13.1 (0.4)
Other impairments (drug exposure, fetal alcohol effect, fetal alcohol syndrome, or visually/hearing impaired)	8.1	5.4 (0.3)*	15.9	4.7 (1.1)*	10.3	5.2 (0.4)*	6.4 (0.3)
Sample size	111	333	44	171	155	504	659

*Statistically significant Casey and state difference at $p < .05$. Washington, Oregon, and Combined tested separately.

2. Physical or learning disability
3. Other impairments (including prenatal drug exposure, fetal alcohol effects, fetal alcohol syndrome, or visual/hearing impairment)

Of the three problems examined, alumni were most often diagnosed with ADHD (13.7%), a physical or learning disability (13.1%), and other impairments (6.4%). Casey alumni were more often diagnosed with all three problems than state alumni.

Summary

One of the primary research questions for the Northwest Alumni Study concerns the association between foster care experiences and outcomes. Before examining that relationship, it is important to understand what factors were associated with poor long-term outcomes. This chapter detailed those risk factors that must be accounted for prior to examining the aforementioned relationship. As findings in this chapter indicate, alumni in this study experienced enormous childhood adversity (risk factors). Some risk factors included:

- High rates of criminal justice system involvement and incarceration for the birth mothers and fathers of alumni
- Low numbers of alumni who lived in a household with both birth parents
- High rates of substance abuse by alumni birth parents
- High rates of unemployment for alumni birth parents
- Unusually high rate of sexual abuse experienced by alumni
- Alumni mental and physical health diagnoses in childhood

Agency differences were noted, and any agency comparison of outcomes should account for these risk factors. In addition to the use of these risk factors as control variables, the relationship between the risk factors and outcomes is examined in O'Brien et al. (2009b). Regardless of the outcome, it is clear that many of the alumni experienced childhoods before foster care characterized by chaos and obstacles not conducive to optimal development.

Acknowledgment.   Dan Torres contributed to this chapter.

PART IV

OUTCOME FINDINGS

6

Mental and Physical Health Functioning

[The foster parents needed] more understanding. Many children coming into foster homes have serious physical and emotional problems. The foster parents ignored them or put them down. They didn't attempt to understand. They didn't care.

Overview

There are long-term consequences of child abuse or neglect on mental and physical health. While some maltreated youth show resilience in the face of such adversity, others struggle. For literature on the effects of child maltreatment upon child development and adult functioning, see Kendall-Tackett and Giacomoni (2003) and Pecora, Wiggins, Jackson, and English (2009b). Based on alumni interviews, this chapter reports on the mental and physical health functioning of alumni, thus providing more empirical data about the short-term and long-term functioning of maltreated youth who were placed in foster care. The primary hypothesis was that alumni would exhibit mental and physical health difficulties that would be more severe than those of the general population.

Mental Health

According to the National Institute of Mental Health (2006a), mental disorders are common in the United States. An estimated 26.2% of Americans age 18 and older—about one in four adults (57.7 million people)—suffer from a diagnosable mental disorder in a given year (DeNavas-Walt, Proctor, & Lee, 2005; Kessler, Chiu, Demler, & Walters, 2005b; National Institute of Mental Health, 2006a).[53] More Americans suffer from mental health disorders than from cancer or diabetes. Further, mental disorders are among the leading cause of disability in the United States and Canada among persons aged 15 to 44 (World Health Organization, 2004). Lastly, many people suffer from more than one mental disorder at a given time: 45% of those with any mental health disorder suffer from two or more disorders (roughly one in eight Americans) (Kessler et al., 2005b). Other national mental health statistics include:

- Almost half of all Americans (46.4%) will experience a emotional, behavioral or substance abuse disorder at some point in their lives (Kessler et al., 2005b).
- Even though emotional, behavioral or substance abuse disorders are widespread in the population, the main burden of illness is concentrated in a much smaller proportion—about 6%, or one in 17—who suffer from a serious emotional disturbance.
- The average delay between the onset of a emotional, behavioral or substance abuse disorder and treatment is often considerable, ranging from six to eight years for mood disorder (e.g., depression) and nine to 23 years for anxiety disorders (e.g., posttraumatic stress disorder) (Wang et al., 2005).

In addition to the pain and suffering of those with mental health disorders, there are economic consequences. The annual economic cost of mental health conditions is estimated at $79 billion, approximately $63 billion of which reflects the loss of productivity as a result of these illnesses (Rice & Miller, 1996), as cited in the President's New Freedom Commission on Mental Health (2003). Further, the *Global Burden of Disease* study developed a measure called the Disability Adjusted Life Years (DALYs). DALYs measure lost years of healthy life regardless of whether the years were lost to premature death or disability. For example, it was found that disability caused by major depression was equivalent to blindness or paraplegia. Major depression ranked second only to ischemic heart disease in magnitude of disease burden in established market economies. Additionally, major depression was the leading cause of *disability* (measured by the number of years *lived* with a disabling condition) worldwide among persons aged five and older (Murray & Lopez, 1996; National Institute of Mental Health, 2006a).

Very little research has systematically estimated the burden of mental illness in children and adolescents. In 1998, however, the direct costs for the treatment of child mental health problems (emotional and behavioral) were approximately $11.75 billion, or $173 per child (Ringel & Sturm, 2001; Sturm et al., 2000).[54] The costs for youth in foster care may be much higher because of the significant effects of child maltreatment upon physical and mental health.

In comparison to the general population findings above, data on the mental health functioning of youth in foster care and alumni of care are scarce. Data do exist from a study of 406 17-year-olds in foster care in Missouri. McMillen et al. (2004) reported that 37% met DSM-IV criteria for a psychiatric diagnosis in the previous year and 61% met similar criteria for a lifetime disorder, with the highest rates for disruptive disorders (such as Conduct Disorder [CD], Oppositional Defiant Disorder [ODD], major depression, and attention deficit hyperactivity disorder). Additionally, Brandford and English (2004), in a study of 19- to 20-year-olds, found that although most youth participated in counseling services, 42% had indicators for depression. Meanwhile, self-reports of mental health functioning made by older adolescents in foster care have indicated rates of approximately 25% for borderline clinically significant internalizing behavioral problems and 28% for externalizing behavioral problems (Auslander et al., 2002; White et al., 2007).

Another disorder that is underexamined is substance abuse. In the only national interview study of foster care alumni ever conducted, Cook et al. (1991) found that 17% of alumni with a median age of 21 years had some kind of drug problem. Additional data were provided by Barth (1990), who found that 19% of youth were drinking once a week or more. Further, Jones and Moses (1984) found that 6% reported a current problem with alcohol, while 13% had had a problem in the past. Festinger (1983) found that 81.2% of the males and 66.4% of the females had used drugs of some sort in the year preceding the study; almost 29% of the males and 14% of the females had used at least one drug practically every day (p. 195). (See Table 6.1 for a summary of foster care studies reporting prevalence or incidence rates of mental, emotional, and behavioral disorders.)

Anxiety, PTSD, Social Phobia, and Depression[55]

Overview

This section presents types, definitions, and the prevalence of major mental, emotional, and behavioral disorders that were measured by the Northwest Alumni Study. For prevalence rates in the general population, see National Institute of Mental Health (2006b). A few of these conditions are highlighted because of high prevalence rates among children placed in foster care.

Anxiety Disorders

Anxiety disorders, as a group, are the most common emotional disorders that occur in children, adolescents, and adults; they include panic disorder, social phobia, generalized anxiety disorder (GAD), and posttraumatic stress disorder (PTSD). Panic disorder is characterized by feelings of extreme fear and dread that strike unexpectedly and repeatedly for no apparent reason, often accompanied by intense physical symptoms, such as chest pain, pounding heart, shortness of breath, dizziness, or abdominal distress. Social phobia is an extreme fear of being embarrassed or scrutinized by others. People with this disorder are often uncomfortable in new situations and in interacting with strangers and large groups. Social phobia can be especially debilitating

Table 6.1.   Selected Studies of Physical and Mental Health Outcomes of Alumni
of Foster Care

Youth In Transition and Post–Foster Care Functions

General findings	**Courtney et al. (2001):** 47% of youth received mental health services while in care (e.g., counseling, therapy, group therapy or counseling, medication for emotions, substance abuse treatment, and psychiatric hospitalization). Mental Health Inventory scores indicated more psychological distress for youth in care than for peers not in care, as assessed in the Health Insurance Experiment. Provision of mental health services decreased by about half once youth had exited care, although the mental health assessment did not indicate a corresponding decrease in the need for service. (Wisconsin)

Courtney et al. (2004): Youth 17 years of age who had at least one year in care before turning 17. Mental health was assessed by the lifetime version of the CIDI: 31.4% had one or more mental, emotional, and behavioral disorders: PTSD (16.1%), depression—any type (2.9%), generalized anxiety disorder (0%), social phobia (0.4%), alcohol abuse (11.3%), alcohol dependence (2.7%), substance abuse (5.0%), and substance dependence (2.3%).

Service use: 36.5% received psychological or emotional counseling, 22.5% had a prescription for medication for a psychological/psychiatric disorder, and 7.1% spent at least one night in a psychiatric hospital in the past year. (Illinois, Iowa, Wisconsin)

Courtney et al. (2005b): This longitudinal study assessed mental health in a sample of 19-year-olds using the lifetime version of the CIDI. Exactly one-third of all the young adults interviewed were found to have at least one mental, emotional, and behavioral diagnosis.

The most prevalent mental, emotional, and behavioral disorders were PTSD, alcohol abuse, substance abuse, and major depression. Compared to young adults still in care, respondents no longer in care had notably higher lifetime prevalence rates of alcohol dependence ($t = 2.5$, $p < .01$), alcohol abuse ($t = 3.4$, $p < .001$), substance dependence ($t = 2.0$, $p = .04$), and substance abuse ($t = 3.4$, $p < .001$).

There were statistically significant gender differences in lifetime prevalence rates. Alcohol abuse ($t = 2.1$, $p = .03$) and substance abuse ($t = 2.8$, $p = .001$) were more prevalent among males, while major depression ($t = 2.7$, $p = .007$) and PTSD ($t = 4.0$, $p < .001$) were more prevalent among females (pp. 41–42). (Illinois, Iowa, Wisconsin)

Alcohol use, dependence or abuse	**Robins (1966):** Former patients seen at the St. Louis Municipal Psychiatric Clinic between 1924 and 1929 were followed up many years later. Those who had been given a diagnosis of alcoholism reported a higher rate of living away from both parents compared to those with no diagnosis (76% vs. 39%, $p < .05$) (p. 241). However, some of those living away from home were hospitalized or lived with relatives. (Missouri)

Festinger (1983): 29.3% of males and 12.1% of females drank at least three times per week. 62.5% of males and 36% of females had drunk enough during the preceding month to "feel high" (p. 195). (New York City)

Jones and Moses (1984): 6% of youth aged 19 to 28 reported a current problem with alcohol, while 13% had had a problem in the past. Men were more likely to report a problem with alcohol than women (p. 72). (West Virginia)

Barth (1990): 19% of youth were drinking once a week or more. This rate was quite comparable to that of a random sample of high school students (p. 429). (San Francisco Bay area)

(continued)

Table 6.1. Continued

Courtney et al. (2007): 4.8% of females and 9.4% of males had 12-month CIDI diagnoses of alcohol abuse in a study of 21-year-old foster care alumni, with rates for alcohol dependence of 3.5% and 11.6%, respectively (p. 46).

Drug use[59] **Festinger (1983):** 81.2% of males and 66.4% of females had used drugs of some sort in the year preceding the study. (The drugs usually were marijuana and cocaine; tranquilizers were seldom used; p. 195.) Almost 29% of the males and 14% of the females had used at least one drug nearly every day. 45% of respondents had decreased their usage over the years, while 37.3% had increased their usage. (New York City)

Jones and Moses (1984): Only 1% reported a current problem with drugs, while 16% reported having had a problem in the past (p. 72). (West Virginia)

Barth (1990): The proportion of youth using drugs while in foster care (56%) remained the same after leaving care (p. 429). (San Francisco Bay area)

Cook, Fleishman, and Grimes (1991): 17% had some kind of drug problem. (National sample)

Courtney et al. (2007): Drug dependence: 1% of females and 5.1% of males. Drug abuse: 1.9% of females and 5.8% of males.

Depression **Zimmerman (1982):** 47 total responses (14 of the total sample were not questioned about mental health). 34% (16) received help for "nerves," while 13% felt that they needed help but did not seek treatment. Of those who received help, six reported trouble with depression, while eight reported feelings of tension and anger. Twelve of the 16 took medication for their problems, usually valium (p. 75).

Barth (1990): 42% experienced a problem with depression or sadness; 15% sought treatment. 22% reported having suicidal thoughts; only 11% sought treatment (p. 428, Table 3).

Brandford and English (2004): 42% of young adults were depressed 6–12 months after emancipation from foster care, as measured by the Center for Epidemiological Studies Depression Scale (p. 14). This contrasts with national data that 27% of 12th graders feel depressed. (Washington State)

Courtney et al. (2007, p. 46): 7.6% of females and 1.1% of males suffered from major depression (12 months, rates for 23-year-olds).

PTSD **Courtney et al. (2007, p. 46):** 7.9% of females and 3.8% of males had a CIDI diagnosis (12 month for 23-year-olds). Lifetime rates for 19-year-olds were 12.6. (Courtney et al., 2005b, p. 43)

Reinherz, Paradis, Giaconia, Stashwick, and Fitzmaurice (2003): Childhood and adolescent familial and behavioral-emotional factors predicting depression during this critical developmental stage. During the transition to adulthood, 82 participants (23.2%) experienced major depression. Bivariate indicators of later depression included a family history of depression or substance use disorders, family composition, and childhood family environments perceived as violent and lacking cohesiveness. Also significant were self- and mother-reported internalizing behaviors, as well as self-rated anxiety and depressive symptoms. Multivariate analyses showed family violence, family composition, internalizing problems during adolescence, and low family cohesion to be the most salient factors.

to children or young adults who are enrolled in large schools with large class sizes. Generalized anxiety disorder is characterized by persistent, exaggerated worry and tension over everyday events. Given the nature of traumatic stressors that alumni from foster care experienced prior to entering the system, PTSD is an emotional disorder of special importance and is described in more detail below.

Posttraumatic Stress Disorder (PTSD)

The *DSM-IV* (American Psychiatric Association, 1994) reported a general population prevalence of PTSD of between 1% and 14% (depending on the sample), with rates in high-risk samples (people who have experienced trauma) ranging from 3% to 58%. The National Comorbidity Survey Replication (NCS-R) estimated that the lifetime prevalence of PTSD in a nationally representative sample was 7.8% (Molnar, Buka, & Kessler, 2001). Thus, there are large numbers of people who find that PTSD interferes with social relationships, employment, and other areas (American Psychiatric Association, 1994).

Posttraumatic stress disorder has a diagnostic requirement that differentiates it from many other disorders, including other anxiety disorders: the experience of an identifiable stressful event. Various risk factors, however, have been identified as affecting the response to the trauma and the development of PTSD, and they help explain why many people who are exposed to trauma do not suffer from PTSD. These risk factors include a history of prior trauma or mental, emotional, and behavioral disorders, familial mental, emotional, and behavioral disorders, dissociation during the trauma, and autonomic hyperarousal (McFarlane, 2000).

Certain dimensions or types of trauma have been associated with PTSD. For example, interpersonal violence is more likely to result in PTSD than other traumatic events (Kilpatrick et al., 2003), and childhood rape appears more likely to lead to PTSD than childhood molestation (Molnar et al., 2001). Further, it has been found that women are more likely to experience PTSD than men (Kessler, Sonnega, Bromet, Hughes, & Nelson, 1995, as cited in Kilpatrick et al., 2003).

Those who suffer from PTSD may experience the following:

- Memories and images of the traumatic event
- Recurrent dreams, flashbacks, and extreme distress and physiological activity brought on by cues—internal or external—reminiscent of the trauma
- Thoughts or feelings related to the trauma or people, places, or activities that bring back memories of the trauma
- Detachment from others
- Difficulty concentrating or sleeping
- Hypervigilance or being constantly on guard and trying to avoid further trauma

Even though many people with PTSD recover within a couple of years, a substantial proportion continue to have chronic PTSD for many years. The latter pattern is more typical among people who experienced multiple traumas that were prolonged and that happened in childhood (Kessler, Berglund, Demler, Jin, & Walters, 2005a). This has been referred to as *complex PTSD* (Herman, 1997; Jongedijk, 2003).

Major Depression

Although not an anxiety disorder, another potentially debilitating mental, emotional, and behavioral disorder, especially for alumni of foster care, is depression. The *DSM-IV* (American Psychiatric Association, 1994) explains that "the essential feature of a Major Depressive Episode is a period of at least 2 weeks during which there is either depressed mood or the loss of interest or pleasure in nearly all activities" (p. 320). A Major Depressive Episode also involves at least two additional symptoms, which may include changes in appetite, weight, sleep, or activity; decreased energy; feelings of guilt or worthlessness; difficulty in concentration or decision making; and suicidal ideation or behavior. The symptoms occur "most of the day, nearly every day, for at least 2 consecutive weeks" (p. 320). The episode disrupts normal functioning, often preventing the person from going to work or school, taking care of personal hygiene, or even getting out of bed. Suicide is, of course, relatively common: Up to 15% of people suffering from severe depression complete a suicide. If not better accounted for by a psychotic disorder, a Major Depressive Episode may indicate a diagnosis of Major Depression or Bipolar Disorder.

Depressive symptoms frequently appear with other symptoms and diagnoses, particularly anxiety (American Psychiatric Association, 1994; Kendler, Heath, Martin, & Eaves, 1987; Kessler et al., 2003). The NCS-R reported that the majority of people with current (past year) depression suffered severe role and other serious impairments (Kessler et al., 2003), which may include unemployment and work difficulties (Marcotte, Wilcox-Gök, & Redmon, 1999; Nolen-Hoeksema & Girgus, 1994); school problems (Nolen-Hoeksema & Girgus, 1994); hopelessness; sleep difficulties (Kendler et al., 2003; alcohol problems (Holahan, Moos, Holahan, Cronkite, & Randall, 2004); and interpersonal dysfunction (Reinherz, Giaconia, Hauf, Wasserman, & Silverman, 1999).

Depression can arise from a variety of influences, and often multiple causes are relevant. Genetic factors play a role (Kendler et al., 1987; Plomin, 1989) and many environmental factors have been implicated, including family problems (Billings & Moos, 1982; Hughes & Graham-Bermann, 1998; Kendler et al., 1987; Kilpatrick et al., 2003); marital problems (Christian-Herman, O'Leary, & Avery-Leaf, 2001); life strains such as money problems or parenting issues (Billings & Moos, 1982); health problems (Reinherz et al., 1999); recent severe psychosocial stressors (American Psychiatric Association, 1994); and childhood loss and trauma (Briere, 1992; Molnar et al., 2001; Reinherz et al., 1999). This is not an exhaustive list. Given the differences in life experiences between men and women, there are gender differences in the onset and prevalence of depression (Kilpatrick et al., 2003; Molnar et al., 2001; Nolen-Hoeksema & Girgus, 1994). There is some evidence that depression among older adolescents and young adults is relatively common and increasing in prevalence, and that it tends to last into later adulthood (Reinherz et al., 1999).

Physical Health

There are long-term consequences regarding mental and physical health functioning for many people who have been victims of childhood abuse or neglect. While some maltreated youth show resilience in the face of such adversity, others struggle with mental or physical health issues (Kendall-Tackett & Giacomoni, 2003; Pecora et al., 2009b).

Physical Health Needs of Youth in Foster Care

Serious physical health conditions at entry into foster care require prompt health care screening and treatment. Almost one out of every two children in foster care have chronic medical problems (Halfon, Mendonca, & Berkowitz, 1995; Simms, 1989; Takayama, Wolfe, & Coulter, 1998; United States General Accounting Office, 1999), and the presence of these chronic conditions will greatly increase their likelihood of developing serious emotional problems (Rubin et al., 2004; Rubin, Halfon, Raghavan, & Rosenbaum, 2005). Further, many of these physical health conditions will persist into young adulthood.

In a recent study with a nationally representative sample of 700 children who had been in foster care for one year, caregivers were asked about children's health problems that "lasted or reoccurred." Over one-quarter of the children had some type of recurring physical or mental, emotional, and behavioral disorder; for example, 11% reported general mental and physical health problems, 12% reported some type of gastrointestinal illness, and 4% reported a difficulty beginning before birth or at birth. In addition, 4% had a cardiovascular disorder, and 7% of these children had a neurological, endocrine, or blood disorder (U.S. Department of Health and Human Services, 2001a).

Mental and Physical Health Findings

My first foster mom worked as a psychiatric nurse. She was able to recognize my problems and was able to help me through my suicidal periods.

I feel there should have been more emphasis put on the mental health. I needed resources from adults and guidance—not parents. Some kids who were younger needed parents. I needed counseling and preparation for living on my own.

Overview

This section reports the mental health functioning of the alumni at the time of the interview, primarily based on the CIDI data. Included is a discussion of mental, emotional, and behavioral disorders during the lifetime of the individual, in the past 12 months, recovery rates, use of mental health services, and self-esteem. Most youth enter foster care as a last resort because family support efforts have been unsuccessful. These youth have a family history and life experiences that are detrimental to their well-being and safety. The very act of removal from their parents can be traumatic for the youth, potentially resulting in PTSD and creating a sense of hypervigilance because their lives become unpredictable. While few previous foster care alumni studies have measured PTSD, a number of other mental, emotional, and behavioral disorders have been documented (see Table 6.1). Therefore, it was hypothesized that a high proportion of alumni would be struggling with mental, emotional, and behavioral disorders (see Garland et al., 2001; Leslie et al., 2000).

Mental, Emotional, and Behavioral Disorders During the Lifetime

The Northwest Alumni Study compared the mental health functioning of alumni aged 20 to 33 with that of individuals of similar age and ethnicity and the same gender in the general population (from the NCS-R). Based on questions from the CIDI, both the Northwest Alumni Study and the NCS-R assessed lifetime and 12-month mental, emotional, and behavioral disorder prevalence rates. This analysis takes the NCS-R data matched to ages 20–33 and poststratifies the NCS-R data to match the Northwest distribution of Race $\times$ Sex $\times$ Age. The NCS-R prevalence estimates were then run on this poststratified data set. For lifetime prevalence, highlights include the following (see also Table 6.2):

- The prevalence of mental, emotional, and behavioral disorders among alumni exceeded that of the general population on all nine mental, emotional, and behavioral disorders that were assessed.
- The prevalence of lifetime PTSD was significantly higher among alumni (30.0%) than among the general population (7.6%). This lifetime PTSD rate was comparable to that of Vietnam War veterans (30.9% for male veterans and 26.9% for female veterans) (Kulka, Fairbank, Jordan, & Weiss, 1990).
- The prevalence of lifetime major depression was significantly higher among alumni (41.1%) than among the general population (21.0%).
- In addition to PTSD and major depression, over one in five alumni had one of the following during his or her lifetime: panic syndrome, modified social phobia, or drug dependence.

Lifetime mental, emotional, and behavioral disorder prevalence rates for the agency subsamples are presented in O'Brien et al. (2009a). Recent mental health data on older alumni from foster care are scarce. However, while age at

Table 6.2. Mental Health Functioning: Rates for Lifetime Symptoms, Symptoms in the Past 12 Months, and Lifetime Recovery[a]

Mental Health Outcomes	Northwest Alumni			NCS-R (General Population)		
	Northwest Alumni Study: % Who Had Symptoms—Lifetime	Northwest Alumni Study: % Who Had Symptoms in Last 12 Months	Northwest Alumni Study: % Recovered	Gen. Pop. (NCS-R) for Ages 20–33: % Who Had Symptoms—Lifetime	Gen. Pop. (NCS-R) for Ages 20–33: % Who Had Symptoms in Last 12 Months	Gen. Pop. (NCS-R): % Recovered[b]
CIDI diagnosis[c]	—	54.4 (2.7)	—	—	22.1 (1.0)[*d]	—
Three or more CIDI diagnoses[c]	—	19.9 (2.3)	—	—	2.9 (0.5)[*d]	—
Major depression episode	41.1 (2.8)	20.1 (2.3)	51.0 (4.5)	21.0 (1.4)[*]	11.1 (0.8)[*]	48.3 (2.2)
Panic syndrome	21.1 (2.2)	14.8 (1.9)	30.1 (5.4)	4.8 (0.5)[*]	3.5 (0.4)[*]	30.4 (4.7)
Modified social phobia	23.3 (2.5)	17.1 (2.3)	26.6 (5.2)	15.9 (1.6)[*]	9.4 (1.0)[*]	36.7 (3.1)[*]
Generalized anxiety disorder	19.1 (2.4)	11.5 (2.0)	39.6 (7.3)	7.0 (0.8)[*]	4.0 (0.6)[*]	39.8 (3.8)
PTSD[e]	30.0 (2.5)	25.2 (2.5)	15.7 (2.4)	7.6 (0.7)[*]	4.6 (0.5)[*]	41.9 (4.1)[*]
Alcohol problem	Not measured	11.9 (1.6)	—	Not measured	Not measured	—
Alcohol dependence	11.3 (1.2)	3.6 (0.6)	67.9 (4.5)	7.1 (0.1)[*]	2.3 (0.6)	63.4 (5.4)

Drug problem	Not measured	12.3 (2.2)	—	Not measured	Not measured	—
Drug dependence	21.0 (2.3)	8.0 (1.8)	61.8 (6.6)	4.5 (0.7)*	0.7 (0.2)*	80.4 (4.8)*
Anorexia[f]	1.2 (0.3)	0.0	100.0	0.3 (0.1)*	0.0	—
Bulimia	4.9 (1.4)	3.6 (1.3)	25.8 (1.1)	0.8 (0.2)*	0.5 (0.2)*	48.3 (13.6)*
SF-12® mental health score of 50 or above	—	50.6 (2.8)	—	—	—	—
Sample size	479				1601	

* Indicates a significant difference between the Northwest Alumni Study and the NCS-R, $p < .05$, two-tailed.

[a] This analysis takes the NCS-R data matched to ages 20–33 and poststratifies those data to match the Northwest distribution of Race × Sex × Age. The NCS-R prevalence estimates were then run on this poststratified data set. These numbers are slightly different from the NCS-R mental health comparison statistics published previously in the Northwest Alumni Study report (Pecora, Kessler, Williams, O'Brien, Downs, English, et al. 2005) because those original numbers did not take into account the poststratification.

[b] Alumni were considered to have recovered if the lifetime occurrence of a mental health symptom was not present in the past 12 months.

[c] Because alcohol and drug problems were not assessed during the lifetime, the CIDI diagnosis and three or more CIDI diagnoses could not be computed for the lifetime; consequently, no recovery rate could be computed for either item.

[d] Not adjusted by race or gender.

[e] The NCS-R PTSD section included some additional specific trauma items, but the Northwest Alumni Study version of the CIDI PTSD items included some general questions that were designed to identify potentially traumatic events. The purpose was to help the respondent identify at least one event, so the focus was on measuring whether the reactions to any of these events constituted PTSD rather than measuring the number or type of items per se. The measures, therefore, should be comparable.

[f] Anorexia is extremely rare in the general population.

the time of the interview was younger, the Midwest Evaluation of the Adult Functioning of Former Foster Youth study used many of the same mental health assessment instrument subscales as the Northwest Alumni Study (the CIDI) [Courtney et al., 2005b] assessed the mental health of the 19-year-olds in their sample using the lifetime version of the CIDI. Table 6.3 presents the overlapping CIDI diagnoses in the Midwest and Northwest studies. The most prevalent mental, emotional, and behavioral disorders in the Midwest study were PTSD, major depression, and alcohol dependence. Although prevalence rates were lower than those in the Northwest Alumni Study, this may be largely attributable to the age difference in subjects between the two studies (all 19-year-olds for the Midwest study compared to an average age of 24.2 years for the Northwest Alumni Study).

Table 6.2 indicates reasonably high rates of recovery for the Northwest Alumni Study alumni from certain mental, emotional, and behavioral disorders, including alcohol dependence (67.9%), drug dependence (61.8%), and major depression (51.0%). However, other mental, emotional, and behavioral disorders have endured, with lower recovery rates for generalized anxiety disorder (39.6%), social phobia (26.6%), bulimia (25.8%), and PTSD (15.7%). In comparison, recovery rates were statistically significantly higher for the general population on five of the eight mental health outcomes that were tested. There were no significant differences on the other three.

The Midwest study also measured short-term recovery rates but on a much shorter time basis. So, these short-term recovery rates may in fact reflect more of the stresses of emancipation, the fact that a slightly higher-functioning group of youth may still be in care, and a lack of opportunity to recover. For example, compared to young adults still in care, respondents no longer in care had notably *higher* lifetime prevalence rates of alcohol dependence ($t = 2.5$, $p < .01$), alcohol abuse ($t = 3.4$, $p < .001$), substance dependence ($t = 2.0$, $p = .04$), and substance abuse ($t = 3.4$, $p < .001$) (Courtney et al.,

Table 6.3. Lifetime CIDI Diagnoses From the Midwest and Northwest Foster Care Studies

	Lifetime CIDI Prevalence Rate[a]	
Mental Health Outcomes	*Midwest Study*	*Northwest Study*
Major depression	10.3	41.1
Modified social phobia	0.0	23.3
Generalized anxiety	0.0	19.1
PTSD	12.5	30.0
Alcohol dependence	6.2	11.3
Drug dependence	5.3 (substance)	21.0
Sample size	**321 (age = 19)**	**479 (mean age = 24.2)**

[a]Source: Courtney et al. (2005, p. 42). Note that the most recent Midwest Study (Courtney et al., 2007) only used the CIDI 12-month prevalence questions. As a result, lifetime prevalence rates were not available.

2005a). So, in contrast to the lifetime recovery rates of the Northwest Alumni Study, the short-term trajectory of the Midwest alumni is negative, no doubt exacerbated by the stresses of trying to live in the community with insufficient supports so soon after leaving foster care.

Supplemental Information About PTSD in American War Veterans

The PTSD rates of alumni from foster care and U.S. war veterans must be compared cautiously. The National Vietnam Veterans Readjustment Survey study reported the following information about PTSD among Vietnam War veterans: The estimated lifetime prevalence of PTSD among American Vietnam theater veterans is 30.9% for men and 26.9% for women. An additional 22.5% of men and 21.2% of women have had partial PTSD at some point in their lives. Thus, more than half of all male Vietnam veterans and almost half of all female Vietnam veterans—about 1,700,000 Vietnam veterans in all—have experienced "clinically serious stress reaction symptoms." In addition, 15.2% of all male Vietnam theater veterans (479,000 out of 3,140,000 men who served in Vietnam) and 8.1% of all female Vietnam theater veterans (610 out of 7,200 women who served in Vietnam) are "currently" diagnosed with PTSD. (*Currently* here means 1986–1988, the period when the survey was conducted.)

Briere (2004) argues, however, that the incidence of PTSD is difficult to determine because the clinical data on PTSD often predate the modern PTSD criteria. But some data do exist. Kulka et al. (1990) estimated rates of PTSD for Vietnam theater veterans at 15.2% for males and 8.5% for females (current prevalence) and at 30.6% for males and 26.9% for females (lifetime prevalence). Hoge et al. (2004) have also published current PTSD rates of American war veterans. Additionally, some studies of victims of child maltreatment address the topic of PTSD, such as Boney-McCoy and Finkelhor (1996) and McCloskey and Walker (2002).

Mental, Emotional, and Behavioral Disorders During the Past 12 Months

During the 12 months prior to being interviewed, with only two exceptions (alcohol dependence and anorexia), mental health functioning was significantly poorer for the Northwest alumni than for the general population. Highlights of findings include the following (see also Table 6.2):

- Over half of the alumni (54.4%) had a current mental, emotional, or behavioral disorder compared to less than one-quarter of the general population (22.1%).
- The prevalence of PTSD in the last 12 months was significantly higher among alumni (25.2%) than among the general population (4.6%). By comparison, American war veterans have lower rates of PTSD (Vietnam veterans: 15%; Afghanistan veterans: 6%; and Iraq veterans: 12%–13%) in the past 12 months.[56] (Lifetime rates are more similar.)

- The prevalence of major depression within the past 12 months among alumni (20.1%) was nearly double that of the general population (11.1%).

Twelve-month mental, emotional, and behavioral disorder prevalence rates for the agency subsamples are presented in O'Brien et al. (2009a).

Other Aspects of Additional Mental Health Findings

Use of Mental Health Services

Research indicates that many alumni of foster care *(1)* have met the criteria for a mental, emotional, and behavioral disorder and *(2)* have sought out various kinds of mental health services. For example, a recent study of Alaska alumni found that 79% reported ever using mental health or substance abuse services, including 27% in the past year (Williams, Pope, Sirles, & Lally, 2005). Similarly, and despite lack of health insurance coverage (see Chapter 8), Northwest alumni had accessed or obtained the following in the past year:

- Self-help group or hotline for mental health, alcohol, and drug treatment (11.6%).
- Outpatient professional help (23.3%), with 59.0% seeing the professional six or more times.
- A small percentage of alumni (11.8%) were currently seeing a helping professional.
- Fewer than 1 in 20 (4.0%) had stayed overnight in a facility for mental health, alcohol, or drug treatment. Over the course of their lifetime, however, almost one in three (31.2%) had sought such treatment (O'Brien et al., 2009a).

Self-Esteem

The Rosenberg scale score was used to assess self-esteem (one item was omitted accidentally during instrument preparation[57]). The 10 items are answered on a 4-point scale: from *strongly agree* to *strongly disagree*. Scores on the Rosenberg scale range from 10 to 40, with higher scores indicating higher self-esteem. It was found that many alumni had average self-esteem (average score 29.4), but over a quarter (27.0%) had a score of less than 27 (O'Brien et al., 2009a).

Physical Health Findings

Although 27.5% of the alumni reported a chronic health disorder, most of the alumni (68.8%) had a physical health SF-12® scale score of 50 or higher, indicating good physical health (Ware, Kosinski, & Keller, 1998) (see Table 6.4). Further, many (59.0%) rated their health as somewhat or much better now compared to the previous year. The general health ratings seem similar to those of the general population, at least in Oregon. For example, in the

Table 6.4.   Physical Health Functioning

Physical Health	Northwest Alumni % (SE)
No chronic physical disorder[a]	72.5 (2.4)
SF-12® physical health score of 50 or above	68.8 (2.5)
Does not smoke currently	57.2 (2.6)
Smokes fewer than 10 cigarettes per day	75.3 (2.0)
Does not drink currently	53.1 (2.8)
Drinks fewer than 150 drinks per year	75.9 (2.2)
Sample size	**479**

[a]Chronic physical disorder includes heart disease, high blood pressure, chronic lung disease, ulcers, and human immunodeficiency virus. It does not include diabetes or asthma.

1998 Oregon Risk Factor Surveillance System Survey, overall, 57.4% of the respondents reported being in either excellent or very good general health. The percentage was 65.6% for those aged 18–24 and 62.7% for those aged 25–34 (and 63.4% for those between the ages of 18 and 34) (Centers for Disease Control and Prevention [CDC], 1998a).

Smoking

Over 40% of the alumni (42.8%) were smoking at the time of the interview, with 24.7% of the sample smoking more than 10 cigarettes per day (see Table 6.4). This is similar to the rate in the general population: 40.2% of 18- to 25-year-olds currently smoke one or more cigarettes per day (National Center for Health Statistics, 2004).

Drinking

Almost half of the alumni (46.9%) currently drank alcohol, with 24.1% drinking more than 150 drinks per year. Some aspects of this prevalence are lower than those of the general population, where, for example, 61.4% of 18- to 25-year-olds had had at least one drink recently (National Center for Health Statistics, 2004). Also, in the 1998 Oregon Behavior Risk Factor Surveillance System Survey, 63.7% respondents aged 18 to 34 had had at least one drink of any alcoholic beverage in the past month (Centers for Disease Control and Prevention [CDC], 1998a). Physical health prevalence rates for the agency subsamples are presented in O'Brien et al., (2009a).

Summary

Main Findings

A key research question in this study was "How are youth placed in foster care faring as young adults?" Despite the challenges of child maltreatment, childhood adversity, and placement instability, many of the alumni demonstrated positive outcomes in terms of good mental and physical health. Over 50% of alumni with a lifetime diagnosis had recovered from major depression, alcohol dependence, drug dependence, and anorexia. But recovery rates in the five other mental health areas were lower for alumni than for the general population.

Many alumni did, however, face significant challenges in these areas. Specifically, over half of the Northwest alumni had had a diagnosable mental, emotional, and behavioral disorder in the past year, and one in five had three or more disorders. Of particular concern were the high rates of depression and PTSD, which exceeded the rates of war veterans. Of further concern is that a recent study estimated that PTSD and other anxiety disorders cost the U.S. economy $42 billion per year. Patients with PTSD were three to five times more likely to go to a doctor and six times more likely to be hospitalized than those without anxiety disorders (Greenberg et al., 1999, as cited in Kendall-Tackett ,1996).

Given the investment that child welfare agencies have made in high-quality services, why are the prevalence rates of mental illness so high and the recovery rates so low in some areas? First, we need to consider the severe child maltreatment and domestic violence that these persons may have experienced. Second, the initial trauma may have been exacerbated by frequent placement changes, as documented in Williams, Herrick, Pecora, and O'Brien (2009). Third, it may be that agency treatment approaches have not been matched well with the particular needs of certain youth. Despite the widespread use of standard psychological assessments, child welfare and mental health agencies have only recently begun to pay more careful attention to disorders like PTSD and social phobia. And evidence-based treatment training for these disorders has become more widely available only in the past five years. Fourth, therapists experienced in many of the child mental, emotional, and behavioral disorders identified in this study are scarce.

In terms of physical health, although over 1 in 4 alumni currently had a chronic health disorder, almost 7 in 10 indicated good physical health as assessed by a standardized scale. Smoking and drinking rates appear on par with those of the general population, which many health experts would say are too high.

Limitations[58]

Two study limitations need to be highlighted. First, the event(s) that precipitated the mental, emotional, and behavioral disorders may have occurred at any time during the life of the alumnus or alumna—before, during, or after care. Measurement of mental health functioning or standardized diagnostic information on the young adults prior to and during foster care was not available. Second, because sample members were served in foster care before 1999 and the bulk of the interviews were conducted in 2001, it is possible that more recent federal regulations and agency enhancements may have changed the way mental, emotional, and behavioral disorders among foster children are addressed, which would potentially result in different outcomes for those children served from 1999 on.

Acknowledgment.   Eva Hiripi, Tamera Wiggins, Nancy Gebler, Catherine Roller White, and Ellen Walters contributed to this chapter.

7

Educational Achievements

QUESTION: Could anything have been done to improve the move from foster care to living on your own?

ANSWER: Offer independent living classes much earlier, like at age 14. Make sure kids are really, really well prepared for first year of college, not just the simple college orientation. I only had $200 in the bank when I got to college.

Overview

Educational achievement is a powerful determinant of future life success for all youth. Specifically, high school dropouts are seriously at risk of being unemployed (National Center for Educational Statistics, 1996; Stern, Paik, Catterall, & Nakata, 1989) and on public assistance (National Center for Educational Statistics, 1996; Service, 1995). Youth who are at risk for school failure are also at high risk for drug abuse, delinquency, violence (Hawkins & Catalano, 1992; Institute of Medicine [IOM] Committee on Prevention of Mental Disorders, 1994; Maguin & Loeber, 1996), and poor long-term adjustment (Jackson, 1994). The Adolescent Health (Add Health) study of 90,000 adolescents from 134 schools across the United States that began in the mid-1990s found that youth who have problems with schoolwork are more likely than others to experience or be involved with *every* health risk studied, regardless of race and ethnicity (Blum, Beuhring, & Rinehart, 2000).

This chapter presents the educational experience and achievements of the Northwest alumni. Children in foster care are at high risk for school failure because of childhood deprivation and other adversities, frequent school changes, and lack of educational supports (Altshuler, 1997; Ayasse, 1995; Cohen, 1991; Jackson, 1994; Stein, 1994; Stein, Rae-Grant, Ackland, & Avison, 1994). Because of the extended time in care (an average of over six years), educational achievement is particularly relevant for the Northwest alumni. The educational achievement of alumni is tabled at the end of the chapter, while agency breakdowns and additional educational information are tabled in O'Brien et al. (2009a).

Where possible, education data are contrasted with findings from other foster care follow-up studies. Currently, there are few studies with which to compare data for older foster care alumni, but the data are slowly building because of longitudinal follow-up studies of public agency alumni in certain midwestern states (Courtney et al., 2001, 2004b, 2007) and in Washington (Brandford & English, 2004). Other child welfare agencies have also been conducting studies on the East Coast (Casey Family Services, 2004), in Nevada (Reilly, 2003), and in some other western states (Casey Family Programs, 2004).

Further, general population comparison data (from the U.S. Census, Department of Labor, and the National Center for Educational Statistics) are included when those statistics are available. In addition, because many of the children placed in foster care are part of low-income families, comparison data for children living in poverty are also provided when possible. Lastly, when comparing any educational data, the racial composition of the study is important. Because high school completion rates for African-American, Hispanic/Latino, and Native American youth are generally lower in the general population, the racial/ethnic breakdown of studies should be considered.

Educational Achievement

Foster Care Alumni Comparison Data

One of the few national U.S. foster care follow-up studies found that only 54% of the alumni had completed high school (Cook, 1991). In a Wisconsin study, 63% of the alumni had completed high school 12 to 18 months after discharge (Courtney et al., 2001). The high school completion rate among emancipated youth in West Virginia was 63% compared with 73% of all youth aged 18 to 24 in West Virginia (Jones & Moses, 1984).

A recent study of 213 Washington State alumni found that half of the young adults had completed high school or earned a GED during their first 6 to 12 months out of care, with an additional 19% working toward a high school diploma or GED. Additionally, about one in four (28%) had started some college classes or vocational training (Brandford & English, 2004, p. 4). Researchers also found high rates of special education status, school interruptions and mobility, low reading ability, and poor grades, all factors that severely limit postsecondary school access and success.

While the high school educational achievement presented above may be troubling, a recent report of youth in foster care in Illinois, Iowa, and Wisconsin found high school completion rates of 74.5% for males and 79.3% for females (11.3% and 8.3% GED only for males and females, respectively) at age 21 (Courtney et al., 2007, p. 28), and in a survey of the same group at 19 years of age, the researchers estimated that about over 86% aspired to attend college or to enroll in a postsecondary training program (Courtney et al., 2004b). Gaining access to college opportunities and overcoming the many academic, financial, health, and personal barriers have been difficult for alumni. Students coming from state or privately sponsored foster care are underrepresented significantly in the postsecondary education and training settings that could provide them with better opportunities for employment or higher-paying jobs. Youth in foster care are less likely to be enrolled in college preparatory classes than youth not in care (15% versus 32%), even when they have similar test scores, and they are significantly underrepresented in postsecondary programs (Sheehy et al., 2002).

Unfortunately, other data on postsecondary education of alumni from foster care are sparse and difficult to compare; estimates range widely for college enrollment rates (7%–74%) and graduation rates (1%–8%) (Casey Family Services, 1999; Courtney et al., 2004b, 2007; Reilly, 2003). One reason for these ranges is the young age at which educational achievement is assessed, usually at 19 or 20. Thus, the age of young adults at follow-up is important to note when comparing data. Nevertheless, previous studies do provide benchmarks for the educational achievement of the Northwest alumni.

School Experience of Northwest Alumni from Foster Care

Before detailing the educational achievement of the Northwest alumni, it is important to review the educational challenges they faced (see O'Brien et al., 2009a). For example, many alumni:

- Attended three or more different elementary schools (63.5%)
- Were in special education classes for students needing extra help (35.6%)
- Received tutoring or other supplemental educational services (48.1%)
- Repeated a grade in school (31.3%)

Another obstacle that alumni encountered was placement instability, which may increase the likelihood of additional school moves and educational failure and further complicates educational attainment (Cadoret & Riggins-Caspers, 2002; De Bellis, 2001; Lansford et al., 2002). For example, almost one-third of the alumni (30.2%) experienced 10 or more school changes, indicating serious disruptions in the continuity of their education.

High School Completion

When possible, many agencies providing foster care encourage youth to complete high school (or obtain a GED) before leaving care. According to case record data for those who left care after 17.25[60] years of age (84.5% of alumni), half (49.6%) had completed high school (O'Brien et al., 2009a). At follow-up, alumni reported completing high school at a surprisingly high rate (84.8%), which was roughly comparable to that of a group of 18- to 24-year-olds who were not currently enrolled in high school (86.6%) (National Center for Education Statistics, 2004) and that of 18- to 29-year-olds in the general population (87.3% in 2000; National Center on Education Statistics, 2003; see Table 7.1). The high school completion rate was even higher for alumni aged 25 and older (90.8%), who have had more time to complete classes or their GED (O'Brien et al., 2009a). This figure compares favorably to the high school completion rate for the general population for all adults aged 25 and older in 2000 (80.4%) (U.S. Census Bureau, 2000a).

A more appropriate comparison group would be children who were from chaotic, poor, and socially disorganized families but who were not placed in foster care. However, since these data are not available, general population statistics from the U.S. Census are used as comparisons. Alternatively, the U.S. Department of Education reports a current population survey data rate of 84.1% for high school completion or GED attainment for those over 25 in 2000 (U.S. Department of Education, 2003).

High School Diploma versus a GED

A concern for youth in care and alumni from care is whether high school is completed with a diploma or a GED. In the United States, the percentage of students obtaining a GED has been on the rise since the early 1990s, increasing from about 400,000 to over 500,000 in 1999 (U.S. Department of Education, 2002). In the general population, the 87.3% of 18- to 29-year-olds who completed high school was split into two groups: (1) completion with a diploma (82.2%) and (2) completion with a GED (5.1%) (National Center on Education Statistics, 2003). In Oregon, for the period 1998–2000, the general population high school completion rate for 18- to 24-year-olds not currently enrolled in high school was 82.3%. For the same age group at that time in Washington, the rate was 87.4% (Kaufman, Alt, & Chapman, 2001). (Note that the Northwest Alumni Study data were not adjusted for those not currently enrolled in high school.)

A substantial proportion of Northwest alumni (28.5%) obtained a GED instead of a high school diploma, a rate five times that of the general population (5%).[61] While having a GED is more beneficial than not completing high school (Smith, 2003), research indicates that people who obtain a diploma instead of a GED are more successful as adults. While postsecondary enrollment rates for GED recipients are much higher than the rates of other dropouts, completion rates tend to be far lower than those of traditional high school graduates. Furthermore, compared to those with high school diplomas, GED completers have lower educational attainment and lower earnings:

- While two-thirds of those obtaining a GED claim that they take the exam to gain access to postsecondary educational programs, their persistence and completion rates tend to be low for all but vocational programs (Boesel,

Table 7.1. Educational Outcomes for Northwest Alumni and Comparison Groups[a]

Educational Outcomes	Total % (SE)	Census Bureau Data %	%	Other Alumni Studies — Study
Completed high school— high school diploma or GED	84.8 (1.9)	Between 70– and 87, depending upon the age range and study	71% at 36.7 years old	Buehler et al. (2000)
			77% at 22 years old; 90% at 22.8 years old	Blome (1997) national study of alumni; Casey Family Services (1999) with long-term extended alumni from foster care
			44% at 22.8 years old	Casey Family Services (1999) with non-extended alumni from foster care[b]
			63% at about 20 years old	Courtney et al. (2001) Wisconsin study of high school completion 12 to 18 months after discharge
			40%	Mech and Fung (1999)
			69% at 20.2 years old	Reilly (2003)
			54% at 21 years old	Cook, Fleishman, and Grimes (1991) Westat National Study of alumni
Completed high school— high school diploma only	56.3 (2.7)	About 75	28.6%	Mech (2003) (Very few alumni studies have delineated completion of diplomas vs. GEDs.)
Completed high school— with a GED	28.5 (2.5)		11%	Mech and Fung (1999)
Any education past high school (any type of post-secondary education)	42.7 (2.7)	About 52—some college (ages 25 and older)	27% at 22 years old; 45% at 22 years old	Alexander and Huberty (1993) alumni with some college or vocational training; Blome (1997) national study of alumni

			73% at 22.8 years old	Casey Family Services (1999) with long-term extended alumni from care[b]
			18% at 22.8 years old	Casey Family Services (1999) with non-extended alumni from foster care[b]
			12.6%	Frost and Jurich (1983) with some college
			7% at 20 years old	Jones and Moses (1984) with some college
			30% at 20.2 years old	Reilly (2003)
			33%	Cook et al. (1991) Westat National Study of alumni
			11.5%, 19–29 years old	Zimmerman (1982) with some college
Completed any degree/ certificate beyond high school (vocational, BA, etc.)	20.6 (1.8)		N/A	N/A
Completed college or more (has BA or more)	1.8 (0.4)	24 (ages 25 and older)	8%	Casey Family Services (1999) with non-extended alumni from foster care[b]
			5.4%	Festinger (1983)
			2.1%	Frost and Jurich (1983)
			1%	Jones and Moses (1984)
			2% at 21 years old	Cook et al. (1991) Westat National Study of alumni
			1.6%	Zimmerman (1982)
Sample size	**479**			

[a]These comparative data from the earlier studies must be viewed with special caution, as only the Blome (ages 22 and older) and Westat studies (up to age 24) included older alumni.

[b]In the Casey Family Services study, two main groups were differentiated: (1) those who were placed with the agency for a long period of time and (2) those alumni who had left the program early.

Alsalam, & Smith, 1998, as cited in Smith, 2003, p. 376). Specifically, GED completers, compared to those with a high school diploma, were only half as likely to complete an associate's degree and much less likely to complete a bachelor's degree (Smith, 2003). (See Table 7.2.)

- GED recipients were more than twice as likely as those with high school diplomas to not enroll in postsecondary education (Bozick & DeLuca, 2005).
- Much of the widely reported research by economists finds that GED graduates have labor market outcomes closer to those of noncredentialed high school dropouts than to those of graduates holding traditional diplomas (Cameron & Heckman, 1993; Maloney, 1993, as cited in Smith, 2003, p. 376).
- Those with GEDs also have lower incomes than those with diplomas (Grubb, 1999).

Despite the less favorable results, obtaining a GED is better than dropping out of high school and may be the only viable alternative for some young people. In the United States, GED holders complete vocational programs at slightly higher rates than those with high school diplomas (15.4% versus 11.1%; Smith, 2003). Other results for GED graduates include the following:

- GED recipients have higher basic literacy skills than high school dropouts (Smith, 2003, p. 388), and current and future recipients scored higher on the Armed Forces Vocational Aptitude Battery (Smith, 2003, p. 389).
- Over time, the wages of GED graduates grew more rapidly than they would have had the individuals not earned a GED. Among disadvantaged high school youth, Bos (1995, 1996) found 8%–10% increases in earnings (Smith, 2003, p. 390).

There are many legitimate reasons why youth in foster care may feel it necessary to pursue a GED. According to open-ended responses, some alumni report that after being bounced between five or 10 different schools, they just wanted to complete their education in the most efficient manner possible. For others, towering over their classmates because they were two grades behind them was embarrassing. Some alumni discussed the fact that mental health issues like social phobia or depression made it difficult to attend traditional schools—especially schools with large class sizes and teachers who did not understand their situation. Educational advocates have also raised

Table 7.2.   General Population Dropout Rates for Postsecondary Education

Degree	Percent with Regular Diploma	Percent with GED
Vocational certificates	11.1	15.4
Had not completed a degree within five years after first enrollment (GED holders also had been enrolled for fewer months.)	56.1	70.9

Source: Smith (2003, p. 386).

the concern that some schools are "counseling out" their most academically challenged students to try to maximize their school or district test scores (Smithgall, Gladden, Goerge, & Courtney, 2004). Youth in foster care may be among the students most vulnerable to this kind of discrimination.

There are several important points about GED completion. First, the proportion of those obtaining a GED in the general population has been increasing for many years (U.S. Department of Education, 2002). Recent analysis indicates a relationship between the local, state, and national focus on testing (which has high-stakes funding consequences) and graduation (Bracey, 2004). In addition to the focus on testing, Bracey points to the dramatic rise in dropout rates under the federal No Child Left Behind Act, which has not been bolstered with academic remediation or tutoring services. Second, among the Northwest alumni, Casey alumni obtained a diploma more frequently than state alumni (68.0% versus 52.7%), but both were substantially below the rate of the general population figure cited above (82.2%) (O'Brien et al., 2009a).

Third, because of frequent moves or other obstacles that place them behind (e.g., a delay in transferring school records), there are foster youth obtaining a GED who have little, if any, hope of graduating from high school (John Emerson, personal communication, October 7, 2004). At the same time, others are dropping out or pursuing a GED when they could be in high school. In sum, the system is not providing effectively for these youth. For example, youth who commit to obtaining a GED when they could be in school may not be receiving appropriate support and accommodations. Such support might have afforded many youth the chance to obtain a high school diploma (Conger & Rebeck, 2001).

Postsecondary Enrollment and Completion

While high school completion rates for the Northwest alumni were relatively high, the college enrollment and college completion rates for alumni in the current study were low. The proportion of alumni aged 25 and older that has completed any postsecondary education (45.3%) is substantially lower than that (57%) of the general population in the same age group who completed some college coursework (U.S. Census Bureau, 2000h).[62] (Note that the alumni group statistic includes vocational training, while the general population statistic does not. Therefore, the difference between the two groups is underestimated.) Meanwhile, only 2.7% of the alumni aged 25 and older completed a bachelor's degree or higher, a rate substantially lower than that of the general population group in the 25–34 age range (24.4% in 2000) (O'Brien et al., 2009a; U.S. Census Bureau, 2000a). Also, although no general population comparison is available, three in 10 alumni aged 25 and older completed some type of postsecondary degree (29.9%). Lastly, almost one in five alumni (17.2%) were in school currently, and more than one in 10 (12.1%) were enrolled in college currently (O'Brien et al., 2009a).

As demonstrated above, the college dropout rate was substantial. Therefore, it is critical that agencies track completion and enrollment. Data from the 1995–1996 entry cohort reported that only 63% of students in the general population beginning a four-year college program actually graduate within six years (National Center on Education Statistics, 2003, p. 12). Caution should be exercised because that percentage only includes high school seniors who graduated earlier that year; nevertheless, enrolling but not completing postsecondary education is a problem.

The Casey National Alumni Study, which included both young and older alumni placed between 1966 and 1998 in all Casey field offices, also found a high rate of college enrollment (49.3%) but a fairly low completion rate for a bachelor's degree or higher (10.8%) (Pecora et al., 2003b, p. 28). Clearly, more work needs to be done to help youth complete their college or vocational degrees. In Chapters 11 and 12 the factors predictive of educational success are explored. This will help identify the strategies that must be implemented to improve these outcomes.

Summary

Maltreated children have elevated risks of ending up homeless, experiencing substance abuse problems, having health and mental health disorders, becoming involved with the corrections system, and having their children placed in foster care (Felitti et al., 1998; Roman & Wolfe, 1997; Widom, Weiler, & Cottler, 1999). Yet, these unfortunate outcomes are not inevitable. The most promising mechanism to mitigate such risks is likely to be a good education. As mentioned earlier, research shows that education is a leading indicator of successful youth development and adult self-sufficiency. Educational outcomes, such as high school graduation, literacy/basic reading skills, taking high school courses necessary for college admission, and postsecondary education or job training, are some of the best indicators of future well-being and successful transition to adulthood for youth from foster care as well. Yet, youth in foster care are:

- More than twice as likely as youth not in care (37% vs. 16%) to drop out of high school.
- Less likely to be enrolled in college preparatory classes (15% vs. 32%), even when they have test scores and grades similar to those of youth not in care.
- Significantly underrepresented in postsecondary programs.
- Often at least one grade level behind their peers in basic academic achievement.
- Much more likely than their peers to be in special education classes.[63]

For youth in foster care, poor educational outcomes are often due to lack of school stability caused by frequent home placement disruptions, frequent school absences, inadequate educational advocacy, inadequate support, and educators' lack of awareness of the special circumstances of youth in care

(Altshuler, 1997; Seyfried, Pecora, Downs, Levine, & Emerson, 2000). Youth in foster care, perhaps more than other students, need a solid education to help ensure a successful future.

Almost one-third (31%) of America's youth who exited foster care in federal fiscal year 2001 had been in care for two years or more, and 44% of those who were still in care in 2001 had been there for two years or more (U.S. Department of Health and Human Services, 2003). Many of these youth had been moved from foster family to foster family several times, which, for a school-age youth, can mean changing elementary and/or high schools. This supports the study's finding that almost one-third (30.2%) of the alumni had 10 or more school changes, indicating serious disruptions in the continuity of their education. Research shows that changing schools during high school diminishes academic progress and decreases the chances for graduation (Noble, 1997).

Nationally, about 80% (given all of the different calculations mentioned earlier) of adults in the general population have a high school diploma or GED. Decisive national data on high school graduation rates for children in foster care, however, are not currently available. But as more studies of older alumni from foster care are completed, we predict that the graduation rate for youth in foster care will likely be at or below 80% until these challenges are addressed.

In summary, more than four out of five alumni had completed high school via a diploma or GED, a rate that compares favorably to that of the general population and is much higher than the rates found by other foster care studies (partly due to age differences among alumni studies). However, more than one out of four alumni obtained a GED, a rate five times higher than that of the general population. Because national research has found that adults with a diploma are more likely to earn an associate's and a bachelor's degree, the relatively high GED rate found in the Northwest Study is of great concern.

Although the overall high school completion rate was quite good, alumni completion rates for postsecondary education were low. Fewer than one in five alumni completed a vocational degree and about one in 50 completed a bachelor's degree, a rate substantially below that of the general population. Also of concern was the high number of youth who began a postsecondary education program but did not obtain a degree. For information on the differences in educational outcomes between alumni served in Casey and alumni served in state systems, see Working Paper No. 5 (O'Brien et al., 2009a) and Kessler et al. (2008).

Acknowledgment.   Catherine Roller White contributed to this chapter.

8

Employment and Finances

QUESTION: Could anything have been done to improve the move from foster care to living on your own?

ANSWER: Yeah, spend more time teaching me what the real world was like versus glossing it over. I would live rich for two days and poor for five. I still struggle with that now.

Overview

Previous research has shown that youth who have been placed in foster care experience a wide range of economic-related adversities after leaving care such as homelessness, unemployment, and low wages and income. Table 8.1 summarizes studies that have examined some of these adversities. This chapter will present current alumni achievement and functioning with respect to homelessness and living situation, employment, public assistance, and finances. Findings are compared not only to those of other foster care follow-up studies but also to general population information gathered from the U.S. Census Bureau. Currently, there are few studies with which to compare follow-up data (especially for older alumni), but the literature is slowly building, with longitudinal follow-up studies such as the Midwest study (Courtney et al., 2007) and studies that use state employment or other databases (e.g., Goerge et al., 2002; The Urban Institute, University of California Berkeley, & University of North Carolina at Chapel Hill, 2008).

Homelessness and Living Situation

Homelessness

While most of the Northwest alumni were in stable and positive living situations at the time of the interview, many have experienced challenges to

Table 8.1. Previous Studies of Homelessness, Employment, and Income of Foster Care Alumni

		Study Details	
Outcome	*Author(s)*	*Findings*
Homelessness	Barth (1990)	29% of the respondents reported that they currently had no home or that they moved every week or more. 39% reported experiencing problems with housing at some time. Running out of money or food was a major worry for 64%. On average, participants had moved six times since leaving foster care.
	Brandford and English (2004)	13% of respondents reported being homeless.
	Cook (1994)	25% of 18- to 24-year-old respondents reported having experienced homelessness.
	Courtney et al. (2001)	12% of respondents reported being homeless.
Employment	Alexander and Huberty (1993)	A 49% employment rate compared with a U.S. population rate of 67% for 18-to 24-year-olds (U.S. Census Data, 1991). Current students (13%) and Supplemental Security Income (SSI) recipients (9.4%) accounted for one-quarter of the study population.
	Barth (1990)	About 75% were employed, with most working full-time, but many in low-paying jobs without benefits, compared with a California employment rate of 64.2% in 1989 (U.S. Census Bureau, 1991, Table 636).
	Cook (1994)	The Westat National Study found that 49% of the 18- to 24-year-olds were working.
	Courtney et al. (2007)	51.5% of the 23-year-old alumni were currently employed, versus 63.9% in the National Adolescent Health Study (p. 31).
	Festinger (1983)	Excluding disabled respondents and those in school, employment rates were about 75% among males and 81% among females when homemakers are counted among the employed, 62.7% when disabled and homemakers are removed from the numbers. The employment rates for New York City in 1983 for those over age 16 were 91.4% for men and 91.9% for women (U.S. Census Bureau, 1984) (Table 657).
	Goerge et al. (2002)	30% of alumni from foster care in Illinois, 23% in California, and 14% in South Carolina were unemployed when they left foster care.

(continued)

Table 8.1. Continued

| | Study Details | |
Outcome	Author(s)	Findings
	Jones and Moses (1984)	21% of subjects were employed full-time, with more men than women working; 12% were employed part-time. 28% of the alumni had had no jobs since leaving high school. 43% of the total population was employed in West Virginia in 1983 (U.S. Census Bureau, 1984, Table 657). 26% of alumni were looking for work, which exceeds the unemployment rate of West Virginia in 1983, with 21.1% for men and 13% for women (U.S. Census Bureau, 1984, Table 657).
	The Urban Institute, University of California at Berkeley, and University of North Carolina at Chapel Hill (2008)	Youth who age out of foster care continue to experience poor employment outcomes at age 24. Compared to youth nationally and even to youth from low-income families, they are less likely to be employed or employed regularly, and, not surprisingly, they earn very little. At age 24, average monthly earnings for youth who age out of foster care who work are $690 in California, $575 in Minnesota, and $450 in North Carolina compared to $1,535 for youth nationally. Employment and earnings differences between youth who age out of foster care and youth from low-income families remain in California and Minnesota even when controlling for demographic factors. Case history factors do not appear to play an important role in influencing employment outcomes. Overall, about one-third to one-half of these youth follow a path that leads to relatively positive employment outcomes by age 24. At the same time, the other one-half to two-thirds of these youth exhibit patterns leading to poorer outcomes at age 24.
	Zimmerman (1982)	59% of the men were employed (Table 6.7), a figure lower than Louisiana's 76.3% labor force participation rate in 1981 (U.S. Census Bureau, 1982, Table 628). 48% of women were employed (Table 6.7), equal to the 47.4% labor force participation rate in Louisiana in 1981 (U.S. Census Bureau, 1982, Table 628).

(continued)

130

Table 8.1.   Continued

Outcome	Study Details	
	Author(s)	*Findings*
Wages and income	Alexander and Huberty (1993)	81% of those employed were working in unskilled or semiskilled service sector jobs. 61.2% rated their income as adequate to live decently.
	Courtney et al. (2007)	The mean average hourly wage for 21-year-old alumni was $8.85 (median, $8.00) versus the National Adolescent Health Study findings (mean $9.99, median $9.12)
	Jones and Moses (1984)	Wages ranged from $0.75/hour to $10.00/hour. The average was $3.50/hour. 25% worked in a bar or restaurant and 17% worked as unskilled laborers. 24% hoped for a job in skilled labor and 22% hoped for professional work.
	Zimmerman (1982)	60% earned a yearly income of $9,000 or less (including public assistance). Only 9% earned over $20,000/year.
Public assistance	Alexander and Huberty (1993)	14.2% of alumni living in Indiana received some form of public assistance (AFDC, food stamps, General Assistance) compared to only 5% of the state's population in 1992 (U.S. Census Bureau, 1994, Table 599).
	Courtney et al. (2007)	8.8% of women and no men were receiving TANF; 53.8% of women were receiving Women and Infants and Children. 11.3% of females and 12.9% of males were receiving SSI (p. 39).
	Courtney et al. (1998)	12–18 months after leaving care, 32% were receiving public assistance.
	Dworsky and Courtney (2000)	2% received AFDC TANF cash assistance within two years of emancipation.
	Festinger (1983)	20.6% were receiving public assistance; an additional 20.6% had received it in the past but were not current recipients compared with 7.4% of the New York State population who were receiving public assistance in 1980 (U.S. Census Bureau, 1981, Table 561).
	Jones and Moses (1984)	6% received public assistance at the time of the study, with 50% having received it at one time. This matches the 6% rate of the population in West Virginia receiving public assistance in 1983 (U.S. Census Bureau, 1984, Table 640). 25% had received food stamps at the time, with 38% having received them at some point (Table 18).

(continued)

Table 8.1.   Continued

Outcome	Study Details	
	Author(s)	Findings
	Zimmerman (1982)	25% were receiving some form of public support (AFDC, SSI, prison; Table 6.8); this rate was high in that 7.3% of the total population of Louisiana were receiving AFDC or SSI in 1982 (the 1981 figure was unavailable) (U.S. Census Bureau, 1983, Table 653). [Note: Zimmerman included alumni in prison in those under public support.]
Health insurance	Alexander and Huberty (1993)	47.1% had no health insurance compared to a U.S. uninsured population rate of 51.9% for those aged 18 to 24.
	Courtney et al. (2007)	Of the 21-year-old alumni who were working, only 48.2% received health insurance from their employer (p. 34). Only 50.7% of the alumni had health insurance of any kind, with the exception that 70.3% of the alumni had Medicaid or state medical assistance coverage (p. 43).
Other forms of economic instability	Goerge et al. (2002)	Alumni from foster care in Illinois, California, and South Carolina were often underemployed when they left foster care, with mean earnings below the poverty level and less than those of youth in similar age comparison groups.

achieve their current quality of life. Alumni experienced a troubling rate of homelessness after leaving foster care. Of particular concern: More than one in five alumni (22.2%) were homeless for one or more nights within a year after leaving care (see Table 8.3). Although not an exact comparison, the rate of homelessness found by Courtney et al. (1998) in alumni 12–18 months after leaving care was 12%. For the 21-year-old alumni the current rate was 1%, but 17.7% had been homeless since exiting care. Of the alumni who had ever been homeless, 51.9% had been homeless for more than one week (Courtney et al., 2007, p.16) (see Table 8.1). In the general population, the homelessness rate is estimated at 1% per year. For example, according to estimates developed from the 1996 National Survey of Homeless Assistance Providers and Clients, at least 2.3 million adults and children (nearly 1% of the U.S. population) are likely to experience a spell of homelessness at least once during a year (Burt et al., 1999).[64] In that study, 21% reported that their first period of homelessness occurred prior to their 18th birthday, and 27% of these homeless adults reported living in foster care, a group home, or another institutional setting for part of their childhood (12% reported being in foster care, 10% in a group home, and 16% in residential institutions).

Growing national data show that foster care placement is one of the risk factors for homelessness. A study of homelessness in Minneapolis (Piliavin, Sosin, Westerfelt, & Matsueda, 1993) found that 39% of the 331 homeless persons aged 18 or over who were interviewed reported being in a childhood foster care placement (foster home, group home, or institution). Foster care placement had the strongest relationship to the length of homelessness. Further, research in Chicago found that 14% of the homeless reported being in foster care as a child (Sosin, Colson, & Grossman, 1988). In New York City, the figure was 23% (Susser, Struening, & Conover, 1987).

Living Situation

Alumni were asked to specify whether they owned or rented their house or apartment. Approximately one in 10 alumni (9.3%) owned their home or apartment (see Table 8.2). In contrast, in the United States, the rate of home ownership for householders under age 35 was 41.2% (under age 25: 22.4%; for all adults: 67.5%) (U.S. Census Bureau, 2000f). For the western United States, where the overall home ownership rate is less for all adults (61.7%), the rate for those less than 25 years old was 17.4% and for those less than age 35 it was 33.6% (U.S. Census Bureau, 2000g).[65]

Employment

Question: Could anything have been done to improve the move from foster care to living on your own?

Answer: Yeah, sure. I don't know what. I just remember feeling very, very alone. I had no one. When I moved out I lived with my boyfriend. When that didn't go well, I lived in my car until I found a friend's mom who I could stay with.

Answer: Working in a restaurant owned by my foster family [led to my success in life]. It introduced me to the working world. I learned to cook and how to interact with the public. It was great for learning communication skills.

Answer: My construction teacher got me to think I could be more than I am. He said I could own a house before I was 25. I bought a house at age 19. My teacher explained how real estate works. My boyfriend and his mom—they taught me how to build credit. She helped me sign papers for the house and buy my truck. My mom has eight kids—my boyfriend's mom took me in.

Contributing to the low home ownership rate of the Northwest alumni was the difficulty of finding an occupation that paid a living wage. Only seven in 10 alumni (70.3%) who were eligible for work were employed. This rate is significantly lower than the national average of 95% for persons aged 20–34 in the general population.[66] Rates varied somewhat, depending on gender and school enrollment for the men and women in this study (ranging from 66.4% to 76.8% for six subgroups) (see Table 8.3). With one exception,

Table 8.2.   Living Situation for Northwest Alumni and Comparison Groups

Type of Home Ownership	Total Alumni % (SE)	Census Bureau Data
Owns home or apartment	9.3 (1.6)	• U.S. Census: 22.4% of those under age 25 own their house, compared to 41.2% of those under age 35 and 67.5% of all adults (U.S. Census Bureau, 2000f). • For the western United States, where the overall home ownership rate is less (61.7%), the rate for those under age 25 was 17.4% and for those under age 35 it was 33.6% (U.S. Census Bureau, 2000g).
Rents home or apartment	81.8 (1.9)	• 33.8% (U.S. Census Bureau, 2000b) of U.S. households.
Other[a]	8.9 (1.0)	—
Sample size	479	

[a]Other consisted of living with friends or family, or in housing paid for by their employer.

a recent study of older alumni between the ages of 20 and 51 (mean, 30 years) that found that 88.1% of the alumni eligible for work were working part- or full-time (Pecora et al., 2003b, 2006), data from comparison studies are equally troubling, showing that too few young alumni of the foster care system are employed. For example, the Westat National Study found that only 49% of the 18- to 24-year-olds were working (Cook, 1994), while a study using administrative data found that 30% of alumni from care in Illinois, 23% in California, and 14% in South Carolina were unemployed when they left foster care (Goerge et al., 2002). Many alumni are part of a large group of marginalized youth in society today: In the United States, 3.8 million young people between the ages of 18 and 24 are neither employed nor in school—roughly 15% of all young adults (Nelson, 2004).

Types of Jobs

The occupations of alumni were coded into one of over 500 potential categories, which were clustered into 13 major groups and six summary groups. For example, a *legislator* is an initial category, *Executive, Administrative, and Managerial Occupations* is a major group, and *Managerial and Professional Occupations* is a summary group. The top 10 most common positions that alumni held are presented in Table 8.4. Of the alumni who were working and had personal incomes of more than $17,918 per year, the three most common job categories were:

- Financial records processing occupations: 14.3%
- Service occupations (excluding protective jobs such as police and household jobs such as a cleaning service): 18.1%
- Sales occupations: 16.3%

Table 8.3.   Homelessness, Public Assistance, Finance, and Employment Outcomes for Northwest Alumni and Comparison Groups

Employment and Finance	Total Alumni % (SE)	Census Bureau Data
Homelessness		
Homeless for one or more nights at any time within a year after leaving foster care	22.2 (2.1)	
Owns house or apartment	9.3 (1.6)	40.8% (those under age 35)
Employment (within subgroups defined on the basis of gender, student status, and marital status)[a]		
Males in school	76.8 (3.0)	
Single females in school	74.0 (4.1)	
Married females in school	68.9 (6.1)	
Males *not* in school	75.1 (3.2)	
Single females *not* in school	70.4 (4.6)	
Married females *not* in school	66.4 (6.3)	
Employment for all alumni (in workforce)	70.3 (2.6)	95% (ages 20–34)
Public Assistance		
Ever received any public assistance or welfare (AFDC/TANF) since turning 18	51.7 (2.8)	
Receiving public assistance (AFDC/TANF) at the time of the interview	16.8 (2.2)	
Anyone in household received public assistance in the past six months	47.8 (2.8)	
Finance		
Household income at or above the poverty level	66.8 (2.6)	
Household income greater than three times the poverty level	21.3 (2.2)	
Has health insurance of any kind	67.0 (2.6)	75% (those 25 to 34 years old)
Sample size	**479**	

[a]Employment was examined separately for men and women and, within each gender, in subgroups defined by whether or not the respondent was still a student and, among women, marital status. Marital status was used only among women because typically women have a legitimate role as homemaker if they are married and their husband earns enough money to support the family, whereas men typically have no equivalent role. Employment results are reported by subgroup because not having a job outside the home is not necessarily a poor outcome for a married woman or for a student.

A disproportionately high percentage of alumni were serving in the military (1.8% compared to 0.5% of those aged 16 and older in the general population [U.S. Census Bureau, 2000d]). There is very little comparison

Table 8.4.   Type of Alumni Employment

Most Frequent Occupational Categories and Jobs[a]	Total Alumni (%)
Service occupations (not including protective and household)	18.1
Nursing aides, orderlies, and attendants	3.5
Waiters and waitresses	3.2
Cooks	3.2
Sales occupations	16.3
Cashiers	5.5
Supervisors and proprietors	3.2
Sales workers	2.0
Financial records processing occupations	14.3
Bill and account collectors	2.0
Administrative support occupations	2.0
Traffic, shipping, and receiving clerks	1.7
Sample size *(number of alumni with jobs)*	343

[a]The most common job was *Managers and Administrators*, but it did not fall into one of the most frequently occurring occupations, which are the categories listed above.

data on military service by alumni from foster care except for a recent study that found that 6.1% of alumni who left care at age 18 or older went into the military (Casey Research Services, 2005).

Public Assistance

When they were unable to pay for basic living expenses, many alumni turned to public assistance. At the time of the interview, about one in six (16.8%) alumni were receiving cash public assistance, either from Temporary Assistance to Needy Families (TANF) or General Assistance[67] (see Table 8.3). This rate was five times higher than the 2000 general population rate of 3.4% (U.S. Census Bureau, 2000c)[68] but lower than the 26% reported by a long-term follow-up study of alumni on the East Coast (Casey Family Services, 1999, p. 13) and one conducted in 1998 involving Wisconsin youth 18 months after leaving foster care using state administrative data; in that study, 39% were unemployed and 32% were receiving public assistance (Courtney et al., 1998).

Another study by Dworsky and Courtney (2000) tracked the employment and public assistance use of a cohort of youth in foster care in Wisconsin; they found that very few had received cash assistance and/or food stamps within two years of leaving care. However, they found that there were significant race and regional effects, with African American youth and youth from Milwaukee being more likely to use Aid to Families with Dependent Children (AFDC)/TANF or food stamps.

Other comparison data are equally sobering. Alexander and Huberty (1993) found that 14.2% of youth from care in Indiana received some form of public assistance (AFDC, food stamps, General Assistance) compared to only 5% of the general population in that state (U.S. Census Bureau, 1994, Table 599). Additionally, Festinger (1983) found that one in five alumni (20.6%) were receiving public assistance; an additional 20.6% had received it in the past but were not current recipients compared with 7.4% of the New York State population who were receiving public assistance in 1980 (U.S. Census Bureau, 1981, Table 561). About half (47.8%) of the Northwest Alumni Study participants indicated that they or someone living with them had received help from a federal, state, or local agency in the past six months (see Table 8.3).

Finances

Income

Although findings from this study dispel the notion that a high percentage of alumni are unemployed or in jail, personal and household incomes reflect the difficulties that many alumni encounter. For example, two-thirds of alumni (66.8%) were living in households at or below the poverty line (see Table 8.3). In comparison, the 2000 poverty rate for the United States was 11%. [Poverty began at $8,959 for a U.S. household of one in that year. For two adults and one child, the poverty line was $13,861 (U.S. Census Bureau, 2001).]

Health Insurance

Being uninsured has serious consequences; a recent Institute of Medicine study (2003) noted that about 18,000 Americans die prematurely each year from illness that could have been treated by better access to health care through insurance coverage.[70] Given the mental health difficulties of alumni from care and their inability to find occupations that pay a living wage, finding and using health insurance is critical. Two out of three alumni (67.0%) had health insurance (see Table 8.3), meaning that nearly twice as many alumni lacked health care coverage compared to the general population aged 18 to 44 (18%). Young adults (19–34) are those most likely to be uninsured (Institute of Medicine, 2001, p. 2). This is a serious national problem—one not confined to alumni of foster care. For example, in the Oregon Behavioral Risk Factor Surveillance System Survey, 84.7% of all respondents indicated that they had some kind of health care coverage, but the percentage insured was only 75% for those in the 25–34 age group (Centers for Disease Control and Prevention [CDC], 1998b). As a further comparison, 47.1% of alumni had no health insurance compared to a U.S. population rate of 51.9% for those aged 18–24 (Alexander & Huberty, 1993). Additional information on homelessness as well as personal and household incomes is available in Working Paper No. 5 (O'Brien et al., 2009a).

Summary

While a high proportion of alumni are working and have health insurance, many alumni are in fragile economic situations. After accounting for alumni who were not in the workforce (e.g., full-time students and homemakers), the employment rate was 80.1%. This rate is lower than that of persons aged 20–34 in the general population (95%). One-third of the alumni (33.2%) had household incomes at or below the poverty level, which is three times the national poverty rate. One-third (33.0%) had no health insurance, which is double the national rate of 18% for those aged 18–44. More than one out of five alumni (22.2%) experienced homelessness after leaving foster care. The next chapter presents findings about the relationships and social supports of the alumni.

Acknowledgment.   Catherine Roller White contributed to this chapter.

9

Relationships, Social Support Networks, and Parenting

One interviewer was impressed by a 21-year-old father who was very gracious to his wife and their three young daughters. He spoke very gently to them and of them, and expressed how much he enjoyed his young family and how they made him feel like he belonged. He said that by marrying and having children he'd finally found the family he'd "never been allowed" to have when he was growing up. This respondent takes pride and pleasure in working hard to provide for his family so his wife can be the homemaker, and he finds enjoyment in his family and weekend gatherings of extended family. He said that it was one particular social worker who made the difference. The social worker was a young man with a happy family, who obviously enjoyed his wife and kids and who included the respondent in some of their activities. This man showed the respondent how things might be, and inspired him to seek the same.

Overview

Prior chapters have reported on alumni functioning in terms of physical and mental health, education, and employment and finances. This chapter focuses on the nature and quality of the relationships that alumni have with key groups of people such as spouses or partners, birth family, and former foster parents. Sources and types of social support available to alumni are examined, as well as child-rearing status, parenting, and placement of children of alumni in foster care.

As a multidimensional construct, social support has been categorized into several types of support: *tangible* (material assistance or actions), *emotional* (expression of feelings of concern or empathy), *appraisal* (information relevant to self-evaluation), and *informational* (factual and educational aid) (House, 1981; Jung, 1997; Tardy, 1985). Additional categories include *guidance* and *feedback* (direction and advice) (Barrera, Sandler, & Ramsay, 1981).

Social support is both given and received, and although it is common to consider social networks as wholly positive, research has shown that social support can have both positive and negative elements. In fact, some relationships are quite asymmetrical, with one person continually providing support and the other receiving support (Turkington, 1985). Continual provision of support can be an emotional drain on one person in the relationship and thus can be internalized as a negative element of social support (Kessler, McLeod, & Wethington, 1985). It is important to consider the balance between received and provided support (Jung, 1997). Some research has shown that negative support—such as unequal support provision or high rates of conflict or disagreement—can have a larger impact on well-being than positive support (Beach, Martin, Blum, & Roman, 1994; Horwitz, McLaughlin, & Raskin White, 1998; Stack, 1974). However, Jung (1997) found that well-being was not necessarily greater for those who were receiving more support than they were providing. Social support is often viewed under the assumption that "if some is good, more is better," but this is not necessarily the case (McIntosh, 1991). In a study examining different properties of social support (amount of support, adequacy of support, and number of people providing support), McIntosh (1991) found that too many people willing to provide support may in fact increase strain rather than reduce it.

While evidence suggests that social support can have both positive and negative impacts, much research indicates that the presence of social support in general does reduce stress, increase physical functioning, increase subjective well-being, increase life expectancy, and mitigate risk behaviors and psychological distress (DePanfilis, 1996; Mann, 2003; McIntosh, 1991; Michael, Colditz, Coakley, & Kawachi, 1999; Peeters, Buunk, & Schaufeli, 1995; Ross & Mirowsky, 2002). For example, in the National Longitudinal Study of Adolescent Health (*Add Health*) of 90,000 adolescents across the United States, the most consistent protective factor against risk behaviors was the presence of a positive parent-family relationship (Blum et al., 2000).

Theoretical Frameworks for Understanding the Importance of Positive Relationships[71]

Resilience

Providing a framework that is useful for evaluating interventions for youth in foster care, Luthar and Cicchetti (2000) defined resilience as "a dynamic process wherein individuals display positive adaptation despite experiences of significant adversity or trauma" (p. 858). Although resilience has been shown to be related to biological factors such as temperament or environmental factors such as attachment, researchers have also found that new strengths or vulnerabilities can appear in an individual through the experience of age- and gender-related physical and psychological changes or as life circumstances change (Luthar & Cicchetti, 2000).

In evaluating the long-term efficacy of interventions with youth in foster care, it is helpful to examine recent research that has attempted to gain an understanding of resilience as a process rather than a set of traits or factors. The developmental perspective is focused on the role of the environment in the development of resilience. This expansion of resilience allows for the provision of services to enhance evidence-based protective factors in children and adolescents who may have previously had a poor outlook because of multiple community and individual risk factors. Community risk factors include low neighborhood socioeconomic status, poor school climate, and limited social resources. Individual risk factors include antisocial relationships with peers, negative family involvement, and child maltreatment.

In addition, Noam and Hermann (2002) identified a number of factors that they believe are predominantly influential in the development of resilience. One of those factors is "the capacity to engage in productive relationships and to be supported by people and institutions that are attentive and make a positive contribution to an individual's development and well-being" (p. 871).

Although this developmental resilience model has not been directly applied to youth in care, there is reason to believe that it could be useful for this population. Based on the available literature, the model appears to be particularly suited to the unique needs of children in foster care. It encompasses developmental stages and accounts for individual differences in development. It allows for adaptation to meet the special needs of youth in care, who are likely to have been maltreated, to suffer from various mental and physical health conditions, and to already be experiencing educational or social difficulties (Courtney et al., 2001; Rashid, 2004; Shin, 2004; Zetlin, Weinberg & Kimm, 2004).

Research on resilience has demonstrated the importance of supportive relationships as a protective factor against adverse life situations in at-risk youth in general (Furstenberg, Cook, Eccles, Elder, & Sameroff, 1999; Gilligan, 1999). Early relationships of youth in care are likely to have been characterized by physical, emotional, or sexual abuse. In addition, multiple placement changes may mean that these youth lack opportunities to develop long-lasting, stable, and positive relationships with caring adults. Caring adults not only serve as role models and mentors, they also provide guidance, information, and emotional support to youth as the young people struggle with obstacles and transition through developmental stages—in particular, the many hurdles that youth in care must overcome before becoming self-sufficient adults (Shin, 2004).

Social Support and Relationships as Important Risk and Protective Factors for Youth in Care and Alumni of Foster Care

Social support is associated with providing protective factors related to physical and mental well-being. Greater levels of social support have been shown to increase subjective life expectancy (Ross & Mirowsky, 2002). Individuals who are married, and thus are experiencing a high level of social attachment, tend to be healthier than unmarried people (Haring-Hidore, Stock, Okun, & Witter, 1985). Lacking close friends or relatives or a confidant has been associated with a reduction in physical functioning (Michael et al., 1999). Further, certain types of social support have been shown to buffer, to a degree, work-related stresses (Himle, Jayaratne, & Thyness, 1991; McIntosh, 1991).

The *Add Health* study of adolescents found that children who report feeling connected to a parent are protected against many different kinds of health risks including emotional distress and suicidal thoughts and attempts; cigarette, alcohol, and marijuana use; violent behavior; and early sexual activity (Blum & Rinehart, 1997, p. 16). Another study of youth aged 12 to 21 found that family bonding is important in protecting against illicit drug use among youth, especially those aged 12 to 18; by contrast, youth with low family bonding are three times more likely to use illicit drugs than youth with high family bonding (Mann, 2003). Conversely, as an example of how certain aspects of social support networks can have negative effects, Mann found that involvement with antisocial peers increases the risk of drug initiation in youth. Research has also indicated consistently that perceived social support is highly correlated with self-esteem and self-concept (Sarason et al., 1991). Sarason, Pierce, Bannerman, and Sarason (1993) state that feeling cared about and valued by others is important in creating a positive self-image.

Prior chapters have reported that adults in the Northwest Alumni Study endured child maltreatment that was often multifaceted, severe, and long-term. Many alumni experienced multiple moves and other kinds of disruptions while growing up. These alumni faced more risks than most children of their age. Past and present risk factors can limit the positive effects of the protective factors and services received. For example, Nollan, Pecora, Nurius, and Whittaker (2001) argue that these risk factors, and a lack of social supports or other protective factors, are linked to inadequate development of life skills. They found that protective factors—such as good relationships with foster parents, high self-esteem, and involvement in social groups—were associated with greater self-sufficiency skills among youth placed in long-term foster care, while risk factors—such as ADHD, special education, many placement changes, and abuse and neglect—were associated with fewer self-sufficiency skills. Thus, the protective aspects of social support are especially valuable to alumni of foster care. Specifically, social support has been shown to have an interactive effect on adjustment and well-being (Heller, Swindle, & Dusenbury, 1986), and such support can decrease the impact of childhood sexual and physical abuse on adult psychopathology (Runtz & Schallow, 1997). Child victims of neglect, poverty, and violence have been found to use social support as an important factor in their successful adjustment later in life (Mrazek & Mrazek, 1987; Werner & Smith, 1989; Zimrin, 1986).

Interviews with alumni of foster care illustrate the importance of caring relationships with adults. For example, one study found that when alumni were asked what was the most positive or helpful factor or experience in foster care, a significant number stated that a feeling of belonging and an emotionally supportive relationship with the foster family, a social worker, or a case worker while in care were important and positive factors (Wedeven et al., 1997). Maintaining relationships (both providing and receiving care) with siblings, from childhood to adulthood, has also been found to be an important form of support for maltreated youth (Muller, Goh, Lemieux, & Fish, 2000).

Importance of Social Support in Adults

Adults develop an expanded social network, drawing social support from various relationships such as those with marital partners, children, peers, parents, and siblings. Weiss (1974) identified six roles of relationships—attachment, social integration, reliable alliance, guidance, reassurance of worth, and opportunity for nurturance—and determined that deficiencies in any of these lead to personal distress.

Social support is causally related to health maintenance, psychological well-being, and treatment prognosis (for reviews, see Cohen & Wills, 1985; Tracy & Whittaker, 1987; Whittaker & Garbarino, 1985). In particular, Wahler and his colleagues have found that failures in parenting training are correlated with "parental insularity," or a lack of social support (Wahler, 1980; Wahler, Leske, & Rogers, 1979). Furthermore, social support networks that place heavy demands upon families or are the source of criticism have been linked to higher family stress and difficulty in becoming self-sufficient (e.g., Stack, 1974; Whittaker, Tracy, & Marckworth, 1989).[72]

For many, adulthood brings with it the additional responsibilities of parenthood. Factors that influence parenting behaviors are especially important when considering alumni of foster care, as it is most often the failure of the birth parents' parenting that leads to youth placement in foster care; therefore, alumni of foster care have usually experienced poor parenting role models. Additionally, the parenting behaviors exhibited by foster parents or guardians are important in shaping the lives of the youth in their care. Research indicates that the nature of the relationship between children and their parents has an effect on children's personality development (Daniels, 1986) and that individuals' perceptions of the availability of social support are related to the way family members view them (Sarason et al., 1993).

One study found that children of mothers with high levels of perceived social support were much more likely to function better (in terms of behavioral and developmental outcomes) than those whose mothers had low perceived social support (Runyan et al., 1998b). Additionally, several studies that investigated the causes of child maltreatment showed that "social support networks both directly and indirectly influence parenting adequacy" (DePanfilis, 1996, p. 37). Furthermore, Dumas, Wahler, and others have reported that socially isolated families are doubly at risk of treatment failure because they are not just isolated: They are embedded in coercive interactions with bill collectors, landlords, protective services caseworkers, food stamp clerks, counselors, police, and other social-control agents (Dumas, 1984; Dumas & Albin, 1986; Dumas & Wahler, 1983; Wahler & Dumas, 1989). The lack of social support is thought to affect both the psychological and material resources that insular families may bring to bear in solving financial, housing, health, child care, and other problems. Thus, insular families are hypothesized to be more likely to fail to respond to treatment (Fraser, Pecora, & Haapala, 1991). Regardless of the lack of current conclusions about their precise functioning, social networks, supports, and relationships are clearly an intricate part of successful parenting.

The implications of this research are clear: If communities intend to help alumni of foster care succeed, life skills to develop and sustain positive, noncoercive relationships must be taught.[73]

Relationships and Social Support Networks

They could've instilled values in me. I had to learn the hard way about friendships and [to] not leave children unattended in the bathtub: They could drown.

When you're 18 it's very hard to live by the rules. I don't really think we parted on the best of terms. It could have been nicer. I was looking forward to leaving and I think they were looking forward to me leaving too, so it felt awkward. I felt bad about that. I wanted to keep in touch but since things felt awkward when I left I didn't follow up.

Marriage and Cohabitation

Nearly one-third (30.4%) of the alumni reported being currently married (see Table 9.1). This is lower than the general population rate (43.4% of the population aged 20–34; U.S. Census Bureau, 2004). Research shows that marriage provides financial and health benefits (Reardon-Anderson, Stagner, Macomber, & Murray, 2005) but it may have little association with a person's subjective sense of well-being (i.e., perceived happiness, morale, quality of life, or life satisfaction). This may be mediated by the amount of satisfaction derived from the marriage (Haring-Hidore et al., 1985). Similarly, Ross (1995) found that although being in a relationship generally improves well-being, being in an unhappy relationship is worse than being in no relationship. These findings exemplify the complexity of social support in relationships.

While just over 30% of alumni were married, it is important to note that many people were not married but were in committed relationships. Ross (1995) reported that being in a socially attached relationship provided emotional and economic support that significantly reduced distress but that there was no significant difference between living with a partner and being married. Nearly half of the alumni (47.1%) were either married or cohabitating at the time of the study, which is slightly less than the general population rate (Kessler & Walters, 2002). Only 0.5% of respondents reported being in a same-sex relationship. Almost two-thirds (62.7%) of married or cohabitating alumni reported being very satisfied with their relationship. These data suggest that the majority of alumni are involved in positive supportive relationships with their partners.

Table 9.1.   Marriage, Relationships, and Parenting Variables Used in the Multivariate
Analyses

Marriage, Relationships, and Parenting Outcomes	Total Alumni % (SE)	General Population NCS-R and Other Comparison Data
Relationships and Social Supports		
Alumni married	30.4 (2.5)	43.4 (U.S. Census)
• No violence in the relationship	61.2 (5.0)	68.1 (NCS-R)
		84 (Straus et al, 1996)
• Alumni married or cohabitating	47.1 (2.8)	64 (U.S. Census, 5.2 + 58.8)
		40.1 (NCS-R)
• Very satisfied with the relationship	62.7 (4.1)	
• Not socially isolated (has three or more friends)	85.7 (2.0)	
Alumni single and not cohabiting	52.9 (2.8)	59.9 (NCS-R)
• Not socially isolated (has three or more friends)	74.8 (3.3)	
No serious fighting with anyone in past 12 months	88.2 (1.9)	
Negative social support (receives high demands, stress, and arguments from friends and relatives)	25.0 (2.7)	32.9[78] (NCS-R)
Positive social support (receives high understanding, help from friends and relatives)	49.2 (2.8)	38.2[79] (NCS-R)
Parenting		
No children before age 18	92.7 (1.3)	91.6[80] (NCPTP)
No children before marriage	82.0 (1.9)	65.4 (NCHS)
Alumni with children	63.0 (2.6)	
• Does many activities with children	25.7 (3.5)	
• Frequently displays nurturance/affection to children	27.0 (3.4)	
• Has not had a child of his or her own placed in foster care	91.8 (1.2)	
Sample size	479	Varied

Note: NCS-R = National Comorbidity Survey Replication; NCPTP = National Campaign to Prevent Teen and Unplanned Pregnancy; NCHS = National Center for Health Statistics.

Further supporting this idea, the vast majority (85.7%) of alumni who were married or cohabitating were not socially isolated (that is, they had three or more friends). Alumni who were single and not cohabitating (52.9%) had a slightly higher rate of social isolation (74.8% had three or more friends).

Among those alumni who were married or cohabitating, about three in five (61.2%) reported having no violence in their relationship, as measured using the psychological aggression and physical assault subscales from the revised Conflict Tactics Scale (Straus, 1979; Straus & Gelles, 1989). However, the proportion of alumni experiencing violence in their relationships (38.8%) was more than double that of the general population (16%) (Straus et al., 1996). The rate found in the current study is closer to the 31.9% found in people of the same age in the general population by the National Comorbidity Study (Nancy Sampson, personal communication, October 16, 2008). While gender differences in domestic violence were not a focus of this study, they were briefly examined. Of the alumni who were currently married, a higher percentage of men (70.5%) reported having no violence in their relationship compared to women (57.3%). However, this difference did not reach statistical significance. Domestic violence is not only detrimental to the parents' relationship, but their children are at risk of witnessing this violence, which can strain the relationship between parents and children and increase the children's chances of entering the child welfare system.

While much literature has suggested that adult partner violence can be explained by intergenerational transmission (Widom, 1989b), research also indicates that most people who were raised in violent families do not become violent partners themselves. Lackey and Williams (1995) found that men from violent families who are attached to their partner, friends, and relatives are less likely to engage in partner violence as adults. Findings in the current study are consistent with the literature that suggests that most adults from violent families do not engage in partner violence as adults; however, these alumni of foster care, many of whom were physically abused (64.6%; see Chapter 5), did engage in partner violence at rates higher than the general population.

Social Support From Friends and Relatives

In addition to support from a spouse or partner, people derive social support from relationships with others, including friends, peers, neighbors, and other relatives (Lackey & Williams, 1995; Ross & Mirowsky, 2002; Wellman & Wortley, 1990). When considering alumni's social support networks of friends and relatives, it is important to examine both positive and negative aspects. Positive social support was defined as receiving strong understanding and help from friends and relatives, while negative social support entailed demands, stress, and arguments.

Support experienced by alumni was mixed. One-half of alumni (49.2%) reported receiving positive social support from friends and relatives, while one-quarter (25.0%) experienced negative social support. These numbers are similar to those reported by the National Comorbidity Survey Replication (NCS-R): 42.5% reported receiving positive support and 31.3% reported receiving negative support.[74] The vast majority of alumni (88.2%) reported no serious fighting with anyone in the past 12 months.

Contact With Birth Family

The potential harm and benefit of contact with birth families has been the topic of much research. Many studies find great benefit for youth who maintain some contact with their birth families. As discussed in Chapter 2, maintaining positive connections to birth families, siblings, and kin is critical in the development of youth regardless of how long they have been in out-of-home care before achieving permanency (Bernstein, 2000; Berrick et al., 1998; Casey Family Programs, 2000). While the research base is not extensive, some studies have shown that youth in out-of-home care who are placed with their siblings and who have contact with their birth parents while in care have better outcomes than youth who do not (Barth, 1986; Fanshel et al., 1990; Iglehart, 1994; Leathers, 2005). This may be because interacting with birth families gives youth an identity, a sense of cultural self, and a historical connection. In some cases, contact with the birth family is not recommended. This may be because of child safety concerns or because the child has been emotionally abandoned by family members for some reason, such as past behavior, the child's report of maltreatment, or homophobia that has led to rejection of the child.

Alumni in this study had more contact with their siblings (58.6%) than with either of their birth parents, which suggests relatively strong ties between alumni and their siblings. As discussed previously in this chapter, victims of child abuse derive great support from their relationships with siblings through adulthood (Muller et al., 2000). Mothers experienced the second most frequent contact (40.9% of alumni reported being in contact with their mothers at least a few times a month). Birth fathers were contacted least often (20.5%). Two-thirds of alumni were in contact with other relatives who were not in their household at least a few times a month. This underscores the importance of connecting youth in foster care with other relatives and the potentially greater roles that these relatives could play in terms of providing guidance and ongoing support, or becoming legal guardians or adoptive parents.

Contact With Foster Parents and the Former Child Welfare Agency

The majority of alumni reported having some contact with their former foster parents (61.9%). Of these, 35.8% had contact about once a month or less, and 26.0% had contact a few times a month or more. The percentage of alumni in contact with their former foster parents is higher than for any other category of birth family members, even siblings. For more information about contact with former foster parents and the former child welfare agency, see O'Brien et al. (2009a).

However, only 21.9% of alumni said that a child welfare agency had been helpful to them since leaving foster care. This suggests that the majority of alumni developed lasting relationships with their foster parents and that their foster parents are part of the alumni's social support networks. At the same time, most alumni do not appear to have continuing support from the child welfare system at an organizational level.

Parenting

Child-Rearing Status and Parenting Scale Scores

While most alumni reported not having had a child before age 18 (92.7%) or before marriage (82.0%), a large proportion of alumni (63.0%) were parents at the time of their interview (see Table 9.1). A recent large study of 19-year-old alumni (a much younger sample than in the current study) of foster care found that 23.4% had children (Courtney et al., 2005b). In the general population, 91.6% of women did not have a child before the age of 20 (National Campaign to Prevent Teenage Pregnancy, 2004), while the National Center for Health Statistics (2005) reports that 34.6 % of births in 2003, to women aged 15 to 44, involved unmarried women.

Using parenting scales[75] that measured the frequency with which alumni performed certain parenting behaviors, one-fourth of alumni with children (25.7%) reported that they do many activities with their children (e.g., doing dishes together, going to the store together, looking at books or reading stories with them). Just over a quarter (27.0%) of alumni with children reported that they frequently display nurturance and affection toward their children (e.g., hugging or showing physical affection, verbally expressing love). These percentages are lower than would be expected of parents with healthy, positive relationships with their children.

Placement of Children of Alumni in Foster Care

As predicted by the Northwest Alumni Study's conceptual framework and previous research on the importance of positive support networks, a disproportionately high rate of children of alumni are placed in foster care. Of alumni with children, 8.2% had a child placed in foster care; nationally, approximately 1.1% of children are placed in foster care every year. Note that the two rates may actually differ less if the general population rate is aggregated over a 10-year period, which is the post–foster care period covered by the Northwest Alumni Study.[76]

The relatively high rate of placement of children of alumni in foster care, along with the low scores on the parenting scales, indicates that there may be a small but notable multigenerational cycle of placement in foster care—at least in this sample. Some alumni have not been able to avoid repeating the child-rearing mistakes of their parents or have become overwhelmed by poverty or mental illness. Many theories might explain the parenting styles of youth from foster care. It may be that a dearth of positive role models in the lives of these youth results in a lack of the skills necessary to parent their own children. Alternately, because they realize how important a positive relationship with a parent or caring adult is, alumni may be conscientious in providing this to their own children; if they didn't, the rate would be even higher (Casey Family Programs, 2005a).

In general, parenting efficacy has been shown to be related to the degree of familial discord experienced by mothers. Satisfaction with social support from family and friends may enhance parenting efficacy (Ortega, 2002). Effective parenting eliminates the need to place children in the child welfare system.[77]

Other Areas of Social Support

In addition to the primary means of social support discussed above (marriage, cohabitation, and parenting), alumni draw on other relationships and institutions for support. These variables were not included in the multivariate analysis, but they are presented here because of their potential importance and impact as social supports for alumni. These variables include religiosity and ethnic identity.

Religiosity

Religion can be a very powerful form of support for an individual. Regular church attendance by families has been shown to significantly improve children's functioning (Runyan et al., 1998b). Other researchers have found that weekly religious attendance is associated with a statistically significant increase in quitting smoking, becoming more physically active, avoiding depression, increasing the number of personal relationships, and getting married (Strawbridge, Sherma, Cohen, & Kaplan, 2001). Over one-third of the alumni interviewed (34.5%) said that they attended religious services at least once per month. Over two in five alumni (42.2%) said that they often or almost always seek spiritual comfort when they experience difficulties in their family, work, or personal lives. Additionally, nearly two-thirds of alumni (63.6%) reported having volunteered in the community or church at some point in their lives (O'Brien et al., 2009a). This is not unlike what White et al. (2007) found in a study of adolescents in foster care.

However, not all religions, belief systems, and other spiritual traditions are appropriate for all youth in foster care. For instance, some fundamentalist belief systems reject youth who identify as gay, lesbian, bisexual, transgendered, or questioning (GLBTQ; e.g., Child Welfare League of America, 2006a; Downs, 2006). Caseworkers and parents should carefully match youth with belief systems that work best for them.

Ethnic Identity

Ethnic identity has been regarded as an important part of child development that may help children remain strong and resilient during difficult times (Gonzales & Cauce, 1995; Rodriguez, Cauce, & Wilson, 2000). Alumni of color comprised over half (54.4%) of the Northwest Alumni Study sample. Almost three-fourths (74.3%) of the alumni of color reported that they identified somewhat or strongly with their own ethnic group. More than half of the alumni of color (56.3%) felt that they fit into groups of people of only their own ethnicity, and over one-third (36.5%) felt that they fit into a white-only group.

Summary

While definitive literature is lacking on the importance of each of the dimensions of social support, substantial research indicates that social support networks help mediate stress, as well as enhance mental and physical health. Children entering foster care because of physical abuse, sexual abuse, neglect, or any other reason experience enormous changes and a great deal of stress. In addition to being separated from their family, many children are unable to maintain relationships with friends and community members upon initial placement (Johnson, Yoken, & Voss, 1995). Changing homes because of placement disruption compounds the immeasurable sense of loss that these children must face by repeatedly leaving relationships behind (Festinger, 1983; Herrick & Piccus, 2005). Social supports can act as a buffer against the negative effects of these highly stressful situations. In fact, young adults who were maltreated as youth have been found to achieve better psychological adjustment when they have high levels of current perceived social support (e.g., Runtz, 1991; Runtz & Schallow, 1997).

The data reveal a mixed picture of both supports and stresses in relationships with relatives, foster parents, and others. For example, alumni in the Northwest Alumni Study had fairly high rates of marriage (although lower than that of the general population) and cohabitation. They reported high rates of satisfaction with their relationships; however, twice as many alumni reported marital violence as the general population. The alumni with children reported low rates of nurturing and affection for their children, and nearly 1 in 10 of those with children (8.2%) had their children placed in foster care. This lends support to the idea of intergenerational transmission of poor parenting skills despite the high levels of marital and cohabitative supports present.

Alumni reported receiving positive social support more frequently than negative social support from friends and relatives. Of all living relatives, the highest percentage of alumni are in contact with their siblings, followed by contact with their birth mother. Almost two-thirds of alumni are in contact with their former foster parents. Alumni report low rates of social isolation, though higher rates are reported by single alumni than by married or cohabitating alumni. More than half of alumni reported being involved in religious activities such as attending religious services and volunteering in a community or church or seeking spiritual comfort in times of difficulty. See O'Brien et al. (2009b) for the effects of demographics and risk factors on outcomes and Chapter 11 for the effects of the foster care experience on outcomes.

Acknowledgment.   Catherine Roller White, A. Chris Downs, and Anne Havalchak contributed to this chapter.

10

Relation Between Agency Membership
and Outcomes

QUESTION: If you could tell children coming into the foster care agency anything right now, what would you tell them?

ANSWER: Take advantage of the school programs and all of the extracurricular programs, because they are not going to get all of that when they get out on their own.

Overview

This chapter examines the third major research question: Is one foster care program approach better than another in terms of outcomes? It was hypothesized that Casey alumni would exhibit more desirable outcomes than state alumni. To test this hypothesis, the relation between the location in which alumni were served (agency and state) and outcomes (e.g., PTSD in last 12 months, current employment) was examined after controlling for demographics and risk factors that were significant in a stepwise logistic regression (see Chapters 3 and 5 for a description of those variables).

Odds Ratios

An odds ratio is a measure of the relative proportion of people with a positive score on a dichotomous (yes-no) outcome among people who differ on a predictor variable. If we define p_1 as the proportion of respondents in predictor group 1 who have a positive score on a given outcome and p_2 as the comparable proportion in predictor group 2 (e.g., where group 1 consists of males and group 2 of females and we are examining the predictive effect of gender on the outcome), then the unadjusted (i.e., without controls for other variables) odds ratio of the predictor (Group 1: Group 2) with the outcome equals the odds p_1/q_1 (where q_1 is the additive reciprocal of p_1 and the sum $p_1 + q_1 = 1.0$) divided by the odds p_2/q_2. The upper end of the odds ratio is unbounded, while the lower bound is 0.0. The odds ratios presented in this volume are largely used to quantify the relative odds of diverse dichotomously defined outcomes among alumni served by Casey compared to those served by the public programs. For example, if 80% of the Casey alumni were currently employed and 60% of the state alumni were currently employed, the odds ratio would be (80 / 20) / (60 / 40)] = 2.7. We would interpret this as telling us that Casey alumni have a 2.7 times higher odds of being currently employed than state alumni. The odds ratios we report were all obtained using logistic regression analysis (Hosmer & Lemeshow, 2004). Logistic regression coefficients can be interpreted as the natural logarithms of odds ratios. We consequently exponentiated the logistic regression coefficients to obtain odds ratios. Ninety-five percent confidence intervals (95% CI) of the odds ratios are also reported routinely in all tables that present odds ratios.

To ease interpretation of the odds ratios, all outcomes are phrased positively (e.g., *no PTSD in last 12 months, no major depression in last 12 months*) and are coded such that the preferable outcome is 1 and the less preferable outcome is 0. The agency variable is coded as Casey = 1 and state = 0. Therefore, an odds ratio greater than 1.0 means that alumni from Casey had significantly higher odds of a positive outcome than the state ($p < .05$, two-tailed). If the odds— the proportion of those with versus without the outcome—are equivalent, this odds ratio will be 1.0; this means that there is no association between the foster care program (Casey or state) and the outcome.

The relation between outcomes and foster care agency (Casey vs. state) was examined by separately regressing each outcome on agency membership (after controlling for demographics and risk factors) in a series of logistic regressions. As described in Chapter 4, data were weighted to adjust for non-random survey non-response and to adjust for differences in Casey and state samples in baseline characteristics.

Odds ratios evaluating these relations are presented in Tables 10.3–10.7. Each odds ratio shows the relative likelihood of attaining an outcome given a participant's service from a particular agency (Casey or state) and/or in a particular state (Washington or Oregon) compared to an alternative agency and/or state. Specifically, odds ratios were calculated for the following three conditions:

1. Interaction (always tested prior to subsequent conditions): tested whether the relation between agency and outcomes differed by state (Washington or Oregon)
2. Agency Main Effect (examined only if the Interaction was *not* significant): tested whether outcomes differed by agency (all Casey alumni compared to all state alumni averaged across the two states)
3. Within State Agency Effects (examined only if the Interaction was significant): tested whether outcomes differed by agency (Casey compared to state) separately in Washington and in Oregon.

When the Interaction was not statistically significant for an individual outcome, the Agency Main Effect is presented, while Within State Agency Effects are not presented (thus, the cells are blank). Conversely, when the Interaction was significant, the Agency Main Effect is not presented (thus, the cells are blank), and Within State Agency Effects are presented. For example, in Table 10.3, the Interaction was significant for the outcome *no generalized anxiety in last 12 months* but was not significant for *no drug dependence in last 12 months.* Therefore, for *no generalized anxiety in last 12 months,* Within State Agency Effects were examined. For the two Within State Agency Effects comparisons, no statistically significant difference was found between Casey and state alumni in Washington, but a significant difference was found between Casey and state alumni in Oregon. In Oregon, the odds of Casey alumni having *no generalized anxiety in last 12 months* were 11.9 times greater than those of state alumni. In contrast, because the Interaction for *no drug dependence in last 12 months* was not significant, only the Agency Main Effect was examined. No significant difference was found between Casey and the state. (These odds ratios do not imply a causal relationship between variables.)

Limitations

As described in Chapter 4, study findings should be viewed with some caution because of the following potential study limitations:

1. Comparisons between Casey and the state agencies should be interpreted with caution because Casey field offices were not operating under the workload pressures of achieving a permanent placement in the same way that the public agency staff were. Namely, because the children referred to Casey were those that the state agency and the juvenile court determined were unable or unwilling to be adopted or be reunified with their parents, Casey staff had the goal of stabilizing and preserving the placement.
2. The Northwest Alumni Study focused on alumni who had spent one year or more in foster care as adolescents. Many of these youth tend to stay in care for longer periods of time or enter care as adolescents (e.g., at age 16) and emancipate from care in *both* public and private systems. This was a study of a group of alumni who spent a year or more in care as *adolescents;* therefore, participants do not represent the full spectrum of children served in foster care.
3. There were differences between Casey and state alumni in certain risk factors and foster care experiences. For example, Casey alumni stayed in care an average of two years longer than state alumni, and there were differences in child maltreatment history in the birth family (e.g., more Casey youth had been sexually abused than youth in the state agencies). Weighting and propensity score matching were conducted to minimize these differences; however, the full range of differences may not have been addressed by these statistical techniques.

The Effects of Location on Outcomes

Expected Results

As discussed in Chapter 2, it was hypothesized that Casey alumni would exhibit more desirable outcomes than their state counterparts due to their access to additional resources. Before this Agency Main Effect could be examined, the Interaction was tested. The Interaction tested whether the relation between agency and outcomes differed by state, which was not expected. The expectations for each condition described above are presented in Table 10.1. Further, Tables 10.3–10.7 are set up such that odds ratios greater than 1.0 (and statistically significant) were expected. The reference group was the group least likely to achieve desirable outcomes. Although the State Main Effect could have been examined, those data are not presented because it was not a question of interest.

Because of the large number of odds ratios, data were summarized for each of the five outcome domains and across all outcome domains. The percentages of expected and unexpected results are presented for the Interaction, Agency Main Effect, and Within State Agency Effects. For example, as discussed previously, it was expected that the Interaction would not be significant. Table 10.2 presents the percentage of time the Interaction was not statistically significant (labeled "Exp." for "expected" in the table) and the percentage of time the Interaction was significant (labeled "Unexp." for "unexpected" in the table; "Exp." plus "Unexp." equals 100%). If the Interaction was not significant for every individual outcome within a domain (i.e., "Exp." equals 100.0%), the Within State Agency Effects were not applicable ("N/A") because only the Agency Main Effect needed to be examined. However, if the Interaction was not significant for some variables in a domain and was significant for other variables in the domain, the Agency Main Effect and Within Agency Effects were both evaluated. Within each state, Casey alumni were expected to exhibit more desirable outcomes. Because the focus of this chapter is the Agency Main Effect, specific examples highlighting differences between Casey and state outcomes are presented.

Mental Health

1. *Interaction*: As presented in Table 10.2, the interaction was not statistically significant for 8 of 10 mental health items (80.0%) (labeled "Exp." for "expected").
2. *Agency Main Effect*: Casey alumni exhibited significantly more desirable results ($p < .05$, two-tailed) when compared to state alumni on four individual Mental Health outcomes (50.0% of eight Mental Health outcomes for which the Interaction was not statistically significant) (labeled "Exp." for "expected"); state alumni exhibited significantly more desirable results when compared to Casey alumni on zero of eight (labeled "Unexp." for "unexpected"); and there was no statistically significant difference between alumni served by the two agencies on four (50.0%). The percentage of outcomes with no significant differences between Casey and the state is not presented in the table, but it can be calculated by the following computation: 100 – (Exp. + Unexp.). As seen in Table 10.3, when compared to alumni served by the state, alumni served by Casey had

   - 1.5 times higher odds of having *no 12-month CIDI diagnosis*
   - 1.8 times higher odds of having a *total number of 12-month CIDI diagnoses fewer than three*

Table 10.1. Key for Interpreting Findings Presented in Table 10.2

Condition	Comparison	Reference Group	Expectation	Definition in Table 10.2	
				Expected	Unexpected
Interaction	Casey alumni served in Washington compared to all other alumni	All alumni except Casey alumni served in Washington	The Interaction would not be significant	Interaction not significant	Interaction significant
Agency Main Effect	Agency (Casey alumni compared to state alumni)	State alumni	Casey alumni would exhibit more desirable outcomes compared to state alumni	Casey alumni would exhibit more desirable outcomes compared to state alumni	State alumni would exhibit more desirable outcomes compared to Casey alumni
Within State Agency Effects	In Washington (Casey alumni compared to state alumni)	State alumni in Washington	Casey alumni served in Washington would exhibit more desirable outcomes compared to state alumni served in Washington	Casey alumni served in Washington would exhibit more desirable outcomes compared to state alumni served in Washington	State alumni served in Washington would exhibit more desirable outcomes compared to Casey alumni served in Washington
	In Oregon (Casey alumni compared to state alumni)	State alumni in Oregon	Casey alumni served in Oregon would exhibit more desirable outcomes compared to state alumni served in Oregon	Casey alumni served in Oregon would exhibit more desirable outcomes compared to state alumni served in Oregon	State alumni served in Oregon would exhibit more desirable outcomes compared to Casey alumni served in Oregon

Table 10.2. Expected and Unexpected Results for Each of the Three Conditions (%)

		Outcome Domain										
		Mental Health (10)		Physical Health (6)		Education (5)		Employment and Finances (14)		Relationships and Social Supports (13)		All Outcomes (48)	
Conditions		Exp.	Unexp.	Exp.	Unexp.	Exp.	Unexp.	Exp.	Unexp.	Exp.	Unexp.	Exp.	Unexp.
Interaction		80.0	20.0	100.0	0.0	100.0	0.0	42.9	57.1	76.9	23.1	72.9	27.1
Agency Main Effect[a]	Agency	50.0	0.0	16.7	16.7	80.0	0.0	33.3	16.7	10.0	40.0	34.3	17.1
Within State Agency Effects[b]	Washington	0.0	0.0	n/a	n/a	n/a	n/a	0.0	25.0	66.7	0.0	15.4	0.0
	Oregon	100.0	0.0	n/a	n/a	n/a	n/a	87.5	0.0	66.7	0.0	84.6	0.0

Note: For the Interaction, Exp. (expected) is the percentage of time the Interaction was significant, while Unexp. (unexpected) is the percentage of time the Interaction was significant.

For the Agency Main Effect, Exp. is the percentage of time Casey alumni exhibited more desirable outcomes than state alumni, while Unexp. is the percentage of time state alumni exhibited more desirable outcomes than Casey alumni.

For the Washington Within State Agency Effect, Exp. is the percentage of time Casey alumni in Washington exhibited more desirable outcomes than state alumni in Washington, while Unexp. is the percentage of time state alumni in Washington exhibited more desirable outcomes than Casey alumni in Washington.

For the Oregon Within State Agency Effect, Exp. is the percentage of time Casey alumni in Oregon exhibited more desirable outcomes than state alumni in Oregon, while Unexp. is the percentage of time state alumni in Oregon exhibited more desirable outcomes than Casey alumni in Oregon.

Except for the test of the Interaction (where Exp. and Unexp. sum to 100%), odds ratios that were not significant were not included in this table. However, they can be determined by adding the expected and unexpected significant percentages together for an area and domain and subtracting from 100.

[a]The Agency Main effect was examined only when the Interaction was not significant.

[b]Within State Agency Effects were examined only when the Interaction was significant.

Table 10.3. The Relationship between Location and Mental Health Outcomes[a]

	Mental Health Outcomes: Odds Ratios (95% CIs)				
Conditions	No 12-Month CIDI Diagnosis	Total Number of 12-Month CIDI Diagnoses Was Fewer Than Three	No Major Depression in Last 12 Months	No Panic Syndrome in Last 12 Months	No Modified Social Phobia in Last 12 Months
I. Interaction					
Casey x Washington (compared to Others[b])	0.6 (0.2–1.4)	0.4 (0.1–1.9)	1.4 (0.4–4.1)	0.4 (0.1–1.6)	0.3 (0.1–1.4)
II. Agency Main Effect					
Casey (compared to state)	1.5 (1.0–2.1)*	1.8 (1.1–3.0)*	2.0 (1.2–3.4)*	1.5 (0.9–2.3)	1.8 (1.1–3.0)*
III. Within State Agency Effects					
Washington Casey (compared to Washington State alumni)					
Oregon Casey (compared to Oregon State alumni)					

Mental Health Outcomes: Odds Ratios (95% Confidence Intervals)

Conditions	No Alcohol Dependence in Last 12 Months	No Drug Dependence in Last 12 Months	No PTSD in Last 12 Months	No Generalized Anxiety in Last 12 Months	SF-12 Mental Health Score of 50 or Above
Interaction					
Casey x Washington (compared to Others[b])	0.0 (0.0–0.0)*	0.4 (0.1–2.5)	0.5 (0.2–2.0)	0.1 (0.0–0.7)*	2.3 (0.9–5.6)
Agency Main Effect					
Casey (compared to state)		1.4 (0.6–3.1)	1.4 (0.9–2.1)		1.0 (0.7–1.4)
Within State Agency Effects					
Washington Casey (compared to Washington State alumni)	0.6 (0.3–1.1)			1.5 (0.8–2.8)	
Oregon Casey (compared to Oregon State alumni)	>100 (—)*			11.9 (2.1–66.0)*	

*Significant at p < .05, two-sided.

[a]Cells with darker shading indicate findings in the expected direction: for the interaction, it was expected that the odds ratios would not be significant; for all other effects, it was expected that odds ratio would be significant. Cells with lighter shading indicate that the odds ratio is significant and in the unexpected direction. If a cell is not shaded, the odds ratio was not significant.

[b]Compared to Casey x Oregon, State x Washington, and State x Oregon.

[c]For this cell, the odds ratio and the lower bound limit of the CI exceeded 100 and was excluded from the table due to its large size.

- 2.0 times higher odds of having *no major depression in last 12 months*
- 1.8 times higher odds of having *no modified social phobia in last 12 months*

3. *Within State Agency Effects*: In Washington, there was no statistically significant difference between Casey and state alumni on the two Mental Health items (i.e., *no alcohol dependence in last 12 months* and *no generalized anxiety in last 12 months*) where the Interaction was significant (100.0%, not presented in Table 10.2). Within Oregon, Casey alumni exhibited more desirable results on both of these Mental Health outcomes.

Physical Health

1. *Interaction*: As presented in Table 10.2, the interaction was not significant for any of the six Physical Health outcomes.
2. *Agency Main Effect*: Casey alumni exhibited significantly more desirable results when compared to state alumni on one Physical Health outcome (16.7% of the six Physical Health outcomes for which the Interaction was not statistically significant), and state alumni exhibited significantly more desirable results when compared to Casey alumni on one Physical Health outcome (16.7%). There was no significant difference between alumni served by the two agencies on four individual Physical Health outcomes (66.7%). For example, as seen in Table 10.4, Casey alumni had 1.8 times higher odds of having *no chronic physical disorder* (such as heart disease, high blood pressure, or human immunodeficiency virus/acquired immunodeficiency virus [HIV/AIDS]) compared to state alumni, while state alumni had 2.5 times higher odds[81] of *smoking fewer than 10 cigarettes per day* compared to Casey alumni.
3. *Within State Agency Effects:* Not applicable. These are not presented because Interactions were not significant for all outcomes.

Education

1. *Interaction*: As presented in Table 10.2, the Interaction was not significant for any of the five Education outcomes.
2. *Agency Main Effect*: Casey alumni exhibited more desirable results when compared to state alumni on four Education outcomes (80.0% of the five Education outcomes for which the Interaction was not statistically significant); state alumni exhibited more desirable results when compared to Casey alumni on zero outcomes; and there was no significant difference between alumni served by the two agencies on one outcome (20.0%). For example, as seen in Table 10.5, when compared to alumni served by the state, alumni served by Casey had

- 2.4 times higher odds of having *completed high school with a diploma*
- 2.0 times higher odds of having *any education past high school*
- 2.6 times higher odds of having *any degree/certificate beyond high school*
- 3.7 times higher odds of having *completed college or more (has BA or more)*

3. *Within State Agency Effects:* Not applicable. These are not presented because interactions were not significant for all outcomes.

Table 10.4. The Relationship Between Location and Physical Health Outcomes[a]

	Physical Health Outcomes: Odds Ratios (95% CI)					
Conditions	No Chronic Physical Disorder	SF-12 Physical Health Score of 50 or Above	Does Not Smoke Currently	Smokes Fewer Than 10 Cigarettes Per Day	Does Not Drink Currently	Drinks Fewer Than 150 Drinks Per Year
I. Interaction						
Casey x Washington (compared to Others[b])	1.7 (0.7–4.2)	0.4 (0.2–1.2)	1.3 (0.6–3.0)	1.9 (0.7–5.2)	1.2 (0.5–3.1)	1.3 (0.5–3.7)
II. Agency Main Effect						
Casey (compared to state)	1.8 (1.2–2.7)*	1.0 (0.7–1.4)	0.8 (0.5–1.0)	0.4 (0.3–0.6)*	0.7 (0.5–1.0)	0.8 (0.6–1.2)
III. Within State Agency Effects						
Washington Casey (compared to Washington State alumni)						
Oregon Casey (compared to Oregon State alumni)						

*Significant at $p < .05$, two-sided.

[a]Cells with darker shading indicate findings in the expected direction: for the interaction, it was expected that the odds ratios would not be significant; for all other effects, it was expected that odds ratio would be significant. Cells with lighter shading indicate that the odds ratio is significant and in the unexpected direction. If a cell is not shaded, the odds ratio was not significant.

[b]Compared to Casey x Oregon, State x Washington, and State x Oregon.

Table 10.5. The Relationship Between Location and Educational Outcomes[a]

Conditions	Educational Outcomes: Odds Ratios (95% Confidence Intervals)				
	Completed High School—High School Diploma or GED	Completed High School—High School Diploma Only	Any Education Past High School	Completed Any Degree/Certificate Beyond High School	Completed College or More (Has BA or More)
I. Interaction					
Casey x Washington (compared to Others)[b]	1.0 (0.3–2.9)	0.5 (0.2–1.4)	1.1 (0.4–2.7)	0.5 (0.2–1.4)	1.1 (0.2–5.6)
II. Agency Main Effect					
Casey (compared to state)	1.2 (0.7–1.9)	2.4 (1.6–3.4)*	2.0 (1.4–2.9)*	2.6 (1.8–3.7)*	3.7 (2.0–6.9)*
III. Within State Agency Effects					
Washington Casey (compared to Washington State alumni)					
Oregon Casey (compared to Oregon State alumni)					

*Significant at $p < .05$, two-sided.

[a]Cells with darker shading indicate findings in the expected direction: for the interaction, it was expected that the odds ratios would not be significant; for all other effects, it was expected that odds ratio would be significant. Cells with lighter shading indicate that the odds ratio is significant and in the unexpected direction. If a cell is not shaded, the odds ratio was not significant.

[b]Compared to Casey x Oregon, State x Washington, and State x Oregon.

Employment and Finances

1. *Interaction*: As presented in Table 10.2, the interaction was not significant for 6 of 14 Employment and Finances outcomes (42.9%).
2. *Agency Main Effect*: Casey alumni exhibited significantly more desirable results when compared to state alumni on two Employment and Finances outcomes (33.3% of the six Employment and Finances outcomes for which the Interaction was not significant); state alumni exhibited more desirable results when compared to Casey alumni on one (16.7%); and there was no significant difference between alumni served by the two agencies on the other three (50.0%). For example, as seen in Table 10.6, Casey alumni had 1.7 times higher odds of not being *homeless within one year after leaving foster care* than state alumni. Meanwhile, state alumni had 2.5 times higher odds of *owning a house or apartment* than Casey alumni.
3. *Within State Agency Effects*: In Washington, Casey alumni exhibited more desirable results when compared to state alumni on zero of the eight Employment and Finances outcomes where the Interaction was significant; state alumni exhibited more desirable results when compared to Casey alumni on two (25.0%); and there was no significant difference on six (75.0%). Given that Casey resources for life-skills development and subsidized youth employment experience were increased during the study period, this was not expected. In Oregon, Casey alumni exhibited more desirable results when compared to state alumni on seven Employment and Finances outcomes (87.5%); state alumni exhibited more desirable results when compared to Casey alumni on zero; and there was no significant difference on one (12.5%).

Relationships and Social Supports

1. *Interaction*: As presented in Table 10.2, the interaction was not significant for 10 of 13 Relationships and Social Supports outcomes (76.9%).
2. *Main Effect*: Casey alumni exhibited more desirable results than state alumni on one Relationships and Social Supports outcome (10.0% of the 10 Relationships and Social Supports outcomes for which the Interaction was not significant); state alumni exhibited more desirable results when compared to Casey alumni on four (40.0%); and there was no significant difference between alumni served by the two agencies on five (50.0%). For example, as seen in Table 10.7, Casey alumni had 1.9 times higher odds of having *frequent displays of nurturance/affection with children* (among alumni with children). Meanwhile, when compared to alumni served by Casey, alumni served by the state had

   • 2.5 times higher odds of being *not socially isolated if married or cohabitating*
   • 1.4 times higher odds of *experiencing positive social support from friends/ relatives*
   • 1.4 times higher odds of having *no children before marriage*
   • 2.0 times higher odds of having *no children of their own placed in foster care*

3. *Within State Agency Effects*: In Washington, Casey alumni exhibited more desirable results when compared to state alumni on two of the three Relationships and Social Supports outcomes where the Interaction was significant (66.7%); state alumni exhibited more desirable results when

Table 10.6. The Relationship Between Location and Employment and Finances Outcomes[a]

| | | Employment and Finances: Odds Ratios (95% CIs) | | | | | | | |
| | | Public Assistance | | | Household Income Greater Than: | | | |
Conditions	Not Homeless Within One Year After Leaving Care	Never on Public Assistance After Age 18	Currently Does Not Receive Cash Public Assistance	No One in Household Received a Form of Public Aid in the Last Six Months	Household Income Above the Poverty Level	Household Income Greater Than Three Times the Poverty Level	Has Health Insurance of Any Kind	Owns House or Apartment
I. Interaction								
Casey x Washington (compared to Others[b])	2.1 (0.6–6.8)	0.2 (0.1–0.4)*	0.3 (0.1–0.8)*	0.2 (0.1–0.6)*	0.5 (0.2–1.2)	0.1 (0.0–0.2)*	0.9 (0.3–2.7)	0.5 (0.1–3.0)
II. Agency Main Effect								
Casey (compared to state)	1.7 (1.1–2.5)*				1.4 (0.9–2.1)		1.4 (0.9–2.1)	0.4 (0.2–0.8)*
III. Within State Agency Effects								
Washington Casey (compared to Washington State alumni)		0.4 (0.3–0.6)*	0.9 (0.5–1.4)	0.8 (0.5–1.2)		0.3 (0.2–0.5)*		
Oregon Casey (compared to Oregon State alumni)		2.3 (1.0–5.5)	3.2 (1.2–8.4)*	3.5 (1.4–8.3)*		3.5 (1.4–9.0)*		

Employment and Finances (for Gender Subgroups): Odds Ratios (95% CIs)

	Employed (Studying)			Employed (Not Studying)		
		Females			Females	
Conditions	Males	Not Married	Married	Males	Not Married	Married
I. Interaction						
Casey x Washington (compared to Others[b])	0.5 (0.1–2.6)	0.0 (0.0–0.0)*	1.2 (0.2–7.3)	0.1 (0.0–0.7)*	0.0 (0.0–0.0)*	0.1 (0.0–0.9)*
II. Agency Main Effect						
Casey (compared to state)	0.6 (0.3–1.1)		2.5 (1.1–6.0)*			
III. Within State Agency Effects						
Washington Casey (compared to Washington State alumni)		1.0 (0.4–2.5)		0.7 (0.3–1.3)	1.8 (0.8–4.0)	0.7 (0.3–1.7)
Oregon Casey (compared to Oregon State alumni)		>100 (—)*		6.4 (1.1–38.1)*		4.6 (1.1–18.9)*

*Significant at p < .05, two-sided.

[a] Cells with darker shading indicate findings in the expected direction: for the interaction, it was expected that the odds ratios would not be significant; for all other effects, it was expected that odds ratio would be significant. Cells with lighter shading indicate that the odds ratio is significant and in the unexpected direction. If a cell is not shaded, the odds ratio was not significant.

[b] Compared to Casey x Oregon, State x Washington, and State x Oregon.

[c] For this cell, the odds ratio and the lower bound limit of the CI exceeded 100 and was excluded from the table due to its large size.

Table 10.7.   The Relationship Between Location and Relationships and Social Supports Outcomes[a]

			Relationships and Social Supports: Odds Ratios (95% CIs)				
			Married or Cohabitating				
Conditions	No Violence in Relationship	Married or Cohabitating	Very Satisfied in Relationship	Not Socially Isolated	No Social Isolation Among Single and Not Cohabitating	No Serious Fighting With Anyone in Last 12 Months	No Neg. Social Support	Pos. Social Support
I. Interaction								
Casey x Washington (compared to Others[b])	0.3 (0.1–1.5)	0.9 (0.4–2.2)	1.1 (0.3–3.8)	0.4 (0.1–3.5)	0.0 (0.0–0.0)*	0.4 (0.1–2.1)	0.9 (0.3–2.5)	0.6 (0.3–1.4)
II. Agency Main Effect								
Casey (compared to state)	0.6 (0.3–1.2)	1.3 (0.9–1.9)	1.4 (0.8–2.5)	0.4 (0.2–0.6)*		1.0 (0.6–1.6)	0.7 (0.5–1.0)	0.7 (0.5–1.0)*
III. Within State Agency Effects								
Washington Casey (compared to Washington State alumni)					2.4 (1.2–5.0)*			
Oregon Casey (compared to Oregon State alumni)					>100 (—)*			

Relationships and Social Supports: Odds Ratios (95% CIs)

Conditions	Among Alumni with Children				
	No Children Before Age 18	No Children Before Marriage	Does Many Activities With Children	Frequent Displays of Nurturance/Affection With Children	Did Not Have His or Her Own Child Placed in Foster Care
I. Interaction					
Casey x Washington (compared to Others)[a]	0.0 (0.0–0.0)*	0.8 (0.2–2.6)	6.3 (1.7–23.4)*	0.7 (0.2–2.2)	1.1 (0.1–8.4)
II. Agency Main Effect					
Casey (compared to state)		0.7 (0.4–1.0)*		1.9 (1.1–3.4)*	0.5 (0.3–1.0)*
III. Within State Agency Effects					
Washington Casey (compared to Washington State alumni)	1.5 (0.8–2.8)		2.8 (1.5–5.5)*		
Oregon Casey (compared to Oregon State alumni)	>100 (—)*[c]		0.4 (0.1–1.4)		

*Significant at *p* < .05, two-sided.

[a]Cells with darker shading indicate findings in the expected direction: for the interaction, it was expected that the odds ratios would not be significant; for all other effects, it was expected that odds ratio would be significant. Cells with lighter shading indicate that the odds ratio is significant and in the unexpected direction. If a cell is not shaded, the odds ratio was not significant.

[b]Compared to Casey x Oregon, State x Washington, and State x Oregon.

[c]For this cell, the odds ratio and the lower bound limit of the CI exceeded 100 and was excluded from the table due to its large size.

compared to Casey alumni on zero; and there was no significant difference between alumni served by the two agencies on one (33.3%). In Oregon, Casey alumni exhibited more desirable results when compared to state alumni on two outcomes (66.7%); state alumni exhibited more desirable results when compared to Casey alumni on zero; and there was no significant difference between alumni served by the two agencies on one (33.3%).

Results for All Outcomes

1. *Interaction*: As presented in Table 10.2, the interaction was not significant for 35 of 48 outcomes (72.9%).
2. *Agency Main Effect*: Casey alumni exhibited more desirable results when compared to state alumni on 12 outcomes (34.3% of the 35 outcomes for which the Interaction was not significant; see above and Table 10.8); state alumni exhibited more desirable results when compared to Casey alumni on six outcomes (17.1%; see above and Table 10.8); and there was no significant difference between alumni served by the two agencies on 17 outcomes (48.6%).
3. *Within State Agency Effects*: In Washington, Casey alumni exhibited more desirable results when compared to state alumni on two of the 13 outcomes where the Interaction was significant (15.4%); state alumni exhibited more desirable results when compared to Casey alumni on two outcomes (15.4%); and there was no significant difference between alumni served by the two agencies on nine outcomes (69.2%). In Oregon, Casey alumni exhibited more desirable results when compared to state alumni on 11 outcomes (84.6%); state alumni exhibited more desirable results when compared to Casey alumni on zero; and there was no significant difference between alumni served by the two agencies in Oregon on two outcomes (15.4%).

Location Hypothesis

The question "Is one foster care program approach better than another in terms of outcomes?" has been partially answered by the data above. The numbers presented thus far may be inflated because differences between Casey and the state were evaluated only if the Interaction was not significant. In Table 10.8, no such adjustment was made. For example, in the analyses above, the Interaction was significant for 35 of 48 outcomes. When the Agency Main Effect was examined, 12 outcomes favored Casey, six favored the state, and there was no difference on 17. These numbers were divided by 35. A more conservative approach is presented in Table 10.8; this uses 48 outcomes as the total and includes all items in the analyses regardless of whether the Interaction was significant. Because it was hypothesized that Casey alumni would exhibit more desirable outcomes than state alumni, this may be a more appropriate evaluation. Every outcome examined is listed in Table 10.8 according to which alumni group fared better: Casey, the state, or no difference. It was found that Casey alumni exhibited more desirable outcomes on 12 of the 48 outcomes (25.0%), the state alumni on six of the 48 (12.5%), and there was no difference on 30 (62.5%). Most of the outcomes that favored Casey were in Mental Health and Education; those favoring the state were in Relationships and Social Supports; and no substantial difference was found for Physical Health and Employment and Finances.

Table 10.8. Summary of Casey and State Differences Across Outcomes[a]

	Outcome Domain					
	Mental Health		Physical Health		Education	
Effect	Item	% (out of 10)	Item	% (out of 6)	Item	% (out of 5)
Casey Better	• No 12-month CIDI diagnosis • Total number of CIDI diagnoses was fewer than three • No major depression in last 12 months • No modified social phobia in last 12 months	40.0	• No chronic physical disorder	16.7	• Completed high school—high school diploma only • Any education past high school (any type of post-secondary education) • Completed any degree/certificate beyond high school (vocational, BA, etc.) • Completed college or more (has BA or more)	80.0
State Better		0.0	• Smokes fewer than 10 cigarettes per day	16.7		0.0
No Difference	• No panic syndrome in last 12 months • No alcohol dependence in last 12 months • No drug dependence in last 12 months • No PTSD in last 12 months • No generalized anxiety in last 12 months • Short Form Health Survey 12 (SF-12) mental health score of 50 and above	60.0	• SF-12 physical health score of 50 or above[c] • Does not smoke currently • Does not drink currently • Drinks fewer than 150 drinks per year	66.7	• Completed high school diploma or GED	20.0

(continued)

Table 10.8.   Continued

| | Outcome Domain | | | | |
| | Employment and Finances | | Relationships and Social Supports | | Total |
Effect	Item	% (out of 14)	Item	% (out of 13)	% (out of 48)
Casey Better	• Not homeless within one year after leaving foster care • Employment for married women in school[b]	14.3	• Frequent displays of nurturance affection with children	7.7	25.0
State Better	• Owns house or apartment • Employment for single women *not* in school[b]	7.1	• No children before marriage • Did not have his or her own child placed in foster care • Not socially isolated in married or cohabiting relationship • Positive social support from friends and relatives	30.8	12.5
No Difference	• Never on public assistance after age 18 • Not receiving cash public assistance currently • No one in household on public assistance in last six months • Household income above the poverty level • Household income greater than three times the poverty level • Has health insurance of any kind • Employment for men *not* in school[b] • Employment for married women *not* in school[b] • Employment for men in school[b] • Employment for single women in school[b]	78.6	• Alumni married or cohabiting • No violence relationship • Very satisfied with marriage or cohabiting relationship • Not socially isolated if single and *not* cohabiting • No serious fighting with anyone in past 12 months • No negative social support from friends and relatives • No children before age 18 • Does many activities with children	61.5	62.5

[a] This table only reports main effects.

[b] The impact of Casey vs. state agency on employment outcomes was examined separately for men and women and within each gender, in subgroups defined by whether or not the respondent was still a student and, among women, by marital status. Marital status was used only among women because typically women have a legitimate role as homemaker if married and the husband makes enough money to support the family, whereas men typically have no equivalent role. Employment results are reported by subgroup because not having a job outside the home is not necessarily a poor outcome for a married woman or for a student.

[c] A score of 50 or higher indicates good physical or mental health (depending upon the particular SF-12 subscale).

Cost-Benefit Analyses

Service quality matters. In a recently competed set of analyses of the Northwest Alumni Study data, we found that quality foster care services for children pay big dividends when they become adults. More specifically, the mental and physical health of children placed in foster care improved when they were supported by child welfare programs with highly trained staff who had low caseloads and good access to supplementary services.

The Northwest Study supports a major assertion of Casey Family Programs' 2020 Strategy, which seeks better outcomes for children in care while moving to reduce the need for out-of-home care. The study demonstrated that key investments in quality foster care for adolescents are associated with dramatic reductions in the rates of mental disorders and substance abuse later in life. If child welfare agencies reinvest savings accrued through reduction of child placements, public and private agencies will be able to implement key program components linked with positive adult outcomes.

The hypothesis was that the alumni who received services from a program with a greater investment in the workforce and services would produce better outcomes. This was based on the assumption that alumni would experience foster care more favorably as a result of having social workers with graduate social work degrees and lower caseloads; foster parents with fewer turnovers and more training; and youth access to a wide array of education, mental health, and other services. Although there were many similarities in the way alumni experienced care and the outcomes they achieved, significant outcome differences were found in important areas. Specifically, Kessler et al. (2008) found that alumni who received higher-quality services

- Had significantly fewer placement changes.
- Were substantially less likely to experience adverse events such as a reunification failure during comparable periods of time in foster care.
- Were at lower risk of foster parent neglect, physical abuse, and sexual abuse.
- Had 50% reductions in rates of adult major depression and substance use disorders. They also had significantly fewer ulcers and cardiometabolic disorders but more respiratory disorders.
- Were more likely to have completed years of education beyond high school and to be employed.

These recent analyses document the economic advantages of high-quality foster care programs. For most of the outcomes listed above, a monetary value can be attached, allowing comparison with costs. For the outcomes for which financial data were available, the estimated present value of the enhanced foster care services exceeded their extra costs. More specifically, except for one health condition, all of the outcome differences expressed in monetary terms favored the alumni served by a program where there had been a greater fiscal investment and provision of high-quality services. The net aggregate benefits for the enhanced quality program were large at $206,305 per alumnus. In addition to the more positive education and employment outcomes, the cost savings from fewer chronic physical and mental disorders contribute to the net benefits. This finding is consistent with the study's hypothesis that the high-quality services produced better long-term outcomes.

Further, findings suggest that additional funds provided to state programs, or reinvestments in program improvements funded by savings from reduced foster care placement rates, may represent a worthwhile social investment. About 100,000 adolescents ages 12–17 enter foster care each year. If all of them were to receive enhanced foster care services including but not limited to lower caseloads for social workers, better-trained staff, fewer foster care placement changes, and fewer school changes, the long-term saving for a single cohort of these children would be about $6.3 billion (in 2007 dollars; Zerbe et al., 2009).

> *Question: If you could tell children coming into the foster care agency anything right now, what would you tell them?*
>
> *Answer: If it's [state foster care], then, "Forget it, good luck." If it's Casey and they're just joining the foster care system, "You're lucky; not many kids have the opportunity to be in a program like it."*

> *Question: Could anything have been done to improve the move from foster care to living on your own?*
>
> *Answer: Actually, no, they helped quite a bit. It was my fault when I messed up.*
>
> *Answer: Helped me when I was emancipated by giving me something. They gave me nothing and something needed to be done. It really sucks to be at such a young age and have to do it all yourself. Classes for skills, job corps. Being taught life skills, like balancing a checkbook, writing a check, etc. I had to learn on my own—I wasn't taught and it wasn't easy.*

Summary

This set of analyses enabled us to test one of the key hypotheses of this study, namely: Would the greater availability of support sources, lower worker and foster parent turnover, and other agency differences described in Chapter 1 enable Casey alumni to achieve more desirable outcomes as adults than state alumni? Although Casey alumni did exhibit more desirable outcomes overall, state alumni exhibited more desirable outcomes in some areas. And for the majority of outcomes, there was no difference between the performance of Casey and state alumni. However, as the cost-benefit analyses demonstrated, some of the outcome areas where Casey alumni were more positive are important, such as mental health, educational achievements, and physical health; these results produce a substantially positive cost-benefit ratio for the Casey model of foster care.

The next chapter will provide some insights into what foster care experiences—regardless of agency membership—may be most responsible for positive outcomes.

Acknowledgment.   Catherine Roller White and Eva Hiripi contributed to this chapter.

11

Relation Between Foster Care Experience and Outcomes

I was not into it. I wouldn't let anyone help me. If I would have, [the foster parents] may have been there. I don't know. It took a couple of tries to get to a home that was decent. By that time I was spoiled—I was so negative and closed up.

Overview

This chapter examines the third primary research question: Are there key factors or program components that are linked with better functioning in adulthood? It was hypothesized that a more positive foster care experience would be related to more desirable outcomes. These include:

1. A more stable placement history
2. Educational stability and more access to educational tutoring supports
3. More access to therapeutic service and supports
4. More involvement with the foster family
5. Greater preparation for leaving care (e.g., employment training and support)
6. More tangible resources upon leaving care (e.g., $250 in cash and a driver's license)
7. A positive relationship with an adult while growing up

This chapter examines the relation between a set of foster care experience variables and outcomes by summarizing 1,680 odds ratios. While some interpretation of unusual variables or findings is included, implications and recommendations are presented in Chapter 13. Each outcome (e.g., *no PTSD in last 12 months, no major depression in last 12 months*) was examined separately after controlling for demographics and risk factor variables that were significant in a stepwise logistic regression: agency serving the youth, the state in which the youth was served, and the Interaction between agency and state. The foster care experience variables and areas are listed below. (For more information about these variables, see Williams, Herrick, Pecora, & O'Brien, 2009).

Foster Care Experience Areas

1. Placement History
   - *Number of placements*
   - *Length of time in care (in years)*
   - *Placement change rate*
   - *Number of reunification failures*
   - *Number of runaways*
   - *Number of unlicensed living situations with friends or relatives*
2. Educational Services and Experience
   - *Could participate in supplemental educational services/tutoring*
   - *Total number of school changes from elementary through high school* (some changes may have occurred prior to entry into foster care)
3. Therapeutic Service and Supports
   - *Could participate in therapeutic service and supports*
4. Activities with Foster Family
   - *Participated often in activities with foster family*
5. Preparation for Leaving Care
   - *Degree of preparation for leaving care*
6. Leaving Care Resources
   - *Number of resources upon exiting care* (i.e., driver's license, $250 in cash, dishes and utensils)
7. Foster Family and Other Nurturing Support While in Care
   a. Parenting style of both foster parents, coded as
      - *Authoritative*
      - *Permissive*
      - *Authoritarian*
      - *Disengaged*
      - *Other*
   b. Other supports
      - *Felt loved while in foster care*
      - *Overall, foster parents were helpful*
      - *Foster family helped with ethnic issues*
      - *Had a close relationship with an adult while growing up*
   c. Child maltreatment while in foster care
      - *Child maltreatment while in foster care*

Odds Ratios

As discussed in Chapter 10, an odds ratio is a measure of relative risk—it quantifies how much higher or lower are the odds that one group will exhibit an outcome compared to another group. More simply, odds ratios are a way of comparing the risk that, for example, alumni with certain experiences (e.g., a low number of placements) will be currently employed compared to alumni with different experiences (e.g., a high number of placements). To ease interpretation of the odds ratios, all outcomes are phrased positively (e.g., *no PTSD in last 12 months, no major depression in last 12 months*) and are coded such that the preferable outcome is 1 and the less preferable outcome is 0.

The independent variables (foster care experiences) are coded such that the preferable experience is 1 and the less preferable experience is 0. Therefore, an odds ratio greater than 1.0 means that alumni with a more positive foster care experience (e.g., a low number of placements) had higher odds of a positive outcome than alumni with a less positive foster care experience (e.g., a high number of placements). If the odds—the proportion of those with versus without the outcome—are equivalent, this odds ratio will be 1.0; this means that there is no association between the particular foster care experience and the outcome.

The relation between outcomes and foster care experiences was examined by separately regressing each outcome on each foster care experience (after controlling for demographics, risk factors, and agency) in a series of logistic regressions. As described in Chapter 4, data were weighted to adjust for non-random survey nonresponse and to adjust for differences in Casey and state samples in baseline characteristics. Odds ratios are presented in a special Working Paper available on the Casey website (O'Brien et al., 2009c). For these analyses, the *reference group* for all foster care experience variables is the one theorized to be most likely to lead to undesirable outcomes. For example, having a close relationship with an adult while growing up is a more optimal, less at-risk situation than not having a close relationship with an adult, so *not* having a close relationship is the reference group. For foster care experience variables, levels of the variables (e.g., low, medium, and high) were determined based on theory, past research, and distributions of the data. The tables in O'Brien et al. (2009c) are set up such that odds ratios greater than 1.0 (and statistically significant, $p < .05$, two-tailed) were expected. For example, the first row of data in O'Brien et al. (2009c) shows that alumni who experienced a low number of placements had 1.8 times higher odds, compared to alumni who experienced a high number of placements, of having *fewer than three CIDI diagnoses* and *no major depression in last 12 months*.

There is only one exception to the design of odds ratio scores—parenting style (in the Foster Family and Other Nurturing Support While in Care area). For this variable, the reference group was "other" parenting style for the foster parents. It was expected that authoritative foster parents would have better outcomes than "other" foster parents but that "other" foster parents would have better outcomes than permissive, authoritarian, and disengaged foster parents. Therefore, it was expected that the odds ratios would be greater than 1.0 (and significant) when comparing authoritative to "other" and would be less than 1.0 (and significant) when comparing permissive, authoritarian, and disengaged to "other."

Analyses were conducted so that each foster care experience area (e.g., Placement History, Educational Services and Experience) was examined independently of other areas, meaning that analyses within one foster care experience area did not control for foster care experience variables in another area. Individual variables within an area (e.g., *number of placements, length of time in care*) are presented using the following significance convention

($p < .05$): * for bivariate X^2 and † for multivariate X^2. The bivariate X^2 (labeled as *Gross X^2*) evaluated the relation between an individual variable and an individual outcome, while the multivariate X^2 (labeled as *Net X^2*) evaluated the relation between an individual variable and an individual outcome after controlling for other variables in that foster care experience area. When there was only one variable in a foster care experience area (e.g., Therapeutic Service and Supports), no multivariate X^2 was needed; therefore, only a bivariate X^2 is presented.

The tables in O'Brien et al. (2009c) report bivariate odds ratios (and the bivariate confidence intervals, in parentheses) only when the bivariate X^2 was statistically significant at the .05 level; otherwise, no odds ratios are presented. The significance of the bivariate odds ratios is designated by a * placed outside the parentheses containing the confidence intervals. Multivariate odds ratios, which controlled for other variables within that foster care experience area (but not between areas), were tested for significance. Although the multivariate odds ratios are not reported, their significance is designated by a † placed outside the parentheses containing the bivariate confidence intervals.

For example, in O'Brien et al. (2009c), the relation between *number of placements* and *no major depression in last 12 months* was examined (see the first few rows in the fourth column of Table 1 of the working paper. Because the Gross X^2 (bivariate X^2) of 8.8 was significant (the multivariate X^2 of 1.1 was not), the bivariate odds ratios and confidence intervals were presented for two comparisons: alumni with a medium number of placements compared to alumni with a high number of placements and alumni with a low number of placements compared to alumni with a high number of placements. Neither comparison achieved multivariate significance (thus, there is no † outside the parentheses containing the confidence interval) but, at the bivariate level, alumni with a low number of placements had 1.8 times higher odds than alumni with a high number of placements of having *no major depression in last 12 months*. The significance of this comparison is designated by a * placed outside the parentheses containing the confidence interval for the bivariate odds ratio (1.2–2.7)*.

A distinction must be made here between a large association, indicating that there is a strong relation between the two variables, and a clear causal relation, where one might infer that one factor clearly causes an outcome to occur. These odds ratios do not imply a causal relationship between variables.

The Relation Between the Foster Care Experience and Outcomes

I don't really think there was anything in foster care that led to my success. Once I reached 18 and had a child of my own, I realized I needed to grow up. When I was in foster care, I learned how to hate people.

I got a phone call when I turned 18 from my caseworker saying they dropped my case and that was it. There was no training for when you turn 18, this is what happens. Then I didn't have a job and had to move home 'cause I couldn't pay bills.

Because of the large number of odds ratios to be evaluated, the odds ratios are summarized in this chapter across foster care experience area (e.g., Placement History) and outcome domain (e.g., Mental Health) (see Table 11.1) and for each foster care experience variable (e.g., *number of placements, length of time in care*) and outcome domain (see Tables 11.2–11.5). First, the relation between the seven foster care experience areas and five outcome domains is presented. This includes summaries of the 18 individual foster care experience variables and the 48 individual outcomes. Because of the way the foster care experience variables were distributed into levels (yes/no; low, medium, high; etc.), a total of 1,680 odds ratios is summarized. These odds ratios were divided into three categories: *(1)* significant in the expected direction, *(2)* significant in the unexpected direction, and *(3)* not significant.

Table 11.1 summarizes the findings from subsequent tables (Tables 11.2–11.5) by presenting the percentage of expected and unexpected significant results for the relation between foster care experience areas and outcome domains. For example, the two cells in the bottom right-hand corner of Table 11.1 (shaded) show that 26.4% of all odds ratios were significant in the expected direction, while 9.5% of all odds ratios were significant in the unexpected direction. Therefore, 64.1% [100 − (26.4 + 9.5)] of all odds ratios were not significant. This indicates an association between the foster care experience areas and outcomes a quarter of the time and no relationship about 64% of the time.

As seen in the last two columns of Table 11.1, when foster care experience areas are examined across all outcomes, two areas of foster care experience— Therapeutic Service and Supports and Leaving Care Resources—predicted outcomes in the expected direction over 40% of the time (41.7% and 49.0%, respectively). It was expected that 5% would be statistically significant by chance, so these results indicate a meaningful level of association between these variables. Further, only 4.2% of the Therapeutic Services and Support odds ratios were in the unexpected direction, while 10 times as many were in the expected direction. These findings reinforce the importance of certain service components hypothesized to predict alumni outcomes, including:

- More access to therapeutic services and supports
- More tangible resources upon leaving care (e.g., $250 in cash and a driver's license)

Meanwhile, Preparation for Leaving Care predicted outcomes in the expected direction 22.9% of the time and in the unexpected direction 8.3% of the time. Similarly, Foster Family and Other Nurturing Support While in

Table 11.1 Summary Table for the Percentages of Significant Expected and Unexpected Bivariate Odds Ratios for the Relation Between Foster Care Experience Areas and Outcome Domains

| | Outcome Domain | | | | | | | | | | | |
| Foster Care Area | Mental Health | | Physical Health | | Education | | Employment and Finances | | Relationships and Social Supports | | Across All Outcomes | |
	Exp.	Unexp.	Exp.	Unexp.	Exp.	Unexp.	Exp.	Unexp.	Exp.	Unexp.	Exp.	Unexp.
Placement history	30.8	3.3	22.2	2.8	41.7	0.0	24.4	6.5	21.8	8.3	26.6	5.2
Educational services and experience	56.7	0.0	44.4	0.0	26.7	13.3	40.5	7.1	25.6	7.7	38.9	5.6
Therapeutic service and supports	60.0	0.0	50.0	0.0	0.0	20.0	35.7	0.0	46.2	7.7	41.7	4.2
Activities with foster family	10.0	0.0	83.3	0.0	40.0	0.0	28.6	7.1	23.1	7.7	31.3	4.2
Preparation for leaving care	15.0	5.0	8.3	8.3	30.0	20.0	32.1	3.6	23.1	11.5	22.9	8.3
Leaving care resources	50.0	0.0	33.3	8.3	80.0	0.0	53.6	0.0	38.5	3.8	49.0	2.1
Foster family and other nurturing support while in care	17.1	7.9	22.6	1.2	18.6	18.6	21.4	27.0	17.6	15.9	19.3	15.9
Across all foster care areas	28.0	4.6	26.7	2.4	31.4	10.3	27.1	14.1	22.2	11.2	26.4	9.5

Note: Exp. = expected, Unexp. = unexpected. Odds ratios that were not statistically significant are not included in this table. However, they can be determined by adding the expected and unexpected significant percentages together for an area and domain and subtracting from 100.

Care predicted outcomes in the expected direction 19.3% of the time and in the unexpected direction 15.9% of the time. These two foster care experience areas predicted outcome domains in the expected direction least often and in the unexpected direction most often.

The Relation Between Placement History and Outcomes

Table 11.2 summarizes the relation between Placement History and outcome domains. Six variables defined this foster care experience area in the current study: *(1) number of placements, (2) length of time in care, (3) placement change rate, (4) number of reunification failures, (5) number of runaways,* and *(6) number of unlicensed living situations with friends/relatives.* Highlights of this table are presented below. Overall, Placement History predicted outcomes in the expected direction over one-quarter of the time (26.6%), in the unexpected direction about 5% of the time (5.2%), and not significantly almost 70% of the time (68.2%). For specific outcome domains, Placement History had the highest rate of prediction in the expected direction for Education (41.7% of the time), and it had the highest rate of prediction in the unexpected direction for Relationships and Social Supports (8.3% of the time).

For specific Placement History variables (see Table 11.2), *placement change rate* had the highest rate of prediction in the expected direction across all outcomes (47.9%). It was exceptional at predicting Mental Health and Education in the expected direction (60.0% of the time for each). The relationships with placement history and specific outcomes are presented in O'Brien et al. (2009c). For example, alumni who experienced a low or medium placement change rate had 1.7 and 1.4 times higher odds, respectively, than those who experienced a high placement change rate of having *no 12-month CIDI diagnosis.* Further, alumni who experienced a low or medium placement change rate had 4.6 and 2.7 times higher odds, respectively, than those who experienced a high placement change rate of *complet[ing] high school with a diploma* (see O'Brien et al., 2009c). This underscores the growing concern in the field about the damaging effects of placement change (e.g., Ryan & Testa, 2005).

Number of unlicensed living situations with friends and relatives had the lowest rate of prediction in the expected direction (13.5%) and the highest rate of prediction in the unexpected direction (13.5%; see Table 11.2). Specifically, it had high rates of prediction in the unexpected direction for Employment and Finances and Relationships and Social Supports outcomes (21.4% and 19.2% of the time, respectively). Specific relations are presented in O'Brien et al. (2009c). For example, alumni who had never had an *unlicensed living situation with friends/relatives* had 3.5 times higher odds than those who had two or more such living situations of having *no major depression in last 12 months,* but those with two or more had 2.5 times higher odds than those with none or one of *own[ing] a house or apartment* (see Tables 1 and 4 in O'Brien et al., 2009c). The lack of clear directionality in the association between this placement experience factor and some outcome areas indicate that unlicensed

Table 11.2 Summary Table for the Percentages of Significant Expected and Unexpected Bivariate Odds Ratios for the Relation Between Placement History and Outcome Domains

| | Outcome Domain | | | | | | | | | | | |
| Placement History (six variables) | Mental Health | | Physical Health | | Education | | Employment and Finances | | Relationships and Social Supports | | Across All Outcomes | |
	Exp.	Unexp.	Exp.	Unexp.	Exp.	Unexp.	Exp.	Unexp.	Exp.	Unexp.	Exp.	Unexp.
Number of placements	30.0	0.0	33.3	0.0	50.0	0.0	35.7	0.0	23.1	0.0	32.3	0.0
Length of time in care	40.0	0.0	25.0	8.3	30.0	0.0	0.0	10.7	23.1	3.8	20.8	5.2
Placement change rate	60.0	0.0	41.7	0.0	60.0	0.0	39.3	0.0	46.2	3.8	47.9	1.0
Number of reunification failures	5.0	0.0	8.3	0.0	40.0	0.0	28.6	0.0	11.5	15.4	17.7	4.2
Number of runaways	10.0	10.0	25.0	8.3	60.0	0.0	28.6	7.1	26.9	7.7	27.1	7.3
Number of unlicensed living situations with friends/relatives	40.0	10.0	0.0	0.0	10.0	0.0	14.3	21.4	0.0	19.2	13.5	13.5
Across all placement history variables	30.8	3.3	22.2	2.8	41.7	0.0	24.4	6.5	21.8	8.3	26.6	5.2

Note: Exp. = expected, Unexp. = unexpected. Odds ratios that were not statistically significant are not included in this table. However, they can be determined by adding the expected and unexpected significant percentages together for an area and domain and subtracting from 100.

placement with relatives or family friends may be a positive or negative experience, depending on the situation (this is different from kinship care, which is a licensed situation). While some research literature supports this idea (e.g., Hegar & Scannapieco, 1998), more research is needed to understand what makes one situation positive and another negative.

The Relation Between Educational Services and Experience and Outcomes

Table 11.3 summarizes the relation between Educational Services and Experience and outcome domains. Two variables defined this foster care experience area: *(1)* [alumni] *could participate in supplemental educational services/tutoring* and *(2) total number of school changes from elementary through high school.* Highlights of this table are presented below. Overall, Educational Services and Experience predicted outcomes in the expected direction nearly 40% of the time (38.9%), in the unexpected direction slightly over 5% of the time (5.6%), and not significantly over 50% of the time (55.5%). For specific outcome domains, Educational Services and Experience had the highest rate of prediction in the expected direction for Mental Health and Physical Health (56.7% and 44.4% of the time, respectively) and had the highest rate of prediction in the unexpected direction for Education (13.3% of the time).

As described in Working Paper No. 4 (Williams et al., 2009), a measure of access to certain therapeutic or remedial services was used in lieu of a measure of actual service use because youth who manifest problems that are often associated with poor outcomes may be more likely to receive these services. When the two variables in this foster care experience area were examined separately (see Table 11.3), [alumni] *could participate in supplemental educational services/tutoring* predicted in the expected direction across all outcomes nearly half the time (47.9%). It was exceptional at predicting Mental Health and Employment and Finances in the expected direction (60.0% and 64.3% of the time, respectively). Specific relations are presented in O'Brien et al. (2009c). For example, alumni who had *access to supplemental educational services/tutoring* had 1.8 times higher odds than those who did not of having *a total number of 12-month CIDI diagnoses fewer than three* and had 8.8 times higher odds of *own[ing] a house or apartment* (see Tables 1 and 4 in O'Brien et al., 2009c). Given that many youth placed in foster care are one to three grade levels behind in reading, math, and/or science (Emerson, 2007), the value of access to educational supports is understandable. The degree of association with many adult outcomes underscores the strategic value of these supports. This variable did not predict in the unexpected direction at all (0.0%).

Therefore, when the foster care experience area of Educational Services and Experience did predict in the unexpected direction, it was a result of the *total number of school changes from elementary through high school.* This variable predicted the outcome domains of Education, Employment and Finances, and of Relationships and Social Supports, in the unexpected direction over 10%

Table 11.3 Summary Table for the Percentages of Significant Expected and Unexpected Bivariate Odds Ratios for the Relation Between Educational Services and Experience, Therapeutic Service and Supports, and Outcome Domains

| | Outcome Domain | | | | | | | | | | | |
| | Mental Health | | Physical Health | | Education | | Employment and Finances | | Relationships and Social Supports | | Across All Outcomes | |
Educational/Therapeutic	Exp.	Unexp.	Exp.	Unexp.	Exp.	Unexp.	Exp.	Unexp.	Exp.	Unexp.	Exp.	Unexp.
Educational Services and Experience (two variables)												
Could participate in supplemental educational services/tutoring	60.0	0.0	50.0	0.0	20.0	0.0	64.3	0.0	30.8	0.0	47.9	0.0
Total number of school changes from elementary through high school	55.0	0.0	41.7	0.0	30.0	20.0	28.6	10.7	23.1	11.5	34.4	8.3
Across both Educational Services and Experience variables	56.7	0.0	44.4	0.0	26.7	13.3	40.5	7.1	25.6	7.7	38.9	5.6
Therapeutic Service and Supports (one variable)												
Therapeutic Service and Supports	60.0	0.0	50.0	0.0	0.0	20.0	35.7	0.0	46.2	7.7	41.7	4.2

Note: Exp. = expected, Unexp. = unexpected. Odds ratios that were not statistically significant are not included in this table. However, they can be determined by adding the expected and unexpected significant percentages together for an area and domain and subtracting from 100.

of the time (20.0%, 10.7% and 11.5%, respectively; see Table 11.3). This variable did, however, predict in the expected direction for all outcome domains (including those predicted in the unexpected direction) more than one-third of the time (34.4%). It was exceptional at predicting Mental Health and Physical Health in the expected direction (55.0% and 41.7% of the time, respectively). Specific relations are presented in O'Brien et al. (2009c). For example, alumni who experienced a low number of school changes had 1.9 times higher odds than those who experienced a high number of school changes of *complet[ing] high school with a diploma* and had 3.7 times higher odds of *completing college or more*. However, those with a high number of school changes had 1.7 times higher odds than those with a low number of *complet[ing] any degree/certificate beyond high school*[82] (see Table 3 in O'Brien et al., 2009c). This mixed pattern suggests that those youth who experienced a low number of school changes may have completed a more typical educational trajectory: completing high school with a diploma and sometimes completing a college degree. Meanwhile, those alumni experiencing a high level of educational disruption completed a less typical educational trajectory: GED and a postsecondary degree that does not involve a college degree.

The Relation Between Therapeutic Service and Supports and Outcomes

Table 11.3 also summarizes the relation between Therapeutic Service and Supports and outcome domains. One variable defined this foster care experience area in the current study: *could participate in therapeutic service and supports*. This variable, focused on service access, predicted outcomes in the expected direction over 40% of the time (41.7%), in the unexpected direction less than 5% of the time (4.2%), and not significantly over 50% of the time (54.1%). For specific outcome domains (see Table 11.3), Therapeutic Services and Support had the highest rate of prediction in the expected direction for Mental Health, Physical Health, and Relationships and Social Supports (60.0%, 50.0%, and 46.2% of the time, respectively) and had the highest rate of prediction in the unexpected direction for Education and Relationships and Social Supports (20.0% and 7.7% of the time, respectively). This foster care experience area did not predict any outcomes in the Education domain in the expected direction (0.0%). Specific relations are presented in O'Brien et al. (2009c). For example, alumni who had more access to therapeutic services and supports had 2.5 times higher odds than those with less access of having *no major depression in last 12 months* and 1.7 times higher odds of *smoking fewer than 10 cigarettes per day*. However, those with less access had 3.3 times higher odds than those with high access of *complet[ing] college or more* (see Tables 1, 2, and 3 in O'Brien et al., 2009c).

Comments from alumni reviewers suggested that much of the individual therapy they received was not helpful. This mixed view of the value of therapy may partially explain why having higher access to these services was a strong predictor of many but not all alumni outcomes.

The Relation Between Activities With Foster Family and Outcomes

Table 11.4 summarizes the relation between Activities with Foster Family and outcome domains. One variable defined this foster care experience area: [the youth in care] *participated often in activities with foster family.* This variable predicted outcomes in the expected direction over 30% of the time (31.3%), in the unexpected direction less than 5% of the time (4.2%), and not significantly almost 65% of the time (64.5%). For specific outcome domains (see Table 11.4), Activities with Foster Family had the highest rate of prediction in the expected direction for Physical Health and Education (83.3% and 40.0% of the time, respectively), and it had a modest rate of prediction in the unexpected direction for Employment and Finances and Relationships and Social Supports (7.1% and 7.7% of the time, respectively). Specific relations are presented in O'Brien et al. (2009c). For example, alumni who participated more in *activities with foster family* had 1.7 times higher odds than those who participated less of *not smok[ing] currently* and 1.8 times higher odds of *completing high school with a diploma* (see Tables 2 and 3 in O'Brien et al., 2009c).

The Relation Between Preparation for Leaving Care and Outcomes

The emphasis on developing life skills for independent living at an early age grew in the 1990s and was reinforced by the passage of the Independent Living Act of 1999. Table 11.4 also summarizes the relation between Preparation for Leaving Care and outcome domains. One variable defined this foster care experience area: *degree of preparation for leaving care.* The types of preparation that constituted this variable were *(1)* access to employment training or job location services, *(2)* access to independent training groups or workshops, *(3)* alumni reporting that they were somewhat or very prepared for independent living, and *(4)* alumni with health insurance at exit.

This variable predicted outcomes in the expected direction over 20% of the time (22.9%), in the unexpected direction almost 10% of the time (8.3%), and not significantly almost 70% of the time (68.8%). For specific outcome domains (see Table 11.4), Preparation for Leaving Care had the highest rate of prediction in the expected direction for Employment and Finances and Education (32.1% and 30.0% of the time, respectively), and it had the highest rate of prediction in the unexpected direction for Education and Relationships and Social Supports (20.0% and 11.5% of the time, respectively).

Specific relationships are presented in O'Brien et al. (2009c). For example, alumni who had a medium or high *degree of preparation for leaving care* had 1.6 and 2.3 times higher odds, respectively, than those who had a low degree to *not be homeless within one year after leaving care* and 2.0 and 1.8 times higher odds, respectively, than those who had a low degree to *complete*

Table 11.4 Summary Table for the Percentages of Significant Expected and Unexpected Bivariate Odds Ratios for the Relation Between Activities with Foster Family, Preparation for Leaving Care, and Leaving Care Resources, and Outcome Domains

Activities With Foster Family/ Preparation for Leaving Care/ Leaving Care Resources	Outcome Domain											
	Mental Health		Physical Health		Education		Employment and Finances		Relationships and Social Supports		Across All Outcomes	
	Exp.	Unexp.	Exp.	Unexp.	Exp.	Unexp.	Exp.	Unexp.	Exp.	Unexp.	Exp.	Unexp.
Activities With Foster Family (one variable)												
Participated often in activities with foster family	10.0	0.0	83.3	0.0	40.0	0.0	28.6	7.1	23.1	7.7	31.3	4.2
Preparation for Leaving Care (one variable)												
Degree of preparation for leaving care	15.0	5.0	8.3	8.3	30.0	20.0	32.1	3.6	23.1	11.5	22.9	8.3
Leaving Care Resources (one variable)												
Leaving care resources	50.0	0.0	33.3	8.3	80.0	0.0	53.6	0.0	38.5	3.8	49.0	2.1

Note: Exp. = expected, Unexp. = unexpected. Odds ratios that were not statistically significant are not included in this table. However, they can be determined by adding the expected and unexpected significant percentages together for an area and domain and subtracting from 100.

high school with a diploma. However, alumni who had a low *degree of preparation for leaving care* had 2.0 and 1.4 times higher odds, respectively, than those who had a medium or high degree of *complet[ing] any degree/certificate beyond high school* (see Tables 3 and 4 in O'Brien et al., 2009c).

The data confirm the connection between life-skills preparation and later adult success in two areas typically stressed in this era of incomplete life skills preparation: educational attainment and employment. Since passage of the Foster Care Independence Act of 1999, agencies have gradually moved to adopt more comprehensive life-skills curricula and standardized assessment approaches like the Daniel Memorial and the Ansell-Casey Life Skills Assessment (ACLSA).

The Relation Between Leaving Care Resources and Outcomes

Table 11.4 also summarizes the relation between Leaving Care Resources and outcome domains. One variable defined this foster care experience area in the current study: *leaving care resources.* Leaving care resources included *(1)* a driver's license, *(2)* \$250 in cash, and *(3)* dishes and utensils. This variable predicted outcomes in the expected direction almost 50% of the time (49.0%), in the unexpected direction only about 2% of the time (2.1%), and not significantly almost 50% of the time (48.9%). For specific outcome domains (see Table 11.4), Leaving Care Resources had the highest rate of prediction in the expected direction for Education, Employment and Finances, and Mental Health (80.0%, 53.6%, and 50.0% of the time, respectively) and had the highest rate of prediction in the unexpected direction for Physical Health (8.3% of the time). Specific relations are presented in O'Brien et al. (2009c). For example, alumni who had a medium or high number of *resources when leaving care* had 6.2 and 17.7 times higher odds, respectively, than those who had a low number of *complet[ing] college or more* and 2.3 and 3.6 times higher odds, respectively, than those who had a low number of not *receiving public assistance currently.*

The Relation Between Foster Family and Other Nurturing Support While in Care and Outcomes

Table 11.5 summarizes the relation between Foster Family and Other Nurturing Support While in Care and outcome domains. Six variables defined this foster care experience area: *(1) parenting style of both foster parents; (2)* [alumni] *felt loved while in care; (3) overall, foster parents were helpful; (4) foster family helped with ethnic issues; (5)* [alumni] *had a close relationship with an adult while growing up;* and *(6) child maltreatment while in care (by foster family or other caregiver).* Overall, Foster Family and Other Nurturing Support While in Care predicted outcomes in the expected direction almost 20% of the time (19.3%), in the unexpected direction over 15% of the time (15.9%), and not significantly almost 65% of the time (64.8%). For specific outcome domains, Foster Family and Other Nurturing Support While in Care had the highest rate of prediction in the expected direction for Physical Health (22.6% of the time), and it had the highest rate of prediction in the unexpected direction for Employment and Finances (27.0% of the time).

Foster Family and Other Nurturing Support While in Care predicted outcomes significantly in the unexpected direction more than any other foster care experience area. Upon inspection of the summary table (Table 11.5), of the six variables that define Foster Family and Other Nurturing Support While in Care, three predicted in the expected direction consistently and three predicted in the unexpected direction consistently.

The three variables that predicted in the expected direction consistently were [alumni] *felt loved while in care; overall, foster parents were helpful;* and *foster family helped with ethnic issues.* Among these variables, [alumni] *felt loved while in care* had the highest rate of prediction in the expected direction across all outcomes at nearly 40% of the time (39.6%). It predicted Employment and Finances and Relationships and Social Supports in the expected direction more than half the time (57.1% and 53.8% of the time, respectively). Specific relations are presented in O'Brien et al. (2009c). For example, alumni who *felt loved while in foster care* had 2.0 and 3.4 times higher odds, respectively, than those who did not of having *health insurance of any kind* and of having *no violence in married or cohabitating relationship* (see Tables 4 and 5 in O'Brien et al., 2009c).

The three variables that predicted in the unexpected direction consistently were *parenting style of both foster parents,* [alumni] *had a close relationship with an adult while growing up,* and *child maltreatment while in care.* Of these variables, *child maltreatment while in care* had the highest rate of prediction in the unexpected direction across all outcomes at almost one-quarter of the time (23.3%), followed by *parenting style* (18.2%), and [alumni] *had a close relationship with an adult while growing up* (16.7%). Specific relations are presented in O'Brien et al. (2009c). For example, alumni who had foster parents with an "other" parenting style had 1.7 times higher odds than those who had foster parents with an authoritative parenting style of *complet[ing] any education past high school* (see Table 3 in O'Brien et al., 2009c). In looking at the underlying pattern of results, it appears that the way foster parenting style was measured may not adequately capture the complexities or realities of the dynamics, as this variable had counterintuitive results.

The rate of prediction in the unexpected direction for *child maltreatment while in care* was exceptionally high for Employment and Finances and Relationships and Social Supports (37.1% and 32.3% of the time, respectively). Predictions at the variable level are presented in Working Paper No. 7 (O'Brien et al., 2009c). For example, alumni who experienced sexual abuse (with no other type of abuse) had 3.3 and 10.0 times higher odds, respectively, than those who experienced sexual abuse and at least one other type of abuse of *not be[ing] homeless within one year after leaving care* and of *not receiv[ing] negative social support* (see O'Brien et al., 2009c). The reference group for this experience was "sexual

Table 11.5 Summary Table for the Percentages of Significant Expected and Unexpected Bivariate Odds Ratios for the Relation Between Foster Family and Other Nurturing Support While in Care and Outcome Domains

Foster Family and Other Nurturing Support While in Care (six variables)	Outcome Domain											
	Mental Health		Physical Health		Education		Employment and Finances		Relationships and Social Supports		Across All Outcomes	
	Exp.	Unexp.	Exp.	Unexp.	Exp.	Unexp.	Exp.	Unexp.	Exp.	Unexp.	Exp.	Unexp.
Parenting style of both foster parents	10.0	5.0	8.3	4.2	0.0	20.0	16.1	39.3	15.4	11.5	12.0	18.2
Felt loved while in foster care	20.0	10.0	0.0	0.0	40.0	20.0	57.1	0.0	53.8	0.0	39.6	4.2
Overall, foster parents were helpful	45.0	0.0	33.3	0.0	30.0	30.0	35.7	3.6	26.9	0.0	34.4	4.2
Foster family helped with ethnic issues	40.0	0.0	16.7	0.0	20.0	0.0	28.6	7.1	30.8	7.7	29.2	4.2
Had a close relationship with an adult while growing up	0.0	40.0	16.7	0.0	0.0	0.0	0.0	21.4	23.1	7.7	8.3	16.7
Child maltreatment while in care	10.0	8.0	36.7	0.0	28.0	20.0	15.7	37.1	4.6	32.3	15.4	23.3
Across all foster family and other nurturing support while in care variables	17.1	7.9	22.6	1.2	18.6	18.6	21.4	27.0	17.6	15.9	19.3	15.9

Note: Exp. = expected, Unexp. = unexpected. Odds ratios that were not statistically significant are not included in this table. However, they can be determined by adding the expected and unexpected significant percentages together for an area and domain and subtracting from 100.

abuse and/or physical abuse and physical neglect." It is possible that the type of abuse is less important than if abuse occurred in some instances.

Of particular note for this foster care experience area was the low rate of prediction for [alumni] *had a close relationship with an adult while growing up* in the expected direction (only 8.3% of time). For three of the five outcome domains—Mental Health, Education, and Employment and Finances—[alumni] *had a close and confiding relationship with an adult while growing up* did not predict any outcomes (0.0%) in the expected direction. This pattern of results does not support one of the main study hypotheses. This counterintuitive finding may, in part, be the result of the way the variable was measured. More precise assessments of the type, duration, and nature of the relationship(s) may be needed to obtain a more accurate picture of the conditions under which positive adult relationships may have beneficial longer-term effects.

Note of Caution When Interpreting These Odds Ratios

The pattern of odds ratios for many of the foster care experience factors indicates that they are strongly linked with a number of key alumni outcomes. While many practitioners believe that these factors are important, they may actually be indicators of other crucial underlying factors for success, signs of something much deeper or more personal that makes the difference in becoming a successful adult after living in foster care. The variables examined do not completely explain why certain services had a more positive effect in some outcome areas, indicating that some unmeasured phenomena affected alumni outcomes.

In addition, the study team introduced controls for the process variables considered here into the equations predict outcomes from Casey-versus-state differences in order to see if processes of care could explain the better performance of Casey alumni. (That is, did the Casey-versus-state odds ratios change with these controls?) The processes of care variables were significant in some areas but were not universally significant predictors of the Casey–state agency differences. So, while we know more now about how processes of care predict good outcomes from this chapter, and that Casey alumni do better than state alumni (as described in Chapter 10), this new analysis shows that this benefit of the Casey program is not due to the fact that these processes of care are more common in the Casey program. A question then arises: Are these processes of care more common in the Casey program than in the state program? We examined that as well, and the answer was yes, but the differences were not so great as to explain the full benefit of the Casey program. So, these processes are part of the story, but not the whole story. Future studies should try to systematically vary and test some of these agency and service factors to better understand how they affect child development and adult outcomes.

Summary

In summary, when each of the foster care experience areas was tested individually, more than one-quarter of the odds ratios were found to be significant and in the expected direction, while nearly 1 in 10 of the odds ratios were significant and in the unexpected direction; this is two times what would be expected by chance. Some important findings with implications for practice, however, are evident. Of the seven foster care experience areas, three predicted outcomes in the expected direction at nearly 40% of the time or more: Educational Services and Experience, Therapeutic Service and Supports, and Leaving Care Resources. Two more predicted outcomes in the expected direction at least one-quarter of the time: Activities with Foster Family and Placement History.

The two foster care experience areas that had the lowest rates of prediction in the expected direction were Preparation for Leaving Care and Foster Family and Other Nurturing Support While in Care. Although they were lower than others, these foster care experience areas predicted in the expected direction nearly one-fifth of the time. The implications of these findings, placed in the context of other results and previous research, are discussed in Chapter 13.

For two foster care experience areas (Preparation for Leaving Care and Foster Family and Other Nurturing Support While in Care), the prediction of outcomes in the unexpected direction, at 8% and 16%, respectively, is of particular concern. That these areas did not demonstrate greater prediction of outcomes in the expected direction, and the propensity of these areas to predict outcomes in the unexpected direction, make these findings disconcerting. Closer inspection of the data reveals that three variables within the area of Foster Family and Other Nurturing Support While in Care carry the weight of counterintuitive findings (low expected and high unexpected odds ratios) for this area: *parenting style of both foster parents,* [the youth in care] *had a close relationship with an adult while growing up,* and *child maltreatment while in care.* As discussed earlier in this chapter, these counterintuitive findings may result from flaws in the way these concepts were operationalized. Alternatively, some of these variables may function differently than hypothesized. Dimensions of some of these variables that are part of a larger variable may act in ways that lower the likelihood of certain positive alumni outcomes. For example, certain specific dimensions or types of parenting behavior, while bundled within a specific parenting style, may in fact be harmful to many children in foster care.

Acknowledgment.   Catherine Roller White and Eva Hiripi contributed to this chapter.

12

Effects of Optimizing the Foster Care Experience on Outcomes

I wish I would have been given the tools to manage my adult life effectively. I could have been taught that my actions and choices create my present and future rather than merely being a victim of circumstance.

Overview

Child welfare administrators and practitioners want to know which aspects of service delivery to target in order to improve long-term success for youth in care. One way to address this issue is to ask "What outcomes would be achieved had alumni received an ideal (optimal) level of care?" To examine this question, statistical simulations were conducted to estimate the degree to which optimizing foster care experiences would affect alumni outcomes (see Table 12.1). Note that the outcomes in this chapter are all phrased negatively, unlike the outcomes in the rest of the book. This is because the optimization analyses were designed to estimate *decreases* in *undesirable outcomes* (not increases in desirable outcomes).

Each of the seven foster care experience areas was optimized: *(1)* Placement History, *(2)* Educational Services and Experience, *(3)* Therapeutic Service and Supports, *(4)* Activities with Foster Family, *(5)* Preparation for Leaving Care, *(6)* Leaving Care Resources, and *(7)* Foster Family and Other Nurturing Support While in Care (see Tables 12.4–12.8).

Optimization involved changing observed data on process variables so that they reflected the ideal situation for foster care experiences and using regression coefficients to generate proportions of expected outcomes in the outcome variables listed in Table 12.1. Optimal levels of all foster care experience variables, presented in Table 12.2, were defined based on theory, the distribution of the data, and practice perspectives about what is more likely

Table 12.1. Outcomes Domains and Individual Outcomes Within Domains

Outcome Domain (Number of Individual Outcomes)	Individual Outcome
Mental Health (10)	had at least one 12-month CIDI diagnosis
	total number of 12-month CIDI diagnoses was three or more
	major depression in last 12 months
	panic syndrome in last 12 months
	modified social phobia in last 12 months
	alcohol dependence in last 12 months
	drug dependence in last 12 months
	PTSD in last 12 months
	generalized anxiety in last 12 months
	SF®-12 mental health score below 50
Physical Health (6)	has a chronic physical disorder
	SF®-12 physical health score below 50
	smokes currently
	smokes 10 or more cigarettes per day
	drinks currently
	drinks 150 or more drinks per year
Education (5)	did not complete high school—high school diploma or GED
	did not complete high school with a diploma
	no education past high school
	did not complete any degree/certificate beyond high school
	did not complete college or more (BA or more)
Employment and Finances (9)[a]	homeless within one year after leaving foster care
	public assistance after age 18
	currently receives cash public assistance
	household received a form of public assistance in past six months
	household income below the poverty level
	household income less than three times the poverty level
	does not have health insurance of any kind
	does not own house or apartment
	not employed or self-employed (note: split into six subgroups)
Relationships and Social Supports (13)	not married or cohabiting
	violence in relationship
	not very satisfied with marriage or cohabiting relationship
	among alumni married or cohabitating: socially isolated
	among single and not cohabitating alumni: socially isolated
	serious fighting with anyone in past 12 months

(continued)

Table 12.1.   Continued

Outcome Domain (Number of Individual Outcomes)	Individual Outcome
	negative social support
	no positive social support
	had children before age 18
	had children before marriage
	among alumni with children: does not do a lot of things with children
	among alumni with children: infrequent displays of nurturance/affection with children
	among alumni with children: had a child of their own placed in foster care

[a]For the Employment and Finances domain, there were 14 variables. For simulation analyses at the outcome domain level, the six employment subgroups were collapsed into one employment variable. For simulation analyses at the individual outcome level, employment status for all six subgroups were used as individual outcomes (see Table 12.7 for subgroup description).

to result in positive outcomes. Optimal levels of individual variables were purposely set at levels that most child welfare agencies would be able to attain, although most agencies would not likely be able to attain optimal levels of *all* foster care experience variables simultaneously.

The seven areas of foster care experience were optimized independently of other areas (e.g., Placement History was optimized but no other area was optimized) *and* simultaneously (all areas optimized at the same time). When a foster care experience area was optimized, every variable in that area was optimized. For example, optimizing Placement History involved optimizing all six variables in this foster care experience area: *(1) number of placements; (2) length of time in care; (3) placement change rate; (4) number of reunification failures; (5) number of runaways;* and *(6) number of unlicensed living situations with friends/relatives.* When all foster care experience areas were optimized simultaneously, every variable in every foster care experience area was optimized at the same time. In contrast, optimizing foster care experience areas independently provided an index of the extent to which alumni outcomes could be improved if only one foster care experience was optimized, which is a more likely scenario than optimization of all foster care experiences for agencies with limited resources. Optimizing foster care experience areas simultaneously provided an index of the extent to which alumni outcomes could be improved had the entire foster care experience been ideal.

In this chapter, two separate analyses are presented that examine the effects of optimizing the foster care experience on outcomes: *(1)* at the outcome domain level (e.g., Mental Health), which involved creating a domain-level undesirable outcome score (described below), and *(2)* at the individual outcome level (e.g., *PTSD in last 12 months*). (See Table 12.1 for a list of all

Table 12.2. Outcomes Domains and Individual Outcomes Within Domains

Foster Care Experience Area	Foster Care Experience Variables	Optimal Level
Placement history	number of placements	Low (3 or fewer)
	length of time in care (in years)	Low (fewer than 3.6)
	placement change rate (placements per year)	Low (fewer than 0.61)
	number of reunification failures	Low (0)
	number of runaways	Low (0)
	number of unlicensed living situations with friends/relatives	Low (0)
Education services and experience	total number of school changes elementary through high school	Low (3 to 6)
	could participate in supplemental educational services/tutoring	Had access
Therapeutic service and supports	had access to all of the following:	Had access to all
	1. counseling and mental health services	
	2. alcohol and drug treatment programs	
	3. group work or group counseling	
Activities with foster family	participated in a lot of activities with foster family	Participated in both enjoyable and religious activities
Preparation for leaving care	degree of preparation for leaving care	High (had 3 or 4)
	1. access to employment training or job location services	
	2. access to independent living training groups or workshops	
	3. being somewhat or very prepared for independent living	
	4. had health insurance at exit	
Leaving care resources	number of resources when left care	High (had 2 or 3)
	1. a driver's license	
	2. $250 in cash	
	3. dishes and utensils	
Foster family and other nurturing support while in care	positive parenting by foster parents	High
	felt loved while in foster care	Felt loved
	overall, foster parents were helpful (rated from 1 to 7)	A lot (7)
	had a close relationship with an adult while growing up	Had a relationship
	foster family helped with ethnic identity	Foster family helped
	child maltreatment while in foster care	No child maltreatment

individual outcomes.) In both sets of analyses, prior to optimizing foster care experiences, demographics and risk factor variables that were statistically significant in a stepwise logistic regression were controlled; this was the same set of control variables in the analyses described in Chapter 11.

Additionally, the agency serving the youth, the state in which the youth was served, and the interaction between the state and the agency were controlled. After controlling for these variables, both sets of analyses optimized foster care experience areas separately (to estimate the effect of optimizing only a particular area) and simultaneously (to estimate the effects of optimizing all foster care areas). This is a conservative and important analytical approach that is rare in child welfare research. *This analysis identifies the potential effects of key program refinements when differences in alumni demographics, risk factors, Casey/state agency differences, and interactions among these variables were controlled.*

The Effects of Optimizing the Foster Care Experience on Outcome Domains

Question: Could anything have been done to improve the move from foster care to living on your own?

Answer: I think if they had actually explained what to do, what to look for. I had to learn how to budget on my own. They were so focused on "don't do drugs," "don't get pregnant" that they didn't focus on those issues.

Answer: They could have helped with getting an apartment, with some money to get started. Getting some kind of medical card or something.

Answer: I got moved every six months, that's why I became so bad.

Procedure

The first step in the simulations at the domain level was to create a score for each alumnus or alumna that summed the number of undesirable (negative) items within each of the five outcome domains and across all domains— Mental Health, Education, Physical Health, Employment and Finances, and Relationships and Social Supports. This Total Undesirable Outcome Score could range from 0 to 43 (see Table 12.3). For example, the Education outcome domain score summed the five individual education outcome variables listed in Table 12.1. Scores in this domain could range from 0 (alumnus or alumna achieved all individual education outcomes) to 5 (alumnus or alumna achieved no individual education outcomes). All individual outcomes were operationalized in the undesirable direction (e.g., *depression in last 12 months, did not complete high school, homeless within one year after leaving foster care*); therefore, summing within a domain reflected the total number of undesirable outcomes in that domain.

Additionally, individual alumni outcomes were summed across all domains (tantamount to adding summed outcome-domain scores) and reflected the total number of undesirable outcomes across all domains (Total Undesirable Outcome Score). For the Employment and Finances domain, there were

14 variables. For this analysis only, the six employment subgroups (which are all mutually exclusive) were collapsed into one variable reflecting the employment status of the alumnus or alumna. Therefore, this domain score ranged from 0 to 9.

The second step in the simulation was to regress separately the five outcome domain scores and the Total Undesirable Outcome Score on actual foster care experiences (after controlling for demographics, risk factors, and agency variables). This created a separate regression equation for each of the summed outcome scores, each estimating the number of undesirable outcomes that each alumnus or alumna actually achieved based on observed data (e.g., observed time in care—low, medium, or high; observed number of schools—low, medium, or high).

Next, the coefficients for each of the separate regression equations created above were used to calculate the number of undesirable outcomes that each alumnus or alumna would be estimated to have achieved based on an optimal foster care experience (e.g., a *low* time in care and a *low* number of schools attended). That is, all alumni foster care experience data were manually changed to be optimal. Optimal levels for each foster care experience are listed in Table 12.2.

In the last step of the simulation, the estimated number of undesirable outcomes achieved before and after optimization was compared. The change (i.e., increase, decrease, or no change) in the number of outcomes before and after optimizing the foster care experience areas represents the estimated *effect* of optimizing these foster care experiences.[83] A distinction must be made here between a large association, indicating that there is a strong relationship between the two variables, and a clear causal relationship (established through an experimental study design), where one might infer that one factor clearly causes an outcome to occur.

"No effect" for a foster care experience area occurred when none of the individual variables defining that area significantly predicted outcome domains. Further, although some of the percentages in parentheses appear negligible (or zero), some of the variables within that foster care experience area did significantly predict outcomes for the domains. However, when examined in combination with other variables within that foster care experience area, the effects canceled each other out (i.e., optimizing some of the variables within the foster care experience area decreased undesirable outcomes, while optimizing others increased undesirable outcomes).

Results

Table 12.3 presents a summary of the estimated outcome domain scores before optimizing the foster care experiences and the percent change in the estimated number of undesirable outcomes after optimization. This provides an estimate of the percentage of undesirable outcomes that can be prevented (or, alternatively, worsened) if the foster care experience is optimized. Negative values in the table represent the estimated percent decrease in undesirable outcomes, while positive values represent the estimated percent increase in undesirable outcomes. For example, the Mental Health domain score before optimization was 2.2 (out of 10). Optimization of Placement History produced an estimated decrease in 22.0% of undesirable mental outcomes. Given that the observed number of undesirable mental health outcome was 2.2, a 22.0% decrease in such outcomes results in 1.7 undesirable outcomes (or 8.3 desirable outcomes, compared to 7.8 desirable outcomes before optimization). Note that this assumes that the associations between placement characteristics and alumni outcomes found in the regression analyses simulations are indeed due to the effects of the placement experiences and not to some unmeasured factor.

Optimization of Placement History produced the greatest reduction in undesirable outcomes on the Mental Health outcome domain (-22.0%), produced large reductions for Education and Physical Health (-17.8% and -16.0%, respectively), and produced the smallest reduction for Relationships and Social Supports (-3.0%). For the Total Outcome Score, Placement History reduced the estimated number of undesirable outcomes by 9.1%.

When the foster care experience area of Educational Services and Experience was optimized, the greatest reduction in the estimated number of undesirable outcomes was found for the Physical Health outcome domain (-19.4%) and the smallest reduction was found for Relationships and Social Supports and Education (-1.8% and no effect, respectively). For the Total Outcome Score, optimization of Educational Services and Experience reduced the estimated number of undesirable outcomes by 6.6%.

When the foster care experience area of Therapeutic Service and Supports was optimized, very modest effects were observed. The greatest reduction in the estimated number of undesirable outcomes was found for the Mental Health outcome domain (-3.1%), and the smallest reduction was found for Physical Health and Education (-0.9% and no effect, respectively). For the Total Outcome Score, optimization of Therapeutic Service and Support reduced the estimated number of undesirable outcomes by only 1.3%.

When the foster care experience area of Activities with Foster Family was optimized, very modest effects were observed. The greatest reduction in the estimated number of undesirable outcomes was found for the Physical Health outcome domain (-6.5%). Surprisingly, optimization of Activities with Foster Family increased the estimated number of undesirable outcomes for Mental Health and Relationships and Social Supports (6.4% and 1.0%, respectively). For the Total Outcome Score, Activities with Foster Family had no effect on the estimated number of undesirable outcomes. This aspect of the foster care experience may have been measured insufficiently; alumni reviewers have emphasized the value of being placed with an active and nurturing family. Alternatively, other measured factors may be more closely associated with helping alumni achieve key outcomes as adults.

Table 12.3. Summary Table for Percent Decrease in the Estimated Number of Undesirable Outcomes When Foster Care Experience Areas Are Optimized

Foster Care Area	Outcome Domain					
	Mental Health (10)	Physical Health (6)	Education (5)	Employment and Finances (9)[a]	Relationships and Social Supports (13)	Total Undesirable Outcome Score (43)
Prevalence rate prior to optimization	2.2	2.1	2.7	3.8	6.1	17.0
Percent decrease in undesirable outcomes						
Placement history	-22.0	-16.0	-17.8	-6.8	-3.0	-9.1
Educational services and experience	-13.0	-19.4	—	-7.2	-1.8	-6.6
Therapeutic service and supports	-3.1	-0.9	—	-1.5	-1.1	-1.3
Activities with foster family	6.4	-6.5	-4.2	—	1.0	0.0
Preparation for leaving care	-4.9	1.6	—	-3.0	1.2	-0.5
Leaving care resources	—	6.9	-14.6	-12.2	-3.4	-5.4
Foster family and other nurturing support while in care	2.2	-13.7	7.0	3.2	-4.3	0.0
All foster care experience areas optimized	-38.0	-48.0	-25.5	-27.9	-11.4	-22.2

Note: — indicates no effect for a foster care experience area. Although some of the percentages appear negligible (or zero), some of the variables within that foster care experience area did significantly predict outcomes for the domains. However, when examined in combination with other variables within that foster care experience area, the effects canceled each other out (i.e., some of the variables within the foster care experience area decreased undesirable outcomes, while others increased undesirable outcomes).

[a] For the Employment and Finances domain, there were 14 variables. For this analysis only, the six employment subgroups were collapsed into one employment variable (see Table 12.7 for subgroup description and breakdown).

When the foster care experience area of Preparation for Leaving Care was optimized, very modest effects were observed. The greatest reduction in the estimated number of undesirable outcomes was found for the Mental Health outcome domain (–4.9%), supporting a study hypothesis about the value of life-skills preparation. Surprisingly, optimization of Preparation for Leaving Care slightly increased the estimated number of undesirable outcomes for Physical Health and Relationships and Social Supports (1.6% and 1.2%, respectively). For the Total Outcome Score, optimization of Preparation for Leaving Care reduced the estimated number of undesirable outcomes by only 0.5%.

When the foster care experience area of Leaving Care Resources was optimized, the greatest reduction in the estimated number of undesirable outcomes was found for the Education and Employment and Finances outcome domains (–14.6% and–12.2%, respectively). Surprisingly, optimization of Leaving Care Resources increased the estimated number of undesirable outcomes for Physical Health by 6.9%. For the Total Outcome Score, Leaving Care Resources reduced the estimated number of undesirable outcomes by 5.4%.

When the foster care experience area of Foster Family and Other Nurturing Support While in Care was optimized, the greatest reduction in the estimated number of undesirable outcomes was found for the Physical Health outcome domain (–13.7%). Surprisingly, optimization of Foster Family and Other Nurturing Support While in Care increased the estimated number of undesirable outcomes for Education, Employment and Finances, and Mental Health (7.0%, 3.2%, and 2.2%, respectively). For the Total Outcome Score, Foster Family and Other Nurturing Support While in Care did not reduce the estimated number of undesirable outcomes (0.0%). As discussed previously, this may be due to flaws in the conceptualization of the variables in this area.

When all of the foster care experience variables were optimized *simultaneously*, large reductions in the estimated number of undesirable outcomes were found. Nearly half (–48.0%) of the estimated number of undesirable outcomes were reduced for the outcome domain of Physical Health, and almost 40% (–38.0%) of the undesirable outcomes were reduced for Mental Health. The smallest reduction (but still a substantial effect) of the estimated number of undesirable outcomes was found for the outcome domain of Relationships and Social Supports (–11.4%). For the Total Outcome Score, when all foster care experience variables were optimized simultaneously, over one-fifth of the estimated number of undesirable outcomes was reduced (–22.2%). This represents an increase in the number of estimated desirable outcomes across all domains from 26.0 to 29.7.

The Effects of Optimizing the Foster Care Experience on Individual Outcomes

Summarizing findings on how optimizing foster care experiences affects outcomes at the domain level was useful globally. Equally useful is examining the effects of optimizing foster care experiences in a similar fashion for each of the 48 outcomes separately.[84] The procedure for calculating the change in the estimated prevalence rate for each of the 48 outcomes was similar to the procedure for examining the effects of optimizing the foster care experiences at the domain level. The primary difference was that estimated individual undesirable outcome prevalence rates were examined rather than undesirable outcome summary scores.

Procedure

The first step in this set of simulations was to regress separately each of the 48 outcomes on actual foster care experiences, controlling for the same set of control variables used in the analyses described in Working Paper No. 6 (O'Brien et al., 2009b) (demographics and risk factors variables that were statistically significant in a stepwise logistic regression, agency serving the youth, the state in which the youth was served, and the interaction between agency and state). This created a separate regression equation for individual outcomes, each estimating the outcome's prevalence rate. Next, the coefficients for each of the separate regression equations created above were used to estimate each outcome's prevalence rate had the foster care experience been optimal (see Table 12.2 for optimal levels). The estimated prevalence rate before and after optimization was then compared. The change in the estimated prevalence rate of each outcome represents the estimated effect of optimizing these foster care experiences. For example, the estimated effect of optimizing Placement History on *at least one 12-month CIDI diagnosis* (in the Mental Health outcome domain) is presented in the first data column of Table 12.4. Prior to optimization, the estimated prevalence rate of the Northwest alumni with *at least one 12-month CIDI diagnosis* was 54.9%. When optimized separately, Placement History reduced the estimated prevalence rate of those alumni with a *12-month CIDI diagnosis* by nearly one-fifth (–18.5%). Given that the estimated prevalence of alumni with at least one 12-month CIDI diagnosis was 54.9%, an 18.5% decrease in undesirable outcomes results in 44.7% of alumni with at least one 12-month CIDI DSM diagnosis (55.3% with none).

The change in prevalence rates reflects the difference in the predicted prevalence rate of the undesirable form of the outcome (having PTSD). These differences are presented in Tables 12.4–12.8 and represent one of three changes in the predicted prevalence rates of undesirable outcomes: *(1)* a decrease (change value is negative); *(2)* an increase (change value is positive); and *(3)* no change (change value is 0.0).

Because the analyses examined the effects of optimizing seven foster care experience areas separately and simultaneously across 48 outcomes, a total of 384 data points are summarized [(7 + 1) * 48]. Each data point represents the change (i.e., increase, decrease, or no change) in the estimated prevalence rate of an individual undesirable outcome. To describe all of these changes in prevalence rates in the text would be too cumbersome (although some detail is provided below). A more useful summary is provided in the last two columns of Tables 12.4–12.8, which summarize the effects of optimizing the foster care experience area across each individual outcome within an outcome domain. Specifically, the percentage of time that the optimization of a foster care experience area decreased the estimated prevalence rate of undesirable outcomes or increased the estimated prevalence rate of undesirable outcomes is reported. For example, as seen in Table 12.4, across the 10 individual Mental Health outcomes, optimizing Placement History resulted in a decrease in the estimated prevalence rate for nine of 10 undesirable Mental Health outcomes (–90.0%) while increasing the estimated prevalence rate of undesirable Mental Health outcomes for only one outcome (10.0%). The percentage of time that no change in the estimated prevalence rate of undesirable outcomes was found is not reported, but it can be calculated by subtracting the above percentages from 100 [100 – (90 + 10) = 0%].

Results

The Effects of Optimizing the Foster Care Experience on Mental Health

As presented in Table 12.4, optimization of the foster care experience areas of Placement History and Educational Services and Experience decreased the estimated prevalence rate for the 10 undesirable Mental Health outcomes most frequently (90.0% and 80.0% of the time, respectively). The estimated prevalence rate for two undesirable outcomes, *alcohol dependence in last 12 months* and *total number of 12-month CIDI diagnoses of three or greater,* decreased by nearly half when Placement History was optimized (–49.2% and –48.8%, respectively). The estimated prevalence rate of *drug dependence in last 12 months* decreased by nearly 60.0% when Educational Services and Experience was optimized (–58.7%).

In contrast, optimization of the foster care experience area of Activities with Foster Family did not decrease the estimated prevalence rate of any of the 10 undesirable Mental Health outcomes; instead, it increased the estimated prevalence rate of three of them (30.0%). Meanwhile, optimization of Foster Family and Other Nurturing Support While in Care decreased the estimated prevalence rate of 40.0% of the undesirable Mental Health outcomes while increasing the estimated prevalence rate of 50.0% of the undesirable Mental Health outcomes.

When all foster care experience variables were optimized simultaneously, the estimated prevalence rate for nine of 10 undesirable Mental Health outcomes was decreased (90.0%). The decreases ranged from –18.7% for *SF®-12 mental health score below 50* to –87.7% for *drug dependence in last 12 months.* Only the prevalence rate of *generalized anxiety in last 12 months* was increased

Table 12.4. Summary Table for Percent Change in the Estimated Prevalence Rate of Mental Health Outcomes When Foster Care Experience Areas Were Optimized

Foster Care Area	Mental Health Outcomes										Foster Care Area Summary[a]	
	Had at Least One 12-Month CIDI Diagnosis	Total Number of CIDI Diagnoses Was Three or More	Major Depression in Last 12 Months	Panic Syndrome in Last 12 Months	Modified Social Phobia in Last 12 Months	Alcohol Dependence in Last 12 Months	Drug Dependence in Last 12 Months	PTSD in Last 12 Months	Generalized Anxiety in Last 12 Months	SF®-12 Mental Health Score Below 50	% Decrease	% Increase
Prevalence rate prior to optimization	54.9	18.2	18.4	16.9	13.9	4.6	5.8	23.8	8.9	49.8	n/a	
Placement history	-18.5	-48.8	-7.1	-38.5	-12.9	-49.2	58.1	-37.7	-41.9	-3.5	90.0	10.0
Educational services and experience	-8.9	-32.9	-13.3	15.7	-31.8	-39.4	-58.7	-25.4	-0.04	0.0	80.0	10.0
Therapeutic service and supports	0.0	-7.2	-9.6	0.0	0.0	8.1	0.0	0.0	-11.8	0.0	30.0	10.0
Activities with foster family	0.0	35.6	0.0	33.0	0.0	0.0	0.0	0.0	40.9	0.0	0.0	30.0
Preparation for leaving care	0.0	-15.8	-16.7	0.0	0.0	-18.8	0.0	-7.0	0.0	-2.0	50.0	0.0

Leaving care resources	0.0	0.0	-4.1	-37.1	0.0	87.6	-64.0	5.6	0.0	-9.0	40.0	20.0
Foster family and other nurturing support while in care	3.7	27.1	-15.7	14.1	0.0	-21.3	-34.5	2.7	79.3	-7.2	40.0	50.0
All foster care experience variables optimized	-20.2	-60.5	-49.7	-34.0	-51.1	-77.9	-87.7	-57.3	12.4	-18.7	90.0	10.0

[a] *Percent decrease* refers to the number of times across Mental Health outcomes that optimizing a foster care area resulted in a reduction in the predicted prevalence rate of undesirable Mental Health outcomes. Conversely, *percent increase* refers to the number of times across Mental Health outcomes that optimizing a foster care area resulted in an increase in the predicted prevalence rate of undesirable Mental Health outcomes. After a foster care experience area was optimized, the predicted prevalence rate of some Mental Health outcomes did not change. This percentage is not included in the table but can be calculated by subtracting the percent increase plus the percent decrease from 100 [no change = [100 − (%decrease + %increase)].

when all foster care experience variables were optimized simultaneously by 12.4%.

The Effects of Optimizing the Foster Care Experience on Physical Health

As presented in Table 12.5, optimization of the foster care experience areas of Placement History and Educational Services and Experience decreased the estimated prevalence rate of the six undesirable Physical Health outcomes most frequently (83.3% of the time). For Placement History, estimated decreases ranged from –13.5% for *SF®-12 physical health score below 50* to –38.6% for *smokes 10 or more cigarettes per day.* For Educational Services and Experience, estimated decreases ranged from –17.6% for *SF®-12 physical health score below 50* to –21.3% for *smokes currently.* Optimizing either of these foster care experience areas did not increase the estimated prevalence rate of any undesirable Physical Health outcomes.

In contrast, optimization of the foster care experience areas of Therapeutic Service and Supports and Leaving Care Resources did not decrease the estimated prevalence rate of any of the six undesirable Physical Health outcomes. Optimization of these areas increased the estimated prevalence rate of none (0.0%) and one-third (33.3%), respectively. Meanwhile, optimization of Foster Family and Other Nurturing Support While in Care again exhibited polarizing effects. It decreased the estimated prevalence rate of 50.0% of the undesirable Physical Health outcomes while increasing the estimated prevalence rate of 33.3% of the undesirable Physical Health outcomes.

When all foster care experience variables were optimized simultaneously, the estimated prevalence rate of all six undesirable Physical Health outcomes was decreased (100%). The decreases ranged from –17.2% for *drinks currently* to –72.9% for *smokes currently.*

The Effects of Optimizing the Foster Care Experience on Education

As presented in Table 12.6, optimization of the foster care experience areas of Placement History and Leaving Care Resources decreased the estimated prevalence rate of the five undesirable Education outcomes most frequently (100.0% and 80.0% of the time, respectively). The estimated prevalence rate of two undesirable outcomes, *not completing high school with a diploma or GED* and *no high school diploma,* decreased by –68.6% and –59.0%, respectively, when Placement History was optimized. The estimated prevalence rate of *not completing high school with a diploma or GED* decreased by nearly 50.0% when Leaving Care Resources was optimized (–47.7%).

In contrast, optimization of the foster care experience areas of Educational Services and Experience, Therapeutic Service and Supports, and Preparation for Leaving Care did not decrease the estimated prevalence rate of any of the five undesirable Education outcomes while increasing the estimated prevalence rate of three (60.0%), zero (0.0%), and two (40%) of them, respectively. Meanwhile, optimization of Foster Family and Other Nurturing

Table 12.5. Summary Table for Percent Change in the Estimated Prevalence Rate of Physical Health Outcomes When Foster Care Experience Areas Were Optimized

	Physical Health Outcomes						Foster Care Area Summary[a]	
Foster Care Area	Has a Chronic Physical Disorder	SF®-12 Physical Health Score Below 50	Smokes Currently	Smokes 10 or More Cigarettes Per Day	Drinks Currently	Drinks 150 or More Drinks Per Year	% Decrease	% Increase
Prevalence rate prior to optimization	23.4	33.1	49.2	28.1	49.8	29.2	n/a	
Placement history	−17.5	−13.5	−27.0	−38.6	0.0	−24.4	83.3	0.0
Educational services and experience	0.0	−17.6	−21.3	−19.6	−18.2	−18.7	83.3	0.0
Therapeutic service and supports	0.0	0.0	0.0	0.0	0.0	0.0	0.0	0.0
Activities with foster family	−14.0	0.0	−9.3	−13.5	0.0	0.0	50.0	0.0
Preparation for leaving care	0.0	0.0	0.0	−7.4	−2.0	0.0	33.3	0.0
Leaving care resources	0.0	0.0	1.4	0.0	18.2	0.0	0.0	33.3
Foster family and other nurturing support while in care	16.9	−10.7	−28.9	−7.6	0.0	6.9	50.0	33.3
All foster care experience variables optimized	−32.9	−47.1	−72.9	−67.9	−17.2	−26.2	100.0	0.0

[a] *Percent decrease* refers to the number of times across Physical Health outcomes that optimizing a foster care area resulted in a reduction in the predicted prevalence rate of undesirable Physical Health outcomes. Conversely, *percent increase* refers to the number of times across Physical Health outcomes that optimizing a foster care area resulted in an increase in the predicted prevalence rate of undesirable Physical Health outcomes. After a foster care experience area was optimized, the predicted prevalence rate of some Physical Health outcomes did not change. This percentage is not included in the table but can be calculated by subtracting the percent increase plus the percent decrease from 100 [no change = [100 − (%decrease + %increase)].

Table 12.6. Summary Table for Percent Change in the Estimated Prevalence Rate of Education Outcomes When Foster Care Experience Areas Were Optimized

			Education Outcomes			Foster Care Area Summary[a]	
Foster Care Area	Did Not Complete High School—High School Diploma or GED	Did Not Complete High School With a Diploma	No Education Past High School	Did Not Complete Any Degree/ Certificate Beyond High School	Did Not Complete College or More	% Decrease	% Increase
Prevalence rate prior to optimization	15.3	40.2	49.5	71.9	97.1	n/a	
Placement history	−68.6	−59.0	−23.9	−4.5	−2.4	100.0	0.0
Educational services and experience	22.4	0.0	0.7	8.0	0.0	0.0	60.0
Therapeutic service and supports	0.0	0.0	0.0	0.0	0.0	0.0	0.0
Activities with foster family	−16.3	−15.2	0.0	0.0	0.0	40.0	0.0
Preparation for leaving care	0.0	3.4	0.0	0.8	0.0	0.0	40.0
Leaving care resources	−47.7	−34.6	−29.4	0.0	−2.7	80.0	0.0
Foster family and other nurturing support while in care	33.3	13.9	19.1	−1.1	−0.2	40.0	60.0
All foster care experience variables optimized	−81.0	−81.7	−36.2	−3.9	−7.2	100.0	0.0

[a] Percent decrease refers to the number of times across Education outcomes that optimizing a foster care area resulted in a reduction in the predicted prevalence rate of undesirable Education outcomes. Conversely, percent increase refers to the number of times across Education outcomes that optimizing a foster care area resulted in an increase in the predicted prevalence rate of undesirable Education outcomes. After optimizing a foster care experience area, the predicted prevalence rate of some Education outcomes did not change. This percentage is not included in the table but can be calculated by subtracting the percent increase plus the percent decrease from 100 [no change = 100 − (%decrease + %increase)].

Support While in Care again exhibited polarizing effects. It decreased the estimated prevalence rate of 40.0% of the undesirable Education outcomes while increasing the estimated prevalence rate of 60.0% of the undesirable Education outcomes.

When all foster care experience variables were optimized simultaneously, the estimated prevalence rate of all five undesirable Education outcomes was decreased (100.0%). The decreases ranged from −3.9% for *no degree/certificate beyond high school* to −81.7% for *no high school diploma*.

The Effects of Optimizing the Foster Care Experience on Employment and Finances

As presented in Table 12.7, optimization of the foster care experience areas of Leaving Care Resources, Placement History, and Educational Services and Experience decreased the estimated prevalence rate of the 14 undesirable Employment and Finances outcomes most frequently (71.4%, 64.3%, and 64.3% of the time, respectively). The estimated prevalence rate of three undesirable outcomes—*unemployment for females not in school and married, unemployment for females in school and not married,* and *unemployment for females not in school and not married*—decreased by nearly 50.0% or more when Leaving Care Resources was optimized (−48.0%, −50.3%, and −55.1%, respectively). The estimated prevalence rate of these same three undesirable outcomes—*unemployment for females in school and not married, unemployment for females not in school and married,* and *unemployment for females in school and married*—decreased by 50.0% or more when Placement History was optimized (−54.1%, −54.1%, and −54.4%, respectively). The estimated prevalence rate of three undesirable outcomes—*unemployment for females in school and not married, unemployment for males not in school,* and *unemployment for females not in school and not married*—decreased by 20.0% or more when Educational Services and Experience was optimized (−20.4%, −22.4%, and −33.0%, respectively).

Optimization of Leaving Care Resources did not increase the estimated prevalence rate of any undesirable Employment and Finances outcomes; however, optimization of both Placement History and Educational Services and Experience increased the estimated prevalence rate of four (28.6%) and two (14.3%) of the 14 undesirable Employment and Finances outcomes, respectively.

Optimization of Foster Family and Other Nurturing Support While in Care again exhibited polarizing effects. It decreased the estimated prevalence rate of 57.1% of the undesirable Employment and Finances outcomes while increasing the estimated prevalence rate of 42.9% of the undesirable Employment and Finances outcomes.

When all foster care experience variables were optimized simultaneously, the estimated prevalence rate of 13 of 14 undesirable Employment and Finances outcomes was decreased (92.9%). The decreases ranged from −1.1% for *household income less than three times the poverty level* to −100.0% for

Table 12.7. Summary Table for Percent Change in the Estimated Prevalence Rate of Employment and Finances Outcomes When Foster Care Experience Areas Were Optimized

| | | | Employment & Finance Outcomes | | | | |
| | Homeless Within One Year After Leaving Foster Care | | Public Assistance | | Household Income Less Than: | | |
Foster Care Area		After Age 18	Currently Receives Cash Public Assistance	Household Received a Form of Public Assistance in Past 6 Months	The Poverty Level	3 Times the Poverty Level	Does Not Have Health Insurance of Any Kind
Prevalence rate prior to optimization	22.1	47.1	15.3	47.0	26.9	76.8	32.8
Placement history	-6.5	1.6	0.0	-26.4	-1.2	7.8	-21.8
Educational services and experience	-12.5	-15.8	-13.7	8.4	0.0	-7.2	0.0
Therapeutic service and supports	0.0	0.0	0.0	-3.8	0.0	-2.3	-4.7
Activities with foster family	0.0	0.0	20.7	0.0	0.0	0.0	0.0
Preparation for leaving care	0.0	0.0	0.0	-4.4	-9.1	0.0	0.0
Leaving care resources	-19.1	-19.1	-33.9	-10.1	-16.3	-8.7	-21.1
Foster family and other nurturing support while in care	-23.5	15.9	12.1	-0.5	-2.4	8.7	-10.7
All foster care experience variables optimized	-64.9	-22.6	-58.1	-34.1	-38.1	-1.1	-61.8

Employment & Finance Outcomes

Foster Care Area	Does Not Own House or Apartment	Not Employed (in School)			Not Employed (Not In School)			Foster Care Area Summary[a]	
		Males	Females		Males	Females		% Decrease	% Increase
			Not Married	Married		Not Married	Married		
Prevalence rate prior to optimization	91.0	25.6	22.9	38.3	27.4	28.0	34.7	n/a	
Placement history	-2.1	46.5	-54.1	-54.4	29.4	-34.4	-54.1	64.3	28.6
Educational services and experience	-7.3	-7.6	-20.4	0.0	-22.4	-33.0	1.6	64.3	14.3
Therapeutic service and supports	0.0	0.0	2.3	0.0	0.0	0.0	0.0	21.4	7.1
Activities with foster family	0.0	0.0	0.0	0.0	0.0	0.0	0.0	0.0	7.1
Preparation for leaving care	-1.9	0.0	0.0	-25.4	6.7	0.0	-36.8	35.7	7.1
Leaving care resources	0.0	0.0	-50.3	0.0	0.0	-55.1	-48.0	71.4	0.0
Foster family and other nurturing support while in care	-0.3	35.6	66.7	-77.8	-0.5	57.2	-46.8	57.1	42.9
All foster care experience variables optimized	-9.8	24.0	-93.7	-100.0	-27.1	-82.4	-100.0	92.9	7.1

[a] Percent decrease refers to the number of times across Employment and Finances outcomes that optimizing a foster care area resulted in a reduction in the predicted prevalence rate of undesirable Employment and Finances outcomes. Conversely, percent increase refers to the number of times across Employment and Finances outcomes that optimizing a foster care area resulted in an increase in the predicted prevalence rate of undesirable Employment and Finances outcomes. After optimizing a foster care experience area, the predicted prevalence rate of some Employment and Finances outcomes did not change. This percentage is not included in the table, but can be calculated by subtracting the percent increase plus the percent decrease from 100 [no change = [100−(%decrease + %increase)].

unemployment for females in school and married and *unemployment for females not in school and married.* Only the prevalence rate of *unemployment for males in school* was increased when all foster care experience variables were optimized simultaneously (by 24.0%).

The Effects of Optimizing the Foster Care Experience on Relationships and Social Supports

As presented in Table 12.8, optimization of the foster care experience areas of Placement History and Foster Family and Other Nurturing Support While in Care decreased the estimated prevalence rate of the 13 undesirable Relationships and Social Supports outcomes most frequently (61.5% and 53.8% of the time, respectively). The estimated prevalence rate of two undesirable outcomes—*serious fighting with anyone in last 12 months* and *children before marriage*—decreased by nearly one-fifth or more when Placement History was optimized (–19.7% and –29.4%, respectively). The estimated prevalence rate of two undesirable outcomes—*socially isolated among alumni married or cohabitating* and *socially isolated among alumni single and not cohabitating*—decreased by 45.0% or more when Foster Family and Other Nurturing Support While in Care was optimized (–45.5% and –67.5%, respectively). Optimization of both Placement History and Foster Family and Other Nurturing Support While in Care increased the estimated prevalence rate of five of the 13 undesirable Relationships and Social Supports outcomes (38.5%).

In contrast, optimization of the foster care experience areas of Educational Services and Experience and Preparation for Leaving Care increased the estimated prevalence rate of the 13 undesirable Relationships and Social Supports outcomes more often than it decreased the estimated prevalence rates. Optimization of both of these foster care experience areas increased the estimated prevalence rates of six undesirable Relationships and Social Supports outcomes (46.2%). Optimization of Educational Services and Experience decreased the estimated prevalence rates of four undesirable Relationships and Social Supports outcomes (30.8%), while Preparation for Leaving Care decreased the estimated prevalence rates of three undesirable Relationships and Social Supports outcomes (23.1%).

When all foster care experience variables were optimized simultaneously, the estimated prevalence rate of 10 of 13 undesirable Relationships and Social Supports outcomes was decreased (76.9%). The decreases ranged from –1.8% for *violence in relationship for alumni married or cohabitating* to –77.3% for *socially isolated for alumni married or cohabitating.* Interestingly, the three undesirable Relationships and Social Supports outcomes for which estimated prevalence rates increased when all foster care experience variables were optimized simultaneously (23.1%) all concerned the subgroup of alumni with children. The three outcomes were *does not do a lot of things with children, had a child of their own placed in foster care,* and *no frequent displays of*

Table 12.8. Summary Table for Percent Change in the Estimated Prevalence Rate of Relationships and Social Supports Outcomes When Foster Care Experience Areas Were Optimized

	Not Married or Cohabitating	Alumni Married or Cohabitating		Socially Isolated	Socially Isolated Among Single and Not Cohabitating	Serious Fighting With Anyone in Last 12 Months	Neg. Social Support
		Violence in Relationship	Not Very Satisfied in Relationship				
Prevalence rate prior to optimization	52.6	33.8	29.9	16.3	15.3	10.3	79.3
Placement history	-5.0	17.5	13.9	-1.9	12.0	-19.7	-7.4
Educational services and experience	6.5	0.1	11.2	25.0	-26.2	0.0	0.0
Therapeutic service and supports	0.0	0.0	8.2	-16.5	11.0	0.0	0.0
Activities with foster family	-13.0	0.0	29.6	0.0	0.0	0.0	0.0
Preparation for leaving care	0.0	11.3	0.0	41.3	-18.1	9.9	2.8
Leaving care resources	0.0	-4.8	0.0	-49.2	41.8	0.0	0.0
Foster family and other nurturing support while in care	-7.3	-17.9	-20.5	-45.5	-67.5	-24.8	0.4
All foster care experience variables optimized	-15.9	-1.8	-39.4	-77.3	-75.7	-58.2	-13.3

(continued)

Table 12.8.   Continued

				Among Alumni With Children			Foster Care Area Summary[a]	
	No Pos. Social Support	Had Children Before Age 18	Had Children Before Marriage	Does Not Do a Lot of Things With Children	Infrequent Displays of Nurturance/ Affection With Children	Had a Child of Their Own Placed in Foster Care	% Decrease	% Increase
Prevalence rate prior to optimization	52.5	4.7	16.4	75.1	76.0	9.6	n/a	
Placement history	4.7	25.7	-29.4	-0.4	-6.8	-11.1	61.5	38.5
Educational services and experience	-4.6	-45.8	-33.0	3.5	0.0	7.3	30.8	46.2
Therapeutic service and supports	-6.6	0.0	0.0	2.4	0.0	-18.5	23.1	23.1
Activities with foster family	8.1	-24.1	0.0	7.0	0.0	-44.9	23.1	23.1
Preparation for leaving care	-5.8	59.4	4.2	0.0	-2.2	0.0	23.1	46.2
Leaving care resources	-3.1	-51.3	-23.5	9.6	0.0	-15.0	46.2	15.4
Foster family and other nurturing support while in care	-12.0	122.6	7.7	6.7	0.0	188.9	53.8	38.5
All foster care experience variables optimized	-20.6	-44.2	-73.8	16.2	3.0	9.2	76.9	23.1

[a] Percent decrease refers to the number of times across Relationships and Social Supports outcomes that optimizing a foster care area resulted in a reduction in the predicted prevalence rate of undesirable Relationships and Social Supports outcomes. Conversely, percent increase refers to the number of times across Relationships and Social Supports outcomes that optimizing a foster care area resulted in an increase in the predicted prevalence rate of undesirable Relationships and Social Supports outcomes. After optimizing a foster care experience area, the predicted prevalence rate of some Relationships Supports outcomes did not change. This percentage is not included in the table, but can be calculated by subtracting the percent increase plus the percent decrease from 100 [no change = [100 − (%decrease + %increase)].

nurturance/affection with children. The increases in estimated prevalence rates were 16.2%, 9.2%, and 3.0%, respectively.

Summary of the Effects of Optimizing the Foster Care Experience on Individual Outcomes

Table 12.9 summarizes the effects of optimizing the foster care experience on individual outcomes. The table includes summary information from the previous five tables (Tables 12.4–12.8) and two new pieces of information. The last two columns in Table 12.9 summarize the change in the estimated prevalence rate across the 48 undesirable outcomes when the foster care experience areas were optimized separately and simultaneously.

Several patterns emerge when this table is examined. First, when optimized separately, four foster care experience areas—Placement History, Access to Educational Services and Experience, Leaving Care Resources, and Foster Family and Other Nurturing Support While in Care—decreased the estimated prevalence rate of the 48 undesirable outcomes half the time or more (75.0%, 54.2%, 50.0%, and 50.0% of the time, respectively). Except for Foster Family and Other Nurturing Support While in Care, these three areas have %-decrease to %-increase ratios of 2:1 or greater. This means that when these foster care experience areas were optimized separately, they decreased consistently the estimated prevalence rate of undesirable outcomes without substantially increasing the rates of undesirable outcomes.

The second pattern that emerged was that, when optimized separately, two foster care experience areas—Therapeutic Service and Supports and Activities with Foster Family—neither increased nor decreased substantially the estimated prevalence rate of undesirable outcomes (none of these percentages exceeded 18.8%).

The third pattern that emerged from the summary table was that, when optimized separately, the foster care experience area of Preparation for Leaving Care modestly decreased the estimated prevalence rate of undesirable outcomes (31.3% of the time) while increasing the number of undesirable outcomes (18.8% of the time).

The fourth pattern that emerged from the summary table was that, when optimized separately, the foster care experience area of Foster Family and Other Nurturing Support While in Care demonstrated a strong but polarized association with outcomes. Specifically, this foster care experience area decreased the estimated prevalence rate of undesirable outcomes exactly half of the time (50.0%), increased the estimated prevalence rate of undesirable outcomes over 40% of the time (43.8%), and exhibited no change in the estimated prevalence rate less than 7% of the time (6.2%).

The fifth and last pattern that emerged from the summary table was that, when optimized simultaneously, having a collectively better set of foster care experiences had dramatic effects on the estimated prevalence rates of the 48 outcomes. Specifically, simultaneous optimization of the foster care

Table 12.9. Summary Table for Percent Change in the Estimated Prevalence Rate across Outcome Domains When Foster Care Experience Areas Were Optimized

	Outcome Domains					
	Mental Health (10)		Physical Health (6)		Education (5)	
Foster Care Area	% Decrease	% Increase	% Decrease	% Increase	% Decrease	% Increase
Placement history	90.0	10.0	83.3	0.0	100.0	0.0
Access to educational services & experience	80.0	10.0	83.3	0.0	0.0	60.0
Access to therapeutic services & experience	30.0	10.0	0.0	0.0	0.0	0.0
Activities with foster family	0.0	30.0	50.0	0.0	40.0	0.0
Preparation for leaving care	50.0	0.0	33.3	0.0	0.0	40.0
Leaving care resources	40.0	20.0	0.0	33.3	80.0	0.0
Foster family & other nurturing supports while in care	40.0	50.0	50.0	33.3	40.0	60.0
All foster care experience variables optimized	90.0	10.0	100.0	0.0	100.0	0.0

| | Outcome Domains | | | | | |
| | Employment & Finance (13) | | Marriage & Relationships (14) | | Foster Care Area Summary (48)[a] | |
Foster Care Area	% Decrease	% Increase	% Decrease	% Increase	% Decrease	% Increase
Placement history	64.3	28.6	61.5	38.5	75.0	20.8
Access to educational services & experience	64.3	14.3	30.8	46.2	54.2	25.0
Access to therapeutic services & experience	21.4	7.1	23.1	23.1	18.8	10.4
Activities with foster family	0.0	7.1	23.1	23.1	16.7	14.6
Preparation for leaving care	35.7	7.1	23.1	46.2	31.3	18.8
Leaving care resources	71.4	0.0	46.2	15.4	50.0	12.5
Foster family & other nurturing supports while in care	57.1	42.9	53.8	38.5	50.0	43.8
All foster care experience variables optimized	92.9	7.1	76.9	23.1	89.6	10.4

[a] *Percent decrease* refers to the number of times across outcomes that optimizing a foster care area resulted in a reduction in the predicted prevalence rate of undesirable outcomes. Conversely, *percent increase* refers to the number of times across outcome that optimizing a foster care area resulted in an increase in the predicted prevalence rate of undesirable outcomes. After foster care experience was optimized, the predicted prevalence rate of some outcomes did not change. This percentage is not included in the table but can be calculated by subtracting the percent increase plus the percent decrease from 100 [no change = [100 − (%decease + %increase)].

experiences decreased the estimated prevalence rate of undesirable outcomes nearly 90% of the time (89.6%) and increased the estimated prevalence rate of undesirable outcomes about 10% of the time (10.4%).

Summary

The simulation analyses described and presented in this chapter attempted to answer the question "What would outcomes be had alumni received an ideal (optimal) level of care?" To address this question, two sets of optimization analyses were conducted: one at the outcome domain level and the other at the individual outcome level. For both sets of analyses, outcomes were regressed on foster care experiences before and after experiences were optimized and the change in the estimated undesirable outcome level was calculated. Further, foster care experience areas were examined separately and simultaneously. This was done to examine the independent effects of optimization of foster care experience areas and to examine the cumulative effects of an ideal foster care experience.

Summary results for simulations at the outcome domain and individual outcome levels are presented in Tables 12.3 and 12.9, respectively. Both tables tell a similar story. First, when optimized separately, Placement History exhibited the greatest decrease in undesirable estimated outcomes at the domain and individual levels. Second, when optimized separately, two other foster care experience areas—Educational Services and Experience and Leaving Care Resources—consistently decreased undesirable estimated outcomes at the domain and individual outcome levels. Third, mixed and modest results were found when three foster care experience areas were optimized: Therapeutic Service and Supports, Activities with Foster Family, and Preparation for Leaving Care. The impact of optimizing these three areas separately varied by outcome domain and is difficult to generalize across all outcomes. Fourth, when optimized separately, Foster Family and Other Nurturing Support While in Care demonstrated a strong but mixed association with outcomes. This foster care experience area changed the percentage of many estimated undesirable outcomes but it was inconsistent: It decreased some undesirable outcomes and increased others. Lastly, when all foster care experiences were optimized simultaneously, dramatic reductions in the estimated levels of undesirable outcomes were observed.

These findings, while complex and at times contradictory, provide statistical evidence of the value of certain program refinements such as reducing placement changes, providing access to educational supports, and developing life skills before youth exit foster care.

Acknowledgment.   Catherine Roller White and Eva Hiripi contributed to this chapter.

13

Summary and Recommendations

Overview

This chapter summarizes the Northwest Alumni Study's main study research questions, hypotheses, and findings. Recommendations tied directly to the study data are discussed, along with other strategies that have been identified through discussions with alumni from foster care, staff, and others. The summary of major study findings is divided into findings from the *(1)* primary research questions and corresponding hypotheses and *(2)* supplemental research questions. Many of the questions and hypotheses concern the overall status of outcomes such as mental health functioning, while other questions concern relations among variables, such as the effect of child maltreatment on future financial health. In addition to answering the questions and testing hypotheses, data presented in previous chapters have provided answers to many unasked questions. These findings are presented where appropriate.

The Northwest Alumni Study was designed to address the lack of objective data available about adolescents who were placed in foster care for longer time periods in the Northwest. By examining extensive information collected through case records and interviews, the Northwest Alumni Study sought to understand how youth formerly in foster care were faring as adults and what experiences in care related to long-term success. The study also sought to discover if there were agency differences in service delivery quality, process, and outcomes—and what factors might account for those differences. This study, therefore, examined the efficacy of a high-quality long-term family foster care program in the particular context of the American Northwest. As such, this is an example of what Donald Campbell called a *local molar causal validity* study (Campbell, 1986). Although this study took place in only two states, these states are similar to many other states in terms of family demographics and service delivery structures. So, we are cautiously optimistic that readers will be able to generalize the findings to other jurisdictions.

Primary Research Questions and Hypotheses

Before addressing any research questions, a review of the basic demographics will help set the context. The age of the alumni was defined by the study design follow-up time period: ages 20 to 33 years (average age: 24.2 years). More women than men participated in the survey (61%), and more than half of the alumni interviewed (54.4%) were people of color, mainly African American, Hispanic/Latino, and American Indian or Alaskan Native.

The primary research questions asked of the alumni described above concern both prevalence rates and relationships between demographics, risk factors, the intervening agency, foster care experiences, and outcomes. The primary research questions are listed in Table 13.1 with highlights of some of the major findings. Due to the large quantity of data and large number of relationships among variables presented in Chapters 6–12, findings are summarized here for each primary research question.

As discussed in Chapter 12 and in O'Brien et al. (2009a), few expectations were generated concerning the relationship between demographics and outcomes. In contrast, it was expected that lower levels of risk factors and higher levels of a positive foster care experience would be related to positive adult outcomes. Further, due to Casey's enhanced resources and financial capacity, it was hypothesized that, in general, Casey alumni would exhibit more positive outcomes than state alumni. These hypotheses were informed by developmental theories and conceptual models, Landsverk's conceptual framework, previous foster care research, and differences between agencies' resources and functioning (described in Chapter 1). Almost all of the hypotheses were supported by the data.

Supplemental Research Questions

A study of this scope and magnitude generates many other interesting and important research questions. While these were not a primary focus, they added important details concerning alumni functioning. Many of the questions are more specific than the primary research questions, often dealing with subgroups of the total sample (see Table 13.2). Each question is grouped according to its type of variable: demographic, risk factor, agency, foster care experience, or outcome. To avoid duplication, any supplemental questions overlapping with the primary research questions were included in the following section (Table 13.1).

Table 13.1. Selected Findings of the Northwest Alumni Study Main Research Questions

Primary Research Questions and Hypotheses	Breakdown	Selected Findings
How are maltreated youth placed in foster care faring as adults? And to what extent are they different from other adults?	Mental Health	• 54.4% experienced symptoms of mental health disorder within the past 12 months. ◦ Alumni had higher rates of most mental health conditions than the general population. • Many alumni have recovered from past mental health problems, and of those who had problems, many report no longer being dependent upon or abusing alcohol (67.9%) and no longer experiencing symptoms of depression (51.0%). (See Chapter 6)
	Physical Health	• Nearly 7 in 10 (68.8%) scored above the mean on the physical health scale of the SF-12®, indicating good physical health. • 72.5% had no chronic diseases (e.g., heart disease, high blood pressure, HIV/AIDS). (See Chapter 6)
	Education	• Alumni completed high school at rates comparable to that of the general population (84.8% vs. 87.3%). • 1.8% completed college or more. (See Chapter 7)
	Employment and Finances	• Over one in five alumni (22.2%) were homeless for one or more nights at some time within a year after leaving foster care. • Almost 1 in 10 (9.3%) owned a house or apartment. • Nearly three in four (74.0%) are working now or in school. • 83.2% do not currently receive cash public assistance. • 67.0% had health insurance. ◦ Alumni had lower rates than the general population of employment, health insurance coverage, and rates of public assistance. (See Chapter 8)
	Relationships and Social Supports	• 88.2% have had no serious physical fighting in the past year. • 91.8% of alumni with children have not had a child placed in foster care. (See Chapter 9)
Hypothesis: It was hypothesized that alumni would exhibit functioning lower than that of general population comparisons but comparable to or better than that of alumni from other studies.		Supported for many outcome areas with the exception of overall high school completion and current rate of problematic alcohol use, which were both comparable to those of the general population.[93] (See Chapters 6–9)

(continued)

Table 13.1.   Continued

Primary Research Questions and Hypotheses	Breakdown	Selected Findings
Which youth are most at risk for poor long-term outcomes based on risk factors that were descriptive of them at the time of first placement?	Mental Health	• Alumni whose mothers had substance abuse problems were more likely to have had alcohol dependence and generalized anxiety in the past 12 months. • Alumni whose fathers had substance abuse problems were more likely to have had alcohol dependence and PTSD in the past 12 months. (See O'Brien et al., 2009a)
	Education	• Alumni who did not know either their mother or father while growing up were less likely to complete high school. (See O'Brien et al., 2009a)
	Employment and Finances	• Alumni who were five years of age or younger when they entered care were more likely to have someone in their household on public assistance. • Alumni who experienced all four abuse types (sexual, physical, and emotional abuse and neglect) were more likely to have someone in their household on public assistance and to have a household income below the poverty level. (See O'Brien et al., 2009a)
Hypothesis: It was hypothesized that lower levels of risk factors such as less severe child maltreatment would be related to more positive outcomes with respect to education and mental health.		Supported for many outcome areas. The following were related to more positive outcomes: • Experiencing only one type of abuse, and not experiencing sexual abuse and another form of abuse. • Not having a physical health or learning disability problem diagnosed while in care. (See O'Brien et al., 2009a)
Is one foster care program approach better than another in terms of outcomes? (See Chapter 10)	Outcomes favoring state care	• Smoked fewer than 10 cigarettes per day • Owned a house or apartment • Not socially isolated (among those married or cohabitating) • Positive social support from friends and relatives • No children before marriage • Did not have a child of their own placed in foster care

Table 13.1.   Continued

Primary Research Questions and Hypotheses	Breakdown	Selected Findings
	Outcomes favoring Casey care	• No 12-month CIDI diagnosis • Total number of 12-month CIDI diagnoses was fewer than three • No major depression in last 12 months • No social phobia in last 12 months • No chronic physical disorder • Received high school diploma • Some education past high school (any type of postsecondary education) • Completed some degree/certificate beyond high school (e.g., vocational, BA) • Completed college or more (has a BA or more) • Not homeless within 12 months after leaving foster care • Employment for married women in school (who are in the workforce) • Frequent displays of nurturance or affection with children

Primary Research Questions and Hypotheses	Selected Findings
Hypothesis: It was hypothesized that, in general, Casey alumni would exhibit more positive outcomes than state alumni.	It was found that Casey alumni exhibited more desirable outcomes on 12 of the 48 outcomes (25.0%), while the state alumni had more favorable outcomes on 6 of the 48 outcomes (12.5%). (See Chapter 10)
Are there key factors or program components that are linked with better functioning in adulthood?	Yes. They include optimizing such key program factors as: • Minimizing placement change rates and child reunification failures. • Providing access to educational tutoring and other key supports. • Building youth skills for independent living and providing opportunities so that youth leave care with some funds and skills to live on their own. • Positive foster family and other nurturing support while in care (this was especially linked with positive physical health outcomes). (See Chapter 12)
Specific Hypotheses. The following experiences while in care were hypothesized to be related to more positive outcomes:	In general, a more positive foster care experience was related to more positive outcomes. (See Chapters 11 and 12 for this finding and the others related to this hypothesis)

(continued)

Table 13.1.   Continued

Primary Research Questions and Hypotheses	Selected Findings
A more stable placement history	**Supported:** Strongly linked with most of the outcome domains and specific variables like mental health diagnoses and educational achievement.
More access to educational tutoring supports and educational stability	**Supported:** Strongly linked with most of the outcome domains and specific variables, including educational outcomes like completing high school and any degree/ certificate beyond high school.
More access to therapeutic service and supports	**Supported:** Linked with many of the outcome domains and specific variables.
More involvement with the foster family	**Supported:** Strongly linked with some of the outcome domains and specific variables within Mental Health, Education, Employment and Finances, and Relationships and Social Supports.
Greater preparation for leaving care (e.g., employment training and support)	**Supported:** Linked with some of the outcome domains and specific variables within Mental Health, Education, Employment and Finances, and Relationships and Social Supports.
More tangible resources upon leaving care (e.g., $250 in cash and a driver's license)	**Supported:** Strongly linked with most of the outcome domains and specific variables.
Had a close relationship with an adult while growing up	**Not supported:** This relationship was in the opposite direction for all but four outcomes in the multivariate analyses. It was a positive predictor for these variables: • Not smoking currently • Not being socially isolated if single and not cohabitating • Not physically fighting within the past 12 months • Doing a lot of things with their children (among alumni with children)

Table 13.2. Supplemental Research Question Findings

Domain	Supplemental Research Questions	Selected Findings
Demographics	What proportion of alumni were deceased at the time of the study?	• Less than 1% were deceased.
Risk Factors		
Birth Family Characteristics	What were the primary characteristics of the birth families of the alumni in this study?	• Alumni came from birth families that had experienced moderate amounts of unemployment, mental health problems, substance abuse, and/or criminal justice involvement. (See Chapter 5)
Child Maltreatment by Birth Parents	Before entering foster care, what were the types, severity, and age of onset of maltreatment experienced? Who were the perpetrators of maltreatment?	• Over half of the alumni had experienced sexual abuse (53.6%); around two-thirds had experienced physical abuse (64.6%) and physical neglect (67.4%); and over four in five (84.5%) had experienced emotional maltreatment. • Almost one in four alumni (23.2%) had experienced all four maltreatment types, while almost one in five (19.0%) had experienced none or one type. • One in 15 (6.7%) alumni had experienced no maltreatment. (See Chapter 5)
Agencies	Were there any systematic differences among the agency samples in the pre–foster care maltreatment experience?	• More Casey alumni had been sexually abused and emotionally maltreated than state alumni. (See Chapter 5)
	Were there systematic differences among the agency samples in maltreatment experience during foster care?	• More Casey alumni had been sexually abused. (See Williams et al., 2009)

(continued)

Table 13.2. Continued

Domain	Supplemental Research Questions	Selected Findings
Foster Care Experiences		
Placement History and Experience	How long were alumni in foster care, and how many placements did they experience?	• The number of placements varied widely; about one-third (31.9%) of the alumni experienced three or fewer placements, but an equal percentage (32.3%) experienced eight or more placements. • Average length of time in foster care was 6.1 years. • Almost one-third of the alumni (32.5%) stayed in foster care for 3.6 years or less. • Alumni exited care at an average age of 18.5 years. (See Williams et al., 2009)
Agency Staff	According to alumni, were the type and frequency of contact between agency staff and youth adequate? Were agency staff members viewed as helpful?	Alumni reported that they: • Were seen by their caseworkers "too little" (53.6%). • Felt strongly that their caseworkers were helpful (29.7%). • Were strongly satisfied with their overall experience in foster care (40.7%). (See Williams et al., 2009)
Foster Parent Characteristics [The interview asked alumni about their most recent placement (if more than three months; otherwise, the longest placement was referenced).	What were the characteristics of the foster parents?	• Ninety-five percent of the alumni had a foster mother in their last foster family, but only 69.2% had a foster father. (See Williams et al., 2009)
	How did their foster parents, especially in their last foster home, treat youth in their care?	• Of their foster parents overall, 64.0% of the alumni rated them as somewhat or very helpful. • The majority of alumni from both agencies (57.9%) agreed that the foster parents (who may have included kinship caregivers) were the people most helpful to them while they were in care. (See Williams et al., 2009)

Table 13.2. Continued

Domain	Supplemental Research Questions	Selected Findings
	Did youth experience differential treatment, including positive or negative favoritism, compared with other youth living in the home?	• Over four in five of the alumni's foster parents had their own children (78.5%); two-thirds of alumni (64.4%) reported that their foster parents treated the alumni the same as they did their birth children. (See Williams et al., 2009)
Educational Services and Experience	What kinds of access to and participation in educational services and supports did youth receive while in care?	• Almost 9 in 10 alumni (89.1%) reported having access to tutoring or other supplemental educational services, while just under half (48.1%) utilized these services. (See Williams et al., 2009)
Therapeutic Service and Supports	What kinds of access to and participation in therapeutic services and supports did youth receive while in care?	• Over four in five alumni (83.6%) reported that they had access to mental health counseling, drug and alcohol treatment, and group work or group counseling. However, a significantly lower proportion actually utilized these services. (See Williams et al., 2009)
Preparation for Leaving Care	What kinds of access to and participation in services and supports for leaving care did youth receive while in care?	Fewer than half of the alumni reported receiving employment, job location, and other independent living-skills preparation. Yet, more than half (56.9%) reported feeling prepared for independent living when they left care. However, at exit from care, only: • One-third (33.3%) had a driver's license. • Fewer than two in five (38.4%) had $250 in cash. • Fewer than one in four (23.7%) had dishes and utensils for establishing a home. • Over two in five had none of these resources (43.5%). (See Williams et al., 2009)

(continued)

Table 13.2.   Continued

Domain	Supplemental Research Questions	Selected Findings
Child Maltreatment by Foster Parent or Other Caregiver While in Care	While in foster care, did further incidents of maltreatment occur?	• Case record data, documented by agency staff members, revealed that 19.2% of the alumni were alleged to have been abused by a foster family member while in care. • 32.8% of alumni reported being maltreated by a foster parent or other caregiver in public or private agency foster care.[a] (See Williams et al., 2009)
	What was the relationship between child maltreatment and adult outcomes?	• Child maltreatment while in foster care had the highest rate of prediction in the unexpected direction across all outcomes. (See O'Brien et al., 2009a)
Outcomes		
Mental Health	What proportion of alumni had been hospitalized in a treatment facility?	• Fewer than 1 in 20 (4.0%) had stayed overnight for mental health, alcohol, or drug treatment in the last 12 months but, in their lifetime, almost 1 in 3 (31.2%) had received such treatment. (See O'Brien et al., 2009a)
	What overall level of self-esteem did alumni have?	• The mean level of self-esteem was comparable to that of alumni in other samples, but over a quarter (27.0%) reported low self-esteem. (See O'Brien et al., 2009a)
Education	How much education had alumni completed?	• A high proportion of alumni (84.8%) had completed high school, and 42.7% had participated in some kind of postsecondary education. (See Chapter 7 and O'Brien et al., 2009a)
	What degrees had they obtained?	• 20.6% had completed some degree/certificate beyond high school (vocational, BA, etc.). • 1.8% had completed college or more. (See Chapter 7)

Table 13.2.   Continued

Domain	Supplemental Research Questions	Selected Findings
Employment and Finances	What jobs did alumni obtain, and what was their income?	The three most common job categories were: 1. Financial records processing: 14.3% 2. Service occupations: 18.1% 3. Sales occupations: 16.3% (See Chapter 8)
Relationships and Social Supports	How many alumni were adopted?	• 5.7% of alumni were adopted before foster care, 9.0% during foster care, and 0.8% after foster care. (See Williams et al., 2009)
	How many alumni became pregnant or fathered a child?	• While most alumni reported not having a child before they were 18 (92.7%) or before marriage (82.0%), a large proportion of alumni (63.0%) were parents at the time of their interview. (See Chapter 9)
	How well do alumni parent their offspring?	• One-fourth of alumni with children (25.7%) reported that they do a lot of things with their children. • Just over a quarter of alumni with children (27.0%) reported that they frequently display nurturance and affection with their children. (See Chapter 9)
	What percentages of alumni were in significant relationships? What types of relationships were these? What was the level of satisfaction with their current relationship?	• 30.4% of the alumni reported being married currently. • Nearly half of the alumni (47.1%) were either married or cohabitating at the time of the study, which is slightly less than that of the general population. • Almost two-thirds (62.7%) of married or cohabitating alumni reported being very satisfied with their relationship. (See Chapter 9)
	What contact did alumni have with their birth families?	• 58.6% of alumni were in contact with siblings. • 40.9% of alumni were in contact with birth mothers. • 20.5% of alumni were in contact with birth fathers. (See Chapter 9) (continued)

Table 13.2.   Continued

Domain	Supplemental Research Questions	Selected Findings
	Did alumni have contact with their foster parents after exiting care?	• 61.9% were in contact with their former foster parents. (See Chapter 9)
	To what extent were alumni connected with organized religion or with other sources of spiritual comfort?	• Over one-third of alumni (34.5%) reported attending religious services at least once per month. • Over two in five alumni (42.2%) reported that they often or almost always seek spiritual comfort when they experience difficulties in their family, work, or personal lives. (See Chapter 9)

Supplemental Outcomes

Domain	Supplemental Research Questions	Selected Findings
Post-emancipation Services	What kinds of services and supports were provided to alumni after leaving foster care?	• Only 21.9% of alumni said that a child welfare agency had been helpful to them since leaving foster care. (See Chapter 9)
	What kinds of professional services had adult alumni received during the previous 12 months?	• Over 1 in 10 was currently seeing a helping professional (11.8%). Alumni had accessed or obtained the following in the past year: • Self-help group or hotline for mental health, alcohol, drug treatment (11.6%). • Outpatient professional help (23.3%). (See Williams et al., 2009)
Criminal Justice Involvement	How many alumni (of the original sample) were in jail or prison at the time of the study interviews?	• 20 (3.0%) were currently in prison. (See Chapter 3)
Giving Back	Have alumni contributed to their communities while in foster care or as adults?	• 63.6% reported having volunteered in the community or church at some point in their lives. (See Chapter 9)

[a] The case record data may have included others in the home, such as a foster sibling, whereas the interview data were limited to adult caregivers as perpetrators. Neither data collection instrument identified the agency charged with the care of the alumnus or alumna at that time (most Casey alumni were served previously by a state agency).

Defining Success

Adult outcomes for any child are varied. One person might judge college completion as signifying success, while another might focus on employment, relationships, or parenting. To create a more comprehensive set of success indicators, the following list was developed to represent all the major outcome domains. While very few alumni achieved all criteria and the proportion of alumni succeeding in a particular area may be low in relation to the general population, a majority (57.5%) achieved seven (or more) of the criteria.

A. Mental Health
    1. 45.6% had no 12-month mental health diagnosis.
    2. 50.6% had an SF-12® mental health score of 50 or above.[85]
B. Physical Health
    3. 68.8% had an SF-12® physical health score of 50 or above.
    4. 75.3% smoked fewer than 10 cigarettes a day.
    5. 75.9% drank fewer than 150 drinks per year (slightly fewer than 3 drinks per week).
C. Education
    6. 20.6% had received some degree or certificate past high school.
D. Employment and Finances
    7. 67.0% had health insurance.
    8. 21.3% had a household income at least three times the poverty level.
    9. 83.2% did not currently receive cash public assistance.
    10. 74.0% were working or were in school.
E. Relationships and Social Supports
    11. 88.2% had had no serious physical fighting resulting in medical treatment in the past year.

The proportion of the alumni who achieved all 11 indicators, or who achieved 10 indicators, and so on, is presented in Table 13.3.

Although some of these outcomes were not included in the composite approach to success above, they are provided here as examples of success among alumni:

- High percentages of alumni had recovered from mental health problems in the areas of alcohol dependence (67.9%) and depression (51.0%).
- 68.8% scored above the mean on the physical health scale of the SF-12®.
- 72.5% had no chronic diseases (e.g., heart disease, high blood pressure, HIV/AIDS).
- 91.8% of alumni with children had not had a child placed in foster care.
- 97% were not currently in prison.
- 63.6% had volunteered in their communities or church.

In summary, the Northwest Alumni Study documented a number of areas where alumni were successful, as well as areas in which program refinements are needed to help youth develop positive social support networks, complete educational programs, and obtain jobs with a living wage and health care

Table 13.3.   Proportion of Alumni Who Have Achieved Certain
Outcomes[a]

Criteria Achieved	Proportion of Alumni
At least 1 of 11	100.0
At least 2 of 11	99.8
At least 3 of 11	97.9
At least 4 of 11	92.8
At least 5 of 11	84.9
At least 6 of 11	73.1
At least 7 of 11	57.5
At least 8 of 11	37.1
At least 9 of 11	19.1
At least 10 of 11	6.8
All 11	1.8

[a] The outcome domains and indicators were:
  • Mental Health (no 12-month mental health diagnosis; SF-12®
    mental health score of 50 or above)
  • Physical Health (SF-12® physical health score of 50 or above; smoke
    fewer than 10 cigarettes a day; drink fewer than 150 drinks per year)
  • Education (received some degree or certificate past high school)
  • Employment and Finances (have health insurance; have household
    income at least three times the poverty level; do not currently receive
    cash public assistance; are working or are in school)
  • Relationships and Social Supports (have had no serious physical
    fighting resulting in medical treatment in the past year)

benefits. While some program critics have chosen to focus exclusively on the
negative outcomes of foster care, substantial numbers of alumni are coping
well as adults. Many alumni told the interviewers that had they not been
placed in out-of-home care, their outcomes would have been significantly
worse. For example: "If not for my foster parents, I would be dead." "Foster
care saved my life."

As a de facto parent for children placed in foster care, the child welfare
system needs a comprehensive and accurate picture of adult functioning of
those it has served (Bullock, Courtney, Parker, Sinclair, & Thoburn, 2006).
Few follow-up studies of young adults who have been in foster care have
interviewed persons who were 22 years of age and older. The Northwest
Alumni Study interviewed older alumni in order to assess more long-term
outcomes that are important to society as a whole, and the comprehensive
measures enabled the study team to document a wide range of successes.
This could not have been accomplished, of course, without the assistance of
hundreds of alumni from care who wanted to help improve care by sharing
their stories.

Program, Policy, and Practice Recommendations by Study Outcome Domain

Question: If you could tell children coming into the foster care agency anything right now, what would you tell them?
Answer: Let them know they're in a position now to make a decision—they can either use the stuff that has happened in their life as a crutch or as a stepping stone.

Answer: Hmm… "Good luck." (laughs). I don't know. For me, I had no control over anything, really. What can you tell someone in that circumstance? Seek out someone they can talk to, definitely that, if there's anyone they can trust.

Answer: To me, longevity is the primary indicator for having a significant connection. In a system that regards permanency as the best answer for children, there is an amazing amount of impermanence. As my case moved from one work unit to the next, or from one agency to the next, so did I… new people, new homes, new schools, new neighborhoods, new rules and all that. In retrospect, this system that was striving so hard and so quickly for permanence would have been better off taking more time. Would I have had two failed adoptions if more front-end work had been done? I'll never know. What eventually worked in my favor was having a voice, and having a social worker that listened.

The overarching question for the child welfare system is this: What can agencies and communities do to improve outcomes for youth who are currently in care? And with the recent passage of Public Law 110-351, the "Fostering Connections to Success and Increasing Adoptions Act" of 2008 agencies want to know how best to support 18- to 21-year-olds who are in foster care or those recently emancipated (see Table 13.4). To answer these questions, the following recommendations are first clustered by the major outcome domains—Mental Health, Physical Health, Education, Employment and Finances, and Relationships and Social Supports—and then by the sources of the recommendations. The recommendations stem from the basic descriptive outcomes of the study, the foster care experience statistical simulations, and conversations with stakeholders.

The stakeholders included groups of young adults who had been in foster care, foster parents, caseworkers, and agency executives, as well as clinical and policy specialists from each of the three collaborating organizations and other public child welfare agencies.[86] The study team asked these stakeholders to help identify the stories behind the numbers and to solidify the study recommendations.

Mental and Physical Health

Recommendations Based on Descriptive Outcomes

Findings from the National Survey of Child and Adolescent Well-Being (NSCAW) study indicate that despite high rates of mental health service

Table 13.4. Highlights of the Provisions of the Fostering Connections to Success and Increasing Adoptions Act (P.L. 110–351)

The Fostering Connections to Success and Increasing Adoptions Act (P.L. 110–351) will help hundreds of thousands of children and youth in foster care by promoting permanent families for them through relative guardianship and adoption and improving education and health care. Additionally, it will extend federal support for youth to age 21. The act will also offer for the first time many American Indian children important federal protections and support.

The Fostering Connections to Success and Increasing Adoptions Act will improve outcomes for children and youth in foster care by:

Promoting Permanent Families for Children in Foster Care

With Relatives

- **Notice to Relatives When Children Enter Care.** Increases opportunities for relatives to step in when children are removed from their parents and placed in foster care by ensuring they get notice of this removal.
- **Kinship Navigator Programs.** Guarantees funds for Kinship Navigator programs, through new Family Connection grants, to help connect children living with relatives, both in and out of foster care, with the supports and assistance they need.
- **Subsidized Guardianship Payments for Relatives.** Helps children in foster care leave care to live permanently with grandparents and other relative guardians when they cannot be returned home or adopted and offers federal support to states to assist with subsidized guardianship payments to families for these children, generally to age 18. In certain circumstances, children may continue to receive guardianship assistance to age 21. Clarifies that all children who, as of September 30, 2008, were receiving federally supported subsidized guardianship payments or services in states with Child Welfare Demonstration Waivers will be able to continue to receive that assistance and services under the new program. Clarifies that children who leave foster care after age 16 for kinship guardianship are eligible for independent living services and makes them eligible for education and training vouchers.
- **Licensing Standards for Relatives.** Clarifies that states may waive non-safety related licensing standards for relatives on a case-by-case basis and requires the Department of Health and Human Services (DHHS) to report to Congress on the use of licensing waivers and recommendations for increasing the percentage of relative foster family homes that are licensed.

With Adoptive Families

- **Incentives for Adoption.** Increases incentives to states to find adoptive families for children in foster care, especially those with disabilities or other special needs and older youth.
- **Adoption Assistance.** Increases opportunities for more children with special needs to receive federally-supported adoption assistance without regard to the income of the birth families from whom they were originally removed.

With Birth Families and Other Relatives

- **Establishes New Family Connection Grants.** Increases resources for Kinship Navigator programs, as described above. Also provides grants for Family Group Decision-making meetings, Intensive Family Finding activities, and Residential Family-Based Substance Abuse Treatment, all of which can help children stay safely with family members and out of foster care or, once in care, return safely to their parents or find permanence with other relatives.
- **Siblings Together.** Preserves the sibling bond for children by requiring states to make reasonable efforts to place siblings together when they must be removed from their parents' home, provided it is in the children's best interests. In the case of siblings not placed together, states must make reasonable efforts to provide for frequent visitation or other ongoing interaction, unless such interaction would be harmful to any of the siblings.

Improving Outcomes for Children and Youth in Foster Care

- **Foster Care for Older Youth.** Helps youth who turn 18 in foster care without permanent families to remain in care, at state option, to age 19, 20, or 21 with continued federal support to increase their opportunities for success as they transition to adulthood.
- **Educational Stability.** Helps children and youth in foster care, guardianship and adoption achieve their educational goals by requiring that states ensure that they attend school and, when placed in foster care, they remain in their same school where appropriate, or, when a move is necessary, get help transferring promptly to a new school; also provides increased federal support to assist with school-related transportation costs.
- **Health Care Coordination.** Helps improve health care for children and youth in foster care by requiring the state child welfare agency to work with the state Medicaid agency to create a plan to better coordinate health care for these children in order to ensure appropriate screenings and assessments and follow-up treatment and to assure sharing of critical information with appropriate providers and oversight of prescription medications.

Increasing Support for American Indian and Alaska Native Children

- **Direct Access to Federal Support for Indian Tribes.** Offers, for the first time, many American Indian and Alaska Native children federal assistance and protections through the federal foster care and adoption assistance programs that hundreds of thousands of other children are eligible for already.
- **Technical Assistance and Implementation Services.** Requires DHHS to provide technical assistance and implementation services dedicated to improving services and permanency outcomes for Indian children and their families.

Improving the Quality of Staff Working With Children in the Child Welfare System

- Extended federal support for training of staff. Expands the availability of federal training dollars, on a phased-in basis, to reach more of those caring for and working with children in the child welfare system, including relative guardians, staff of private child welfare agencies, court personnel, attorneys, guardian ad litems, and court appointed special advocates.

Source: Adapted from Children's Defense Fund and Center for Law and Social Policy. (2009). Fostering Connections to Success and Increasing Adoptions Act Will Improve Outcomes for Children and Youth in Foster Care. Retrieved April 6, 2009 from: http://www.childrensdefense.org/helping-americas-children/child-welfare/fostering-connection-success-increasing-adoptions-act-overview.html. Reprinted with permission.

needs in comparison with community studies, three of four youth in child welfare who meet a stringent criterion for need were not receiving mental health care within 12 months after a child abuse and neglect investigation (Hurlburt et al., 2004; Landsverk, Burns, Stambaugh, & Rolls-Reutz, 2006). When assessed as adults, the rates of mental health problems in alumni were higher than those of the general population. It is critical to examine why mental health problems are so prevalent in this group. Recommendations related to mental health are the following:

1. Increase the access of youth in care and alumni to evidence-based mental health treatment. This study contributes new findings: Major depression and PTSD may be the most far-reaching mental health conditions for alumni in young adulthood. Depression and PTSD may contribute to difficulty in gaining or retaining employment, and their prevalence underscores the need to improve mental health in many ways, including the following:
   a. Child welfare systems should develop procedures to assess children/ youth upon entry into the foster care system to determine the needs of and appropriate services for youth who have borderline/clinical indications of service need.
   b. Child welfare workers should receive training to enable them to identify those children/youth who may need more formalized assessment and treatment for PTSD, depression, social phobia, and other disorders.
   c. Reform systems to increase mental health insurance coverage and Medicaid (see below for further discussion of Medicaid for alumni from foster care). A disproportionate number of these alumni suffer from PTSD, panic syndrome, generalized anxiety, major depression, and drug dependence. Federal and state governments should examine barriers to mental health care—including eligibility requirements that limit access to funding and worker capacity that may be insufficient to treat mental health problems—so that youth in care and alumni have greater access to effective treatment.
   d. Provide specialized training to Medicaid-funded and other therapists to enable them to properly assess and treat PTSD, depression, social phobia, and other disorders.
   e. Expand early and ongoing evidence-based treatment to help alleviate mental health disorders. The field needs more interventions that have been documented as effective by rigorous practice research (Kazdin & Weisz, 2003; Landsverk et al., 2006). Treat youth with validated approaches, and validate promising new interventions.
   f. Help youth in care access opportunities and services that promote mental health functioning. This public health approach is gaining support (National Research Council and Institute of Medicine, 2009).
   g. Help ensure that the mental health needs of young adults are met through state-funded mental health treatment. Because mental health problems continue into adulthood for many alumni, an age extension through the Chafee Medicaid Option is needed for all alumni whose jobs do not provide coverage. Currently, fewer than 18 states have implemented this option.

h. Improve physical health screenings and follow-up care. And given the high rates of premarital pregnancy and parenthood, reproductive health and family planning urgently need to be overhauled.

Many youth in foster care are forced to leave care at age 18, while they are still in high school, because they will not graduate by their 19th birthday. Many others find themselves unable to sustain stable housing and employment because they do not have any adult support during these critical years. Fortunately, a new Federal law (PL110-351) now allows for youth to stay in care until age 21. Medicaid coverage for children receiving foster care now can be extended past 18.

To ensure that young people have a fair chance to achieve productive citizenship, investment in their care during the transitional years is critical. The new extension of Title IV-E assistance should result both in reduced human cost for youth who are abandoned by their only source of support and in reduced financial burdens to the homeless, welfare, mental health, and health systems. This extension would also ensure that these youth maintain their Medicaid eligibility. New federal legislation provides states with the option of extending Title IV-E assistance to former youth from care up to age 21 as long as they are working or enrolled in educational programs and have a plan to become completely self-sufficient. Funds should be used for programs designed to promote the education, training, or employment of these youth. At a state's option, youth should maintain their eligibility for Medicaid (Child Welfare League of America, 2005).

Recommendations Based on Foster Care Experience Statistical Simulations

1. Help maintain placement stability, which appears to have a large positive effect on adult mental health. Optimizing the Placement History variables resulted in a very large decrease in predicted negative mental health outcomes. While many factors influence placement stability, minimizing placement changes while a youth is on his or her way to a permanent living situation warrants greater attention because of the apparent association of fewer changes with fewer mental health problems. Strategies that are not based strictly on the findings but that could help youth achieve some of the living situation stability outcomes mentioned above include:
   a. Strengthen initial placement decisions so that youth are less likely to move. Child welfare workers need to understand the consequences of unplanned moves for children.
   b. Child welfare systems should provide services to stabilize current placements rather than operate on a *presumptive move* policy wherein a child is automatically moved when there are problems in the placement setting. This approach would be more effective when foster parents are trained in the methods of implementing social learning and other interventions that will minimize placement disruptions (Briere, 2004; Chamberlain, Moreland, & Reid, 1992; Cohen, Mannarino, Zhitova, & Capone, 2003; Kazdin & Weisz, 2003; Price, Chamberlain, Landsverk & Reid, 2009).

Foster parents need to be aware of the importance of their role in ensuring placement stability and enhancing the child's birth family relationships to promote the child's mental health.

 c. Provide opportunities for youth to form positive attachments, and teach them skills for maintaining healthy relationships.

 d. Continuous relationships with adults can facilitate youth development. If caseworkers help youth form and maintain healthy relationships with birth parents and siblings through regular visits, provide transportation for visits (e.g., bus passes), and provide phone cards while they are in care, youth may be less likely to run away or otherwise need to be moved.

2. Increase educational services and experiences. Optimizing Educational Services and Experience (i.e., by providing access to supplemental education services and tutoring and by having a low number of school changes) resulted in a decrease in negative mental health outcomes. Stability and support in the school environment may therefore have a positive effect on adult mental health. This result, for example, supports efforts to maintain youth in the same school even if a placement change is deemed necessary.

Reactions and Recommendations Based on Conversations With Stakeholders

1. Improve foster parent orientation and training with respect to youth mental health. Agencies should provide foster parents with more comprehensive information about how to identify and address mental health difficulties that children in foster care experience (Pasztor, Hollinger, Inkelas, & Halfon, 2006). Training areas include:

 a. Use a broad developmental context; inform foster parents about difficulties their child may encounter and about how they can help manage emotional and behavioral problems.

 b. Provide advocacy training so that foster parents know what the youth's rights are regarding access to mental health services in their community.

 c. Increase the availability of respite care services so that foster parents can have a break from caregiving as well as timely crisis intervention services to help when problems arise suddenly.

2. Provide comprehensive daily emotional support to youth in care. Strategies include:

 a. Help reduce the stigma that youth in foster care feel by helping them understand what alumni have told us: that depression, anxiety, and other mental health conditions are a "natural reaction to an unnatural situation" and that mental health problems can be managed with proper support and intervention.

 b. Encourage youth to grieve at their own pace. Youth need to be allowed to discuss the positive aspects of their birth family and to process their grief over entering foster care.

 c. Inform and involve youth in decisions concerning their mental health problems and treatment regimen.

d. Be vigilant about confidentiality concerns. This issue is complicated by the fact that a youth's relationship with his or her therapist may be undermined by the sharing of information between the therapist and caseworker and/or foster parents. The youth, therefore, may feel that it is not safe to speak openly.

3. Address gaps in the skills of caseworkers and other professional workers.

a. Provide group work and other evidence-based treatment approaches to help youth grieve about losses, understand their thoughts and feelings, and learn new ways of coping with mental health problems (Clarke, DeBar, & Lewinsohn, 2003; Kazdin & Weisz, 2003). There has not been an enduring focus on these areas, especially for adolescents.

b. Caseworkers and counselors who are largely funded by Medicaid need more adequately funded training, clinical supervision, and quality improvement initiatives to improve the diagnosis and treatment of PTSD, generalized anxiety, and other common mental health disorders.

c. Given the higher rate of unmet mental health needs among children of color (Ringel & Sturm, 2001), it is important to develop, evaluate and integrate culturally responsive mental health services with foster care programs.

Education

Although their high school graduation rate was quite high, the rate at which alumni completed high school with a GED credential was disproportionately higher than that of the general population. In addition, while a considerable number of alumni began vocational and college studies, few completed these programs.

Recommendations Based on Descriptive Outcomes

1. Encourage youth not to settle for a GED credential. Those who complete a GED generally attain less education and earn less than individuals who have high school diplomas. Without unduly limiting their role in making key life decisions, youth need to be made aware of the consequences of certain kinds of educational decisions. From a less personal but equally powerful vantage point, labor market outcomes among GED credential holders have been shown to be closer to those of noncredentialed high school dropouts than to those of graduates with traditional diplomas. High school completion is an important milestone:

Most high school dropouts see the result of their decision to leave school most clearly in the slimness of their wallets. The average annual income for a high school dropout in 2005 was $17,299, compared to $26,933 for a high school graduate, a difference of $9,634 (U.S. Bureau of the Census, 2006). The impact on the country's economy is less visible, but it is nevertheless staggering.

If the nation's secondary schools improved sufficiently to graduate all of their students, rather than the 70 percent of students who are currently graduated annually (Editorial Projects in Education, 2008), the payoff would be significant. ***For instance, if the students who dropped out of the Class of 2008 had graduated, the nation's economy would have benefited from an additional $319 billion in income over their lifetimes.*** [Emphasis in original.] (Alliance for Excellent Education, 2008, p.1).

As described above, the economic impact is not trivial. (For the impact on crime reduction and earnings, see Alliance for Excellent Education, 2006.)

Strategies for increasing the rate at which youth obtain a high school diploma include:

a. Examine why GED credentials are more common among alumni from foster care. Alumni have said that some of these reasons may include mental health disorders (e.g., PTSD, depression, social phobia) and difficulty transferring records when changing schools. Some youth in care end up in alternative types of high school settings that offer GED programs as a more efficient and quicker way to complete high school—especially for those who have had to move and see nothing but big holes in their remaining credit requirements. (Sometimes a GED is their last opportunity to complete high school in any type of format.) One issue is to examine what could be done to minimize those situations so that more youth can graduate with diplomas.

b. Make greater efforts to include graduation from high school in service plans. The Washington State Public Policy Institute (2004) issued a cost-benefit analysis of social programs and argued strongly for investments in helping youth complete high school and plan their careers (also see Bos, 1995, 1996; Lee, Aos, & Miller, 2008; Smith, 2003).

c. Support better preparation for, access to, and success in postsecondary education programs. Caseworkers, foster families, and other stakeholders should encourage young people in foster care to plan for college or vocational school and help them become adequately prepared for higher education and training. Inform older youth about local college-preparatory programs, such as GEAR UP, TRIO, and Upward Bound, and help them enroll in these programs (Casey Family Programs, 2003a). The recently passed Higher Education Act (HEA) included a requirement for TRIO programs to do better outreach to youth in foster care and made it somewhat easier for youth in care to qualify as an independent household to obtain financial aid.

d. Inform youth about scholarships (federal, state, county, private, Chafee, etc.) designed exclusively for youth from care.

Recommendations Based on Foster Care Experience
Statistical Simulations

1. Minimize placement change. Optimizing the Placement History variables predicted a decrease in negative education outcomes. If youth do not change homes and schools, they do not have to adjust to a new school environment and a new curriculum, there is no need to transfer school records,

and youth are less likely to fall behind. Placement instability is a result of poor administrative processes, low agency support of foster parents, and behavioral problems of youth. All of these factors need to be studied and addressed (James, 2004; Pecora & Huston, 2008).

2. Provide concrete resources to youth as they leave care. In statistical simulations, optimizing the Leaving Care Resources foster care experience area resulted in a decrease in negative education outcomes. It may be that having concrete resources such as a driver's license, $250 in cash, and dishes and utensils results in more financial stability, allowing alumni to pursue their education goals. This foster care experience variable is likely a proxy for more comprehensive independent living preparation and engagement in the foster care experience; the value of that training is underscored and is worth investigating further. We need to help ensure that youth have caring adults in their lives to guide and support them as they move through the very complicated postsecondary education world.

Reactions and Recommendations Based on Conversations With Stakeholders

1. Increase the likelihood of completing high school with a diploma. Alumni have suggested these strategies:

   a. Every child who enters foster care should have a thorough neuro-cognitive assessment to identify his or her strengths and areas of need. Too often crucial skill or ability gaps may be overlooked, thus contributing to children's falling further behind in their schooling. But clearly, identifying skill gaps is not sufficient; youth need to actually receive the appropriate supplemental supports. Improve identification and treatment of mental health problems that may act as barriers to classroom success (e.g., social phobia, depression, and the sleep and attention problems that accompany PTSD). The appropriate services must then be provided—either through an Individualized Education Plan, Section 504 plan, or other methods that are not stigmatizing for the youth.

   b. Educate school personnel about the challenges that youth in foster care face and the ways they can advocate for these youth.[87] There appears to be a high need for school counselors who have mental health training and who are people of color so that students of color will be more likely to seek treatment. A review of race/ethnicity and mental health treatment by Garland, Landsverk, and Lau (2003) suggests that there is consistently lower use of mental health care for African American youth when controlling for need. Evidence from a national study suggests that coordination between child welfare and mental health agencies may increase the effect of clinical factors and decrease nonclinical factors such as race/ethnicity in the use of mental health care (Hurlburt et al., 2004). Teachers also need training in these situations; very few classroom teachers understand the disorders that may disproportionately impact children in care.

   c. Maintain enrollment in the same school, even if the foster home placement changes. Sometimes placement change is necessary, but agencies should make efforts to minimize its secondary effects. Federal legislation and, in some cases, state legislation are supportive of this issue (see the Legal Center for Foster Care and Education for more information: http://www.abanet.org/child/education/home.shtml).

   d. Maintain an educational profile or "passport" for all children in foster care that moves with them. This will ensure the proper transfer of important records should a child need to change schools.

   e. To help reduce the stigma of being a foster child, ensure that youth have access to high quality public or private schools. Place youth in alternative school settings only if it is absolutely necessary. Youth who have left school should receive support in reenrolling, even if they have turned 18.

   f. When public education is not feasible, provide schooling in alternative schools or programs that have smaller class sizes, nontraditional teaching practices, and more one-on-one instruction. This is particularly warranted for those foster children whose comprehensive evaluations have uncovered learning and/or attention difficulties.

   g. Provide mentors and tutors to promote study and career skills. Focus tutoring and skills development in areas of greatest need and at times when the youth may be most receptive to the assistance (e.g., some youth are not ready to learn about financial issues at age 11 but are prepared at age 14 or 16). "Every child should have the opportunity and supports needed to read fluently and with comprehension before they enter middle school. Worry much less about who is going to go to college and pay more attention to comprehension and fluency. We would then have more children finishing high school and going to college" (Hildy Ayers, personal communication, March 15, 2006).

   h. Advocate for youth to enroll in courses required for graduation, to succeed in postsecondary training, and to explore a full range of education options (e.g., classes beyond high school completion). We see a real need for an "education advocate"—someone who can guide youths' choices and decisions in a meaningful way. This person can be a foster parent, relative, paid education advocate, or other adult but must be someone who is knowledgeable and consistent.

2. Support youth in care by targeting education outcomes to increase completion of vocational training and college programs. Ways to enhance these supports include:

   a. Maximize the use of Chafee funds by state child welfare agencies if not already maximized.

   b. Provide Title IV-E education vouchers. (These funds can help youth meet basic needs like housing so that they can focus on their schoolwork.)

   c. Promote enhanced career planning and support through TRIO and GEAR UP programs.[88] Both TRIO and GEAR UP target disadvantaged students and are extremely important in identifying youth for college awareness opportunities. Neither program specifically emphasizes youth in foster care as a population that requires special attention because of a new clause in the HEA. Youth from care deserve to receive special attention because they tend to move frequently from school to school, have difficulty learning in a traditional classroom setting, and come from impoverished and broken homes.

   d. Increase the use of existing vocational training and college scholarships.

e. Improve the HEA and the Free Application for Federal Student Aid (FAFSA) form layout to make it easier for alumni from foster care to apply and qualify for special scholarships and loans.[89] The HEA can be vital in helping youth in foster care access degree programs at both two- and four-year institutions.[90]

f. Encourage more colleges to keep dorms open during holidays and other vacation periods for alumni who have nowhere to go. Stories of alumni with no place to live during college holiday breaks provide stark remind-ers of the importance of this service. Schools should diligently help alumni make and maintain connections to other adults, such as aca-demic advisors and peer mentors. See a guide for college personnel for helping foster care alumni at http://www.casey.org.

g. Extend or eliminate the age limit at which alumni can receive aid from scholarship programs. Some youth pursue scholarship programs imme-diately after they emancipate, largely because such programs may not be available to them later. Alumni have suggested that this may be a setup for failure since short-term access to scholarships may compel them to begin postsecondary schooling before they are emotionally, socially, and economically ready.

3. Promote formal and informal vocational education for all youth in care. Even those going to college need job skills. Recommendations include:

a. Ensure that agency staff, foster parents, and youth are aware of voca-tional options.

b. Strengthen agency and youth connections to the working world through special agreements and internships and by taking youth to potential job sites. (See the *It's My Life: Employment* guide at http://www.casey.org or http://www.caseylifeskills.org).

Employment

I think the way my foster mother and father transitioned me was great. It was a really smooth transition. In the months before I moved out, they taught me things about money, housework and independent living skills, etc. They thought about getting me ready to go in advance.

They didn't have any screening for her to become a foster parent; she didn't know how to discipline children or deal with problems. [They should] provide ongoing parenting classes for people without children. I never met my social worker, so I had no resources or anyone to talk to about problems. I didn't know what to expect from the foster family—like what they should be giving me. They were always trying to push us to go back with our families and if we wanted to go back, we would have. They could have invested that energy into our future.

Although employment rates were quite high, the income of many alumni was quite low, and the rates at which alumni were receiving public assistance were disproportionately higher than those of the general population. In addi-tion, almost one in four alumni had experienced one or more days of home-lessness within a year of leaving foster care.

Recommendations Based on Descriptive Outcomes

1. Strengthen housing programs and other supports to prevent homelessness after leaving care.
   a. Perform further research to determine what factors might prevent homelessness.
   b. Encourage youth to pursue lifelong relationships with foster parents and other supportive adults so that they have a place to go during difficult times. This may require after-care provisions for the foster parents to help support this key activity.
   c. Reform systems to strengthen transitional housing and public/community housing systems. Government agencies can work with local Section 8 landlords to help allocate apartments for low-income alumni from foster care (Choca et al., 2004; Van Leeuwen, 2004). Like other groups whose special needs have been recognized (such as battered women), alumni would benefit from new housing models that provide not only housing subsidies but also home-based case management or other adult guidance, such as scattered-site, sober living, Master-Lease Models, and Housing and Urban Development (HUD), Section 8 housing assistance (Casey Family Programs, 2005b; Clark & Davis, 2000; Massinga & Pecora, 2004; Polcin, 2001; Shirk & Stangler, 2004).
2. Overhaul independent living preparation. As evidenced by the uneven findings for employment preparation, life-skills preparation, education, and income, alumni varied widely in their level of readiness for emancipation from foster care.
   a. Federal and state funds are being spent on a variety of untested life-skills training, employment services, and education supports. Redirect these funds to the most promising programs, and rigorously evaluate them and replicate successful models.
   b. For every youth, develop a comprehensive transition development plan that includes planning for supportive relationships, community connections, education, life-skills assessment and development (http://www.caseylifeskills.org), identity formation, housing, employment experience, physical health, and mental health (Casey Family Programs, 2001; Massinga & Pecora, 2004; Mech, 2003).
   c. Begin life-skills assessment and training as soon as the youth enters the system and ensure that all relevant adults (e.g., judges, teachers, caseworkers, mentors) are involved.
   d. Use youth-centered or youth-directed models of independent living preparation whenever practical and reasonable (Casey Family Programs, 2001).
   e. Increase youth access to Individual Development Accounts (IDAs), special "youth opportunity passports," and asset-accumulation strategies like debit accounts (see Polcin, 2001).
   f. Implement "booster session" programs that provide a toll-free phone number and various fallback services to alumni after they turn 21. This service could also include ongoing access to special job or housing search help well beyond the current age limitations. Information and referral could also be provided inexpensively and readily through special Web sites.

Recommendations Based on Foster Care Experience
Statistical Simulations

1. Minimize placement change. Optimizing the Placement History program components decreased negative employment and financial outcomes. Having fewer placement changes may allow youth in care to develop better social support networks, which can assist them in finding employment and can serve as a safety net when a youth encounters financial difficulties.
2. Optimize education services and experiences. Optimizing the Education Services and Experience program area decreased negative outcomes. Having better school experiences may lead to better education outcomes, which in turn can improve employment and finances.
3. Provide youth who are exiting care with concrete resources. The study's optimization of the Leaving Care Resources program area indicated that having a critical mass of such resources is important (e.g., a driver's license, $250 in cash, dishes and utensils).

Reactions and Recommendations Based on Conversations
With Stakeholders

1. To lower rates of homelessness and unemployment, consider a range of permanency options to help youth establish lifelong connections. Strategies include:
   a. Expand permanency options to include guardianship, placement with family members, ways of maintaining connections with foster parents, and other forms of permanent connections that are most appropriate for the individual child or adolescent (Brooks, 1994; Casey Family Programs, 2003a; Geen, 2004; Grizenko & Pawliuk, 1994; Rutter, 1987; Werner, 1993). Promote strong family and social support networks to help buffer stress and provide support such as employment leads, financial advice, help with laundry, and so on (Chaskin, 2001; Geen, 2004). Help youth to connect to birth and extended family members in a positive way, even if they are unable to live with them. For gay, lesbian, bisexual, transgendered, and questioning (GLBTQ) youth, this may be especially challenging since homes of origin often reject these youth and are not viable permanency options. In such instances, fostering or guardianship may be better permanency placements (Child Welfare League of America, 2006a,b; Downs, 2006; Mallon, 1999).
   b. Continuously revisit the option to be adopted throughout foster care and beyond.
2. Begin life-skills training and access to employment opportunities at an earlier age, with repeated exposures.
   a. Provide youth in high school with the tutoring and employment experience they need to show them the importance of education and vocational training for earning a living wage (Williams, Stenslie, Abdullah, Grossman, & Shinn, 2002).[91] This may require changes in some aspects of the Child Labor Act, which limits employment opportunities for youth. At the same time, avoid involving youth in employment before

they understand fully how to handle the relationships that may develop with older staff and customers. It is important to make sure that the employment experience is properly supervised. There are compelling findings from Steinberg and others (Steinberg & Avenevoli, 1998; Steinberg & Cauffman, 1995) that exposing young children to these low-wage jobs also exposes them to people (aged 19 to 23) who have cars, apartments, and drugs—some of whom are the children's higher-status shift managers.

b. To help youth gain employment skills, improve coordination between child welfare and local workforce board–sponsored employment programs. Youth in foster care should be a priority population to be served by workforce programs. This will help expand the number of jobs that are available to youth in care via special agreements with local employers, stipends, summer internships, and other strategies.

c. Provide youth who are preparing to emancipate with greater access to experiential life-skills training (e.g., employment and driver's education) in addition to classroom-based training. The MacArthur Foundation transition scholars have documented that major American institutions have not kept pace with societal changes in removing barriers to youths' transition to adulthood.[92]

d. Establish mentoring programs that connect youth with individuals who can help them achieve better education and employment outcomes.

3. Help youth find and pay for transportation options to help them get to work.

a. Help youth overcome obstacles to obtaining a driver's license and auto insurance. Very often, affordable auto insurance for youth is contingent on having an adult (usually a parent) as the primary policyholder. Develop strategies for youth who cannot be added to an adult's policy. Youth in care and alumni report that they are often not allowed to drive due to liability concerns, making it difficult to get to job interviews or to work on time.

b. Provide subsidized or free passes for public transportation.

4. Decrease youths' dependence on agency staff and foster parents when it undermines their ability to succeed independently. The sobering employment and income findings of this and other studies underscore the need to be vigilant about the special needs of youth and the progress they are making toward independent living. Providing everything for a youth may not build the personal discipline and self-reliance needed for later success. Foster parents and caseworkers need to prepare youth to negotiate the systems they encounter by providing life-skills training, on-the-job coaching, and other supports.

Relationships and Social Support

Recommendations Based on Descriptive Outcomes

1. Provide youth in care with training in developing and maintaining healthy dating and marital relationships. In particular, training to increase

knowledge about domestic violence would be useful. People who have grown up in violent situations, such as those who have been exposed to child abuse, may not have the resources to deal with conflicts in a nonviolent way. The percentage of married alumni who reported violence in their relationships was higher than that in the general population.

2. Teach youth in care how to develop and maintain healthy relationships with their birth families. While youth are in care, most of their visits with their birth family members are supervised. However, once they leave care, young adults must negotiate their relationships with birth family members without support and supervision. Given that the majority of alumni in this study reported being in regular contact with their siblings and/or birth parents, training and practice in maintaining these relationships would be helpful.

3. Provide foster parents and alumni of foster care with resources for maintaining their relationship after emancipation. About three in five alumni (61.9%) reported having some contact with their former foster parents. Foster parents and alumni could benefit from having a mutual understanding of the nature of their relationship after emancipation. A discussion of this issue could be part of a youth's transition plan.

4. Provide alumni who are parents with resources to prevent the intergenerational transmission of involvement with the foster care system. Although the vast majority of alumni who were parents did not have their children placed in foster care, the percentage of alumni whose children were in foster care was significantly higher than the national average. Future research should investigate the factors that put alumni at risk of having children in foster care so that interventions can be targeted to those who are at greatest risk.

Recommendations Based on Foster Care Experience
Statistical Simulations

1. Provide stable placements for youth in care. In the optimization analyses, a lower placement change rate predicted more positive relationships and social support outcomes. Having a stable place to live may help youth develop better relationship skills that they can use in future relationships.

2. Match youth in care with foster parents who are able to show them love. Optimization analyses indicated that feeling loved while in foster care was related to better relationships and improved social support outcomes.

Summary

According to stakeholders and research data, encouraging youth to establish stable, lifelong connections may be the most important factor in ensuring the overall well-being of youth from foster care. These connections promote social and emotional functioning, as well as improve employment and financial outcomes. In the statistical simulations of the foster care experience, optimizing certain program areas such as placement stability, access to educational supports, independent living preparation, and other areas can lead to positive alumni outcomes. So, striving to achieve the best situation for these key program components and foster care experience variables in all domains is a worthwhile goal.

This chapter has reviewed highlights of the major findings of the Northwest Alumni Study based on the research questions or hypotheses. In terms of key recommendations, the value of maximizing funding and increasing oversight of the state's use of Chafee funds and other independent living programs was underscored to help ensure that:

1. Youth in high school get the tutoring and employment experience they need to show them that education and vocational training do matter for earning a living wage.
2. Youth preparing to emancipate have access to experiential life-skills training in addition to classroom-based training. Curricula should be developed that include competency-based demonstration of skills rather than youth self-report of skill attainment.
3. Youth have greater access to the kinds of mentor programs that work.
4. Challenge grants are issued to help match scholarship funds for alumni from foster care.
5. States fund tuition waivers at community colleges and universities for students who are alumni of care.
6. Local Section 8 landlords allocate some apartments to students who are alumni from foster care and low-income backgrounds.
7. Evaluations are conducted for any major independent living service or skill-development program so that we know what outcomes our tax dollars have purchased.
8. Regular follow-up studies of youth leaving foster care are conducted for older alumni (e.g., at age 25) to assess how well agencies are doing to help youth succeed and what made a difference for them. Legislators need to know if the funds are making any long-term difference.

Future Directions

A next step in the analysis is to examine the relationship between gender and ethnicity and outcomes. While the value of additional program investments in terms of economic benefits to society in the form of mental health service cost savings, additional tax revenue, and other areas was estimated in Chapter 10, future studies could, in a more intentional way, compare different models of foster family care from a cost-benefit perspective.

Work is also needed from other researchers in the field. Specifically, to better understand the mental health of foster care alumni, the field must replicate aspects of this study. Other studies should include, as this project did, the use of multiple data sources (i.e., case records and interviews), standardized measures (e.g., the CIDI), and weighted data to account for imperfect sampling. While the average age of youth in this study at the time of interview was over 24 years, examination of longer-term outcomes such as college completion requires an older sample. Combined, these study features allowed for a comprehensive evaluation of alumni mental health and other adult outcomes.

A number of questions were raised by the study that new research will need to address:

1. *How can agencies and foster parents maximize placement stability?* With the increasing number of studies documenting the negative outcomes associated with placement change, what can be done to lower change rates?

2. *PTSD:* Given that PTSD and other mental health disorders are prevalent in alumni, what are the rates for youth currently in care? What clinical interventions and other supports might be most useful in reducing those rates?

3. *Child attachments:* Relationships and positive child–adult attachments have been identified as essential. To what extent do youth currently in foster care have attachment disorders? What factors help youth build positive attachments? How does placing siblings together or regular sibling contact affect this attachment process?

4. *Cultural identity and other personal identity issues:* These areas are rarely studied in child welfare. A recent analysis of Casey youth in care underscored the importance of cultural identity for youth adjustment and behavior (White et al., 2008). But additional research is needed to understand more fully the dynamics of this developmental process and what practical steps workers and foster parents can take to encourage positive growth, especially for GLBTQ youth (Downs, 2006; White et al., 2007).

5. *Intervention improvements:* To improve interventions that foster life-skills development, the field needs random assignment or quasi-experimental tests of the most promising approaches to find which strategies work best for certain groups of youth and communities. New findings underscore the complexity of life-skills development when at least some youth espouse a "survivalist self-reliance" and are reluctant to be dependent upon others or seek help, especially emotional support (Samuels & Pryce, 2008).

In addition, most evidence-based treatments for mental health disorders have not been tested with large samples of youth in foster care. Studies that may be most able to address comorbid conditions are needed because one in five alumni interviewed in the Northwest Alumni Study had three or more mental health conditions. Those evaluations should be supplemented by more intensive case studies to capture more of the contextual nuances and key implementation issues. In addition, the most effective timing and dosage for psychotropic medications should be evaluated (Crimson & Argo, 2009).

Conclusion

In contrast to what is portrayed in the media and many research reports, some youth placed in foster care benefit from the protection, emotional care, and services provided to them. The state as a "corporate parent" is successful to the extent that some youth are succeeding (Bullock et al., 2006; Stein &

Munro, 2008). Youth grow and develop while in care and, as adults, are now making many positive contributions to their families and communities.

Qualitative research data and personal stories about the many foster parents and staff members who made a difference have been documented. Alumni also had suggestions for what was most beneficial and what could be improved (e.g., more inclusive decision making, greater attention to alumni's perspectives, less movement from home to home).

In summary, this study identifies the strengths and achievements of young adults who have overcome child maltreatment, family instability, school disruptions, and other challenges to become, in many cases, contributing members of their communities across the United States. At the same time, it documents the inability of these service delivery systems to help some alumni find and maintain stability upon leaving care, overcome the psychological effects of maltreatment and childhood instability, or gain the necessary education to help secure and sustain a job that pays a living wage with health insurance. It also showcases areas of agency difference in outcomes and areas for program improvement.

Appendix A

Project Leaders, Staff Members, and Advisors

Northwest Alumni Study Investigators

Peter J. Pecora, PhD, Principal Investigator, Casey Family Programs, and Professor, School of Social Work, University of Washington

A. Chris Downs, PhD, President, The Downs Group, L. L. C. and formerly Co-Principal Investigator, Research Services, Casey Family Programs

Diana J. English, PhD, Co-Principal Investigator, Senior Director of Strategic Consulting, Casey Family Programs; formerly Chief of Research, Washington Department of Social and Health Services, Children's Administration, Division of Children and Family Services

Steven G. Heeringa, PhD, Co-Principal Investigator, Institute for Social Research, University of Michigan

Ronald C. Kessler, PhD, Co-Principal Investigator and Professor, Department of Health Care Policy, Harvard Medical School

James White, PhD, Co-Principal Investigator, Portland State University; formerly with and representing the Oregon Department of Human Services Children, Adults, and Families

Project Coordinators for Northwest and Casey National
Alumni Studies

Kirk O'Brien, PhD, Director of Foster Care Research, Casey Family
Programs

Jason Williams, MS, Doctoral Student Evans School of Public Affairs,
University of Washington

Merrily Wolf, BA, former Casey Alumni Studies Coordinator

Project Staff Members

Carol Brandford, former Research Manager, Washington Department of
Social and Health Services, Children's Administration, Division of Children
and Family Services, Office of Children's Administration Research

Nathaniel Ehrlich, former University of Michigan Study Director

Mary Herrick, former Research Assistant, Casey Family Programs

Eva Hiripi, former Senior Biostatistician, Harvard Medical School

Brian Judd, former Research Assistant, Casey Family Programs

Alisa McWilliams, Survey Manager, University of Michigan

Sarah Morello, former Research Assistant, Casey Family Programs

Nancy Sampson, Senior Research Manager, Health Care Policy, Harvard
School of Medicine

Ellen Walters, former Senior Biostatistician, Harvard Medical School

Catherine Roller White, Research Analyst, Casey Family Programs

Tamera Wiggins, former Doctoral Intern, Casey Family Programs; currently
Psychologist, Psychology Department, Royal Brisbane and Women's
Hospital and Queensland Health, Australia

Wai Tat Chiu, Biostatistician, Harvard Medical School

Agency Administrator Project Advisors

Rob Abrams, Assistant Regional Administrator, Oregon Department of
Human Services; Children, Adults and Families; Community Human
Services

William Bell, Chief Executive Officer, Casey Family Programs

Sherry Brummel, Research Manager, Washington DSHS Office of Children's Administration Research

Adam Diamond, Staff Assistant, Department of Health Care Policy, Harvard University Medical School

Paul Drews, Regional Administrator for the Metro Region, Oregon Department of Human Services; Children, Adults and Families; Community Human Services

James Edmondson, Managing Director of Field Offices, Casey Family Programs

Steve Gordon, former Chief Operating Officer, Casey Family Programs

Carolyn Graf, Transitional Resources Unit, Oregon Department of Human Services; Children, Adults and Families; Community Human Services

Mark Marsh, former Managing Director of Field Offices, Casey Family Programs

Ruth Massinga, former Chief Executive Officer, Casey Family Programs

Ken Perry, former Senior Manager, Casey Family Programs, currently, senior manager with Idaho Health and Welfare

Acknowledgements

Many conversations with alumni of foster care, foster parents, and child welfare staff have shaped this project over the years. These individuals have guided us toward key issues and paths of inquiry, as well as encouraged us to continue to involve them fully in the data interpretation and data usage phases of the effort. This theme was voiced at a recent gathering of alumni from care: *"Nothing about us without us."* The alumni study team is committed to expanding our strong partnerships with alumni as we move forward, and we are thankful for the leadership that Casey's first Director of Alumni Relations, Misty Stenslie, provided to the organization.

We would like to acknowledge the following researchers and organizations that developed instruments that we drew upon to build the measures for the alumni study:

- Mark Courtney, School of Social Work, University of Washington in Seattle, and Ande Nesmith, the University of Wisconsin at Madison, for their permission to use items from the Wisconsin Young Adult Study
- John Dye, Alumni Location and Case Record Review Specialist, who trained and supervised many of the case record reviewers, guided the study through rough times, and continued to work on the study even after leaving for graduate school

- Nancy Gebler and Tina Mainieri, earlier Study Director and Survey Manager, respectively, at the Institute for Social Research, for their contributions, refinements, and great dedication to the study
- Candace Grossman, former Administrative Assistant, Casey Family Programs, who coordinated budget development and contract management, and who led the initial communications planning efforts
- Jean McIntosh, former Executive Vice President for Strategic Planning and Program Development, Casey Family Programs, for her support throughout much of the project
- Jennifer Murphy, former Casey Research Assistant, who took over for John Dye and began Casey's Contact Information campaign
- Rosie Oreskovich, who led the Washington State Children's Administration for many years and passed away in 2003
- Paulos J. Sanna of the State of Oregon, who served as one of the project representatives during 2001
- Leslie Schockner, former Co-Principal Investigator from the State of Oregon, and Kevin George, Transitional Resources Unit, Oregon Services to Children and Families, who helped develop and guide the project
- John Ware and the New England Medical Center for the use of the SF®-12 Health Survey
- Dionne White, who helped refine the case record review procedure and supervised the reviewers
- Merrily Wolf, who served as the first Casey Project Coordinator and provided the foundation for a successful study
- The Substance Abuse and Mental Health Administration (SAMHSA) "Starting Early Starting Smart" Steering Committee and Data Coordinating Center for the "Service Access and Use" and other sections. The national cross-site evaluation instruments were chosen or developed and the data were collected under cooperative agreements with the Starting Early Starting Smart grantees including the data coordinating center, Evaluation, Management, Training, Inc., Folsom, CA, which was responsible for the national Starting Early Starting Smart cross-site program evaluation per GFA No. 97–004 supported by the SAMHSA, U.S. Department of Health and Human Services and the Casey Family Programs. (See http://ncadi.samhsa.gov/promos/sess/publications.asp)
- The World Health Organization and the team members working with Ron Kessler on the Composite International Diagnostic Interview (CIDI) 3.0
- The University of Maryland Rosenberg Estate Trustees, for their permission to use the Rosenberg Self-Esteem Scale

Project Consultants and National Advisory Committee

The following project consultants provided technical advice during the development of the research design and measurement approach. We thank each of them for their suggestions and encouragement. The project team, however, takes full responsibility for any remaining limitations or errors in the design or measures.

- Byron Egeland, PhD, Department of Psychology, University of Minnesota
- David Fanshel, DSW, Professor Emeritus, School of Social Work, Columbia University
- Steven Finch, PhD, SUNY at Stonybrook
- John Landsverk, PhD, Center for Research on Child and Adolescent Mental Health Services, Children's Hospital, San Diego
- James K. Whittaker, PhD, Professor Emeritus, School of Social Work, University of Washington
- Susan Zuravin, PhD, School of Social Work, University of Maryland

National Scientific Advisory Panel

- Stephen Budde, PhD, Chapin Hall Center for Children, University of Chicago
- Peter R. Correia III, National Resource Center for Youth Services
- Mark Courtney, PhD, Partners for Our Children and School of Social Work, University of Washington
- Renda Dionne, Ph.D, formerly with Indian Child and Family Services, National Indian Child Welfare Agency, Oregon Social Learning Center
- Trudy Festinger, PhD, Ehrenkranz School of Social Work, New York University
- Harold Grotevant, PhD, Family Social Science, University of Minnesota
- Ron Haskins, Brookings Center on Children and Families (former Staff Director, U.S. House of Representatives)
- Penny Maza, PhD, formerly with Federal Children's Bureau/ACYF
- Teresa Miramontes, MD, Special advisor and alumna of Casey Family Programs
- Sandy Oos, Foster Parent, Casey Family Programs
- Alfred Perez, Westat Corporation (and former staff member for the California Youth Connection)
- Jessica Watson-Crosby, National Association of Former Foster Children
- Susan Zuravin, PhD, School of Social Work, University of Maryland

Appendix B

How Child Maltreatment Was Measured and Aggregated in the Northwest Alumni Study

Overview

There is no commonly accepted systematic procedure for describing a child's maltreatment experience; however, there is an emerging consensus (and evidence) on the dimensions of maltreatment that should be examined. These dimensions include severity, frequency, chronicity, duration, type, age of onset, and perpetrator (Barnett et al., 1993; Hanson et al., 1995; National Research Council, 1993). These constructs appear to be the most salient predictors of child outcomes based on research thus far.

Building on the work of others, the LONGSCAN Consortium (Runyan, Cox, Dubowitz, Newton, Upadhyaya, Kotch, et al., 2005; Runyan et al., 1998b) conducted a series of analyses examining different methods of constructing each of the aforementioned dimensions of maltreatment. (See the special issue of *Child Abuse and Neglect* that contains these and other articles: Dubowitz et al., 2005; English et al., 2005b; English, Graham, Litrownik, Everson, & Bangdiwala, 2005c; Hussey et al., 2005; Litrownik et al., 2005; Runyan et al., 2005; Schneider, Ross, Graham, & Derkacz, 2005). This work confirmed the importance of these various dimensions. However, while promising, current research is not definitive. Each approach to defining an individual dimension has its own limitations. Further explorations of these dimensions will be informative, and such explorations are warranted given the status of the dimensions research to date.

Summary of Derived Variables Based Upon
Maltreatment Coding[94]

Based on prior research and the results of the analyses in the LONGSCAN dimensions papers, the following strategies were used as the basis for analysis of maltreatment in the Northwest Alumni Study. The raw material for the descriptions of maltreatment experience under consideration here are the reports of harm referred to the local Child Protective Services (CPS) authority. Trained reviewers carefully scanned CPS intake notes and related materials in case files to record maltreatment according to a version of the structured Modified Maltreatment Coding System (MMCS; English & the LONGSCAN investigators, 1997; modified from Barnett, et al., 1993). This system records systematic information about abuse type, perpetrator, severity, and other appropriate information. From this raw material, researchers may derive a host of variables to describe the maltreatment experience of their sample. This selection of derived variables can be grouped into categories of maltreatment *type, severity,* and *chronicity.* In the Northwest Alumni Study, only variables related to type were utilized.

Some kinds of allegation codes may not imply maltreatment, technically defined, depending on the study site. Washington State legal definitions, for example, exclude educational maltreatment and substance abuse from being accepted at intake as a basis of intervention, and thus these codes were not included in the Northwest Alumni Study. Allegations that can be characterized as moral or legal maltreatment, such as involving a child in a criminal activity, were classified as Neglect. Public referrals for child maltreatment that did not contain allegations that could be coded with the MMCS—for example, reports of incidents not involving maltreatment or reports devoid of enough detail to identify the type—also are excluded from these definitions.

For parsimony, the Northwest Alumni Study analyses focused their work on child maltreatment on the dimension of type. Research, such as that of the LONGSCAN group and others, has demonstrated that the type of maltreatment suffered can differentially affect outcomes. For example, Moran, Vuchinich, and Hall (2004) found that the association between child maltreatment and adolescent substance abuse varied, depending on the type of maltreatment suffered. Types of child maltreatment can be differentiated in many ways. In this section we review the approaches taken to derive variables characterizing the predominant type.

Pure Types

The MMCS captures various types of physical abuse, sexual abuse, neglect, and emotional maltreatment. Neglect includes failure to supervise (e.g., not monitoring a child in what could be a dangerous environment), failure to provide (e.g., food, clothing, shelter, medical care, or hygiene concerns), and moral or legal neglect (e.g., involving a child in one's own criminal activities). One way to describe a child's maltreatment history is to simply list whether the child has suffered each of the four "pure" types. This results in four dichotomous variables.

Expanded Hierarchy Type (EHT) Classification

The LONGSCAN group built on previous research to attempt to derive variables that might describe maltreatment history in a manner both more nuanced and more analytically advantageous (i.e., using as few variables as possible). For type, this has resulted in the Expanded Hierarchy Type (EHT). This is expanded from the Standard Hierarchy of the MMCS system, which assigns higher predominance to certain types (sexual abuse, physical abuse) due to their associations with outcomes. The EHT breaks out two categories with multiple types to capture more of the maltreatment experience in this single variable:

a. Sexual Abuse plus Other
b. Physical Abuse and Neglect

The simplifying decision was made to treat Emotional Maltreatment as a dimension *independent* of Maltreatment Type. Thus, any of the *pure* categories (Sexual Abuse Only, Physical Abuse Only, and Neglect Only) in the EHT definition may or may not also include allegations of Emotional Maltreatment. Correspondingly, for example, having only an Emotional Maltreatment allegation in addition to a Sexual Abuse allegation does *not* qualify a case for the Sexual Abuse plus Other category. Emotional Maltreatment thus is explicitly included only if there are no allegations other than Emotional Maltreatment; if so, the case is classified as Emotional Maltreatment Only.

Based upon the types of allegations made, cases are classified into the following mutually exclusive categories:

1. Sexual Abuse Only (with or without Emotional Maltreatment)
2. Sexual Abuse plus Other (Physical Abuse or Neglect)
3. Physical Abuse Only (with or without Emotional Maltreatment)
4. Neglect Only (with or without Emotional Maltreatment)
5. Physical Abuse and Neglect
6. Emotional Maltreatment Only

Please note that although the EHT-type classification variable was recommended from LONGSCAN efforts, not separating emotional maltreatment from the other subtypes may be seen as a limitation. Some research suggests that a more in-depth analysis separating emotional maltreatment from other types, or coding to indicate if emotional maltreatment is present, would provide valuable differentiation related to outcome. Extending the type classification to account for emotional maltreatment may be a worthwhile pursuit in the future. (See Hart, Binggeli, and Brassard, 1998, for further information.)

Number of Types

While indicating only whether a sample member has suffered more than one type of maltreatment is the simplest characterization of type, it has been shown to have some explanatory power. First, any allegations of Sexual Abuse, Physical Abuse, Neglect, and Emotional Maltreatment are indicated. Then, if allegations of more than one of these types of maltreatment were made, "multiple" is coded as 1. If only one type of allegation was made, however, the variable is coded as 0. (Note that this construction of the variable was used in the LONGSCAN studies, wherein all sample members had suffered maltreatment.)

In the Northwest Alumni Study, however, it became apparent that many of the alumni in the samples had suffered more maltreatment than the typical foster child. In some samples, a count of the number of types might have revealed that most members of the sample had only one type, many fewer had two, and very few had three or four of the pure types—that is, a highly skewed distribution of the count variable. In such a case, dichotomizing the variable would make sense for analytical purposes. In the current study, however, many sample members had suffered multiple types of abuse (see Chapter 5), so it made sense to use the count variable rather than a dichotomized single versus multiple classification.

Summary

The alumni studies team extended the work initiated by the LONGSCAN team and other research efforts. Due to data limitations, it focused on capturing the type of maltreatment endured. This approach to defining the dimensions of maltreatment provides useful information to help understand the dynamics of child maltreatment and the effects of maltreatment on children's growth and development. Considerations of severity and chronicity of maltreatment were beyond the scope of the current investigation but are certainly worthy of other efforts.

Appendix C

Placement History and Foster Care Experience Descriptive Statistics

Question: If you could tell children coming into the foster care agency anything right now, what would you tell them?

Answer: I would say it to the parents so that they're more prepared. They need to be a lot more prepared—it's not like normal parenting. They could've given me classes, like career exploration classes, or opportunities that I could've taken. They could've helped me financially when I first got out, at least for the first three months. I mean, the state is your parent really. They should keep asking you how you're doing and stuff.

One interviewer spoke with a respondent who had been taken from his birth mother for neglect at 1½ and was immediately adopted. After years of cruelty in the adoptive home, CPS put him in foster care at age 12, where he went through 24 placements until he was 16. Then he found his last home. He said he had gotten so used to such displacement, cruelty, and disdain that it took another two years to realize what these people had committed to him. The last foster parents remain his active family, his "real Mom and Dad." He reflected that it was years before he realized his last foster parents just weren't going to hit him or hurt him.

Appendix C provides information on foster care experiences broken into six categories: youth served by Casey in Washington, by the state in Washington State, by Casey in Oregon, by the state in Oregon, by Casey in both Washington and Oregon, and by the state in Washington and Oregon. In addition, the overall (total) percentage is presented. Results of statistical tests showing significant differences between Casey and the state (within Washington, within Oregon, and within both) are also presented.

Table C.1 presents detailed information on placement history. Table C.2 provides information on foster care experiences in each of the six other foster care experience domains (Educational Services and Experience, Therapeutic Service and Supports, Activities with Foster Family, Preparation for Leaving Care, Leaving Care Resources, and Foster Family and Other Nurturing Support While in Care).

Table C.1. Placement History

Placement History Variables		Washington		Oregon		Combined		Total
		Casey	State	Casey	State	Casey	State	
		%	% (SE)	%	% (SE)	%	% (SE)	% (SE)
Number of placements	Low (3 or fewer)	18.0	36.6 (0.7)†	38.6	29.8 (2.3)†	23.9	34.3 (0.9)†	31.9 (0.7)
	Medium (4 to 7)	37.8	37.8 (0.8)	25.0	33.3 (2.4)	34.2	36.3 (1.0)	35.8 (0.7)
	High (8 or more)	44.1	25.5 (0.7)	36.4	36.8 (2.5)	41.9	29.4 (1.0)	32.3 (0.7)
Mean number of placements		7.6	6.1 (0.1)*	5.8	6.6 (0.3)*	7.1	6.3 (0.1)*	6.5 (0.1)
Length of time in care (in years)	Low (fewer than 3.6)	8.1	37.5 (0.7)†	4.5	45.6 (2.5)†	7.1	40.3 (1.0)†	32.5 (0.7)
	Medium (3.6 to 5.9)	12.6	30.3 (0.7)	18.2	34.5 (2.4)	14.2	31.7 (1.0)	27.6 (0.7)
	High (5.9 or more)	79.3	32.1 (0.8)	77.3	19.9 (2.0)	78.7	28.0 (0.9)	39.9 (0.7)
Mean length of time in care (in years)		9.9	5.3 (0.1)*	9.4	4.4 (0.2)*	9.8	5.0 (0.1)*	6.1 (<0.1)
Placement change rate (placements per year)	Low (less than 0.61)	37.8	29.1 (0.8)†	52.3	11.7 (1.6)†	41.9	23.2 (0.7)†	27.6 (0.6)
	Medium (0.62 to 1.23)	34.2	27.9 (0.7)	29.5	28.7 (2.3)	32.9	28.2 (0.9)	29.3 (0.7)
	High (1.23 or more)	27.9	42.9 (0.7)	18.2	59.6 (2.5)	25.2	48.6 (1.0)	43.1 (0.8)
Mean placement change rate (placements/year)		0.9	1.4 (<0.1)*	0.7	1.7 (0.1)*	0.9	1.5 (<0.1)*	1.4 (<0.1)
Number of reunification failures	Low (0)	79.3	71.1 (0.8)†	75.9	57.1 (2.9)†	78.4	66.3 (1.1)†	69.1 (0.9)
	Medium (1)	13.4	16.5 (0.6)	17.2	24.6 (2.6)	14.4	19.3 (1.0)	18.2 (0.7)
	High (2 or more)	7.3	12.4 (0.6)	6.9	18.3 (2.3)	7.2	14.4 (0.9)	12.7 (0.7)
Number of runaways	Low (0)	68.3	62.8 (0.9)†	75.9	57.1 (2.9)†	70.3	60.9 (1.2)†	63.0 (0.9)
	Medium (1)	19.5	17.4 (0.7)	13.8	19.8 (2.4)	18.0	18.2 (0.9)	18.2 (0.7)
	High (2 or more)	12.2	19.8 (0.7)	10.3	23.0 (2.5)	11.7	20.9 (1.0)	18.8 (0.8)

(continued)

Table C.1. Continued

Placement History Variables		Washington		Oregon		Combined		
		Casey	State	Casey	State	Casey	State	Total
		%	% (SE)	%	% (SE)	%	% (SE)	% (SE)
Number of unlicensed living situations with friends/relatives	Low (0)	95.1	76.9 (0.7)†	75.9	72.2 (2.7)	90.1	75.3 (1.0)†	78.7 (0.8)
	Medium (1)	3.7	16.5 (0.6)	17.2	19.8 (2.4)	7.2	17.7 (0.9)	15.2 (0.7)
	High (2 or more)	1.2	6.6 (0.4)	6.9	7.9 (1.6)	2.7	7.1 (0.6)	6.1 (0.5)
Number of kinship care placements	Low (0)	64.9	66.1 (0.8)†	61.4	50.9 (2.5)†	63.9	60.9 (1.0)†	61.6 (0.8)
	Medium (1)	16.2	21.6 (0.7)	25.0	21.6 (2.1)	18.7	21.6 (0.8)	20.9 (0.6)
	High (2 or more)	18.9	12.3 (0.5)	13.6	27.5 (2.3)	17.4	17.5 (0.8)	17.5 (0.6)
Sample size		**111**	**333**	**44**	**171**	**155**	**504**	**659**

*Statistically significant Casey and state difference at $p < .05$. Washington, Oregon, and Combined tested separately.
†Significance when the variable has more than one level, $p < .05$. Washington, Oregon, and Combined tested separately.

Table C.2. Foster Care Experience

Foster Care Experience Variables	Washington Casey % (SE)	Washington State % (SE)	Oregon Casey % (SE)	Oregon State % (SE)	Combined Casey % (SE)	Combined State % (SE)	Total % (SE)
Educational Services and Experience							
Total number of school changes, elementary through high school — Low (3 to 6)	41.5 (3.2)	32.2 (1.8)[†]	37.9 (6.4)	35.6 (3.3)	40.6 (2.9)	33.4 (1.6)[†]	35.0 (1.4)
Medium (7 to 9)	38.3 (3.2)	35.2 (1.9)	33.7 (5.9)	31.9 (3.3)	37.1 (2.8)	34.1 (1.7)	34.8 (1.4)
High (10 or more)	20.2 (2.9)	32.6 (1.8)	28.4 (5.6)	32.4 (3.3)	22.3 (2.6)	32.6 (1.6)	30.2 (1.4)
Could participate in tutoring or other supplemental educational services[a]	93.1 (2.5)	86.2 (1.3)	94.2 (2.4)	90.8 (2.0)	93.4 (1.9)	87.8 (1.1)*	89.1 (1.0)
Therapeutic Service and Supports							
Could participate in all three types of therapeutic service and supports ("a lot")[a,b]	92.8 (1.4)	78.5 (1.5)*	100.0	83.5 (2.5)*	94.7 (1.0)	80.2 (1.3)*	83.6 (1.0)

(continued)

Table C.2. Continued

		Washington		Oregon		Combined		
		Casey	State	Casey	State	Casey	State	Total
		% (SE)	% (SE)	% (SE)	% (SE)	% (SE)	% (SE)	% (SE)
Foster Care Experience Variables								
Activities With Foster Family								
Participated in both enjoyable activities (family sports, outdoors, or community activities) and religious activities with foster family[a]		56.8 (3.3)	44.0 (1.9)*	57.6 (6.4)	39.8 (3.5)*	57.0 (2.9)	42.6 (1.7)*	45.9 (1.5)
Preparation for Leaving Care								
Degree of preparation for leaving care	Low (0 or 1)	9.5 (1.6)	25.5 (1.7)[†]	4.8 (2.0)	11.1 (2.1)[†]	8.3 (1.3)	20.6 (1.3)[†]	17.7 (1.1)
	Medium (2)	27.4 (3.0)	23.9 (1.6)	15.3 (3.7)	26.7 (3.2)	24.3 (2.5)	24.9 (1.5)	24.8 (1.3)
	High (3 or 4)	63.0 (3.2)	50.6 (1.9)	79.9 (4.2)	62.1 (3.4)	67.4 (2.6)	54.6 (1.7)	57.5 (1.5)
Leaving Care Resources[d]								
Sum of leaving care resources	Low (0)	32.2 (3.4)	47.3 (1.9)[†]	27.0 (5.6)	47.3 (3.5)[†]	30.9 (2.9)	47.3 (1.7)[†]	43.5 (1.5)
	Medium (1)	27.4 (2.7)	25.4 (1.6)	36.5 (6.4)	30.1 (3.2)	29.7 (2.6)	27.0 (1.5)	27.7 (1.3)
	High (2 or 3)	40.4 (3.2)	27.2 (1.7)	36.5 (5.9)	22.6 (2.9)	39.4 (2.9)	25.6 (1.5)	28.8 (1.3)
Foster Family and Other Nurturing Support While in Care								
Child Maltreatment While in Care[e]								
No child maltreatment		60.0 (3.5)	67.9 (1.8)[†]	69.5 (6.3)	70.1 (3.1)[†]	62.5 (3.1)	68.6 (1.6)[†]	67.2 (1.4)
Sexual abuse only		8.2 (2.5)	3.1 (0.8)	2.4 (1.4)	2.3 (1.0)	6.7 (1.9)	2.8 (0.6)	3.7 (0.6)
Sexual abuse and other		5.0 (1.2)	5.5 (0.9)	2.4 (1.4)	0.7 (0.5)	4.3 (0.9)	3.9 (0.6)	4.0 (0.5)

Table C.2. Continued

	Washington		Oregon		Combined		
	Casey	State	Casey	State	Casey	State	Total
	% (SE)	% (SE)	% (SE)	% (SE)	% (SE)	% (SE)	% (SE)
Foster Care Experience Variables							
Physical abuse only	7.1 (1.4)	3.2 (0.7)	23.3 (6.3)	5.2 (1.6)	11.3 (2.0)	3.9 (0.7)	5.6 (0.7)
Physical neglect only	4.8 (1.2)	10.3 (1.2)	2.4 (1.4)	14.9 (2.4)	4.1 (1.0)	11.8 (1.1)	10.1 (0.9)
Physical neglect and physical abuse only	14.9 (3.3)	10.0 (1.1)	0.0	6.9 (1.7)	11.0 (2.5)	9.0 (0.9)	9.4 (0.9)
Parenting Style of Both Foster Parents[a,f]							
One or both foster parents was… Authoritative	23.9 (2.5)	28.7 (1.7)	35.6 (5.5)	25.2 (3.0)	27.0 (2.3)	27.5 (1.5)	27.4 (1.3)
Authoritarian	18.7 (2.3)	17.7 (1.5)	2.4 (1.4)	13.0 (2.4)*	14.4 (1.7)	16.1 (1.3)	15.7 (1.1)
Permissive	22.1 (3.0)	14.2 (1.4)*	8.2 (2.8)	13.1 (2.3)	18.4 (2.4)	13.8 (1.2)	14.9 (1.1)
Disengaged	35.1 (3.6)	28.5 (1.7)	34.0 (6.7)	32.4 (3.3)	34.8 (3.2)	29.9 (1.6)	31.0 (1.4)
Other	60.0 (3.4)	72.9 (1.7)*	73.4 (5.0)	70.6 (3.1)	63.5 (2.9)	72.1 (1.5)*	70.1 (1.4)
Positive parenting Low	60.8 (3.0)	50.6 (1.9)†	44.6 (6.5)	49.0 (3.5)†	56.6 (2.8)	50.1 (1.7)	51.6 (1.5)
Medium	21.1 (2.3)	25.0 (1.7)	19.8 (5.3)	30.9 (3.2)	20.8 (2.2)	27.1 (1.6)	25.6 (1.3)
High	18.1 (2.1)	24.3 (1.6)	35.6 (5.5)	20.0 (2.8)	22.6 (2.1)	22.9 (1.4)	22.8 (1.2)
Other Supports							
Foster family helped with ethnic issues[a]	73.1 (3.0)	59.2 (1.9)*	50.7 (6.4)	63.4 (3.4)	67.2 (2.9)	60.7 (1.7)	62.2 (1.5)

(continued)

Table C.2. Continued

Foster Care Experience Variables		Washington		Oregon		Combined		
		Casey	State	Casey	State	Casey	State	Total
		% (SE)	% (SE)	% (SE)	% (SE)	% (SE)	% (SE)	% (SE)
Had a close and confiding relationship with an adult while growing up		39.1 (3.2)	43.3 (1.9)	60.2 (5.8)	51.2 (3.5)	44.6 (2.9)	46.0 (1.7)	45.7 (1.5)
Felt loved while in foster care		84.2 (2.8)	81.3 (1.6)	69.5 (6.3)	83.0 (2.5)*	80.4 (2.6)	81.9 (1.4)	81.5 (1.2)
Overall, foster parents were helpful	A little	37.3 (3.5)	37.8 (1.8)	30.5 (6.3)	32.9 (3.3)†	35.5 (3.1)	36.1 (1.6)	36.0 (1.5)
	Some	27.0 (2.7)	26.9 (1.8)	19.7 (4.3)	33.3 (3.3)	25.1 (2.3)	29.1 (1.6)	28.1 (1.4)
	A lot	35.8 (3.0)	35.3 (1.8)	49.8 (6.4)	33.8 (3.3)	39.4 (2.8)	34.8 (1.7)	35.9 (1.4)
Sample size		82	242	29	126	111	368	479

[a]These data refer to the last placement of at least three months.

[b]To be able to participate "a lot" means the alumnus or alumna had access to (1) counseling or other mental health services; (2) alcohol or drug treatment programs; and (3) group work or group counseling.

[c]Sum of (1) could participate in employment training or job location services; (2) could participate in independent living training groups or workshops; (3) was somewhat or very prepared for independent living; and (4) had health insurance at exit.

[d]Sum of the number of resources available when leaving care: (1) a driver's license; (2) $250 in cash; and (3) dishes and utensils.

[e]See Chapter 5 for an explanation of the Expanded Hierarchical Categorization of maltreatment.

[f]Authoritative, authoritarian, permissive, engaged, and "other" parenting styles were created according to Baumrind (1995). Positive parenting was trichotomized into high, medium, and low based on alumni reports of foster parents' parenting style—authoritative, authoritarian, permissive, disengaged, or "other." High positive parenting occurred only when two foster parents were present in the identified home and they were both authoritative or one was authoritative and one was "other." Medium positive parenting occurred when both were "other" or one was authoritative and one was authoritarian, permissive, or disengaged or only one foster parent was present and s/he was authoritative. Low positive parenting occurred when one parent was "other" and one was authoritarian, permissive, or disengaged or when both were authoritarian, permissive, or disengaged or when only one foster parent was present and s/he was authoritarian, permissive, or disengaged, or "other."

*Statistically significant Casey and state difference at p < .05. Washington, Oregon, and Combined tested separately.

†Significance when the variable has more than one level, p < .05. Washington, Oregon, and Combined tested separately.

Notes

1. *In loco parentis* refers to the right of the state to intervene if the parents do not fulfill their caregiver responsibilities.
2. Placements are being shortened through various permanency planning programs, fiscal incentives, other parameters of the Adoption and Safe Families Act (P.L. 96–272), and changes in child welfare practice.
3. For example, the 1994 Amendments to the Social Security Act (SSA) authorized the U.S. Department of Health and Human Services (DHHS) to review state child welfare programs to ensure conformity with the state plan requirements of Titles IV-B and IV-E of the SSA.
4. For example, American Humane Association et al. (1998); Pecora, Whittaker, Maluccio, Barth, and DePanfilis (2009).
5. The federal government alone spent $13 billion in 2004 for programs within the Administration for Children and Families, which does not include state-only funded programs. (See http://www.whitehouse.gov/omb/budget/fy2006/pdf/budget/hhs.pdf).
6. This review draws from Maluccio, Ainsworth, and Thoburn (2000); Maluccio and Pecora (2006); McDonald, Allen, Westerfelt, and Piliavin (1996), and Whittaker and Maluccio (2002).
7. For examples of international foster care research, see Biehal, Clayden, Stein, and Wade (1992, 1995); Dumaret, Coppel-Batch, and Couraud (1997); Flynn and Biro (1998); Jackson (1994); Vinnerljung, Oman, and Gunnarson (2005).
8. The most relevant federal goal focuses on "no more than two placements for children in care for 12 months or less." Recent federal reviews have found continued wide variations in state performance (see U. S. Department of Health and Human Services, 2008a).
9. Created by the Oregon Legislature and signed by the governor in 1995 (Senate Bill 1).
10. The receipt and screening of reports of possible child abuse and neglect remained a centralized function across the county.
11. Another promising program that was operating in the Multnomah County area during this time was the Partners Project. This project was one of the first to blend funding and

wraparound services for children and families in Oregon. The project brought together county mental health, education system, and child welfare services to provide support services for families who were experiencing difficulties yet did not rise to the level of child welfare intervention. This prevention program helped families by keeping children in school and with their families.

12. These data represent all out-of-home care episodes that closed during the calendar year.
13. Children's Administration Strategic Plan 11/7/05.
14. Adapted from Maluccio and Pecora (2006).
15. This review draws from Maluccio, Ainsworth, and Thoburn (2000; McDonald et al. (1996); Pecora et al. (2009) and Whittaker and Maluccio (2002).
16. The most relevant federal goal focuses on "no more than two placements for children in care for 12 months or less." The current performance goal level: 81% have two or fewer placements in less than 12 months of care. In terms of actual performance, the national median for 2000 was 84%—with a range of 58%–100% (source: http://www.acf.hhs.gov/programs/cb/cwrp/2002cfsrresults.htm), More recent federal reviews have found continued wide variations in state performance (McDonald, Salyers, & Shaver, 2004, p. 7).
17. The Northwest Alumni Study did not examine the effects of placement of siblings but will be undertaking a series of analyses to determine the effects of kinship care. For more information on the value of sibling and kinship placement, see Bernstein (2000); Berrick et al. (1998); Casey Family Programs (2000).
18. The exception to birth family contact is when there are child safety concerns or when the child has been emotionally abandoned by family members for some reason, such as past behavior, their reporting of child maltreatment, or homophobia that has led to rejection of the child.
19. Note that some of these findings were found for only certain geographic sites.
20. This section on the use of risk and protective factors and resilience is adapted from Anctil et al. (2007).
21. Some of the more specific research questions that will be explored subsequently include:

- Are there patterns or characteristics of the alumni who had died by the time the study began?
- *Kinship care.* Were there differences in adult outcomes for youth placed with nonrelative foster parents compared with those who were placed with relatives?
- *Decision making.* Did youth feel they had a role in decisions about their lives? Did youth feel that decisions about them were made without their consent or input?
- Where did alumni move after exit from their last foster home? What were the general neighborhood characteristics where alumni lived?
- *Interest in the foster care agency.* To what extent were alumni interested in or involved with the foster care agency that delivered services to them? Was this interest associated with negative variables such as earlier placement disruption or in-care maltreatment? Was this interest associated with positive variables such as wanting to "reinvest in" or "give back to" youth still in care?
- When certain risk factors and foster care experiences are controlled for, do foster care alumni outcomes vary by ethnic group?

22. Adapted from Maluccio and Pecora (2006).
23. For educational achievement data, see Barth (1990); Blome (1997); Brandford and English (2004); Cook (1992); Courtney et al. (2007); Pecora et al. (2003b); and Reilly (2003), but again, note that few studies have interviewed alumni older than age 22.
24. See Pecora et al. (2003b) for the foster care data and the National Center on Education Statistics (2003) for national GED rates for adults over age 18 as of 2000.
25. Brandford and English (2004); English, Kouidou-Giles, and Plocke (1994); Leibold and Downs (2002); Pecora et al. (2003b).
26. U.S. Department of Health and Human Services (2003, p II-4). In the current NSCAW national study of foster care, over 20% of the youth had allegations of maltreatment, but

only 0.7% were substantiated or found to be perpetrated by a foster parent (Kohl et al., 2005).

27. Cook (1991); Pecora et al. (2003b).
28. Cook (1991); Courtney et al. (2007); Havalchak, White, O'Brien, and Pecora (2006).
29. Geen (2004); Hegar and Scannapieco (1998).
30. Casey National Resource Center for Family Support (2003, p. 1). For more resources, see *Children and Youth Services Review*, 2005, *27*(4); *Child Welfare Watch*, Fall 2002, No. 8, p. 35; and Herrick and Piccus (2005).
31. James, Landsverk, Slymen (2004); Ryan and Testa (2004); Rubin et al. (2004).
32. Wulczyn, Kogan, and Harden (2003).
33. Courtney et al. (2004, 2007); Pecora et al. (2003b).
34. See Blome (1997); Buehler et al. (2000); Casey Research Services (2005); Pecora et al. (2003b); Reilly (2003).
35. Festinger (1983); Jones and Moses (1984); Pecora et al. (2003b).
36. See Casey Research Services (2005); Festinger (1983); Jones and Moses (1984); Pecora et al. (2003b).
37. Brandford & English (2004); Casey Family Services (1999); Courtney et al. (2001, 2004b, 2007).
38. Courtney et al (2001); Pecora et al. (2003b); Reilly (2003).
39. For employment-related outcomes, see Alexander and Huberty (1993, p. 22); Barth (1990, p. 424); Courtney et al. (2001, p. 710); Pecora et al. (2003b, pp. 35–57).
40. Courtney et al. (2001, 2007); Festinger (1983); Pecora et al. (2003b).
41. Goerge et al. (2002); Pecora et al. (2003b).
42. Cook (1991, pp. 1–2 to 1–6, 4–1 to 4–29); English Widom, & Brandford, 2001; Widom and Ames (1994, pp. 307, 310).
43. Barth (1990, p. 428); Courtney et al. (2001, 2004b, 2007); Pecora et al. (2003).
44. Festinger (1983); Zimmerman (1982).
45. One exceptional study that tracked this outcome is Casey Family Services (1999, p. 14).
46. See Thompson, Huefner, Ringle, and Daly (2004).
47. A race/ethnicity classification scheme similar to that used in the census was implemented. Interestingly, there was a difference between the ethnicity reported by the alumni themselves and what was noted in their case files. Despite the fact that a few alumni of Latino origin in Oregon were initially removed from the sample using case record data to match ages of subsamples, a small proportion (4.8%) of both the Casey sample and of the state sample identified themselves as Hispanic/Latino.
48. As described in Chapter 4, to reflect data as if all youth had been interviewed, a nonresponse weight was used to adjust data for those who were or were not interviewed. Data are presented in tables separately for the Washington Casey and state samples, the Oregon Casey and state samples, the combined Casey and state data, and the total for all alumni.
49. For more information about the topics covered in this chapter, please see Pecora et al. (2009a), Working Paper No. 3, at http://www.casey.org/research.
50. See http://www.bsos.umd.edu/socy/rosenberg.html.
51. Due to case record limitations, the timing of maltreatment by the birth family was unable to be determined, meaning that maltreatment could have occurred prior to or during placement in foster care.
52. One of the major differences is that the federal studies distinguished between substantiated and unsubstantiated allegations, while the Northwest Alumni Study did not.
53. In the United States, mental disorders are diagnosed based on the *Diagnostic and Statistical Manual of Mental Disorders, Fourth Edition (DSM-IV)*. See American Psychiatric Association (1994). Adults with a serious mental illness are persons aged 18 and over who, currently or at any time during the past year, have had a diagnosable mental, behavioral, or emotional disorder of sufficient duration to meet diagnostic criteria specified within DSM-III-R (American Psychiatric Association, 1987) that has resulted in functional impairment and that substantially interferes with or limits one or more major life activities. Functional impairment is defined as difficulties that substantially interfere with or limit role functioning in one or

more major life activities, including basic daily living skills (e.g., eating, bathing, dressing); instrumental living skills (e.g., maintaining a household, managing money, getting around the community, taking prescribed medication); and functioning in social, family, and vocational/educational contexts (Section 1912 (c) of the Public Health Services Act, as amended by Public Law 321. S.1306).

54. This study included the cost of services provided by health and mental health professionals to treat mental illness. The authors pointed out that one of the many reasons national health expenditures for child/adolescent mental disorders are difficult to estimate is that mental health services are delivered and paid for not only in the health and mental health sectors but also in the education, child welfare, and juvenile justice sectors, and no comprehensive national data sets exist in this area. Indirect costs associated with mental illness (such as future lost wages as a consequence of worse educational attainment) were not included in the Sturm et al. project. This is an understudied area, but this information is an important component for estimating the economic burden of child/adolescent mental disorders. Child and adolescent preventive interventions have the potential to reduce the economic burden of mental illness by reducing the need for mental health and other related services (economic inputs) and increasing the potential benefits of positive developmental outcomes (economic outputs such as educational attainment, economic productivity), representing net societal savings (National Institute of Mental Health, 2004).

55. Abstracted from O'Brien, Williams, Pecora, English, and Kessler (in preparation).

56. Hoge et al. (2004); Kulka et al. (1990).

57. Item No. 5 from the Rosenberg self-esteem scale was omitted accidentally: "I feel I do not have much to be proud of" (see http://www.bsos.umd.edu/socy/rosenberg.html).

58. Abstracted from O'Brien et al. (in preparation).

59. There is little solid evidence that drug use may be a particular problem for alumni from care compared to suitable controls (e.g., matched for prior social problems, race, and socioeconomic status). Because of increases in drug use in the general population over the past 20 years, more recent alumni studies should find increased prevalence and possibly increased incidence rates. More sophisticated studies and analyses are needed.

60. This age was deemed approximately the youngest age at which a student in a normal track (no grade repetition) could have graduated high school. This number was used since some youth were turning 17 even in February and March of their senior year.

61. The national GED completion rate was 5.1% in 2000, and it was 7.8% in 1998 and 1999 when measured in a different manner (National Center on Education Statistics, 2003). Statistics are for individuals aged 18 to 29.

62. Another study indicates that the college enrollment rate has increased with a new generation: 69% of the 1988 youth cohort in the National Education Longitudinal Study enrolled in postsecondary institution in the year following high school graduation. (U.S. Department of Education, National Education Longitudinal Study of 1988, "Fourth Follow-up" (NELS:88/2000), found at http://nces.ed.gov/pubsearch/pubsinfo.asp?pubid=2003005). Hispanic/Latino rate: 66%, African American: 61%, white: 71%, and Asian: 83%.

63. See, for example, Ayasse (1995); Blome (1997); Cook (1991); Edmund S. Muskie School of Public Service (1999); Noble (1997).

64. Nearly two-thirds of these (62%) are estimated to be adults and more than one-third (38%) are estimated to be children. Of the general homeless population, 49% were in their first episode of homelessness, 17% in their second, and 34% had been homeless three or more times. For 28% of these homeless clients, their current episode had lasted 3 months or less, 26% between 4 and 12 months, 16% between 13 and 24 months, and for 30% it had lasted more than 2 years.

65. In 2000, 66.2% of the households were owner-occupied and 33.8% were renter-occupied. The percent owner occupied was 64.3% in Oregon and 64.6% in Washington. See U. S. Census Bureau (2000b).

66. A weighted average for the general population unemployment rate for the eligible workforce combining the age brackets of 20–24 (92.9%) and 25–34 (96.3%) was calculated. See http://www.bls.gov/lau/table12fu1100.pdf.

67. Income should be examined in relation to the age of the alumni and the cost of living in the communities where alumni are residing. Those breakdowns have not been completed.

68. Defined specifically as only General Assistance, Aid to Families with Dependent Children (AFDC), and its successor, Temporary Aid to Needy Families (TANF).

69. Income thresholds based on 2000 poverty line criteria, adjusted by household size.

70. Also see Institute of Medicine (2002).

71. This section is abstracted with permission from Anctil et al. (2007).

72. This section is adapted from Fraser et al. (1991, p. 74).

73. One practical way to teach these social skills to youth aged 8 and up is to access the Ansell-Casey Life Skills Assessment (ACLSA) at http://www.caseylifeskills.org. The assessment and companion resources offer effective means to teach positive social relationships and to avoid negative relationships.

74. Note that these comparison data for the general population used slightly different variables in their scoring.

75. Items are abstracted from the University of Michigan Panel Study of Income Dynamics Child Development Supplement (PSID-CD).

76. This figure (1.1% of the general population of children placed in foster care every year) is derived using the following statistics: 800,000 children in foster care divided by the total number of children under age 18 in the United States on July 1, 2003 (800,000/73,043,506 = 1.1%). For national foster care data, go to http://www.acf.hhs.gov/programs/cb/ and click on Adoption and Foster Care Statistics. See the Trends in Foster Care and Adoption table. The total number of children under age 18 was downloaded February 21, 2006 from http://www.census.gov/popest/states/tables/STEST2003–01res.xls (Annual Estimates of the Resident Population by Selected Age Groups for the United States and States: July 1, 2003, and April 1, 2000).

77. Valuable assessments and practical learning curricula on parenting can be accessed at www.caseylifeskills.org.

78. Not calculated with all of the same variables.

79. Not calculated with all of the same variables; also, cuts were made at different percentiles.

80. These statistics are for people who did not have children before age 20.

81. One divided by an odds ratio switches the comparison and reference groups. For example, saying that state alumni had 2.5 times (1/0.4) higher odds of *smoking fewer than 10 cigarettes per day* than Casey alumni is equivalent to saying that Casey alumni had 0.4 times lower odds of *smoking fewer than 10 cigarettes per day* than state alumni.

82. One divided by an odds ratio switches the comparison and reference groups. For example, saying that those with a high number of school changes had 1.7 times (1/0.6) higher odds than those with a low number of *complet[ing] any degree/certificate beyond high school* is equivalent to saying the following: Those with a low number of school changes had 0.6 times lower odds than those with a high number of *complet[ing] any degree/certificate beyond high school*.

83. See Little (1982) for more information on this statistical approach.

84. For these analyses, the employment variables for each of the six subgroups were examined separately (see Table 12.7).

85. A score of 50 or higher indicates good physical or mental health.

86. These people were chosen as "key advisers" because of their past work in designing the study or their familiarity with the study design or early findings.

87. For more resources and information, see *A Road Map for Learning: Improving Educational Outcomes in Foster Care* at http://www.casey.org.

88. For more information about TRIO, GEAR UP, and other higher education issues, see http://www.trioprograms.org/abouttrio.html, http://www.ed.gov/about/offices/list/ope/trio/index.html, www.ed.gov/print/programs/gearup/index.html, and Casey Family Programs (2003b). The HEA funds outreach programs to prepare disconnected youth for postsecondary education. For example, two federal TRIO programs are educational opportunity outreach programs designed to motivate and support students from disadvantaged backgrounds to progress through the "academic pipeline." The Talent Search

and Upward Bound programs identify, motivate, and support students as they complete secondary school and undertake a program of postsecondary education. Both programs provide a spectrum of services, including assistance in secondary school reentry, entry into GED programs, assistance in completing college admission and financial aid applications, personal and career counseling, instruction, summer housing, and academic tutorials. GEAR UP is a program designed to increase the number of low-income students who are prepared to enter and succeed in postsecondary education. It gives grants to states and partnerships to provide services at high-poverty middle and high schools. Funds are also used to provide college scholarships to low-income students.

89. See Casey Family Programs (2003b) for further discussion of education and training supports.

90. The national Advisory Committee on Student Financial Assistance is considering recommendations for expanding access for youth from foster care to federal financial aid. One area the advisory committee might examine is the potential barrier to application for financial aid for "informal" youth in care youth—those who are not formally part of the foster care system but who live with caregivers other than their birth parents (i.e., in unpaid kinship care). These youth may be failing to apply for federal financial aid because the application does not have a category for recognizing their special circumstances and includes other categories (e.g., "ward of the state") that could create confusion. The FAFSA should specifically state that "unusual circumstances not shown on this form" include kinship care (as it does in the case of "loss of employment"). This modification of the FAFSA form would make it easier for alumni from foster care who are in kinship care to demonstrate that they meet the special-circumstances test for financial aid. Youth from care would benefit greatly if these "special analyses and activities" of the advisory committee addressed their special needs and circumstances. One area the advisory committee might consider is how more youth in foster care can be encouraged to apply for financial aid and how the application process could be streamlined. The new FAFSA language will go into effect for the 2009–2010 application cycle—one year from now. It will have the "foster care" language instead of the "ward of the court" Language.

91. Bolstering these programs requires that funding for the Title IV-E Independent Living program be increased to match current foster care populations and to ensure that states have adequate resources to provide the skills training that young people must have to succeed. In addition to meeting children's basic needs for food, shelter, and care, we must ensure that young people receive training and support to acquire the knowledge, skills, and attitudes needed for independence. This program provides specific support for independent living skill development, job training, and preparation for employment. It has been shown to increase the ability of youth from care to manage their money, access community resources, and find a job. Funding for the Independent Living program, capped at $70 million, has not kept pace with the population of youth eligible to receive the services. Current allocations to the states remain based on their 1984 population, and overall funds have not been increased since 1992 (Child Welfare League of America, 2005).

92. See http://www.pop.upenn.edu/transad/index.htm for the reports from The Network on Transitions to Adulthood (MacArthur Foundation).

93. Williams et al. (2005) found rates of alcohol use comparable to those of the general population in a recent study of Alaska alumni from foster care too, and at least one other study Barth (1990) has shown alcoholism or use rates among alumni to be comparable to those of the general population or even lower.

94. Adapted from materials developed by Dr. Diana English and Carol Brandford, formerly with the Washington State Office of Children's Administration Research, November 27, 2002.

References

Adam, E. (2004). Beyond quality: Parental and residential stability and children's adjustment. *Current Directions in Psychological Science, 13*(5), 210–213.

Ainsworth, M. D. S. (1989). Attachments beyond infancy. *American Psychologist, 44,* 709–716.

Ainsworth, M. D. S., Blehar, M. C., Waters, E., & Wall, S. (1978). *Patterns of attachment: A psychological study of the Strange Situation.* Hillsdale, NJ: Erlbaum.

Alexander, G., & Huberty, T. J. (1993). *Caring for troubled children: The Villages follow-up study.* Bloomington: The Villages of Indiana.

Alliance for Excellent Education. (2006). *Saving futures, saving dollars: The impact of education on crime reduction and earnings.* Washington, DC: Author.

Alliance for Excellent Education. (2008). The high cost of high school dropouts: What the nation pays for inadequate high schools. *Issue Brief. June 2008.* Retrieved March 24, 2009, from http://www.all4ed.org/publication_material/issue_policy_briefs

Altshuler, S. J. (1997). A reveille for school social workers: Children in foster care need our help. *Social Work in Education, 19*(2), 121–127.

Amato, P. R., & Keith, B. (1991). Parental divorce and the well-being of children: A meta-analysis. *Psychological Bulletin, 110,* 26–46.

American Academy of Pediatrics Committee on Early Childhood Adoption and Dependent Care (AAP). (2000). Developmental issues for young children in foster care. *Pediatrics, 106,* 1145–1150.

American Humane Association, Children's Division, American Bar Association, Center on Children and the Law, Annie E. Casey Foundation, Casey Family Services, et al. (1998). *Assessing outcomes in child welfare services: Key philosophical principles, concepts for measuring results, and core outcome indicators.* Englewood, CO: American Humane Association, Children's Division.

American Psychiatric Association. (1987). *Diagnostic and statistical manual of mental disorders, third edition revised (DSM-III).* Washington, DC: American Psychiatric Press.

American Psychiatric Association. (1994). *Diagnostic and statistical manual of mental disorders, fourth edition (DSM-IV)*. Washington, DC: American Psychiatric Press.

Ammerman, R., Kolko, D., Kirisci, L., Blackson, T., & Dawes, M. (1999). Child abuse potential in parents with histories of substance abuse disorder. *Child Abuse and Neglect, 23,* 1225–1238.

Anctil, T., McCubbin, L., O'Brien, K., Pecora, P. J., & Anderson-Harumi, C. (2007). Predictors of adult quality of life for foster care alumni with physical and/or psychiatric disabilities. *Child Abuse and Neglect, 31,* 1087–1100.

Auslander, W. F., McMillen, J., Elze, D., Thompson, R., Jonson-Reid, M., & Stiffman, A. (2002). Mental health problems and sexual abuse among adolescents in foster care: Relationship to HIV risk behaviors and intentions. *AIDS & Behavior, 6*(4), 351–359.

Ayasse, R. H. (1995). Addressing the needs of foster children: The Foster Youth Services Program. *Social Work in Education, 17,* 207–216.

Barber, J. G., & Delfabbro, P. H. (2003). The first four months in a new foster placement: Psychosocial adjustment, parental contact and placement disruption. *Journal of Sociology and Social Welfare, 30*(3), 69–85.

Barnett, D., Manly, J. T., & Cicchetti, D. (1993). Defining child maltreatment: The interface between policy and research. In D. Cicchetti & S.L.Toth (Eds.), *Advances in applied developmental psychology: Child abuse, child development, and social policy* (pp. 7–74). Norwood, NJ: Ablex.

Barrera, M., Sandler, N., & Ramsay, T. B. (1981). Preliminary development of a scale of social support: Studies on college students. *American Journal of Community Psychology, 9,* 435–447.

Barth, R. P. (1986). *Social and cognitive treatment of children and adolescents.* San Francisco: Jossey-Bass.

Barth, R. P. (1990). On their own: The experience of youth after foster care. *Child and Adolescent Social Work Journal, 7*(5), 419–446.

Baumrind, D. (1995). *Child maltreatment and optimal caregiving in social contexts.* New York: Garland.

Beach, S. R., Martin, J. K., Blum, T. C., & Roman, P. M. (1994). Effects of marital and co-worker relationships on negative effect: Testing the central role of marriage. *American Journal of Family Therapy, 21*(4), 313–323.

Becker, J. V., Alpert, J. L., Bigfoot, D. S., Bonner, B. L., Geddie, L. F., Henggeler, S. W., et al. (1995). Empirical research on child abuse treatment: Report by the Child Abuse and Neglect Treatment Working Groups, American Psychological Association. *Journal of Child Clinical Psychology, 24,* 23–46.

Belsky, J. (1980). Child maltreatment: An ecological integration. *American Psychologist, 35,* 320–335.

Benedict, M. I., Zuravin, S., & Stallings, R. Y. (1996). Adult functioning of children who lived in kin versus non-relative family foster homes. *Child Welfare, 75*(5), 529–549.

Bernstein, N. (2000). *A rage to do better: Listening to young people from the foster care system.* San Francisco: Pacific News Service.

Berrick, J. D., Needell, B., Barth, R. P., & Jonson-Reid, M. (1998). *The tender years: Toward developmentally sensitive child welfare services for very young children.* New York: Oxford University Press.

Besharov, D. J., & Hanson, K. W. (1994). *When drug addicts have children: Reorienting child welfare's response.* Washington, DC: Child Welfare League of America.

Besinger, B. A., Garland, A. F., Litrownik, A. J., & Landsverk, J. A. (1999). Caregiver substance abuse among maltreated children placed in out-of-home care. *Child Welfare, 78*(2), 221.

Biehal, N., Clayden, J., Stein, M., & Wade, J. (1992). *Prepared for living?* London: National Children's Bureau.

Biehal, N., Clayden, J., Stein, M., & Wade, J. (1995). *Moving on: Young people and leaving care schemes.* London: HMSO.

Biehal, N., & Wade, J. (1996). Looking back, looking forward: Care leavers, families and change. *Children and Youth Services Review, 18*(4–5), 425–445.

Billings, A. G., & Moos, R. H. (1982). Psychosocial theory and research on depression: An integrative framework and review. *Clinical Psychology Review, 2,* 213–237.

Blome, W. W. (1994). *A comparative study of high school and post high school experiences of foster care and non foster care youth: A secondary analysis of a national longitudinal study.* Unpublished doctoral dissertation, Catholic University of America.

Blome, W. W. (1997). What happens to foster kids: Educational experiences of a random sample of foster care youth and a matched group of non-foster care youth. *Child and Adolescent Social Work Journal, 14*(1), 41–53.

Blum, R. W., Beuhring, T., & Rinehart, P. M. (2000). *Protecting teens: Beyond race, income and family structure.* Minneapolis: Center for Adolescent Health, University of Minnesota.

Blum, R. W., & Rinehart, P. M. (1997). *Reducing the risk: Connections that make a difference in the lives of youth.* Minneapolis: University of Minnesota, Division of General Pediatrics and Adolescent Health.

Blumenthal, K. (1983). Making foster family care responsive. In B. McGowan & W. Meezan (Eds.), *Child welfare: Current dilemmas—Future directions* (pp. 299–344). Itasca, IL: F. E. Peacock.

Boesel, D., Alsalam, N., & Smith, T. M. (1998). *Educational and labor market performance of GED recipients.* Washington, DC: Department of Education, Office of Educational Research and Improvement.

Boney-McCoy, S., & Finkelhor, D. (1996). Is youth victimization related to trauma symptoms and depression after controlling for prior symptoms and family relationships? A longitudinal, prospective study. *Journal of Consulting and Clinical Psychology, 64*(6), 1406–1416.

Bos, J. M. (1995). *The labor market value of remedial education: Evidence from time series data on an experimental program for school dropouts.* New York: doctoral dissertation, New York University (unpublished dissertation).

Bos, J. M. (1996, December). *Effects of education and educational credentials on the earnings of economically disadvantaged young mothers.* New York: Manpower Demonstration Research Corporation, Working Paper.

Bowlby, J. (1982). *Attachment and loss.* New York: Basic Books.

Bozick, R., & DeLuca, S. (2005). Better late than never? Delayed enrollment in the high school to college transition. *Social Forces, 84*(1), 527–550.

Bracey, G. W. (2004). The 14th Bracey Report on the condition of public education. *Phi Delta Kappan, 86*(2), 149–167.

Braitman, L. E., & Rosenbaum, P. R. (2002). Comparing treatments using comparable groups of patients. *Annals of Internal Medicine, 137*(8), 693–695.

Brandford, C., & English, D. (2004). *Foster youth transition to independence study.* Seattle: Office of Children's Administration Research, Washington Department of Social and Health Services.

Bretherton, I. (1992). The origins of attachment theory: John Bowlby and Mary Ainsworth. *Developmental Psychology, 28*(5), 759–775.

Briere, J. (1992). *Child abuse trauma: Theory and treatment of the lasting effects.* Newbury Park, CA: Sage.

Briere, J. (2002). Treating adult survivors of severe childhood abuse and neglect: Further development of an integrative model. In J. E. B. Meyers, L. Berliner, J. Briere, C. T. Hendrix, C. Jenny, & T. A. Reid (Eds.), *The APSAC handbook on child maltreatment* (2nd ed., pp. 175–204). Thousand Oaks, CA: Sage.

Briere, J. (2004). *Psychological assessment of adult posttraumatic states: Phenomenology, diagnosis, and measurement* (2nd ed.). Washington, DC: American Psychological Association.

Bronfenbrenner, U. (1979). *The ecology of human development.* Cambridge, MA: Harvard University Press.

Bronfenbrenner, U., & Morris, P. A. (1998). The ecology of developmental processes. In W. Damon (Ed.), *Handbook of child psychology* (5th ed., pp. 993–1028). New York: Wiley.

Brooks, R. B. (1994). Children at risk: Fostering resilience and hope. *American Journal of Orthopsychiatry, 64,* 545–553.

Brown, J., Cohen, P., Johnson, J. G., & Salzinger, S. (1998). A longitudinal analysis of risk factors for child maltreatment: Findings of a 17-year prospective study of official recorded and self-reported child abuse and neglect. *Child Abuse and Neglect, 22*(11), 1065–1078.

Bruni, M., & Gillespie, J. M. (1999). *Alcohol, tobacco and other drug survey of state child welfare agencies.* Springfield: Illinois Department of Alcoholism and Substance Abuse.

Buehler, C., Orme, J. G., Post, J., & Patterson, D. (2000). The long-term correlates of family foster care. *Children and Youth Services Review, 22*(8), 595–625.

Bullock, R., Courtney, M., Parker, R., Sinclair, I., & Thoburn, J. (2006). Can the corporate state parent? *Children and Youth Services Review, 28*(11), 1344–1358.

Burns, B. J., Phillips, S. D., Wagner, H. R., Barth, R. P., Kolko, D. J., Campbell, Y., et al. (2004). Mental health need and access to mental health services by youths involved with child welfare: A national survey. *Journal of the American Academy of Child & Adolescent Psychiatry, 43*(8), 960–970.

Burt, M. R., Aron, L. Y., Douglas, T., Valente, J., Lee, E., & Iwen, B. (1999). *Homelessness: Programs and the people they serve.* Washington, DC: Urban Institute.

Cadoret, R. J., & Riggins-Caspers, K. (2002). Fetal alcohol exposure and adult psychopathology: Evidence from an adoptive study. In R. P. Barth, D. Brodzinsky, & M. Freundlich (Eds.), *Adoption of drug exposed children* (pp. 106–129). Washington, DC: Child Welfare League of America.

Cameron, S. V., & Heckman, J. J. (1993). The nonequivalence of high school equivalents. *Journal of Labor Economics, 11*(1), 1–47.

Campbell, D. P. (1986). Relabeling internal and external validity for applied social scientists. In W. Trochim (Ed.), *Advances in quasi-experimental design and analysis* (Vol. 31, pp. 67–78). San Francisco: Jossey-Bass.

Carnegie Council on Adolescent Development. (1989). *Turning points: Preparing youth for the 21st century.* Washington, DC: Author.

Casey Family Programs. (1995). *Mission statement.* Seattle: Author.

Casey Family Programs. (2000). *The Casey model of practice.* Seattle: Author.

Casey Family Programs. (2001). *It's my life: A framework for youth transitioning from foster care to successful adulthood.* Seattle: Author.

Casey Family Programs. (2003a). *Family, community, culture: Roots of permanency—A conceptual framework on permanency from Casey Family Programs.* Seattle: Author.

Casey Family Programs. (2003b). *Higher education reform: Incorporating the needs of foster youth.* Seattle: Author.

Casey Family Programs. (2004). *Young adult study interview schedule.* Seattle: Research Services, Casey Family Programs.

Casey Family Programs. (2005a). Alumni study convening discussion notes. Seattle: Author.

Casey Family Programs. (2005b). *It's my life: Housing—a guide for transition services from Casey Family Programs.* Seattle: Author.

Casey Family Services. (1999). *The road to independence: Transitioning youth in foster care to independence.* Shelton, CT: Author.

Casey Family Services. (2004). *Follow-up study summary.* Shelton, CT: Author.

Casey National Resource Center for Family Support. (2003). *Siblings in out-of-home care: An overview.* Washington, DC: Author.

Casey Research Services. (2005). *Military service of Casey alumni based on the Casey National Alumni Study.* Seattle: Casey Family Programs.

Catalano, R. F., & Hawkins, J. D. (1996). The social developmental model: A theory of antisocial behavior. In J. D. Hawkins (Ed.), *Delinquency and crime: Current theories* (pp. 149–197). New York: Cambridge University Press.

Cauce, A. M., & Gonzales, N. (1993). Slouching towards culturally competent research: Adolescents and families of color in context. *Focus: Psychological Study of Ethnic Minority Issues, 7*(2), 8–9.

Centers for Disease Control and Prevention (CDC). (1998a). *Oregon Behavioral Risk Factor Surveillance System Survey Data.* Atlanta: U.S. Department of Health and Human Services, CDC.

Centers for Disease Control and Prevention (CDC). (1998b). *Oregon Behavioral Risk Factor Surveillance System Survey Data*. Retrieved June 1, 2006, from http://www.dhs.state.or.us/dhs/ph/chs/brfs/brfsdata.shtml

Chaffin, M., Kelleher, K., & Hollenberg, J. (1996). Onset of physical abuse and neglect: Psychiatric, substance abuse and social risk factors from prospective community data. *Child Abuse and Neglect, 20,* 191–200.

Chamberlain, P. (2003). *Treating chronic juvenile offenders: Advances made through the Oregon multidimensional treatment foster care model.* Washington, DC: American Psychological Association.

Chamberlain, P., Brown, C. H., Saldana, L., Reid, J., Wang, W., Marsenich, L., et al. (2008). Engaging and recruiting counties in an experiment on implementing evidence-based practice in California. *Administration and Policy in Mental Health and Mental Health Services Research,* 34 (4), 250–260.

Chamberlain, P., Moreland, S., & Reid, K. (1992). Enhanced services and stipends for foster parents: Effects on retention rates and outcomes for children. *Child Welfare, 71*(5), 387–401.

Chaskin, R. J. (2001, March 1). *The evaluation of "community-building": Measuring the social effects of community-based practice.* Paper presented at the Outcomes Roundtable, Volterra, Italy.

Child Welfare League of America. (1995). *Standards of excellence for family foster care.* Washington, DC: Author.

Child Welfare League of America. (1998). *Alcohol and other drug survey of state child welfare agencies.* Washington, DC: Author.

Child Welfare League of America. (2005). *CWLA policy recommendations regarding the Transition to Adulthood Program Act of 1999, H.R. 671.* Washington, DC: Author.

Child Welfare League of America. (2006a). *Out of the margins: A report on the regional listening forums highlighting the experiences of lesbian, gay, bisexual, transgender, and questioning youth in care.* Washington, DC: Author.

Child Welfare League of America. (2006b). *Position statement on parenting of children by GLBT adults.* Washington, DC: Author.

Choca, M. J., Minoff, J., Angene, L., Byrnes, M., Kenneally, L., Norris, D., et al. (2004). Can't do it alone: Housing collaborations to improve foster youth outcomes. *Child Welfare, 83*(5), 469.

Christian-Herman, J. L., O'Leary, K. D., & Avery-Leaf, S. (2001). The impact of severe negative events in marriage on depression. *Journal of Social and Clinical Psychology, 20,* 24–40.

Cicchetti, D. (1989). How research on child maltreatment has informed the study of child development: perspectives from developmental psychopathology. In D. Cicchetti & V. Carlson (Eds.), *Child maltreatment: Theory and research on the causes and consequences of child abuse and neglect* (pp. 377–431). Cambridge: Cambridge University Press.

Cicchetti, D. (1994). Advances and challenges in the study of the sequelae of child maltreatment. *Development and Psychopathology, 6,* 1–3.

Cicchetti, D., & Lynch, M. (1993). Toward an ecological/transactional model of community violence and child maltreatment: Consequences for children's development. *Psychiatry, 56,* 96–118.

Cicchetti, D., & Toth, S. L. (1995). A developmental psychopathology perspective on child abuse and neglect. *Journal of the American Academy of Child and Adolescent Psychiatry, 34,* 541–565.

Clark, H. B., & Davis, M. (2000). *Transition to adulthood: A resource for assisting young people with emotional or behavioral difficulties.* Baltimore: P. H. Brookes.

Clarke, G. N., DeBar, L. L., & Lewinsohn, P. M. (2003). Cognitive-behavioral group treatment for adolescent depression. In A. E. Kazdin (Ed.), *Evidence-based psychotherapies for children and adolescents* (pp. 120–134). New York: Guilford Press.

Cohen, D. L. (1991). Foster youths said to get little help with educational deficits. *Education Week,* pp. 8–10.

Cohen, J. A., Mannarino, A. P., Zhitova, A. C., & Capone, M. E. (2003). Treating child-abuse related posttraumatic stress and comorbid substance abuse in adolescents. *Child Abuse & Neglect, 27*(12), 1345–1365.

Cohen, S., & Wills, T. A. (1985). Stress, social support, and the buffering hypothesis. *Psychological Bulletin, 98*, 310–357.

Coie, J., Watt, N., West, S., Hawkins, D., Asarnow, J., Markman, H., et al. (1993). The science of prevention: A conceptual framework and some directions for a national research program. *American Psychologist, 48*(10), 1013–1021.

Conger, D., & Rebeck, A. (2001). *How children's foster care experiences affect their education.* New York: New York City Administration for Children's Services.

Cook, R., Fleishman, E., & Grimes, V. (1991). *A National Evaluation of Title IV-E Foster Care Independent Living Programs for Youth. Phase 2 Final Report.* Rockville, MD: Westat Corporation.

Cook, R. J. (1992). Are we helping foster care youth prepare for the future? *Children and Youth Services Review, 16*(3/4), 213–229.

Cook, R. J.; Fleishman, E., & Grimes, V. (1991). *A National Evaluation of Title IV-E Foster Care Independent Living Programs for Youth* (Phase 2 Final Report, Volume 1). Rockville: Westat, Inc.

Cook, R. J. (1994). Are we helping foster care youth prepare for their future? *Children and Youth Services Review, 16*(3–4), 213–229.

Corcoran, K., & Fischer, J. (2000). *Measures for clinical practice: A sourcebook* (3rd ed.). New York: Free Press.

Coulling, N. (2000). Definitions of successful education for the "looked after" child: A multi-agency perspective. *Support for Learning, 15*(1), 30.

Courtney, M. E., Dworsky, A., Cusick, G. R., Keller, T., Havlicek, J., Perez, A., et al. (2007). *Midwest evaluation of adult functioning of former foster youth: Outcomes at age 21.* Chicago: University of Chicago, Chapin Hall Center for Children.

Courtney, M. E., Dworsky, A., Ruth, G., Keller, T., Havlicek, J., & Bost, N. (2005). *Midwest evaluation of the adult functioning of former foster youth: Outcomes at age 19.* Chicago, IL: Chapin Hall Center for Children at the University of Chicago.

Courtney, M. E., Needell, B., & Wulczyn, F. (2004a). Unintended consequences of the push for accountability: The case of national child welfare performance standards. *Children and Youth Services Review, 26*(12), 1141–1154.

Courtney, M., Piliavin, I., Grogan-Kaylor, A., & Nesmith, A. (1998). *Foster youth transitions to adulthood: Outcomes 12 to 18 months after leaving out-of-home care.* Madison: School of Social Work and Institute for Research on Poverty, University of Wisconsin-Madison.

Courtney, M. E., Piliavin, I., Grogan-Kaylor, A., & Nesmith, A. (2001). Foster youth transitions to adulthood: A longitudinal view of youth leaving care. *Child Welfare, 80*(6), 685–717.

Courtney, M. E., Terao, S., & Bost, N. (2004b). *Midwest evaluation of the adult functioning of former foster youth: Conditions of youth preparing to leave state care.* Chicago: Chapin Hall Center for Children at the University of Chicago.

Crimson, M. L., & Argo, T. (2009). The use of psychotropic medication for children in foster care. *Child Welfare, 8*(1), 71–100.

Curtis, C., & Denby, R. (2004). Impact of the Adoption and Safe Families Act (1997) on families of color: Workers share their thoughts. *Families in Society, 85*, 71–79.

Daniels, D. (1986). Differential experiences of siblings in the same family as predictors of adolescent sibling personality differences. *Journal of Personality and Social Psychology, 51*(2), 339–346.

De Bellis, M. D. (2001). Developmental traumatology: The psychobiological development of maltreated children and its implications for research, treatment, and policy. *Development and Psychopathology, 13* (3), 539–564.

Demyttenaere, K., Bruffaerts, R., Posada-Villa, J., Gasquet, I., Kovess, V., Lepine, J. P., et al. (2004). Prevalence, severity, and unmet need for treatment of mental disorders in the

World Health Organization World Mental Health Surveys. *Journal of the American Medical Association, 291*(21), 2581–2590.

DeNavas-Walt, C., Proctor, B. D., & Lee, C. H. (2005). *Income, poverty, and health insurance coverage in the United States: 2004.* Washington, DC: U.S. Government Printing Office.

DePanfilis, D. (1996). Social isolation of neglectful families: A review of social support assessment and intervention. *Child Maltreatment, 1*(1), 37–52.

DeVooght, K., Allen, T., & Geen, R. (2008). *Federal, state, and local spending to address child abuse and neglect.* Washington, DC: Child Trends.

Doucette, A., Tarnowski, E., & Baum, E. (2001). *Casey consumer satisfaction and youth behavior study.* Nashville TN: Vanderbilt University, Center for Mental Health Policy.

Downs, A. C. (2006). The utility of the regional listening forums for policy, practice and research: A tripod. In Child Welfare League of America (Ed.), *Out of the margins: A report on the regional listening forums highlighting the experiences of lesbian, gay, bisexual, transgender, and questioning youth in care* (pp. 133–138). Washington, DC: Child Welfare League of America.

Downs, A. C., & Pecora, P. J. (2004). *Application of Erikson's psychosical development theory to foster care research* (Working Paper No. 2). Seattle: Casey Family Programs.

Dubowitz, H., Pitts, S., Litrownik, A., Cox, C., Runyan, D., & Black, M. (2005). Defining child neglect based on Child Protective Services data. *Child Abuse & Neglect, 29*(5), 493–511.

Dumaret, A. C., Coppel-Batsch, M., & Couraud, S. (1997). Adult outcome of children reared for long-term periods in foster families. *Child Abuse & Neglect, 21*(10), 911–927.

Dumas, J. E. (1984). Interactional correlates of treatment outcome in behavioral parenting training. *Journal of Consulting and Clinical Psychology, 52*(6), 946–954.

Dumas, J. E., & Albin, J. B. (1986). Parent training outcome: Does active parent involvement matter? *Behavioral Research and Therapy, 24*(2), 227–230.

Dumas, J. E., & Wahler, R. G. (1983). Predictors of treatment outcome in parenting training: Mother insularity and socioeconomic disadvantage. *Behavioral Assessment, 5*, 301–313.

Dworsky, A., & Courtney, M. E. (2000). *Self-sufficiency of former foster youth in Wisconsin: Analysis of unemployment insurance wage data and public assistance data.* Washington, DC: Department of Health and Human Services, Office of the Assistant Secretary for Planning and Evaluation.

Eckenrode, J., Laird, M., & Doris, J. (1993). Academic performance and disciplinary problems among abused and neglected children. *Developmental Psychology, 29*, 53–62.

Edgbert, S., Egglin, J., Erickson, T., Fimiani, J., Heim, G., Honse, C., et al. (2004). *Elements used for estimating a per day cost for foster care in Oregon State, Washington State, and Casey Family Programs for 1998.* Seattle: Casey Family Programs, Research Services.

Edmund S. Muskie School of Public Service. (1999). *Maine study on improving the educational outcomes for children in care.* Baltimore: Annie E. Casey.

Emerson, J. (2007). From foster care to college: Supporting independent students. *Leadership Exchange, 4*(4), 4–10. Retrieved March 24, 2009 from www.nasfaa.org/PDFs/2007/FosterSPread.pdf.

Emerson, J., Hightower, A., & Montoya, Y. (2003). *2002–2003 Casey Assigned High School Seniors: Graduation status and postsecondary transition plans* (review draft) Seattle: Casey Family Programs.

English, D. J., Bangdiwala, S. I., & Runyan, D. K. (2005a). The dimensions of maltreatment: Introduction. *Child Abuse and Neglect, 29*, 441–460.

English, D. J., Graham, J. C., Litrownik, A. J., Everson, M. D., & Bangdiwala, S. I. (2005c). Defining maltreatment chronicity: Are there differences in child outcomes? *Child Abuse & Neglect, 29*(5), 575–595.

English, D. J., Kouidou-Giles, S., & Plocke, M. (1994). Readiness for independence: A study of youth in foster care. *Children & Youth Services Review, 16*(3–4), 147–158.

English, D. J., & the LONGSCAN investigators. (1997). Modified Maltreatment Classification System (MMCS). http://www.iprc.unc.edu/longscan

English, D. J., Upadhyaya, M., Litrownik, A., Kotch, J., Marshall, J., Dubowitz, H., et al. (2005b). Maltreatment's wake: The relationship of maltreatment dimensions to child outcomes. *Child Abuse & Neglect, 29*(5), 597–619.

English, D. J., Widom, C., & Brandford, C. (2002). *Childhood victimization and delinquency, adult criminality, and violent criminal behavior: A replication and extension. Grant #97-IJ-CX-0017.* Washington, DC: National Institute of Justice.

Erikson, E. H. (1956). The problem of ego identity. *Journal of the American Psychoanalytic Association, 4*(1), 56–121.

Erikson, E. H. (1963). *Childhood and society* (2nd ed.). New York: Norton.

Erikson, E. H. (1964). *Insight and responsibility.* New York: Norton.

Erikson, E. H. (1968). *Identity: Youth and crisis.* New York: Norton.

Erikson, E. H. (1974). *Dimensions of a new identity.* New York: Norton.

Erikson, E. H. (1975). *Life history and the historical moment.* New York: Norton.

Erikson, E. H. (1985). *The life cycle completed.* New York: Norton.

Ezell, M., Casey, E., Pecora, P. J., Grossman, C., Friend, R., Vernon, L., et al. (2002). The results of a management redesign: A case study. *Administration in Social Work, 26*(4), 61–80.

Fanshel, D., Finch, S. J., & Grundy, J. F. (1990). *Foster children in a life course perspective.* New York: Columbia University Press.

Fanshel, D., & Shinn, E. B. (1978). *Children in foster care: A longitudinal investigation.* New York: Columbia University Press.

Felitti, V. J., Anda, R. F., Nordenberg, D., Williamson, D. F., Spitz, A. M., Edwards, V., et al. (1998). Relationship of childhood abuse and household dysfunction to many of the leading causes of death in adults: The Adverse Childhood experiences (ACE) study. *American Journal of Preventive Medicine, 14*(4), 245–258.

Festinger, T. (1983). *No one ever asked us…A postscript to foster care.* New York: Columbia University Press.

Flynn, R., & Biro, C. (1998). Comparing developmental outcomes for children in care compared with those for other children in Canada. *Children & Society, 12,* 228–233.

Ford, B. M. (1983). An overview of hot-deck procedures. In *Incomplete data in sample surveys* (Vol. 2). In W.G. Madow, I. Olkin, and D.B. Rubin (Eds.), (pp.185–207). New York: Academic Press.

Fraser, M. W., Pecora, P. J., & Haapala, D. A. (1991). *Families in crisis: The impact of intensive family preservation services.* Hawthorne, NY: Aldine de Gruyter.

Freundlich, M., & Wright, L. (2003). *Post-permanency services.* Washington, DC: Casey Family Programs Center for Resource Family Support.

Fromm, S. (2001). *Total estimated cost of child abuse and neglect in the United States—Statistical evidence* (Technical Report). New York: Edna McConnell Clark Foundation.

Frost, A. K., & Pakiz, B. (1990). The effects of marital disruption on adolescents: Time as a dynamic. *American Journal of Orthopsychiatry, 60,* 544–555.

Frost, S., & Jurich, A. P. (1983). *Follow-up study of children residing in The Villages* (unpublished report). Topeka, KS: The Villages.

Furstenberg, F. F. J., Cook, T., Eccles, J., Elder, G. H., & Sameroff, A. J. (1999). *Managing to make it: Urban families and adolescent success.* Chicago: University of Chicago Press.

Gabel, K., & Johnston, D. (1997). *Children of incarcerated parents.* New York: Lexington Books.

Garbarino, J. (1982). *Children and families in the social environment.* New York: Aldine.

Garland, A. F., Hough, R. L., McCabe, K. M., Yeh, M., Wood, P. A., & Aarons, G. A. (2001). Prevalence of psychiatric disorders in youths across five sectors of care. *Journal of the American Academy of Child and Adolescent Psychiatry, 40*(4), 419–426.

Garland, A. F., Landsverk, J. A., & Lau, A. S. (2003). Racial/ethnic disparities in mental health service use among children in foster care. *Children and Youth Services Review, 25*(5–6), 491–507.

Geen, R. (2004). The evolution of kinship care policy and practice. *Future of Children, 14*(1), 130–149.

Gelles, R. J., & Straus, M. A. (1988). *Intimate violence*. New York: Simon & Schuster.

Gilligan, R. (1999). Enhancing the resilience of children and young people in public care by mentoring their talents and interests. *Child & Family Social Work, 4*(3), 187–196.

Goerge, R. M., Bilaver, L. A., Lee, B. J., Needell, B., Brookhart, A., & Jackman, W. (2002). *Employment outcomes for youth aging out of foster care*. Chicago: University of Chicago, Chapin Hall Center for Children.

Goerge, R. M., Wulczyn, F., & Fanshel, D. (1994). A foster care research agenda for the 90's. *Child Welfare, 73*(5), 525–547.

Goldberg, S., Muir, R., & Kerr, J. (Eds.). (1995). *Attachment theory: Social, developmental, and clinical perspectives*. Hillsdale, NJ: Analytic Press.

Gonzales, N., & Cauce, A. M. (1995). Ethnic identity and multicultural competence: Dilemmas and challenges for minority youth. In W. D. Hawley & A. Jackson (Eds.), *Toward a common destiny: Improving race and ethnic relations in America* (pp. 131–162). San Francisco: Jossey-Bass.

Greenberg, P. E., Sisitsky, T., Kessler, R. C., Finkelstein, S. N., Berndt, E. R., Davidson, J. R. T., et al. (1999). The economic burden of anxiety disorders in the 1990s. *Journal of Clinical Psychiatry, 60*, 427–435.

Grizenko, N., & Pawliuk, N. (1994). Risk and protective factors for disruptive behavior disorders in children. *American Journal of Orthopsychiatry, 64*, 534–544.

Grubb, W. N. (1999). *Learning and earning in the middle: The economic benefits of sub-baccalaureate education*. New York: Community College Research Center.

Halfon, N., Mendonca, A., & Berkowitz, G. (1995). Health status of children in foster care. The experience of the Center for the Vulnerable Child. *Archives of Pediatrics & Adolescent Medicine, 149*(4), 386–392.

Hanson, R. F., Smith, D. W., Saunders, B. E., Swenson, C. C., & Conrad, L. (1995). Measurement in child abuse research: A survey of researchers. *The APSAC Advisor, 8*, 7–10.

Haring-Hidore, M., Stock, W. A., Okun, M. A., & Witter, R. A. (1985). Marital status and subjective well-being in adults. *Journal of Family Issues, 11*, 4–35.

Haro, J. M., Arbabzadeh-Bouchez, S., Brugha, T. S., de Girolamo, G., Guyer, M. E., Jin, R., et al. (2006). Concordance of the Composite International Diagnostic Interview Version 3.0 (CIDI 3.0) with standardized clinical assessments in the WHO World Mental Health Surveys. *International Journal of Methods in Psychiatric Research, 15*(4), 167–180.

Hart, S. N., Binggeli, N. J., & Brassard, M. R. (1998). Evidence for the effects of psychological maltreatment. *Journal of Emotional Abuse, 1*(1), 27–56.

Havalchak, A., White, C. R., O'Brien, K., & Pecora, P. J. (2007). *Casey Family Programs Young Adult Survey 2006: Examining outcomes for young adults served in out-of-home care*. Seattle: Casey Family Programs.

Haveman, R., & Wolfe, B. (1994). *Succeeding generations: On the effects of investments in children*. New York: Sage.

Hawkins, J. D., & Catalano, R. S. (1992). *Communities that care*. San Francisco: Jossey-Bass.

Hazan, C., & Shaver, P. (1987). Romantic love conceptualized as an attachment process. *Journal of Personality & Social Psychology, 52*(3), 511–524.

Hegar, R. L. (2005). Sibling placement in foster care and adoption: An overview of international research. *Children and Youth Services Review, 27*, 717–739.

Hegar, R. L., & Scannapieco, M. (Eds.). (1998). *Kinship foster care: Policy, practice, and research*. New York: Oxford University Press.

Heller, K., Swindle, R. W., Jr., & Dusenbury, L. (1986). Component social support processes: Comments and integration. *Journal of Consulting and Clinical Psychology, 54*(4), 466–470.

Herman, J. (1997). *Trauma and recovery: The aftermath of violence from domestic abuse to political terror*. New York: Basic Books.

Herrick, M. A., & Piccus, W. (2005). Sibling connections: The importance of nurturing sibling bonds in the foster care system. *Children and Youth Services Review, 27*, 845–861.

Hill, R. B. (2001, January 9–10). *The role of race in foster care placement*. Paper presented at the Race Matters Forum, University of Illinois at Urbana-Champaign.

Hill, R. B. (2007). *Analysis of racial/ethnic disproportionality and disparity at the national, state and county levels*. Washington, DC: The Casey-CSSP Alliance for Racial Equity and the Center for the Study of Social Policy.

Hillis, S. D., Anda, R. F., Felitti, V. J., & Marchbanks, P. (2001). Adverse childhood experiences and sexual risk behaviors in women: A retrospective cohort study. *Family Planning Perspectives, 33*, 206–211.

Himle, D. P., Jayaratne, S., & Thyness, P. (1991). Buffering effects of four social support types on burnout among social workers. *Social Work Research and Abstracts, 27*(1), 34–37.

Hoge, C. W., Castro, C. A., Messer, S. C., McGurk, D., Cotting, D. I., & Koffman, R. L. (2004). Combat duty in Iraq and Afghanistan, mental health problems, and barriers to care. *The New England Journal of Medicine, 351*(1), 13–22.

Holahan, C. J., Moos, R. H., Holahan, C. K., Cronkite, R. C., & Randall, P. K. (2004). Unipolar depression, life context vulnerabilities, and drinking to cope. *Journal of Consulting and Clinical Psychology, 72*, 269–275.

Holdaway, D. M., & Ray, J. (1992). Attitudes of street kids toward foster care. *Child & Adolescent Social Work Journal, 9*(4), 307–317.

Hornby, H., & Zeller, D. (1992). *Oregon Child Protective Services performance study*. Portland: University of Southern Maine, National Child Welfare Resource Center for Management and Administration.

Horwitz, A. V., McLaughlin, J., & Raskin White, H. (1998). How the negative and positive aspects of partner relationships affect the mental health of young married people. *Journal of Health and Social Behavior, 39*(2), 124–136.

Horwitz, S. M., Simms, M. D., & Farrington, R. (1994). Impact of developmental problems on young children's exits from foster care. *Journal of Developmental & Behavioral Pediatrics, 15*(2), 105–110.

Hosmer, D. W., & Lemseshow, S. L. (1989). *Applied logistic regression*. New York: Wiley.

Hosmer, D. W., & Lemseshow, S. L. (2004). *Applied logistic regression* (2nd ed.). New York: Wiley.

House, J. (1981). *Work stress and social support*. Reading, MA: Addison-Wesley.

Hughes, H. M., & Graham-Bermann, S. A. (1998). Children of battered women: Impact of emotional abuse on adjustment and development. *Journal of Emotional Abuse, 1*(2), 23–50.

Humke, C., & Schaefer, C. (1995). Relocation: A review of the effects of residential mobility on children and adolescents. *Psychology: A Journal of Human Behavior, 32*, 16–24.

Hunter, W., & Knight, E. (1998). *LONGSCAN research briefs: Volume 1*. Chapel Hill, NC: LONGSCAN Coordinating Center.

Hurlburt, M. S., Leslie, L. K., Landsverk, J., Barth, R., Burns, B. J., Gibbons, R. D., et al. (2004). Contextual predictors of mental health service use among children open to child welfare. *Archives of General Psychiatry, 61*, 1217–1224.

Hussey, J. M., Marshall, J. M., English, D. J., Knight, E. D., Lau, A. S., Dubowitz, H., et al. (2005). Defining maltreatment according to substantiation: Distinction without a difference? *Child Abuse & Neglect, 29*, 479–492.

Iglehart, A. P. (1994). Adolescents in foster care: Predicting readiness for independent living. *Children & Youth Services Review, 16*(3–4), 159–169.

Institute of Medicine. (2001). *Coverage matters: Insurance and health care*. Retrieved April 30, 2008, from http://www.iom.edu/CMS/3809/4660/4662.aspx

Institute of Medicine. (2002). *Unequal treatment: Comparing racial and ethnic disparities in health care*. Washington, DC: Author.

Institute of Medicine. (2003). *Hidden costs, value lost: Uninsurance in America*. Retrieved September 24, 2008, from http://www.iom.edu/CMS/3809/4660/12313.aspx

Institute of Medicine (IOM) Committee on Prevention of Mental Disorders. (1994). Illustrative preventive intervention research programs. In P. J. Mrazek & R. J. Haggerty (Eds.), *Reducing risks for mental disorders: Frontiers for preventive intervention research* (pp. 215–313) Washington, DC: National Academy Press.

Jackson, S. (1994). Educating children in residential and foster care. *Oxford Review of Education, 20*(3), 267–279.

Jacobson, E., & Cockerum, J. (1976). As foster children see it: Former foster children talk about foster family care. *Children Today, 42*, 32–36.

James, S. (2004). Why do foster care placements disrupt? An investigation of reasons for placement change in foster care. *Social Service Review, 78*(4), 601–627.

James, S., Landsverk, J., & Slymen, D. (2004). Placement movement in out-of-home care: Patterns and predictors. *Children and Youth Services Review, 26*(2), 185–206.

Jensen, J. M., & Fraser, M. W. (Eds.). (2006). *Social policy for children and families: A risk and resilience perspective.* Thousand Oaks, CA: Sage.

Jessor, R., Van Den Bos, J., Vanderryn, J., Costa, F. M., & Turbin, M. S. (1995). Protective factors in adolescent problem behavior: Moderator effects and developmental change. *Developmental Psychology, 31*(6), 923–933.

Johnson, P. R., Yoken, C., & Voss, R. (1995). Family foster care placement: The child's perspective. *Child Welfare, 74*(5), 959–974.

Jones, M. A., & Moses, B. (1984). *West Virginia's former foster children: Their experiences in care and their lives as young adults.* New York: Child Welfare League of America.

Jongedijk, R. A. (2003). *Evidence-based treatment for trauma victims with complex PTSD. Presentation for Foundation Centrum 45.* Retrieved April 30, 2006, from http://www.estss.org/ewots05/ew05_files/jonge03.pdf

Jung, J. (1997). Balance and source of social support in relation to well-being. *The Journal of General Psychology, 124*(1), 77–90.

Kaufman, J., Yang, B., Douglas-Palumberi, H., Damion Grasso, D., Lipschitz, D., Houshyar, S., et al. (2006). Brain-derived neurotrophic factor-5–HTTLPR gene interactions and environmental modifiers of depression in children. *Biological Psychiatry, 59*(8), 673–680.

Kaufman, P., Alt, M. N., & Chapman, C. D. (2001). *Dropout rates in the United States: 2000.* Retrieved January 2, 2008, from http://nces.ed.gov/pubsearch/pubsinfo.asp?pubid=2002114

Kazdin, A. E., & Weisz, J. R. (Eds.). (2003). *Evidence-based psychotherapies for children and adolescents.* New York: Guilford Press.

Kendall-Tackett, K. A., & Eckenrode, J. (1996). The effects of neglect on academic achievement and disciplinary problems: A developmental perspective *Child Abuse & Neglect, 20*(3), 161–169.

Kendall-Tackett, K. A., & Giacomoni, S. M. (Eds.). (2003). *Treating the lifetime health effects of childhood victimization.* Kingston, NJ: Civic Research Institute.

Kendler, K. S., Heath, A. C., Martin, N. G., & Eaves, L. J. (1987). Symptoms of anxiety and symptoms of depression: Same genes, different environments? *Archives of General Psychiatry, 44*, 451–458.

Kessler, R. C. (1991). The National Comorbidity Survey. *DIS Newsletter, 7*, 1–2.

Kessler, R. C., Berglund, P., Demler, O., Jin, R., Koretz, D., Merikangas, K. R., et al. (2003). The epidemiology of major depressive disorder: Results from the National Comorbidity Survey Replication (NCS-R). *Journal of the American Medical Association, 289*(23), 3095–3105.

Kessler, R. C., Berglund, P., Demler, O., Jin, R., & Walters, E. E. (2005a). Lifetime prevalence and age-of-onset distributions of DSM-IV disorders in the National Comorbidity Survey Replication (NCS-R). *Archives of General Psychiatry, 62*(6), 593–602.

Kessler, R. C., Chiu, W. T., Demler, O., & Walters, E. E. (2005b). Prevalence, severity, and comorbidity of twelve-month DSM-IV disorders in the National Comorbidity Survey Replication (NCS-R). *Archives of General Psychiatry, 62*(6), 617–627.

Kessler, R. C., Davis, C. G., & Kendler, K. S. (1997). Childhood adversity and adult psychiatric disorder in the U.S. National Comorbidity Survey. *Psychological Medicine, 27*(5), 1101–1119.

Kessler, R. C., & Magee, W. (1994). Childhood family violence and adult recurrent depression. *Journal of Health and Social Behavior, 35*, 13–27.

Kessler, R. C., McLeod, J. D., & Wethington, E. (1985). The costs of caring: A perspective on the relationship between sex and psychological distress. In B. R. Sarason (Ed.), *Social support: Theory, research, and applications* (pp. 491–506). Boston: Martinus Nijhoff.

Kessler, R. C., & Merikangas, K. R. (2004). The National Comorbidity Survey Replication (NCS-R). *International Journal of Methods in Psychiatric Research, 13*(2), 60–68.

Kessler, R. C., Pecora, P. J., Williams, J., Hiripi, E., O'Brien, K., English, D., et al. (2008). The effects of enhanced foster care on the long-term physical and mental health of foster care alumni. *Archives in General Psychiatry, 65*(6), 625–633.

Kessler, R. C., Sonnega, A., Bromet, E., Hughes, M., & Nelson, C. B. (1995). Posttraumatic stress disorder in the National Comorbidity Survey. *Archives of General Psychiatry, 52*(12), 1048–1060.

Kessler, R. C., & Üstün, T. B. (2004). The World Mental Health (WMH) Survey Initiative Version of the World Health Organization (WHO) Composite International Diagnostic Interview (CIDI). *International Journal of Methods in Psychiatric Research, 13*(2), 93–121.

Kessler, R. C., & Walters, E. E. (2002). The National Comorbidity Survey. In M. T. Tsuang, M. Tohen, & G. E. P. Zahner (Eds.), *Textbook in psychiatric epidemiology* (2nd ed., pp. 343–361). New York: Wiley.

Kilpatrick, D. G., Ruggiero, K. J., Acierno, R., Saunders, B. E., Resnick, H. S., & Best, C. L. (2003). Violence and risk of PTSD, major depression, substance abuse/dependence, and comorbidity: Results from the National Survey of Adolescents. *Journal of Consulting and Clinical Psychology, 71*, 692–700.

Kohl, P. L., Gibbons, C. B., & Green, R. L. (2005, January 16). *Findings from the National Survey of Child and Adolescent Well-Being (NSCAW): Applying innovative methods to understanding services and outcomes for maltreated children; Safety of children in child welfare services: Analysis of reported and undetected maltreatment over 18 months.* Paper presented at the annual meeting of the Society for Social Work and Research, Miami, FL.

Kulka, R. A., Fairbank, J. A., Jordan, K., & Weiss, D. (1990). *Trauma and the Vietnam War generation: Report of findings from the National Vietnam Veterans Readjustment Study.* New York: Brunner/Mazel.

Kupsinel, M. M., & Dubsky, D. D. (1999). Behaviorally impaired children in out-of-home care. *Child Welfare, 78*(2), 297–310.

Lackey, C., & Williams, K. R. (1995). Social bonding and the cessation of partner violence across generations. *Journal of Marriage and the Family, 57*(2), 295–305.

Lamphear, V. S. (1985). The impact of maltreatment on children's psychosocial adjustment: A review of the research. *Child Abuse & Neglect, 9*, 251–263.

Landsverk, J. (1999). Foster care and pathways to mental health services. In P. Curtis, D. Grady, & J. Kendell (Eds.), *The foster care crisis: Translating research into practic and policy* (pp. 193–210). Lincoln: University of Nebraska Press.

Landsverk, J., Burns, B., Stambaugh, L. F., & Rolls-Reutz, J. A. (2006). *Mental health care for children and adolescents in foster care: Review of research literature.* Seattle: Casey Family Programs.

Landsverk, J., Clausen, J. M., Ganger, W., Chadwick, D., & Litrownik, A. (1995a). *Mental health problems in three California counties.* Unpublished manuscript.

Landsverk, J., Davis, I., Garland, A., Hough, R., Litrownik, A., & Price, J. (1995b). *A developmental framework for research with victims of child maltreatment placed in foster care.* San Diego, CA: Center for Research on Child and Adolescent Mental Health Services, Children's Hospital.

Lansford, J. E., Dodge, K. A., Petit, G. S., Bates, J. E., Crozier, J. C., & Kaplow, J. (2002). Long-term effects of early child physical maltreatment on psychological, behavioral, and academic problems in adolescence. *Archives of Pediatrics and Adolescent Medicine, 156*, 824–830.

Lau, A. S., Leeb, R. T., English, D. J., Graham, C., Briggs, E. C., Brody, K. E., et al. (2005). What's in a name? A comparison of methods for classifying predominant type of maltreatment. *Child Abuse & Neglect, 29*(5), 533–551.

Le Prohn, N., Barenblat, M., Godinet, M., Nicoll, A., & Pecora, P. (1996). *Foster parent report.* Seattle: Casey Family Programs.

Le Prohn, N. S., & Pecora, P. J. (1994). *The Casey foster parent study: Research summary.* Seattle: The Casey Family Program.

Leathers, S. J. (2002). Parental visiting and family reunification: Could inclusive practice make a difference? *Child Welfare, 81*(4), 595–616.

Leathers, S. J. (2005). Separation from siblings: Associations with placement adaptation and outcomes among adolescents in long-term foster care. *Children and Youth Services Review, 27*, 793–819.

Lee, S., Aos, S., & Miller, M. (2008). *Evidence-based programs to prevent children from entering and remaining in the child welfare system: Interim report*. Olympia: Washington State Institute for Public Policy.

Leibold, J., & Downs, C. (2002). *San Antonio PAL classes evaluation report*. Seattle: The Casey Family Program.

Leslie, L. K., Landsverk, J., Ezzet-Lofstrom, R., Tschann, J. M., Slymen, D. J., & Garland, A. F. (2000). Children in foster care: Factors influencing outpatient mental health service use. *Child Abuse & Neglect, 24*(4), 465.

Lindsey, D. (2004). *The welfare of children*. New York: Oxford University Press.

Litrownik, A. J., Lau, A., English, D., Briggs, E., Newton, R., Romney, S., et al. (2005). Measuring the severity of child maltreatment. *Child Abuse & Neglect, 29*(5), 553–573.

Little, R. J. A. (1982). Direct standardization: A tool for teaching linear models for unbalanced data. *The American Statistician, 36*, 38–43.

LONGSCAN investigators. (2006). *LONGSCAN research briefs: Volume 2*. Chapel Hill, NC: LONGSCAN Coordinating Center.

Luthar, S. S., & Cicchetti, D. (2000). The construct of resilience: Implications for interventions and social policies. *Development and Psychopathology, 12*, 857–885.

Maas, H. S., & Engler, R. E. (1959). *Children in need of parents*. New York: Columbia University Press.

Maguin, E., & Loeber, R. (1996). Academic performance and delinquency. In M. Tonry (Ed.), *Crime and justice: A review of the research* (pp. 145–264). Chicago: University of Chicago Press.

Mallon, G. (1999). *Let's get this straight: A gay- and lesbian-affirming approach to child welfare*. New York: Columbia University Press.

Maloney, T. (1993). *Will a secondary education increase the earnings of female dropouts?* Unpublished working paper, University of Auckland, New Zealand.

Maluccio, A. N., Ainsworth, F., & Thoburn, J. (2000). *Child welfare outcome research in the United States, the United Kingdom, and Australia*. Washington, DC: CWLA Press.

Maluccio, A. N., & Pecora, P. J. (2006). Family foster care in the USA. In C. McCauley, P. J. Pecora, & W. E. Rose (Eds.), *Enhancing the well-being of children and families through effective interventions: International evidence for practice* (pp. 187–202). London and Philadelphia: Jessica Kingsley.

Maluccio, A. N., Pine, B. A., & Tracy, E. M. (2002). *Social work practice with families and children*. New York: Columbia University Press.

Mann, A. (2003). Relationships matter: Impact of parental, peer factors on teen, young adult substance abuse. *NIDA Notes, 18*(2), 11–13.

Marcia, J. E. (1966). Development and validation of ego identity status. *Journal of Personality and Social Psychology, 3*(5), 551–558.

Marcia, J. E. (1976). Identity six years after: A follow-up study. *Journal of Youth and Adolescence, 5*(2), 145–160.

Marcia, J. E. (1980). Identity in adolescence. In J. Adelson (Ed.), *Handbook of adolescent psychology* (pp. 158–187). New York: Wiley.

Marcotte, D. E., Wilcox-Gök, V., & Redmon, D. P. (1999). Prevalence and patterns of major depressive disorder in the United States labor force. *Journal of Mental Health Policy and Economics, 2*, 123–131.

Marsh, J. C., & Cao, D. (2005). Parents in substance abuse treatment: Implications for child welfare practice. *Children and Youth Services Review, 27*, 1259–1278.

Massinga, R., & Pecora, P. J. (2004). Providing better opportunities for older children in the child welfare system. *Future of Children, 14*(1), 150–173.

McCloskey, L. A., & Walker, M. (2002). Posttraumatic stress in children exposed to family violence and single-event trauma. *Journal of the American Academy of Child and Adolescent Psychiatry, 39,* 108–115.

McDonald, J., Salyers, N., & Shaver, M. (2004). *The foster care straitjacket: Innovation, federal financing and accountability in state foster care reform.* Urbana-Champaign: Children and Family Research Center at the School of Social Work, University of Illinois at Urbana-Champaign.

McDonald, T. P., Allen, R. I., Westerfelt, A., & Piliavin, I. (1996). *Assessing the long-term effects of foster care: A research synthesis.* Washington, DC: CWLA Press.

McFarlane, A. C. (2000). Posttraumatic stress disorder: A model of the longitudinal course and the role of the risk factors. *Journal of Clinical Psychiatry, 61*(Suppl 5), 15–23.

McIntosh, N. (1991). Identification and investigation of properties of social support. *Journal of Organizational Behavior Management, 12,* 201–217.

McLoyd, V., & Wilson, L. (1991). The strain of living poor: Parenting, social support, and child mental health. In A. Huston (Ed.), *Children in poverty* (pp. 105–135). Cambridge, UK: Cambridge University Press.

McMillen, J. C., Scott, L. D., Zima, B. T., Ollie, M. T., Munson, M. R., & Spitznagel, E. (2004). Use of mental health services among older youths in foster care. *Psychiatric Services, 55*(7), 811–817.

Meadowcroft, P., Thomlison, B., & Chamberlain, P. (1994). Treatment foster care services: A research agenda for child welfare. *Child Welfare, 73*(5), 565–581.

Meadowcroft, P., & Trout, B. A. (Eds.). (1990). *Troubled youth in treatment homes: A handbook of therapeutic foster care.* Washington, DC: Child Welfare League of America.

Mech, E. V. (2003). *Uncertain futures: Foster youth transition to adulthood.* Washington, DC: Child Welfare League of America.

Mech, E. V., & Fung, C. C. (1999). Placement restrictiveness and educational achievement among emancipated foster youth. *Research on Social Work Practice, 9*(2), 213–228.

Michael, Y. L., Colditz, G. A., Coakley, E., & Kawachi, I. (1999). Health behaviors, social networks, and healthy aging: Cross-sectional evidence from the Nurses' Health Study. *Quality of Life Research, 8,* 711–722.

Minty, B. (1999). Outcomes in long-term foster family care. *Journal of Child Psychology & Psychiatry and Allied Disciplines, 40*(7), 991–999.

Molnar, B. E., Buka, S. L., & Kessler, R. C. (2001). Child sexual abuse and subsequent psychopathology: Results from the National Comorbidity Survey. *American Journal of Public Health, 91,* 753–760.

Moran, P. B., Vuchinich, S., & Hall, N. K. (2004). Associations between types of maltreatment and substance abuse during adolescence. *Child Abuse & Neglect, 28,* 565–574.

Mrazek, P., & Mrazek, D. (1987). Resilience in child maltreatment victims: A conceptual exploration. *Child Abuse & Neglect, 11*(3), 357–366.

Muller, R. T., Goh, H. H., Lemieux, K. E., & Fish, S. (2000). The social supports of high-risk, formerly maltreated adults. *Canadian Journal of Behavioural Science, 32,* 1–5.

Murray, C. J. L., & Lopez, A. D. (Eds.). (1996). *The global burden of disease and injury series, Volume 1: A comprehensive assessment of mortality and disability from diseases, injuries, and risk factors in 1990 and projected to 2020.* Cambridge, MA: Harvard School of Public Health on behalf of the World Health Organization and the World Bank, Harvard University Press.

National Campaign to Prevent Teenage Pregnancy. (2004). *General facts and stats.* Retrieved April 18, 2006, from http://www.teenpregnancy.org/resources/data/gen1fact.asp

National Center for Education Statistics. (2003). *The condition of education in 2003 in brief.* Washington, DC.: National Center for Education Statistics.

National Center for Educational Statistics. (1996). *Dropout rates in the United States, 1994.* Retrieved January 2, 2008, from http://nces.ed.gov/pubsearch/pubsinfo.asp?pubid=96863

National Center for Education Statistics. (2003). *Distribution of 18- to 29-year-olds, by high school completion status and selected characteristics: 1997 to 1999.* Washington, DC: Author.

National Center for Education Statistics. (2004). *Table 11. Status completion rates of 18- through 24-year-olds not currently enrolled in high school or below.* Retrieved May 15, 2009 from http://nces.ed.gov/pubs2006/dropout/tables/table_11.asp

National Center for Health Statistics. (2004). *Health, United States, 2004, with chartbook on trends in the health of Americans.* Hyattsville, MD: U.S. Government Printing Office.

National Center for Health Statistics. (2005). *National vital statistics report.* Retrieved April 18, 2006, from http://www.cdc.gov/nchs/data/nvsr/nvsr54/nvsr54_02.pdf

National Institute of Mental Health. (2004). *Preventing child and adolescent mental disorders: Research roundtable on economic burden and cost effectiveness.* Retrieved February 6, 2006, from http://www.nimh.nih.gov/scientificmeetings/economicroundtable.cfm

National Institute of Mental Health. (2006a). *The impact of mental illness on society.* Retrieved February 6, 2006, from http://www.nimh.nih.gov/publicat/burden.cfm

National Institute of Mental Health. (2006b). *The numbers count: Mental disorders in America.* NIH Publication No. 06–4584. Retrieved February 6, 2006, from http://www.nimh.nih.gov/publicat/numbers.cfm#KesslerPrevalence#KesslerPrevalence

National Research Council, Panel on Research on Child Abuse and Neglect. (1993). *Understanding child abuse and neglect.* Washington, DC: National Academy Press.

National Research Council and Institute of Medicine (2009). *Preventing Mental, Emotional, and Behavioral Disorders Among Young People: Progress and Possibilities.* Committee on Prevention of Mental Disorders and Substance Abuse Among Children, Youth, and Young Adults: Research Advances and Promising Interventions. Mary Ellen O'Connell, Thomas Boat, and Kenneth E. Warner, Editors. Board on Children, Youth, and Families, Division of Behavioral and Social Sciences and Education. Washington, DC: The National Academies Press. http://www.nap.edu/catalog.php?record_id=12480

National Resource Center for Family-Centered Practice and Permanency Planning (2008a). *Facts about children in foster care in Oregon.* Retrieved June 20, 2008, from http://www.hunter.cuny.edu/socwork/nrcfcpp/info_services/fact-sheets.html

National Resource Center for Family-Centered Practice and Permanency Planning (2008b). *Facts about children in foster care in Washington.* Retrieved from http://www.hunter.cuny.edu/socwork/nrcfcpp/info_services/fact-sheets.html

Nelson, D. W. (2004). Moving youth from risk to opportunity. In *KIDS COUNT 2004 Data Book.* Baltimore: Annie E. Casey Foundation.

Newton, R. R., Litrownik, A. J., & Landsverk, J. A. (2000). Children and youth in foster care: Disentangling the relationship between problem behaviors and number of placements. *Child Abuse & Neglect, 24*(10), 1363–1374.

Noam, G. G., & Hermann, C. A. (2002). Where education and mental health meet: Developmental prevention and early intervention in schools. *Development and Psychopathology, 14,* 861–875.

Noble, L. (1997). The face of foster care. *Educational Leadership, 54,* 26–28.

Nolen-Hoeksema, S., & Girgus, J. S. (1994). The emergence of gender differences in depression during adolescence. *Psychological Bulletin, 115,* 424–443.

Nollan, K., Pecora, P. J., Nurius, P., & Whittaker, J. K. (2001). Risk and protective factors influencing life-skills among youths in long-term foster care. *International Journal of Child & Family Welfare, 5*(1–2), 5–17.

O'Brien, K., Kessler, R. C., Hiripi, E., Pecora, P. J., White, C. R., & Williams, J. (2009a). *Working Paper No. 5: Agency sub-group results for mental and physical health, education, employment, and relationships.* Retrieved June 15, 2009, from http://www.casey.org/research

O'Brien, K., Kessler, R. C., Hiripi, E., Pecora, P. J., White, C. R., & Williams, J. (2009b). *Working Paper No. 6: The relation between demographics and risk factors and foster care alumni outcomes.* Retrieved June 15, 2009, from http://www.casey.org/research

O'Brien, K., Kessler, R. C., Hiripi, E., Pecora, P. J., White, C. R., & Williams, J. (2009c). *Working Paper No. 7: The effects of foster care experiences on alumni outcomes: A multivariate analysis.* Retrieved June 15, 2009, from http://www.casey.org/research

O'Brien, K., Williams, J., Pecora, P., English, D. J., & Kessler, R. C. (in preparation). Post-traumatic stress disorder among alumni of foster care: Implications for practice and policy.

Olsen, L., Allen, D., & Azzi-Lessing, L. (1996). Assessing risk in families affected by substance abuse. *Child Abuse and Neglect, 20,* 833–842.

Orlofsky, J., Marcia, J., & Lesser, I. (1973). Ego identity status and the intimacy versus isolation crisis of young adulthood. *Journal of Personality and Social Psychology, 27,* 211–219.

Ortega, D. M. (2002). How much support is too much? Parenting efficacy and social support. *Children and Youth Services Review, 24*(11), 853–876.

Pasztor, E. M., Hollinger, D. S., Inkelas, M., & Halfon, N. (2006). Health and mental health services for children in foster care: The central role of foster parents. *Child Welfare, 85*(1), 33–57.

Pecora, P. J. & Huston, D. (2008). Why should child welfare and schools focus on minimizing placement change as part of permanency planning for children. *Social Work Now,* 19–27. (A practice journal for New Zealand.)

Pecora, P. J., Kessler, R. C., Williams, J., O'Brien, K., Downs, A. C., English, D., et al. (2005). *Improving family foster care: Findings from the Northwest Foster Care Alumni Study.* Seattle, WA: Casey Family Programs.

Pecora, P. J., Kessler, R. C., Williams, J., Downs, A. C., Hiripi, E., English, D., et al. (2008a). *Working Paper No. 3: Measurement domains and variables, data sources, and data collection procedures.* Retrieved June 15, 2009, from http://www.casey.org/research

Pecora, P. J., Kingery, K., Downs, A. C., Nollan, K., Touregenau, J., & Sim, K. (2003a). *Working Paper No. 1: Examining the effectiveness of family foster care: A select literature review of post-placement outcomes.* Retrieved June 15, 2009, from http://www.casey.org/research

Pecora, P. J., Whittaker, J. K., Maluccio, A. N., & Barth, R. (2000). *The child welfare challenge: Policy, practice, and research* (2nd ed.). Hawthorne, NY: Aldine de Gruyter.

Pecora, P. J., Whittaker, J. K., Maluccio, A. N., Barth, R. P., & Depanfilis, D. (2009) *The child welfare challenge: Policy, practice and research* (3rd ed.). Piscataway, NJ: Aldine-Transaction.

Pecora, P. J., & Wiggins, T. (2009). *Working Paper No. 1: A summary of foster care research data by outcome domain.* Retrieved June 15, 2009, from http://www.casey.org/research

Pecora, P. J., Wiggins, T., Jackson, L. J., & English, D. (2009b). Working Paper No. 4: *Effects of child maltreatment on children and adults, and physical and mental health of children entering and during foster care: A literature review* Seattle, WA: Casey Family Programs.

Pecora, P. J., Wiggins, T., Jackson, L. J., & English, D. (2009c). *Working Paper No. 2: The effects of child maltreatment on children and adults: A brief literature review.* Retrieved from http://www.casey.org/research

Pecora, P. J., Williams, J., Kessler, R. C., Downs, A. C., O'Brien, K., Hiripi, E., et al. (2003b). *Assessing the effects of foster care: Early results from the Casey National Alumni Study.* Seattle: Casey Family Programs.

Pecora, P. J., Williams, J., Kessler, R. C., Hiripi, E., O'Brien, K., Emerson, J., et al. (2006). Assessing the educational achievements of adults who formerly were placed in family foster care. *Child and Family Social Work., 11*(3), 220–231.

Peeters, M. C. W., Buunk, B. P., & Schaufeli, W. B. (1995). Social interactions and feelings of inferiority among correctional officers: A daily event-recording approach. *Journal of Applied Social Psychology, 25*(12), 1073–1089.

Perry, K., Pecora, P., & Traglia, J. (1992). *Practice guidelines for clinical practice and case management:* Seattle: Casey Family Programs.

Piliavin, I., Sosin, M., Westerfelt, A. H., & Matsueda, R. L. (1993). The duration of homeless careers: An exploratory study. *Social Service Review, 67*(4), 576–598.

Pine, B. A., Healy, L. M., & Maluccio, A. N. (2002). Developing measurable program objectives: A key to evaluation of family reunification programs. In T. Vecchiato, A. N. Maluccio & C. Canali (Eds.), *Evaluation in child and family services: Comparative client and program perspectives* (pp. 86–99). New York: Aldine de Gruyter.

Plomin, R. (1989). Environment and genes: Determinants of behavior. *American Psychologist, 44,* 105–111.

Plomin, R., & Nesselroade, J. R. (1990). Behavioral genetics and personality change. *Journal of Personality 58,* 191–220.

Polansky, N. A., Chalmers, M. A., Buttenweiser, E., & Williams, D. P. (1981). *Damaged parents: An anatomy of child neglect.* Chicago: University of Chicago Press.

Polcin, D. L. (2001). Sober living houses: Potential roles in substance abuse services and suggestions for research. *Substance Use and Misuse, 36*(3), 301–311.

President's New Freedom Commission on Mental Health (2003, February 6). *Achieving the promise: Transforming mental health care in America* (DHHS Publication No. SMA-03-3832). Retrieved April 17, 2008, from http://www.mentalhealthcommission.gov/reports/Finalreport/toc_exec.html

Price, J. M.; Chamberlain, P., Landsverk, L. Reid, J.B., Leve, L.D., & Laurent , H. (2008). Effects of a foster parent training intervention on placement changes of children in foster care. *Child Maltreatment,*13(1), 64–75.

Price, L. M., Chamberlain, P., Landsverk, J., & Reid, J. (2009). KEEP foster-parent training intervention: model description and effectiveness. *Child and Family Social Work, 14*(2), 233–242.

Rashid, S. (2004). Evaluating a transitional living program for homeless, former foster care youth. *Research on Social Work Practice, 14*(4), 240.

Reardon-Anderson, J., Stagner, M., Macomber, J. E., & Murray, J. (2005). *Systematic review of the impact of marriage and relationship programs.* Washington, DC: Urban Institute.

Redding, R. E., Fried, C., & Britner, P. A. (2000). Predictors of placement outcomes in treatment foster care: Implications for foster parent selection and service delivery. *Journal of Child & Family Studies, 9*(4), 425.

Reider, C., & Cicchetti, D. (1989). Organizational perspective on cognitive control functioning and cognitive-affective balance in maltreated children. *Developmental Psychology 25,* 382–393.

Reilly, T. (2003). Transition from care: Status and outcomes of youth who age out of foster care. *Child Welfare, 82*(6), 727–746.

Reinherz, H. Z., Giaconia, R. M., Hauf, A. M. C., Wasserman, M. S., & Silverman, A. B. (1999). Major depression in the transition to adulthood: Risks and impairments. *Journal of Abnormal Psychology, 108,* 500–510.

Reinherz, H. Z., Paradis, A. D., Giaconia, R. M., Stashwick, C. K., & Fitzmaurice, G. (2003). Childhood and adolescent predictors of major depression in the transition to adulthood. *American Journal of Psychiatry, 160,* 2141–2147.

Rice, D., & Miller, L. (1996). The economic burden of schizophrenia: Conceptual and methodological issues, and cost estimates. In M. Moscarelli, A. Rupp & N. Sartorius (Eds.), *Handbook of mental health economics and health policy, Vol. 1: Schizophrenia* (pp. 321–324). New York: Wiley.

Rice, D. L., & McFadden, E. J. (1988). A forum for foster children. *Child Welfare, 67*(3), 231–243.

Ringel, J. S., & Sturm, R. (2001). National estimates of mental health utilization and expenditures for children in 1998. *Journal of Behavioral Health Services & Research, 28*(3), 319–333.

Robins, L. N. (1966). *Deviant children grown up: A sociological and psychiatric study of sociopathic personality.* Baltimore: Williams and Wilkins.

Robins, L. N., Wing, J., Wittchen, H. U., Helzer, J. E., Babor, T. F., Burke, J., et al. (1989). The Composite International Diagnostic Interview: An epidemiologic instrument suitable for use in conjunction with different diagnostic system and in different cultures. *Archives of General Psychiatry, 45,* 1069–1077.

Rodriguez, J., Cauce, A. M., & Wilson, L. (2000). *A conceptual framework of identity formation in a society of multiple cultures.* Seattle: Casey Family Programs.

Roman, N. P., & Wolfe, P. B. (1997). The relationship between foster care and homelessness. *Public Welfare, 55,* 4–9.

Rosenbaum, P. R., & Rubin, D. B. (1984). Reducing bias in observational studies using sub-classification on the propensity score. *Journal of the American Statistical Association, 79*, 516–524.

Rosenberg, M. (1965). *Society and the adolescent self-image*. Princeton, NJ: Princeton University Press.

Ross, C. E. (1995). Reconceptualizing marital status as a continuum of social attachment. *Journal of Marriage and the Family, 57*(1), 129–140.

Ross, C. E., & Mirowsky, J. (2002). Family relationships, social support and subjective life expectancy. *Journal of Health and Social Behavior, 43*(4), 469–489.

Rubin, D. M., Alessandrini, E. A., Feudtner, C., Mandell, D. S., Localio, A. R., & Hadley, T. (2004). Placement stability and mental health costs for children in foster care. *Pediatrics, 113*(5), 1336.

Rubin, D.M., Halfon, N., Raghavan, R., & Rosenbaum, S. (2005). *Protecting children in foster care: Why proposed Medicaid cuts harm our nation's most vulnerable youth*. Seattle: Casey Family Programs.

Rumberger, R., & Larson, K. (1998). Student mobility and the increased risk of high school dropout. *American Journal of Education, 107*(1), 1–35.

Runtz, M. G. (1991). *Coping strategies, social support, and recovery from physical and sexual maltreatment*. Ottawa, Ontario: National Library of Canada.

Runtz, M. G., & Schallow, J. R. (1997). Social support and coping strategies as mediators of adult adjustment following childhood maltreatment. *Child Abuse & Neglect, 21*(2), 211–226.

Runyan, D. K., Cox, C. E., Dubowitz, H., Newton, R. R., Upadhyaya, M., Kotch, J. B., et al. (2005). Describing maltreatment: Do Child Protective Services reports and research definitions agree? *Child Abuse & Neglect, 29*(5), 461–477.

Runyan, D. K., Curtis, P. A., Hunter, W. M., Black, M. M., Kotch, J. B., Bangdiwala, S., et al. (1998a). Improving economic opportunities for young people served by the foster care system: Three views of the path to independent living. *Aggression & Violent Behavior, 3*(3), 275–285.

Runyan, D., Hunter, W., Socolar, R., Amaya-Jackson, L., English, D., Landsverk, J., et al. (1998b). Children who prosper in unfavorable environments: The relationship to social capital. *Pediatrics, 101*(1), 12–18.

Russell, M. (1987). *1987 national study of public child welfare job requirements*. Portland: University of Southern Maine, National Child Welfare Resource Center for Management and Administration.

Rutter, M. (1987). Psychosocial resilience and protective mechanisms. *American Journal of Orthopsychiatry, 57*, 316–331.

Rutter, M. (1989a). Intergenerational continuities and discontinuites in serious parenting difficulties. In D. Cicchetti & V. Carlson (Eds.), *Child maltreatment: Theory and research on the causes and consequences of child abuse and neglect* (pp. 317–348). Cambridge: Cambridge University Press.

Rutter, M. (1989b). Pathways from childhood to adult life. *Journal of Child Psychiatry, 30*(1), 23–51.

Rutter, M. (2001). Psychosocial adversity: Risk, resilience, and recovery. In J. M. Richman & M. W. Fraser (Eds.), *The context of youth violence: Resilience, risk, and protection* (pp. 13–41). Westport, CT: Praeger.

Ryan, J. P., & Testa, M. (2004). *Child maltreatment and juvenile delinquency: Investigating the role of placement and placement instability*. Champaign-Urbana: University of Illinois at Urbana-Champaign School of Social Work, Children and Family Research Center.

Ryan, J. P., & Testa, M. F. (2005). Child maltreatment and juvenile delinquency: Investigating the role of placement and placement instability. *Children and Youth Services Review, 27*, 227–249.

Samuels, G. M., & Pryce, J. M. (2008). "What doesn't kill you makes you stronger": Survivalist self-reliance as resilience and risk among young adults aging out of foster care. *Children and Youth Services Review, 30*(10), 1198–1210.

Sarason, B. R., Pierce, G. R., Bannerman, A., & Sarason, I. G. (1993). Investigating the antecedents of perceived social support: Parents' views of and behavior toward their children. *Journal of Personality and Social Psychology, 65*(5), 1071–1085.

Sarason, B. R., Pierce, G. R., Shearin, E. N., Sarason, I. G., Waltz, J. A., & Poppe, L. (1991). Perceived social support and working models of self and actual others. *Journal of Personality and Social Psychology, 60*(2), 273–287.

Schlesselman, J. J. (1982). *Case control studies: Design, conduct, and analysis.* New York: Oxford University Press.

Schneider, M. W., Ross, A., Graham, C., & Derkacz, A. (2005). Do allegations of emotional maltreatment predict developmental outcomes beyond that of other forms of maltreatment? *Child Abuse & Neglect, 29*(5), 513–532.

Service, E. T. (1995). *Dreams deferred: High school dropouts in the United States.* Princeton, NJ: Author.

Seyfried, S., Pecora, P. J., Downs, A. C., Levine, P., & Emerson, J. (2000). Assessing the educational outcomes of children in long-term foster care: First findings. *School Social Work Journal, 24*(2), 68–88.

Sheehy, A. M., Oldham, E., Zanghi, M., Ansell, D., Correia, P., & Copeland, R. (2002). *Promising practices: Supporting transition of youth served by the foster care system.* Baltimore: Annie E. Casey Foundation.

Shin, S. H. (2004). Developmental outcomes of vulnerable youth in the child welfare system. *Journal of Human Behavior in the Social Environment, 9*(1–2), 39–56.

Shirk, M., & Stangler, G. (2004). *On their own: What happens to kids when they age out of the foster care systems.* Boulder, CO: Westview Press.

Simms, M. D. (1989). The foster care clinic: A community program to identify treatment needs of children in foster care. *Journal of Developmental and Behavioral Pediatrics, 10*(3), 121–128.

Sinclair, R. (1998). Involving children in planning their care. *Child and Family Social Work, 3,* 137–142.

Smith, T. M. (2003). Who values the GED? An examination of the paradox underlying the demand for the general educational development credential. *Teacher's College Record, 105*(3), 375–415.

Smithgall, C., Gladden, R. M., Goerge, R. M., & Courtney, M. E. (2004). *Educational experiences of children in out-of-home care.* Chicago: Chapin Hall Center for Children at the University of Chicago.

Sosin, M., Colson, P., & Grossman, S. (1988). *Homelessness in Chicago: Poverty and pathology, social institutions and social change.* Chicago: University of Chicago, School of Social Service Administration.

Sroufe, L. A. (1990). An organizational perspective on the self. In D. Cicchetti & M. Beegley (Eds.), *The self in transition: Infancy to childhood* (pp. 281–307). Chicago: University of Chicago Press.

Stack, C. (1974). *All our kin: Strategies for survival in the black community.* New York: Harper and Row.

Starr, R. H., & Wolfe, D. A. (1991). *The effects of child abuse and neglect: Issues and research.* New York: Guilford Press.

Stein, E., Rae-Grant, N., Ackland, S., & Avison, W. (1994). Psychiatric disorders of children "in care": Methodology and demographic correlates. *Canadian Journal of Psychiatry, 39*(6), 341–347.

Stein, M. (1994). Leaving care: Education and career trajectories. *Oxford Review of Education, 29*(3), 349–360.

Stein, M., & Munro, E. R. (2008). *Young people's transitions from care to adulthood: International research and practice.* London and Philadelphia: Jessica Kingsley.

Stein, T. (1998). *Child welfare and the law* (Rev. ed.). Washington, DC: Child Welfare League of America.

Steinberg, L., & Avenevoli, S. (1998). Disengagement from school and problem behavior in adolescence: A developmental-contextual analysis of the influences of family and part-time work. In R. Jessor & M. Chase (Eds.), *New perspectives on adolescent risk behavior* (pp. 392–424). New York: Cambridge University Press.

Steinberg, L., & Cauffman, E. (1995). The impact of school-year employment on adolescent development. In R. Vasta (Ed.), *Annals of child development: A research annual* (Vol. 11, pp. 131–166). Philadelphia: Jessica Kingsley.

Stern, D., Paik, I., Catterall, J. S., & Nakata, Y. (1989). Labor market experience of teenagers with and without high school diplomas. *Economics of Education Review, 8,* 233–246.

Straus, M. A. (1979). Family patterns and child abuse in a nationally representative American sample. *Child Abuse & Neglect, 3,* 213–225.

Straus, M. A., & Gelles, R. J. (1989). *Physical violence in American families: Risk factors and adaptations to violence in 8,145 families.* New Brunswick, NJ: Transaction.

Straus, M. A., Gelles, R. J., & Steinmetz, S. K. (1980). *Behind closed doors: Violence in the American family.* New York: Doubleday/Anchor.

Straus, M. A., Hamby, S. L., Boney-McCoy, S., & Sugarman, D. B. (1996). The revised Conflict Tactics Scales (CTS2): Development and preliminary psychometric data. *Journal of Family Issues, 17,* 283–316.

Strawbridge, W. J., Sherma, S. J., Cohen, R. D., & Kaplan, G. A. (2001). Religious attendance increases survival by improving and maintaining good health behaviors, mental health, and social relationships. *Annals of Behavioral Medicine, 23*(1), 68–74.

Sturm, R., Ringel, J., Bao, C., Stein, B., Kapur, K., Zhang, W., et al. (2001. National estimates of mental health utilization and expenditures for children in 1998. In National Advisory Mental Health Council's Workgroup on Child and Adolescent Mental Health Intervention Development and Deployment (Ed.), *Blueprint for change: Research on child and adolescent mental health* (NIH Publication No. 01-4985). Rockville, MD: National Institute of Mental Health.

Susser, E., Struening, E. L., & Conover, S. (1987). Childhood experiences of homeless men. *American Journal of Psychiatry, 144*(12), 1599–1601.

Taber, M. A., & Proch, K. (1987). Placement stability for adolescents in foster care: Findings from a program experiment. *Child Welfare, 66*(5), 433–445.

Takayama, J. I., Wolfe, E., & Coulter, K. P. (1998). Relationship between reason for placement and medical findings among children in foster care. *Pediatrics, 101*(2), 201–207.

Tardy, C. (1985). Social support measurement. *American Journal of Community Psychology, 13,* 187–202.

Testa, M. F. (2002). Subsidized guardianship: Testing an idea whose time has finally come. *Social Work Research, 26*(3), 145–158.

The Urban Institute, University of California Berkeley, & University of North Carolina at Chapel Hill. (2008). *Coming of age: Employment outcomes for youth who age out of foster care through their middle twenties.* Retrieved April 18, 2008, from http://aspe.hhs.gov/hsp/08/fosteremp/index.html

Thompson, R. W., Huefner, J. C., Ringle, J. L., & Daly, D. L. (2004). *Adult outcomes of Girls and Boys Town youth: A follow-up report.* Paper presented at the 17th Annual Florida Mental Health Institute Conference, A System of Care for Children's Mental Health: Expanding the Research Base. Tampa: University of South Florida.

Tracy, E. M., & Whittaker, J. K. (1987). The evidence base for social support interventions in child and family practice: Emerging issues for research and practice. *Children and Youth Services Review, 9,* 249–270.

Turkington, C. (1985). What price friendship? The darker side of social networks. *Monitor on Psychology, 16*(2), 38, 41.

United Nations. (1990). *Convention on the rights of the child.* New York City: Author.

United States General Accounting Office. (1999). *Foster care: Effectiveness of independent living services unknown* (Report No. GAO/HEHS-00-10). Washington, DC: Author.

U.S. Census Bureau. (1981). *Statistical abstract of the United States 1981* (102nd ed.). Washington, DC: U.S. Government Printing Office.

U.S. Census Bureau. (1982). *Statistical abstract of the United States 1982–83* (103 ed.). Washington, DC: U.S. Government Printing Office. Retrieved March 10, 2005, from http://www2.census.gov/prod2/statcomp/documents/1982_83-01.pdf

U.S. Census Bureau. (1983). *Statistical abstract of the United States 1984* (104 ed.). Washington, DC: U.S. Government Printing Office. Retrieved March 10, 2005, from http://www2.census.gov/prod2/statcomp/documents/1984-01.pdf

U.S. Census Bureau. (1984). *Statistical abstract of the United States 1985* (105 ed.). Washington, DC: U.S. Government Printing Office. Retrieved March 10, 2005, from http://www2.census.gov/prod2/statcomp/documents/1985-01.pdf

U.S. Census Bureau. (1991). *Statistical abstract of the United States 1991* (111 ed.). Washington, DC: U.S. Government Printing Office. Retrieved March 10, 2005, from http://www2.census.gov/prod2/statcomp/documents/1991-01.pdf

U.S. Census Bureau. (1994). *Statistical abstract of the United States 1994* (114 ed.). Washington, DC: U.S. Government Printing Office. Retrieved March 10, 2005, from http://www2.census.gov/prod2/statcomp/documents/1994-01.pdf

U.S. Census Bureau. (2000a). *Educational attainment by sex: Census 2000 summary file 3.* Retrieved June 10, 2005, from http://factfinder.census.gov/servlet/QTTable?_bm=y&-geo_id=01000US&-qr_name=DEC_2000_SF3_U_QTP20&-ds_name=DEC_2000_SF3_U&-_sse=on

U.S. Census Bureau. (2000b). GCT-H6. Occupied housing characteristics: 2000. In *Census 2000 Summary File 1 (SF 1) 100-Percent Data* (Ed.). Retrieved March 10, 2005, from http://factfinder.census.gov/servlet/GCTTable?_bm=y&-geo_id=01000US&-_box_head_nbr=GCT-H6&-ds_name=DEC_2000_SF1_U&-redoLog=false&-mt_name=DEC_2000_SF1_U_GCTH5_US9&-format=US-9

U.S. Census Bureau. (2000c). *Profile of selected economic characteristics: 2000.* March 2001 Current Population Survey: Table DP-3.. Washington, DC: U.S. Census Bureau. Retrieved March 10, 2005, from http://factfinder.census.gov/bf/_lang=en_vt_name=DEC_2000_SF3_U_DP3_geo_id=01000US.html

U.S. Census Bureau. (2000d). QT-P24. Employment status by sex: 2000. In *Census 2000 Summary File 3 Matrices P43 and PCT35* (Ed.). Retrieved March 10, 2005, from http://www.factfinder.census.gov/servlet/QTTable?_bm=y&-geo_id=01000US&-qr_name=DEC_2000_SF3_U_QTP24&-ds_name=DEC_2000_SF3_U&-redoLog=false

U.S. Census Bureau. (2000e). Table 1. Median income of households by selected characteristics, race, and Hispanic origin of householder: 2000, 1999, and 1998. In Housing and Household Economic Statistics Division (Ed.). Retrieved March 10, 2005, from http://www.census.gov/hhes/www/income/income00/inctab1.html

U.S. Census Bureau. (2000f). Table 7. Homeownership rates by age of householder, fourth quarter 2000 and 1999. In *Housing vacancy survey* (Ed.).Retrieved March 10, 2005, from http://www.census.gov/hhes/www/housing/hvs/qtr400/q400tab7.html

U.S. Census Bureau. (2000g). Table 19. Homeownership rates for the West, by age of householder, and for married-couple families: 1982 to 2000 In *Housing Vacancy Survey* (Ed.). Retrieved March 10, 2005, from http://www.census.gov/hhes/www/housing/hvs/annual00/ann00t19.html

U.S. Census Bureau. (2000h). *Profile of selected social characteristics—2000* (Table DP-2.). Washington, DC: Author. Retrieved March 10, 2005, from http://factfinder.census.gov/bf/_lang+en_vt_name+DEC_2000_SF3_U_DP2_geo_id=01000US.html

U.S. Census Bureau. (2001). *Poverty thresholds in 2000, by size of family and number of related children under 18 years.* Retrieved March 10, 2005, from http://www.census.gov/hhes/poverty/threshld/thresh00.html

U.S. Census Bureau. (2004). Current population reports. From *Statistical abstract of the United States* (derived from Table No. 53, Marital status of the population by sex and age: 2003). Retrieved March 10, 2005, from http://www.census.gov/prod/2004pubs/04statab/pop.pdf

U.S. Department of Education, National Center for Education Statistics. (2002). *Digest of education statistics, 2001.* NCES 2002–130. Washington, DC: Author. Retrieved March 10, 2005, from http://nces.ed.gov/pubs2002/2002130.pdf

U.S. Department of Education, National Center for Education Statistics. (2003). *Digest of education statistics, 2002* (NCES 2003–060 ed.). Washington, DC: Author. Retrieved March 10, 2005, from http://nces.ed.gov/pubsearch/pubsinfo.asp?pubid=2003060

U.S. Department of Health and Human Services. (2003a). *The AFCARS report: Preliminary FY 2001 estimates as of March 2003.* Washington, DC: Author. Retrieved March 10, 2005, from http://www.afcars.gov/programs/cb

U.S. Department of Health and Human Services. (2007a). *Table A: Data indicators for the Child and Family Services Review.* Retrieved July 13, 2008, from http://www.acf.hhs.gov/programs/cb/cwmonitoring/data_indicators.htm

U.S. Department of Health and Human Services (2008a). *Child welfare outcomes 2002–2005: Report to Congress.* Retrieved January 1, 2009, from http://www.acf.hhs.gov/programs/cb/pubs/cw005/cw005.pdf

U.S. Department of Health and Human Services, Administration for Children and Families. (2000). *Child maltreatment: Online reports from the states to the National Child Abuse and Neglect Data System (NCANDS) and the National Incidence Study.* Washington, DC: U.S. Government Printing Office. Retrieved June 10, 2008, from www.acf.hhs.gov/programs/cb/stats_research/index.htm.

U.S. Department of Health and Human Services, Administration for Children and Families. (2001a). *National survey of child and adolescent well-being: One year in foster care report.* Washington, DC: Author. Retrieved June 10, 2008, from www.acf.hhs.gov/programs/opre/abuse_neglect/nscaw/ - 35k.

U.S. Department of Health and Human Services, Administration for Children and Families, (2007b). *Foster care FY2000—FY2005: Entries, exits, and numbers of children in care on the last day of each federal fiscal year.* Retrieved May 1, 2008, from http://www.acf.hhs.gov/programs/cb/stats_research/afcars/statistics/entryexit2005.htm

U.S. Department of Health and Human Services (2008a). *Child welfare outcomes 2002–2005: Report to Congress.* Retrieved September 11, 2008, from http://www.acf.hhs.gov/programs/cb/pubs/cw005/cw005.pdf

U.S. Department of Health and Human Services, Administration for Children and Families, Children's Bureau. (2001b). *The AFCARS report: Preliminary estimates as of April 2001.* Washington, DC: U.S. Government Printing Office.

U.S. Department of Health and Human Services, Administration for Children and Families, Children's Bureau. (2003b). *Child welfare outcomes 2001: Annual report to Congress.* Washington, DC: U.S. Government Printing Office.

U.S. Department of Health and Human Services, Administration for Children and Families, Children's Bureau. (2003c). *Safety, permanency and well-being—Child welfare outcomes 2000.* Washington, DC: U.S. Government Printing Office.

U.S. Department of Health and Human Services, Administration for Children and Families, Children's Bureau. (2005a). *The AFCARS report: Preliminary FY 2003 estimates as of August 2005.* Washington, DC: U.S. Department of Health and Human Services.

U.S. Department of Health and Human Services, Administration for Children and Families, Children's Bureau. (2005b). *Child maltreatment 2003.* Washington, DC: U.S. Government Printing Office.

U.S. Department of Health and Human Services, Administration for Children and Families, Children's Bureau. (2006). *The AFCARS report No. 13: Preliminary FY 2005 estimates as of September 2006.* Washington DC: U.S. Department of Health and Human Services.

U.S. Department of Health and Human Services, Administration for Children and Families, Children's Bureau. (2008b). *The AFCARS report No. 14: Preliminary FY 2006 estimates as of January 2008.* Retrieved July 1, 2008, from http://www.acf.hhs.gov/programs/cb/stats_research/afcars/tar/report14.htm

U.S. Department of Health and Human Services, Administration for Children and Families, Children's Bureau. (2008c). *Child maltreatment 2006.* Washington, DC: National Child Abuse and Neglect Data System.

U.S. Department of Health and Human Services, Administration for Children and Families, Children's Bureau (2008d). *Trends in foster care and adoption: FY 2002-FY 2007.* Retrieved January 5, 2009, from http://www.acf.hhs.gov/programs/cb/stats_research/afcars/

U.S. Department of Health and Human Services, Administration for Children and Families, Children's Bureau. (2008e). *Child maltreatment 2006.* Washington, DC: National Child Abuse and Neglect Data System.

U.S. Department of Health and Human Services, Administration on Children, Youth and Families. (2006). *Child maltreatment 2004.* Washington, DC: U.S. Government Printing Office.

U.S. Department of Health and Human Services, Administration on Children, Youth and Families. (2009). *Child maltreatment 2007.* Washington, DC: U.S. Government Printing Office.

U.S. Department of Health and Human Services, Children's Bureau. (2001c). *National survey of child and adolescent well-being: State child welfare agency survey.* Washington, DC: Author.

U.S. Government Accountability Office. (2007). *African American children in foster care: Additional HHS assistance needed to help states reduce the proportion in care.* Washington, DC: Author.

Usher, C. L., Randolph, K. A., & Gogan, H. C. (1999). Placement patterns in foster care. *Social Service Review, 73,* 22–36.

Van Leeuwen, J. (2004). Reaching the hard to reach: Innovative housing for homeless youth through strategic partnerships. *Child Welfare, 83*(5), 453–468.

Vaughn, R. (2002). *Consumer perceptions of services: Risk and protective factors present in the lives of Casey youth.* New York: National Center on Addiction and Substance Abuse at Columbia University.

Vinnerljung, B., Oman, M., & Gunnarson, T. (2005). Educational attainments of former child welfare clients—a Swedish national cohort study. *International Journal of Social Welfare, 14,* 265–276.

Wahler, R. G. (1980). The insular mother: Her problems in parent–child treatment. *Journal of Applied Behavioral Analysis, 13,* 207–219.

Wahler, R. G., & Dumas, J. E. (1989). Attentional problems in dysfunctional mother–child interactions: An interbehavioral model. *Psychological Bulletin, 105*(1), 116–130.

Wahler, R. G., Leske, G., & Rogers, E. S. (1979). The insular family: A deviance support system for oppositional children. In L. A. Hammerlynck (Ed.), *Behavioral systems for the developmentally disabled: I. School and family environments* (Vol. 1, pp. 102–127). New York: Brunner/Mazel.

Wald, M. (1975). State intervention on behalf of "neglected" children: A search for realistic standards. *Stanford Law Review, 27,* 985–1000.

Walsh, J. A., & Walsh, R. A. (1990). *Quality care for tough kids: Studies of the Maintenance of Subsidized Foster Placements in The Casey Family Program.* Washington, DC: Child Welfare League of America.

Walton, E., Fraser, M. W., Lewis, R. E., Pecora, P. J., & Walton, W. K. (1993). In-home family-focused reunification: An experimental study. *Child Welfare, 72*(5), 473–487.

Walton, E., Sandau-Beckler, P., & Mannes, M. (Eds.). (2001). *Balancing family-centered services and child well-being: Exploring issues in policy, practice, and research.* New York: Columbia University Press.

Wang, P. S., Lane, M., Olfson, M., Pincus, H. A., Wells, K. B., & Kessler, R. C. (2005). Twelve-month use of mental health services in the United States. *Archives of General Psychiatry, 62*(6), 629–639.

Ware, J., Kosinski, M., & Keller, S. D. (1998). *SF-12®: How to score the SF-12® physical and mental health summary scales* (3rd ed.). Lincoln, RI, and Boston: QualityMetric Incorporated and the Health Assessment Lab.

Washington State Department of Social and Health Services. (1987). *State of Washington child welfare plan, FY 1988–89.* Olympia: Washington State Department of Social and Health Services, Division of Children, Youth and Family Services.

Washington State Department of Social and Health Services. (1989). *State of Washington child welfare plan, FY 1990–91.* Olympia: Washington State Department of Social and Health Services Division of Children, Youth and Family Services.

Washington State Department of Social and Health Services. (1991). *State of Washington child welfare lan, FY 1992–93.* Olympia: Washington State Department of Social and Health Services, Division of Children, Youth and Family Services.

Washington State Department of Social and Health Services. (1993). *State of Washington child welfare plan, FY 1994–97.* Olympia: Washington State Department of Social and Health Services, Division of Children, Youth and Family Services.

Washington State Department of Social and Health Services. (1995a). *Washington State manuals: DCFS practices and procedures guide, 1995.* Olympia: Washington State Department of Social and Health Services, Division of Children, Youth and Family Services.

Washington State Department of Social and Health Services. (1996). *Foster parent feedback on DCFS performance report.* Olympia: Author.

Washington State Department of Social and Health Services. (2004a). *Child and family service review, final report, 2004.* Olympia: Author.

Washington State Department of Social and Health Services. (2004b). *Strategic priorities.* Retrieved February 2, 2005, from www1.dshs.wa.gov/ca/about/abStrategy.asp

Washington State Department of Social and Health Services, Division of Children, Youth and Family Services. (1995b). *State comprehensive child and family services plan, FY 1995–99.* Olympia: Author.

Washington State Public Policy Institute. (2004). *Benefits and cost of prevention and early intervention programs for youth.* Olympia: Author.

Weber, J. M. (1988). The relevance of vocational education to dropout prevention. *Vocational Education Journal, 63*(6), 36–38.

Wedeven, T., Pecora, P. J., Hurwitz, M., Howell, R., & Newell, D. (1997). Examining the perceptions of alumni of long-term family foster care: A follow-up study. *Community Alternatives: International Journal of Family Care, 9*(1), 88–106.

Weinfield, N. S., Ogawa, J. R., & Sroufe, L. A. (1997). Early attachment as a pathway to adolescent peer competence. *Journal of Research on Adolescence, 7*(3), 241–265.

Weiss, R. S. (1974). The provisions of social relationships. In Z. Rubin (Ed.), *Doing unto others* (pp. 17–26). Englewood Cliffs, NJ: Prentice Hall.

Wellman, B., & Wortley, S. (1990). Different strokes from different folks: Community ties and social support. *American Journal of Sociology, 96*(3), 558–588.

Werner, E. E. (1989). High-risk children in young adulthood: A longitudinal study from birth to 32 years. *American Journal of Orthopsychiatry, 59*(1), 72–81.

Werner, E. E. (1993). Risk, resilience, and recovery: Perspectives from the Kauai Longitudinal Study. *Development and Psychopathology, 5,* 503–515.

Werner, E. E., & Smith, R. (1989). *Vulnerable but invincible: A longitudinal study of resilient children and youth.* New York: Adams Bannister Cox.

White, C. R., Havalchak, A., Jackson, L. J., O'Brien, K., & Pecora, P. J. (2008). *Mental health, ethnicity, sexuality, and spirituality among youth in foster care: Findings from the Casey Field Office Mental Health Study.* Seattle: Casey Family Programs.

White, C. R., O'Brien, K., Jackson, L. J., Havalchak, A., Phillips, C. M., Thomas, P., et al. (2008). Ethnic identity development among adolescents in foster care. *Child and Adolescent Social Work Journal, 25*(6), 497–515.

Whittaker, J. K., & Garbarino, J. A. (1985). *Social support networks.* Hawthorne, NY: Aldine de Gruyter.

Whittaker, J. K., & Maluccio, A. N. (2002). Rethinking "child placement": A reflective essay. *Social Service Review, 76*(1), 108–134.

Whittaker, J. K., Tracy, E. M., & Marckworth, M. (1989). *Family support project: Identifying informal support resources for high risk families.* Seattle: University of Washington, School of Social Work.

Widom, C. S. (1989a). The cycle of violence. *Science, 244,* 160–166.

Widom, C. S. (1989b). Does violence beget violence? A critical examination of the literature. *Psychological Bulletin, 106*(1), 3–28.

Widom, C. S. (1991). The role of placement experiences in mediating the criminal consequences of early childhood victimization. *American Journal of Orthopsychiatry, 61*(2), 195–209.

Widom, C. S., & Ames, M. A. (1994). Criminal consequences of childhood sexual victimization. *Child Abuse & Neglect, 18*(4), 303–318.

Widom, C. S., Weiler, B. L., & Cottler, L. B. (1999). Childhood victimization and drug abuse: A comparison of prospective and retrospective findings. *Journal of Consulting and Clinical Psychology, 67,* 867–880.

Williams, J.R. Stenslie, M., Abdullah, M., Grossman, C., & Shinn, C. (2002). *In their own words: Listening to the voices of foster care alumni.* Paper presented at the National Foster Parent Association Annual Education Conference, Las Vegas, NV.

Williams, J. R., Pope, S. M., Sirles, E. A., & Lally, E. M. (2005). *Alaska foster care alumni study.* Anchorage: University of Alaska Anchorage.

Williams, J.R. McWilliams, A., Mainieri, T., Pecora, P., & La Belle, K. (2006). Enhancing the validity of foster care follow-up studies through multiple alumni location strategies. *Child Welfare, 85*(3), 499–521.

Williams, J.R. Herrick, M., Pecora, P. J., & O'Brien, K. (2008). *Working Paper No. 4: Placement history and foster care experience.* Retrieved from http://www.casey.org/research

Wind, T. W., & Silvern, L. (1994). Parenting and family stress as mediators of the long-term effects of child abuse. *Child Abuse & Neglect, 18*(5), 439–453.

Wolfe, D. A., & McGee, R. (1994). Dimensions of child maltreatment and their relationship to adolescent adjustment. *Development and Psychopathology, 6,* 165–181.

Woodruff, K. (2004). *Placement stability definitions to promote consistency in state data reporting for the federal outcome measure.* Washington, DC: Child Welfare League of America National Working Group to Improve Child Welfare Data.

World Health Organization. (1996). *Composite International Diagnostic Interview Version 2.0.* Geneva: World Health Organization.

World Health Organization. (2004). *The World Health report 2004: Changing history, Annex Table 3: Burden of disease in DALYs by cause, sex, and mortality stratum in WHO regions: Estimates for 2002.* Geneva: Author.

Wulczyn, F. H. (1991). Caseload dynamics and foster care reentry. *Social Service Review, 65,* 133–156.

Wulczyn, F. H. (2004). Family reunification. *Future Child, 14*(1), 94–113.

Wulczyn, F. H., Barth, R. P., Yuan, Y. T., Harden, B., & Landsverk, J. (2005). *Beyond common sense: Child welfare, child well-being, and the evidence for policy reform.* Piscataway, NJ: Aldine Transaction.

Wulczyn, F. H., & Brunner, K. (2002). *Topic #1: Foster care dynamics in urban and non-urban counties.* Chicago: University of Chicago, Chapin Hall

Wulczyn, F. H., Kogan, J., & Harden, B. J. (2002). *Placement stability and movement trajectories.* Chicago: University of Chicago, Chapin Hall.

Wulczyn, F. H., Kogan, J., & Harden, B. J. (2003). Placement stability and movement trajectories. *Social Service Review, 77*(2), 212–236.

Wyatt, D. T., Simms, M. D., & Horwitz, S. M. (1997). Widespread growth retardation and variable growth recovery in foster children in the first year after initial placement. *Archives of Pediatrics & Adolescent Medicine, 151*(8), 813–816.

Zerbe, R., Plotnick, R., Kessler, R. C., Pecora, P. J., Hiripi, E., O'Brien, K., et al. (2009. Benefits and costs of intensive foster care services: The Casey Family Program compared to state services. *Contemporary Economic Policy.*(Published online February 16, 2009, at http://www3.interscience.wiley.com/JOURNAL/119880786/issue.)

Zetlin, A., Weinberg, L., & Kimm, C. (2004). Improving education outcomes for children in foster care: Intervention by an education liaison. *Journal of Education for Students Placed at Risk, 9*(4), 421–429.

Zima, B. T., Bussing, R., Yang, X., & Belin, T. R. (2000). Help-seeking steps and service use for children in foster care. *Journal of Behavioral Health Services & Research, 27*(3), 271–285.

Zimiles, H., & Lee, V. E. (1991). Adolescent family structure and educational progress. *Developmental Psychology, 27*(2), 314–320.

Zimmerman, R. B. (1982). *Foster care in retrospect. Studies in social welfare.* New Orleans: Tulane University Press.

Zimrin, H. (1986). A profile of survival. *Child Abuse & Neglect, 10*(3), 339–349.

Zuravin, S., McMillen, C., DePanfilis, D., & Risley-Curtiss, C. (1996). The intergenerational cycle of child maltreatment: Continuity vs. discontinuity. *Journal of Interpersonal Violence, 11*(3), 315–334.

Index

Page numbers appearing in *italics* denote those containing figures; page numbers appearing in **bold** denote those containing tables